ANTHROPOLOGY OF CREASE MORPHOGENESIS

About the Author

Prof. R.S. Bali graduated in Anthropology from University of Delhi (1961) and was awarded Ph.D. from the same University (1965).

Presently he is on the faculty of the Department of Anthropology, University of Saugar for the last two decades he has been doing extensive research in the field of Creases and Dermatoglyphics. He guided several doctoral works on creases. Professor Bali is an accepted name in this field of Anthropology.

ANTHROPOLOGY OF CREASE MORPHOGENESIS

A Scientific Analysis

R.S. BALI
Professor, Department of Anthropology
University of Saugar
SAGAR (M.P.)

CONCEPT PUBLISHING COMPANY, NEW DELHI 110059

ISBN 81-7022-325-3

First Published 1994

Published and Printed by
Ashok Kumar Mittal
Concept Publishing Company
A/15-16, Commercial Block, Mohan Garden
NEW DELHI 110059 (India)

Lasertypeset by
Printing Express
H-13, Bali Nagar
NEW DELHI 110015

PREFACE

IN SPITE OF the fact that creases for the last one century are on the scientific anvil they seem not yet to have earned a place as a means of assessing the biological relationships between human populations.

In the past, creases have never been considered as a consolidated whole, instead their application in anthropology has been in bits, thus limiting the trend of their application for complex population problems.

The existing tools of crease applications are meagre and suffer for want of a single and standard methodological approach.

The rapidly growing mass data is lying uncomparable and its full significance in anthropology has never been realized.

The present book is, perhaps, the first comprehensive attempt towards consolidating informations about all creases in a single volume. Out of the existing schemes of crease classifications, new formulations have been added to deal with all creases (palmar, plantar, bracelet, phalangeal and flexion creases of the toes) with a new element of biological awareness.

The applications part of all the formulations has been tried by the author from the last two decades. This book has been divided into Four parts. The first part deals with crease Morphology, Morphometry and Techniques.

The biological aspect of creases is dealt under this part with full details on morphology, morphometry, embryology and crease variation in primates.

The symmetrical and other aspects of creases have also been discussed under this part.

Part II confines to the Methods and Description of Palmar, Plantar, Phalangeal and Bracelet Creases given by the author along with overview of all existing schemes of crease classifications.

The last five Chapters in this part treats separately the inheritance of palmar, plantar, phalangeal, bracelet and creases of the toes.

The inheritance of morphogenic attributes of creases has also been taken care of.

Part III of the book deals with phenotypic variation, twins and ethnic variability in creases. This part of crease anthropology has been expanded under three Chapters.

Chapter 23 of Part III confines to the problems of crease application in medicine. In this chapter the stress is more on palmar creases. Simian and Sydney lines have also been given the treatment in Chapter 22.

The last part of three Chapters deals with the applicational aspects of the creases.

There are many facts in this book — facts relevant to crease anthropology, crease biology and medicinal aspects; still one fact remains that several important areas of informations have not been taken full care of because the author had no access to many valuable contributions of several scientists currently working in this field of anthropology.

Any errors of omission or commission which remain are my own.

Sources of borrowed illustrations are included in the legends of individual figures, additional courtesies in connection with illustrations are also acknowledged.

I am indebted to my scholars and students without whom this work could never have been completed. To my son Rasmeet Singh I owe my thanks for his help in getting the matter typed.

R.S. BALI

CONTENTS

PART-III
CREASES IN HUMAN BIOLOGY, ETHNIC VARIATION AND MEDICINE

PART-IV
APPLICATIONAL ASPECTS OF THE CREASES

LIST OF TABLES

LIST OF FIGURES

PART I

CREASE MORPHOLOGY, MORPHOMETRY AND TECHNIQUES

1

INTRODUCTION

Crease Antiquity

THE HISTORY of palmar creases bears the testimony of its antiquity. To trace its origin we are carried back to the confines of a pre-historic age. An aboriginal Indian carving found at Nova Scotia, originally cited by Cummins and Midlo (1961) predominantly represents palmar creases (Fig. 1.1). Many such carvings in ancient clay objects signify familiarity of ancient workers with crease characteristics. The magic or conjuring signs of palmar creases or of hand, carved on rocks and clay, must have impressed the early men and for them the human hand might have been of more compelling of attention, and several attributes of hand and palm as such have been emphasised for the purpose of divination. In an ultimate sense, the palmistry was, perhaps, the best known field of human morphology, known to the ancient people.

To ancient thinkers the expressional tendency of human hand might have been most fascinating, thus making its subject matter a star of study of human nature. The popularity of palmistry, right from the times of the ancient civilisations of Rome, Greece, China and India can be traced from its early reference in the literature.

Chinese studied palmistry as early as 3,000 years B.C. [Goafar (1964)] while in India it is as old as Aryans [Cheiros (1966) and Sen (1969)]. During the middle ages several attempts were made to revive palmistry but it is only in 19th century that numerous books appeared on this subject.

Creases and Myth

The known synonymity between creases and palmistry, in fact, has enabled creases to survive but with a stigma of fortune-telling and subsequently debarring them from the scientific courts.

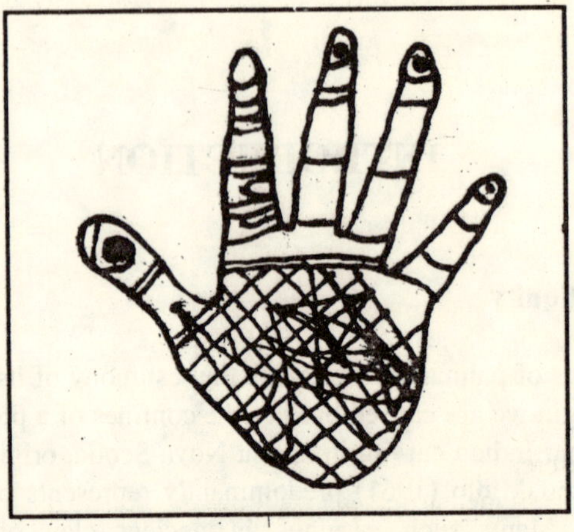

FIG. 1.1: An aboriginal Indian petroglyph (Nova Scotia) representing dermatoglyphics and flexion creases of human hand (Cummins & Midlo, 1961)

The purpose is not to build claims for cheiromancy as a science but to review those factors which kept alive the interest and curiosity of people in this field. The palmists, in vain, tried to build a philosophical structure for logic values, tracing value changes, rational decisions and emotional conflicts back to a person's individual character. Instead of logical interpretation, the study gave birth to divination and occult, thus relegating the entire pursuit as non-scientific.

Without dispelling the element of its obscuritism the palmists pleaded for re-appraisal of palmistry for scientific uses. Scheimen (1972) studied the importance of medical palmistry in the problems of health and diseases. The author claims palmistry as a tool for determining the genetic and the endochronologic make up of an individual. Similar attempts were made by Duell, Sloan and Pearce (1900).

The most frequently quoted palmists, O'Arpentigny, Desbarroses Cheiro, Spier, Sen, St. Germain and Noel Jaquin, have failed to provide a scientific explanation of palmistry.

Crease Anthropology

There is a prevalent but unfounded notion that palmar creases are relevant only to palmists and have no importance beyond their use in palmistry, a popular sport.

Creases are sheer anatomical attributes restricted to the ridged surface of palms, soles and phalanges. They are ridgeless furrows, devoid of dermal configurations and with characteristic features of their own. Cummins and Midlo (1961) exclude creases from dermatoglyphics, branding them as matter for palmistry. On the other hand, the maximum work on palmar flexion creases finds citation under the heading, "dermatoglyphics", because of their close topographical association with dermal configurations. Nonetheless, creases are independent of dermatoglyphic traits, both in their manifestation and application.

Paul Broca (1877) was the first to stir up interest among anthropologists in the simian crease. He introduced the ethnic element in creases. Carrara (1893) and Fere (1900) studied the frequencies of simian creases in Italian and French soldiers, respectively. The single transverse palmar line, which runs across the palm, is typical for most simians and, therefore, gets the name "Simian Crease".

The higher incidence of simian creases among individuals affected by certain diseases and defects were reported by Langdon-Down (1909), Rittmeister (1936), Wurth (1937), Portius (1937) and Tillner (1956). The subsequent findings of Penrose (1967), Weninger and Navratil (1957) confirmed the above results. Simian crease relationship to certain medical syndrome was also attempted by Kervinen (1954), Tunaken (1948), Hale, et al. (1961), Ruth Achs, et al. (1966), Mehas (1972) and Biswas and Bardhan (1966).

To study the ethnic trend of variability of unlike frequencies of simian creases, the work of Crookshank (1924), Buchi (1958), Lestrange (1969), Kimura (1957), Leiber (1960), Kutsuna *op cit*, Kimura (1968) and Walter (1952) are worth mentioning. Lasinski (1960) adapted Poch's formula for the study of crease frequencies. The frequencies of simian creases among different populations were also studied by Battman (1932), Stiffens (1953), Kervine (1954) and Erikson and Norinder (1958).

Wurth (1937) observed that creases are not the functional result of flexion and appear before the embryo moves its hand. Bhumel (1911) also gave the embryonic details of creases, while Schenk and Patzer (1959) studied the embroyology of plantar creases. Similar contributions were made by Usher, et al. (1966) and Nakiela (1972).

Fischer (1949) was first to investigate the genetic aspect of simian creases with the help of twins and family data. Later, Stiffens (1953),

Becker (1952) and Portius (1937) also made their similar observations. Kimura (1968) studied the crease heretability of "M figure", while, Grunberg (1928) studied the simian creases in twins and among families.

Sarkar (1961) describes the simian creases and reviews the studies on palmar creases of anthropoid apes. Buchi (1954) refutes the theory that simian crease is a primitive character. A dominant simian crease concept prevailed over the study of creases for a long time giving a fillip to the simian-oriented crease formulations. These formulations are of Weininger and Navratil (1957), Buchi (1954), Lestrange (1969) and Portius (1937).

Leiber (1960), Kimura (1968), Bali and Chaube (1971) favoured newer trends of crease formulations, thus embracing all possible crease types in their systems of crease classifications. Sydney crease concept introduced by Purvis-Smith (1972) and Menser, Purvis-Smith (1969) tested sydney line in individual with Down's syndrome. The above authors also studied sydney crease in relation to leukaemia (1969).

The creases occurring on plantar and phalangeal surfaces have virtually been ignored. The work on phalangeal flexion crease is relatively more. Okajima (1966-67) studied metacarpel phalangeal creases and also described the technique for obtaining the prints. Penrose (1931) was perhaps the first to study metacarpel phalangeal creases. Cummins and Midlo (1961) reported the absence of metacarpel phalangeal crease. Lambson (1976) and Zizmor (1973) studied the extra phalangeal feature of the crease occurrence. Aue-Hauser (1978) gave a detailed account of this feature. The author based her work on the study of twins.

On the formulation of metacarpel phalangeal creases, Bali (1980, 1984) gave a new system of phalangeal crease classification, which is equally applicable to metatarsel creases. The author also studied the inheritance of metacarpel phalangeal creases.

It is notoriously difficult to obtain good prints of creases on toes.

Plantar creases, like palmar creases are embryonic in nature and are fairly stable in their form and shape. Schenk and Patzer's (1959) attempt appears to be of inceptive nature. Nakiela (1972), has also made observation on plantar creases. Usher, et al. (1966), and Fair, et al., *op cit.* Schaumann and Alter (1976), studied the plantar creases of the new born. Bali and Mishra (1978) gave the formulation of plantar creases and studied the inheritance of plantar creases. Bali, et al. (1983) studied the intra-individual relationship between palmar and plantar creases. Chaube and Bali (1976) made the pioneer attempt in classifying the bracelet creases. The authors also studied the inheritance of bracelet creases.

The creases elucidate various morphological principles, including body symmetry. Creases are heritable traits and have their role in anthropology and other allied sciences. A comprehensive work on human creases, palm, sole, phalanges and bracelet is desired to establish creases as a viable science. The present work is an attempt to highlight the salient features on these directions only.

The text is arranged in four parts. Part I supplies the historical background and deals with crease morphology, crease morphometry and related topics. Part II deals with the methods and description of palmar, plantar, phalangeal and bracelet creases in separate chapters.

Part III is devoted to the application of creases in human biology, ethnic variation and creases as morphological variable.

The last part of three chapters deals with applicational aspects of the creases.

REFERENCES

Aue-Hauser, G., Luigi Gedda, Paolo Parisi, and Rudolf Wytek (1978) : *Twin Research; Clinical Studies*. Alan R.

Bali, R.S. (1983) : *Inheritance of Phalangeal Flexion creases* (Human Biology Recent Advances Vol. 2) (Proc. Internat. Sym. Punjabi University).

Bali, R.S. (1984) : *Creases in Forensic and Criminological Investigation : Anthropology in Indian Context*. Today and Tomorrow's Printers and Publishers.

Bali, R.S. and R. Mishra (1978) : *The study of morphological change in hand, palm and palmar flexion creases of one to eleven years old boys and girls*. Xth Internat. Congr. Anthrop. & Ethno. Sciences, New Delhi, (India).

Bali, R.S. and R. Mishra (1980) : Age change and crease morphogenesis. *Internat. Sym. Dermat*. Punjabi University, Patiala, (India).

Bali, R.S.; A.N. Sharma and R. Chaube (1983) : The Intra-Individual Relationship between Palmar and Plantar Creases (Human Biology Recent Advances Vol. 2) *Proc. Internat.Sym.* Punjabi Univerty.

Bali R.S. and Ramesh Chaube (1971) : *On the formulation of palmar crease. Z. Morph. Anthrop.*, 63 : p. 121.

Becker, E. (1952) : *Zur verebung der Vierfingerfurche*. Homo, 3 : pp. 82-5.

Bettman, S. (1932) : *Zs Anat.* U. Entwicklungsch.

Biswas, P.C. and A. Bardhan (1966) : Palm Prints and Schiozophrenia. *The Anthropologist* 13(1-2) : pp. 1-12.

Bhumel, P. (1911) : *Papillarmuster and psychische Eigenschaften*. Vol. 9. pp. 180-92.

Broca, P. (1877) : *Le pli transversal du Singe dans la main de l'homme, Bull. soc. Anthr.* Paris, Ze Serie, t. XII, pp. 431-32.

Buchi, E.C. (1954) : The Simian crease in India. *Bulletin of the Indian Department of Anthropology*, 3(1) : pp. 39-49.

Carrara, (1893) : *Anomali dei Sochi Palmari hei normali e nei Criminale* (Roma.).

Chaube, R. and R.S. Bali (1976) : *The Bracelet Creases. Z. Morph. Anthrop.* 67. 3 : pp. 353-63.

Cheiros (1966) : *Language of Hand*, Taraporewala, Bombay.

Crookshank (1924) : *The Mongol in our Midst, a study of man and his three faces.* Duffon & Co., New York.

Cummins, H. and C. Midlo (1961) : *Finger Prints, Palms and Soles. An Introduction to Dermatoglyphics*. New York : Dover.

Duel, Sloan and Pearce (1900) : *The Laws of Scientific Hand Reading*. New York.

Eriksson, S.A., and A. Norinder (1958) : *En frekvensundersokning ar handflatans papillari injemonster i thenar-och hypothenarzonerna samt av den s.k. fyrfingerfaran. Nordic Criminology Magazine*. 28: pp. 257-70.

Fere, C. (1900) : *Notes sur les plis de flexion de la paume de la main. C.R. et Mem. Soc. Biol.* Paris, T., 52 : pp. 309-11.

Fischer, E. (1949) : *Bemerkung uber die vierfingrfurche. Zeitschrift fur Morphologie and Anthropologie*. 41 : pp. 268-74.

Goafar (1964) : *Ilm-ul-Kaff.*

Grunberg, H. (1928) : *Die vererbung der menschlichen Tastfiguren. Zeitschrift fur Induktive Abstammungs and Vererbungslebre*. 46 : pp. 285-310.

Hale, A.R., J.H. Phillips and G.E. Burch (1961) : Features of palmar dermatoglyphics in congenital heart disease: report on variants frequently associated with congenital lesions of heart. *Journal of the American Medical Association*. 176 : p. 41.

Kervinen, V. (1954) : The incidence of the four-finger groove in Finland. *Annales Academiae Scientiarum Fennicae* (Helsinki). 40 : pp. 1-2.

Kimura, K. (1968) : A study of palmar creases in Ainus. *Jinruigaku Zassi*. 76 : pp. 60-74.

Kimura, K. (1957) : A study of palmar dermatoglyphics in inhabitants of Sado island *Anthropological Reports* (Niigata) 18 : pp. 51-66 (in Japanese).

Lambson, G. (1976) : Distal displacement of proximal phalangeal flexion creases. *Excerpta Med. Int. Congr. Ser*. 397. p. 203.

Langdon-Down, R.L. (1909) : Mongolian Imbecility. *Brit. Med. J., 12* : p. 665.

Lasinski, W. (1960) : The system of skin furrows on the human palm. *Folia Morphologica*. 11 : 115.124 (in Polish).

Leiber, B. (1960) : *Zur systematic und klinischen Bedentung des menschlichen Handfurch-enbildes. Z. menschi. vererb. u. Konstitution slehre*. 35, pp. 205-32.

Lestrange M. de: (1969) : The transverse creases in Europe-index and comparative study of different sample cited in the Literature. *Amarical Journal of Physical Anthropology*, 30-173-182.

Lestrange M. de (1969) : A propos des plis de flexion de la paume : Classification et rapports entre les differents types decrits. *Bulletin et memoires de la Sociele d Anthropologie de Paris*.

Mehas, K. (1972) : Simian Crease, Acta Pediatra. *Acad. Sci. Hung*. 13, 4 : p. 335.

Menser, M.A., S.G. Purvis-Smith (1969) : Dermatoglyphic defects in children with Leukaemia, *Lancet* 1(7605) : pp. 1076-78.

Nakiela, J. (1972) : Flexion furrows of the feet in poles. *Folia Morphol*. (Warsz.), 31 : p. 301.

Okajima, M. (1966) : A dermatoglyphical study of metacarpophalangeal creases. *Am. J. Phys. Anthropol.*, 24 : pp. 371-80.

Okajima, M. (1967) : Metacarpo-phalangeal and ring crease in twins. *Am. J. Phys. Anthropol.*, 26 : pp. 349-55.

Penrose, L.S. (1931) : The creases on the minimal digit in Mongolism. *Lancet* ii : p. 583.

Penrose, L.S. (1967) : *A suggested use of dermatoglyphic analysis in mongolism.* Boston: Little, Brown.

Portius, W. (1937) : Beitrag zur Frage der Erblichkeit der vierfingerfurche. *Zeitschrift fur Morphologie und Anthropologie.* 36 : pp. 382-90.

Purvis-Smith, S.G. (1972) : The sydney Lines: a significant sign in Down's syndrome. *Australian Paediatric Journal 8* : pp. 190-200.

Rittmeister, J.F. (1936) : *uber die Affenfurche (Vierfingerfurche) mit besonderr Beruchsichtigung der Mikrodegenerationen und des Problems des Mongolismus. Zs. Anat. u. Entwicklungsgesch. Bd.* 106 H. 2: pp. 276-314.

Ruth Achs, Rita and Happer (1966) : Unusual dermatoglyphics associated with Rubella embryopathy, *New England Journal of Medicine*, 274, 3 : p. 148.

Sarkar, S.S. (1961) : The Simian crease. *Zeitschrift fur Morphologie und Anthropologie.* 51(2) : pp. 212-19.

Schaumann, B. and M. Alter (1976) : *Dermatoglyphics in Medical Disorders.* Springer-Verlag, New York. pp. 118-22.

Schenk, H. and H. Patzer (1959) : *Das Fussfurchenbild des Neugeborenen. Kinderarztliche Praxis* 27(4) : pp. 169-73.

Scheimann, E. (1972) : *A doctors' guide to Better Health Through Palmistry*, Vikas Publishing House.

Sen, S.K. (1969) : *Hast Samudrika Shastra, Indian Science of Hand Reading*, Taraporewala, Bombay.

Stiffens, C. (1953) : *Zur Haufigkeit und verebung der vierfingerfurche. Homo*, 4, Band, 3 heft. pp. 126-39.

Tillner, I. (1956) : *Die vierfingerfurche in Beziehung zum verlaug der Handleisten. Anthrop. Anzeiger*, 22 : pp. 260-76.

Tunakan, S. (1948) : *Etude anthropologique des empreintes digitales et palmaires chez les Tures*. Publication de l' universite d' Ankara 15.

Usher, R., F. McLean and K.E. Scott (1966) : Judgement of fetal age. II. Clinical significance of gestational age and an objective method for its assessment. *Pediatr. Clin. North Am.*, 13 : 835.

Walter, H. (1952) : *Betrachtungen, uber die verteilung der vierfingerfurche. Zs. f.* Morphol. u. Anthrop, Bd. XLIV. heft 3-s. pp. 362-68.

Weninger, M. and L. Navratil (1957) : *Die Vierfingerfurche in atiologischer Betrachtung. Anthrop. Gesellsch.* in Wien. Bd., LXXVII : pp. 1-21.

Wurth, A. (1937) : *Die Entstehung der Beugefurchen der menschlichen Hohlhand. Z. Morph. Anthrop.*, 36 : pp. 187-214.

Zizmor, J. (1937) : The extra transverse digital crease asking sign found in Sickle cell disease. *Cutis* (New York) 11 : pp. 447-49.

2

PRINTING TECHNIQUES AND PROCEDURES

ALONG WITH the dermatoglyphics the studies on creases have been appearing in the world literature for over a century. Various printing techniques have been devised for procuring prints of creases on different dermal regions. There are about 60 papers on printing techniques (Mavalwala, 1978). The international concensus for adopting certain techniques has not been specified so far, the reason being simple; the size and shape of various dermatoglyphic areas bearing creases are varied, thus warranting change in technique. It is more so for lifting prints of non-human primates.

A simple 'ink and paper' method is not a viable answer to the problem. Therefore, inkless methods have been devised for good results. The chalk and tape method of Edwards (1978) shows speed, clarity and neatness in application but superior techniques are still being sought.

Some of the prevalent printing techniques, both old and recent, are being considered in this Chapter.

Ink and Paper Method

The procedures for obtaining ink prints of creases and dermal ridges, both for identification and biological studies, have fully been described by Cummins and Midlo (1961). The material essential for making ink prints for palm and sole are: ink, cards or paper, roller, inking slab and a pressure pad. A good quality paper with glazed surface and durability may be selected. To obtain a print of the entire hand or foot the sheet should be measured accordingly. The finger and toe prints should be arranged in natural order. Printed sheets with specified printing spaces are more convenient. The ink best suited is printers ink and a roller is necessary for spreading ink. An inking slab on which ink is rolled into a thin film may be of a glass or polished metallic sheet.

The operator according to his need and preference adapts the printing techniques with certain modifications. But the practice for smearing uniform ink film, pressure regulation against the pad or ridged surface is essential for obtaining good results. Minimum dragging across the paper, cleaning of skin surface before and after printing and keeping the subject in a relaxed mood are the prerequisites for a good printing technique.

The print should be inspected on the spot to check for possible technical defects. Moreover, a foolproof system of recording is needed, especially in case of slips for tce and phalangeal prints.

For biological studies, the emphasis is quite often limited to a particular region of the dermatoglyphics. It is more true in case of creases. The print should be appropriated according to the orientation of crease form and its size. Special attention should be paid to demarcate the essential portion of each crease with respect to its origin and point of termination. For this purpose each crease should be treated as individual. A good crease print should represent its all components, i.e. a complete core, margin, base and terminal point.

To achieve good results commercially available equipments such as finger paste rubber roller, palm printing stamp base, roller for impressing palm print stamp base, universal finger print stamping kit, magnetic magnifier with ridge counting plate and magnifying lense with scale, etc., may be procured. It is true that the above equipments are primarily designed for dermatoglyphic observations, but they can usefully be employed for the study of creases as well. It has already been stated that the simple technique prescribed by Cummins and Midlo is good enough for procuring ink prints of palm, sole, phalanges, toe and bracelet area. In case of palmar creases, the most vulnerable area for defective prints is the radial margin, between interdigital I and II. The subject is made to stretch the thumb at right angles to the palm axis and gentle pressure is applied at the radial margin before the palm is lifted.

Sole Prints: After cleaning, a uniform film of ink is applied on the plantar surface. A glazed paper of appropriate size is attached on the roller (drum) which is moved upward from the heel towards the toes. With a gentle foot pressure, the rolling is manoeuvred in such a way that a portion of the hollow of the sole is also printed (Fig. 2.1a, b).

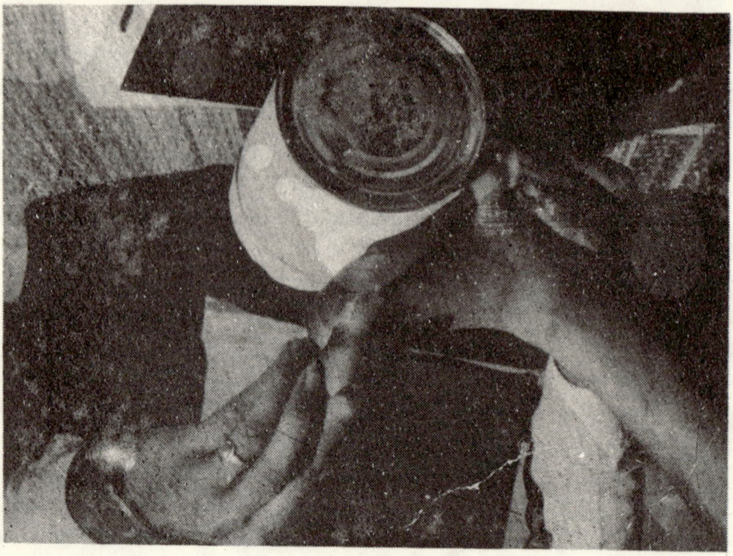

(a)

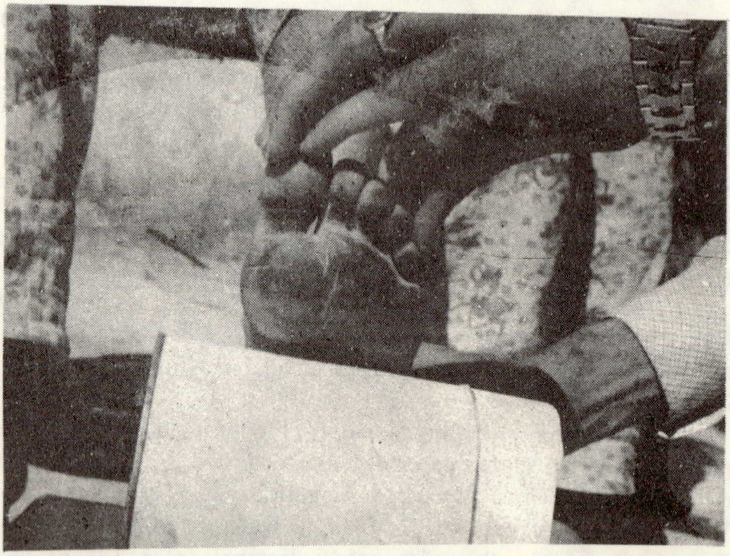

(b)

FIG. 2.1a, b: The technique used in taking a sole print

Bracelet Crease Prints

For procuring prints of bracelet creases, the inking method used by Chaube and Bali (1976) is simple and effective. Before smearing ink on bracelet area, the hand is bent upward, a thin layer of ink is smeared and then hand is straightened again. A paper is wrapped round the wrist with the support of a plastic piece. This method gives good results (Fig. 2.2a, b).

Phalangeal Crease Prints

The procedure for taking phalangeal crease prints as prescribed by Okajima (1966) has proved to have certain disadvantages; the lateral and medial portions of the phalangeal crease areas remain incomplete. After testing several methods the author has come to prefer phalangeal crease printing in two stages.

The prints of distal and middle phalangeal creases are taken by rolling the phalanges to accommodate the lateral and medial margins of the creases (Fig. 2.3).

For proximal phalangeal crease the print is taken along with the palm by stretching the fingers apart, and the interdigital margins are gently pressed before lifting the hand. The pieces of proximal phalangeal crease prints are cut and attached to the respective fingers (Fig. 2.4). The inter-phalangeal creases of the toes are difficult to print. This area is notoriously awkward for procuring good prints. Methews (1928) photo-paper method has been preferred over inking method. Small strips of photo papers of 2×6 cm size are wrapped round the individual crease of each toe. The method gives satisfactory results (Fig. 2.5).

For taking the crease prints of embryo and the new born, the photo-paper method has proved satisfactory.

Inkless Methods

Since the non-inking printing technique shows tidiness over inking method, the technique has widely been accepted.

Cummins and Midlo (1961) provide a detailed procedure for preparation of solution used in this method of printing dermal ridges and creases.

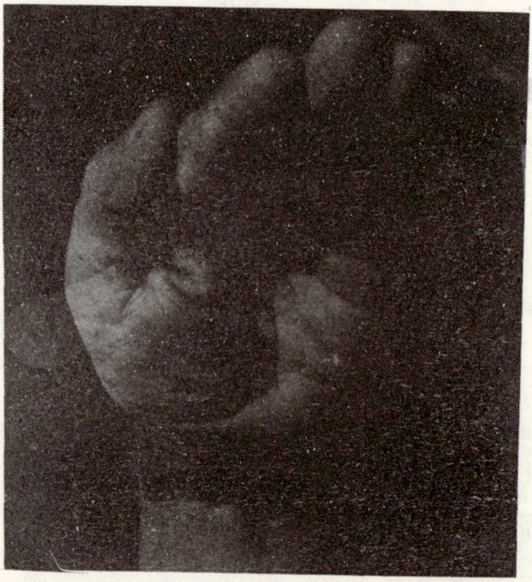

(a)

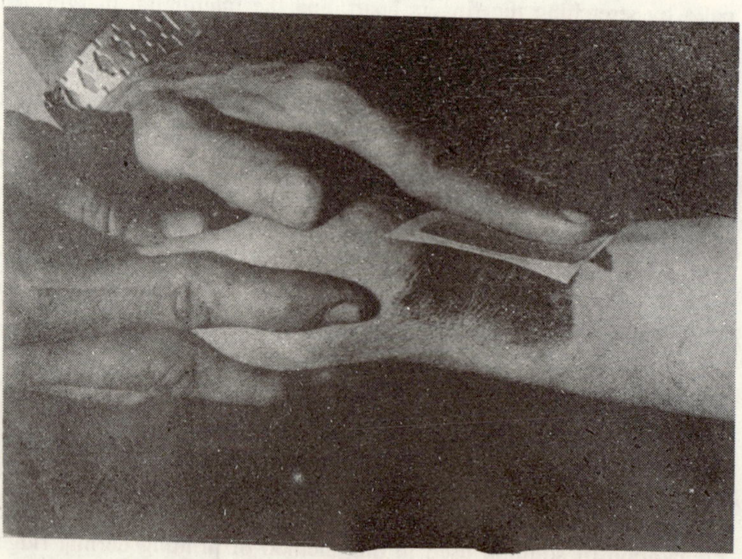

(b)

FIG. 2.2a, b: The technique used in taking bracelet print

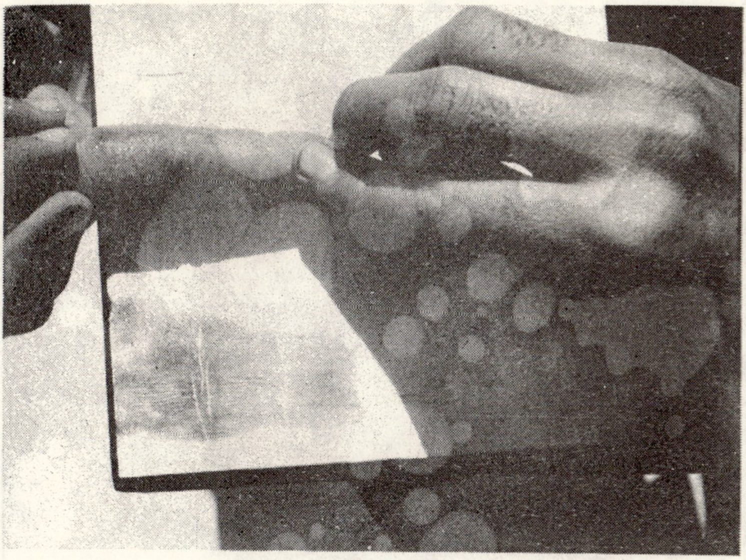

FIG. 2.3: The prints of distal and middle phalangeal creases

Ingredients of the solution are: sodium sulphide, 25 gm; sodium hydroxide (sticks) 5 grams; soluble starch 2 grams; distilled water 100 cc. The sodium sulphide and sodium hydroxide are dissolved in part of the water, the remainder of the water is boiled and the starch is dissolved in it. The starch solution is then added slowly to the first mixture and the material is stirred vigorously and allowed to cool. The working solution is made by adding one part of the stock solution to four or five parts of distilled water. A blotter moistened with this mixture serves as the 'inking slab'. The part to be printed is first pressed against the moist blotter for a few seconds and is then applied against a sheet of photographic paper. For permanence the prints must be fixed in hypo, washed and dried as in the usual photographic procedure. An inkless method of recording dermal ridges and creases traditionally belongs to Böök (1948), Cotterman (1951), Walker (1957).

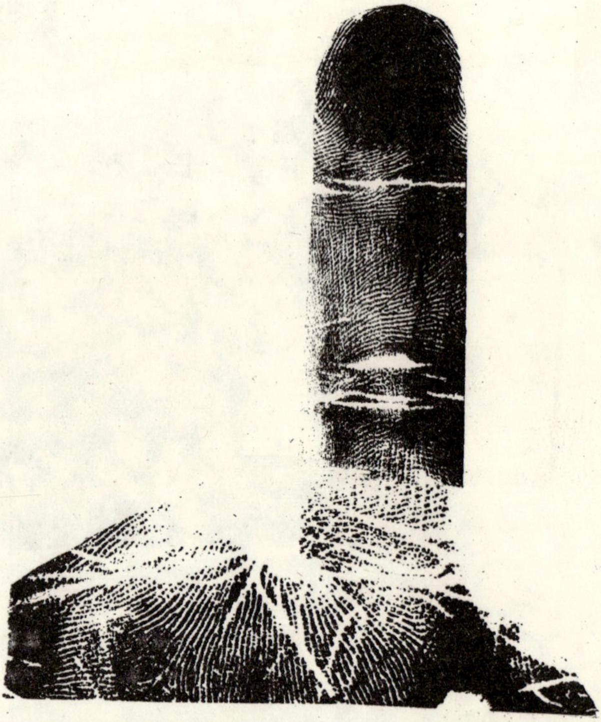

FIG. 2.4: The technique used in taking inter-phalangeal crease prints

Lynn Robertson-Neufeld and Jeffrey Murray (1978) prescribe a modified version of early inkless methods. They use latent print powder and transparent vinyl adhesive sheets.

The latent finger-print powder is dusted lightly on to a cotton ball, which is then tapped gently over the wax paper to remove any excess. The powder cotton ball is rubbed over the plantar and palmar surfaces. The Mactac transparent vinyl adhesive is cut to a desired length, is placed, adhesive side up, on a flat surface and the palm or sole, finger or toe pressed firmly against it. The adhesive is then carefully peeled from the skin and placed, adhesive side down, on a white record sheet. This method provides large number of clear prints in a relatively short time.

A Chalk and Tape Method

The Edward's printing method (1978) is ideally suited for lifting the palm prints of non-human primates, besides printing human palm and sole.

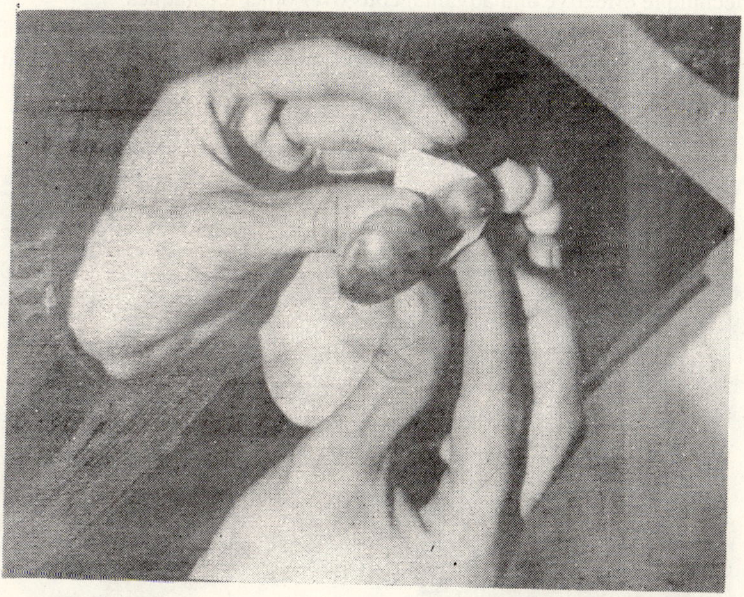

FIG. 2.5: The technique used in taking toe crease prints

The author used acetone, Scotch Brands Magic transparent tape, coloured chalk and index cards for lifting prints on non-human primates.

The size of the tape should be sufficiently wide and long to allow margin on all sides. After cleaning the printing surface thoroughly with acetone it is dried. Colour chalk is applied and plastic tape of appropriate size is applied closely to the surface while it is still dry. The tape is removed and allowed to dry at least for one minute and finally it is applied to a white index card for preservation and analysis.

Magna Brush Technique

This printing technique has been perfected by Aue-Hauser (1979). The method is cheap and simple and its application is valid for any scientific consideration (Fig. 2.6).

The use of magna brush powder (iron filings mixed with carbon powder), powder applicator (a bar-shaped magnet) and liquid vaseline or moisture lotion besides a sheet of white paper can make printing technique effective and advantageous over other techniques.

The procedure is simple. We have to rub first a small amount of liquid vaseline or moisture lotion on one's own hand and smooth it gently over the hand or foot of the proband.

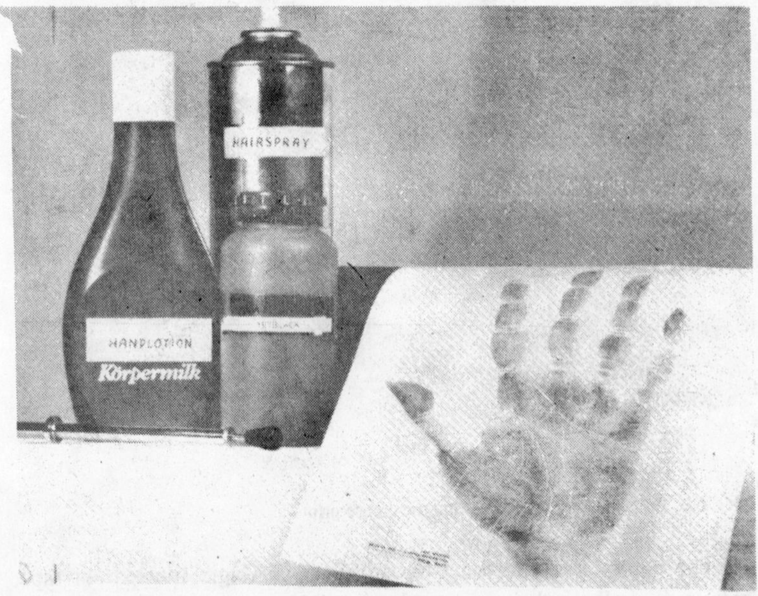

FIG. 2.6: Magna Brush printing technique (after Aue-Hauser)

After the subject's hand or foot has been printed on the paper with vaseline, the brush is lightly moved over the white sheet to make the prints appear on the sheet, which can be fixed through hair spray. This method is more useful in getting prints from hospitalized persons.

The above description of some important inkless printing techniques has proved to have certain advantages over old techniques. The procedure for taking prints of fingers, toes, palm or sole on paper, index cards or transparent tape will essentially remain the same as discussed under inking method.

Crease Tracing

A good print of a crease should represent the complete core and its margins. The splits and branches should be identifiable. The finer details of primary creases are essential for tracing purposes.

A good print on tracing of a crease must provide its anatomy and structural details for the study of crease morphology and crease morphometry. The crease core and its margins, its base and terminal ends conform to a particular orientation, which helps in defining the primary crease.

The crease margin may be straight, serrated, wavy or broken, thus giving varied shapes to crease cores. For tracing the core area of crease surface area, the above features of the crease need to be examined. In case of bifurcation or branching of primary crease at the terminal end, it is difficult to differentiate the main branch from the sister branch. In such cases crease tracing is essential.

The tracing of a crease is done with reference to the middle line which divides the creases longitudinally into two equal halves.

The branch which falls nearer to the projected mid-dotted line is the main branch. The broken or wavy margin is connected to provide equal distance from the mid-reference line (Fig. 2.7).

Crease Examination

Okajima (1978) devised a new technique for examining the dermatoglyphic and crease features of non-human primates. His technique is not a printing method but a chemical treatment of the epidermis. The method, however, cannot be applied to humans and those other primates which lack melanin in the volar epidermis.

The technique provides additional clarity especially for comparing structural relationship between creases and dermal ridges in a more natural situation than is possible with other methods. The equipment for the examination of crease prints by and large are the same as used for examining the dermatoglyphic prints.

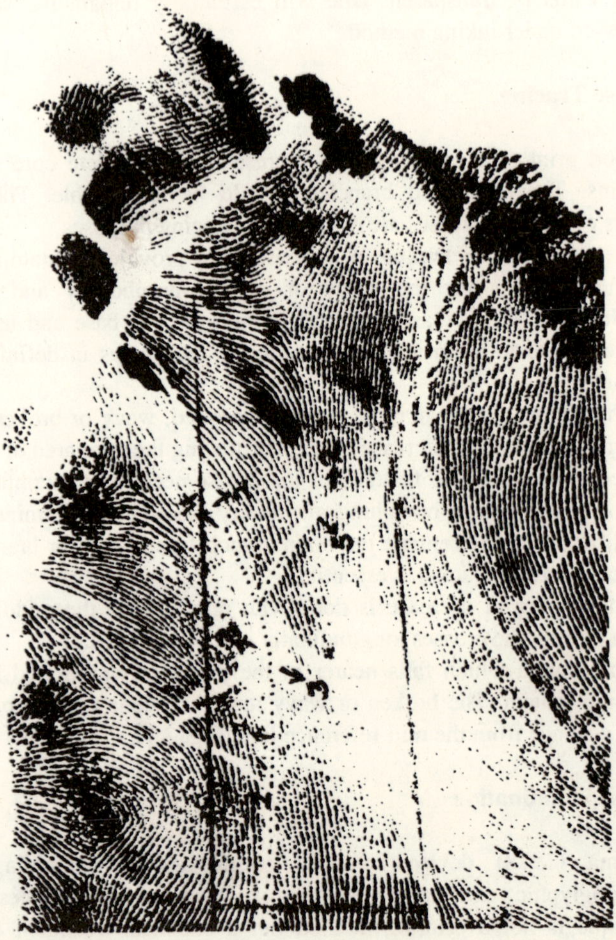

FIG. 2.7: Crease tracing — 1. Primary crease core, 2. Branching - terminal point, 3. Crease border, 4. Main branch, 5. Sub-branch

Apart from magnifying lense certain optical instruments are also available for closer examination of the creases in term of crease border, crease surface area, crease terminal points, for ridge count scale and also for the observation of pseudo crease types.

The age change in creases is a biological phenomenon and conforms to the growth norms (Bali and Mishra, 1978). For systematic and scientific analysis, apart from its configurational interpretation, i.e., crease formulations, the morphometric or quantitative expression of crease form and size is needed and could best be interpreted in term of crease surface area.

For this study, the ordinary inked palmar prints could be appropriated to investigate surface area of a particular crease with the help of planimeter, an instrument used by geomorphologists for interpreting maps, etc. (Fig. 2.8).

The Instrument

A tracer Arm (A) of the Planimeter bears a Tracer point (D) at the end it rests on an adjustable support (D). The Pole arm (E) carries weight or Fulcrum (F) to anchor the instrument (K). There is a measuring wheel (C) appropriately fitted with vernier and a magnifying lens to record the reading.

To study crease morphology in term of crease surface area, i.e., the square centimetre area occupied by a particular crease has been reported first time.

Method of Tracing

The tracing needle (D) is steadily and accurately moved along the crease margin. To cover the entire crease, the tracing needle is fixed at a point and is revolved around its outer margin. This provides the crease surface area in term of square centimetres.

The area encircled by the tracing point is finally recorded in sq. centimetre on measuring wheel. The precautions should be taken to demarcate carefully the boundaries of each crease. The crease split, crease break or crease cut and the crease bifurcation need a closer scrutiny.

The proposed method for calculating the crease surface area with the above instrument purport to interpret crease change in terms of sq. centimetre or per square unit cell count or per square centimetre ridge count. It is the crease morphometry which alone can give us the trend and magnitude of crease change.

FIG. 2.8: Planimeter — A. Tracer arm, C. Measuring wheel, D. Adjustable support, E. Pole arm, F. Weight or fulcrum, K. Anchor

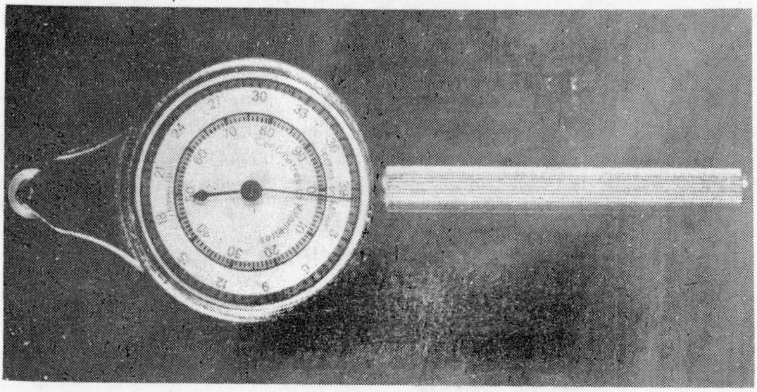

FIG. 2.9: Measurer

Measurer

For measuring crease length (Absolute) accurately and with speed the above instrument is most appropriate (Fig. 2.9). The absolute crease length can also be measured with steel or plastic tape; thread or thin steel wire. But the above method if handled carefully provides direct and accurate readings.

REFERENCES

Aue-Hauser, G. (1979): Magna Brush Technique in Dermatoglyphic Research. *American Journal of Physical Anthropology*. 5 : I.

Bali, R.S. and R. Mishra (1978) : The study of morphological change in hand, palm and palmar flexion creases on one to eleven year old boys and girls. *Xth Internat. Congr. Anthrop. & Ethno, Sciences*, New Delhi, India.

Böök, J.A. (1948) : Finger-print method for genitical studies. *Hereditas* 34 : 368 - 39.

Chaube, R. and R.S. Bali (1976) : The bracelet creases. *Z. Morph. Anthrop*. 67.3 : pp. 353-63.

Cotterman, C.W. (1951): A scotch-tape India ink method for recording dermatoglyphics. *American Journal of Human Genetics* 3(4). pp. 376-79.

Cummins, H. and C. Midlo (1961) : *Finger Prints — palms and soles. An Introduction to dermatoglyphics*, New York: Dover.

Edwards, C.R. (1978) : A Chalk and Tape method for lifting the palm prints of Non-human Primates. *Dermatoglyphics. An Introductional Perspective*. Moutan Publishers, Paris.

Lynn, R. and J. Murray (1978) : *An inkless method of recording dermal ridges: An introductional perspective*. Moutan Publishers, Paris.

Mawalwala, J. (1978) : *Methodology for dermatoglyphics: Finger and Palms. An introductional perspective*. Moutan Publishers, Paris.

Methews, H.H. (1928) : Vide Montgomery, R.B. (1925) : Sole Prints of newborn babies; *Am. Jour. Med. Sci.*; clxix.

Okajima, M. (1966) : A dermatoglyphic study of metacarpophalangeal creases. *Am. J. Phys. Anthrop.* 24: pp. 371-80.

Okajima, M. (1976) : *A new technique for examining Primate dermatoglyphics.* Dermatoglyphics an introductional perspective; Moulton Publishers, Paris.

Walker, N.S. (1957) : Inkless methods of finger, palm and sole printing. *Journal of Pediatrics* 50 : pp. 27-9.

3

CREASES — TERMS AND CONCEPTS

IN SPITE OF numerous studies carried out over almost a century, we must admit that we have not learned very much about creases. After the meeting of the societe d' Anthropologie de Paris held on June 21, 1877, Paul Broca introduced transverse crease concept in anthropology.

More than a hundred years have passed in the course of which numerous anthropologists have interested themselves in the problem of transverse crease and its incidence in various populations, both normal and abnormal.

The simian crease (*affenfurche* or *vierfingerfurche*) has been subject of a large number of recent studies.

Simian Crease Bias

The crease formulation pertains to its configurational types and simian types of crease configurations are the best known formulation among palmar creases. Sydney crease or 'M' figure of Kimura and Hagiya (1958) also reflect the arrangement of major crease types on palm. Apart from these, there are numerous other creases scattered along the entire dermatoglyphic surfaces.

The criteria for assorting primary creases from secondary, tertiary or minutiae have not been specified. So much so, creases have not been supplied with an appropriate definition. The entire work on creases is simian crease oriented, as if it is the only crease type which occurs on the palm. This lopsided approach towards the study of creases has hampered its growth and has rendered this field as ineffective. Sarkar (1961) in his study on simian creases has incorporated the following definitions: The definitions in italics are provided with English version.

Crookshank (1924) in the years following Langdon-Down developed the mongoloid origin of Mongolian Imbecility. He termed the peculiar form of the "Principal fold lines" as "Mongolian or

Orangoid" and defined it as follows: ". . . instead of a distinct line of heart and a distinct line of head, one transverse line only".

Wurth (1937) in the course of his study, on the origin of the palmar flexure line, gave the following definition of the simian crease. ". . . *Eine, Vierfingerfurche (Hesch, Zit. bei Pöch), die gewöhnlich als, Affenfalte "bezeichnet wird, liegt vor, wenn nur eine Querfurche vom Radialrand, entweder zusammenlaufend mit dem Adduktionsabschnitt der Daumenfurche oder gleichlaufend distalwärts davon, zum Ulnarrand die Hand quer durchschneidet. Sie entsteht also dann, wenn der Zeigefingerabschnitt der Fünffingerfurche sich im Hohlhandabschnitt der Dreifingerfurche fortsetzt und wenn dabei die anderen Abschnitte der Fünf-und Dreifingerfurche nicht vorhanden sind.*"

A simian crease is generally regarded as a principal fold line of the palm which runs transversally from the radial end and goes either along the abduction section of the radial longitudinal crease (life line) or runs distally there from across the palm. The merger, fusion or continuous union between the relevant section of distal transverse crease and proximal transverse crease of the palm forms a simian crease.

The above definition is somewhat different from that of Portius (1937), who defines it as follows: "*Von einer Vierfingerfurche sprechen wir dann, wenn an Stelle der Herz-(Dreifingerfurche) und der Kopflinie nur eine einzige quer uber die Hohlhand verlaufende Furche anzutreffen ist.*"

By simian crease we mean that distal transverse and proximal transverse crease meet and make only one line above the upper palmar surface to form a simian crease on meeting.

Tillner (1953) provided a recent definition, which runs as such: "*Unter einer klassischen VFF wird die Verschmelzung der DFF und der FFF verstanden, und zwar derart, daβ sich der Zeigefingerabschnitt der FFF und der Hohlhandabschnitt der DFF zu einer quer über die ganze Handflache verlaufenden Furche verbindet, wobei gleichzeitig der Zwischenfingerabschnitt der DFF und der Hohlhandabschnitt der FFF fehlen.*"

The term classical simian crease complies to a meeting between distal transverse crease and proximal transverse crease to form a simian crease type under the index finger section of proximal transverse crease and the entire palm surface of distal transverse crease to meet and form one line on the entire transverse section of the palm.

Weninger and Navratil (1957) hold nearly the same view as Tillner. They say: "*Statt der beiden beschriebenen transversalen Furchen zieht in seltenen Fällen eine einzige Linie vom ulnaren Rand der Hand quer bis ins erste Interstitum: die Vierfingerfurche (VFF). Nach der allgeme in gültigen Meinung ist sie aus dem Hohlhandabschnitt der DFF und dem Zeigefingerabschnitt der FFF Susammengesetzt, wahrend die anderen Abschnitte der beiden Transversalfurchen fehlen.*"

Their definition is much like Tillner's definition with only difference of showing in rare cases as a single line from ulnar end of the palm towards the first interdigital area of the palm is called simian crease.

According to the generally accepted opinion this is put together from the whole hand section of proximal transverse crease while the other sections of both transverse lines fail.

It will be apparent from the above definition that there is some difference between them. Langdon-Down did not particularise any of the principal fold lines of the palm, Crookshank mentions a single transverse line in place of the head and the heart lines and this is very similar to Portius definition. Tillner's definition almost agrees with the latter part of Wurth's definition, though the former speaks of *Verschmelzung* and the latter *Fortsetzung*, between the relevant sections of *DFF* and of *FFF*. The first part of Wurth's definition is, however, interesting. A transverse line may run from the abduction section of the *DF* or distally therefrom across the palm.

None of the above authors, excepting Crookshank, appears to have taken into account the palmar flexure line in anthropoid apes. Crookshank enquired into these lines in apes and monkeys, and emphasized in italics, that "the Mongoloid line is only found in one: the Orangutan". His photograph of the Orang palm, however, shows, besides the distal transverse line running from the ulnar to the radial end, other smaller ones, as shown in (Fig. 3.1). It is, therefore, worth comparing, first of all, the transverse palmar lines in the anthropoid apes.

Penrose (1949), however, is quite clear in the identification of the palm of a Mongolian imbecile. He mentions "a single transverse crease".

From the few data available to us (Duckworth, (1915); Sonntag, (1924); Wood-Jones, (1929), it is seen that the palm of the apes is characterized by one or more transverse lines.

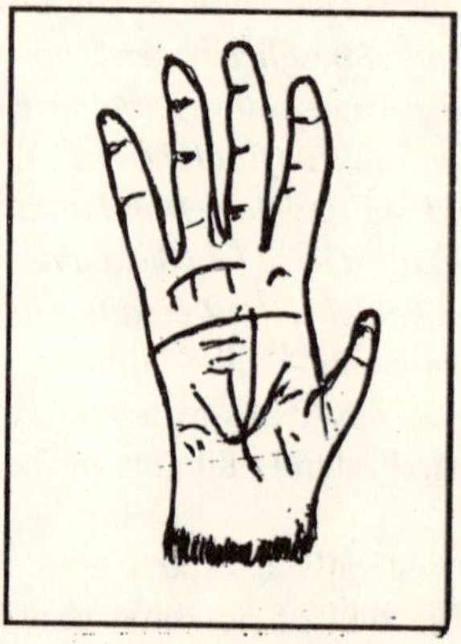

FIG. 3.1: Orang palm (after Crookshanak). (*op cit.* Sarkar)

The Orang palm, figured by Sonntag (Fig. 3.2), shows three transverse lines, all extending from the radial to the ulnar end and are aligned almost parallel. The proximal flexure line is situated almost at the base of the first inter-stitium and the two distal lines are situated close to one another and are at a distance from the proximal line.

It appears to us that the position of the true simian crease has not been satisfactorily defined. There are probably one or more transverse lines, besides, *DFF* and *FFF*, in the anthropoid apes.

Further, the association of criminality and such other anti-social stigmas with the so-called simian line is worth re-considering from the true identification of the above line. A large number of cases appears to have been wrongly diagnosed, since some time the *DFF* running transversely across the palm might have been considered as a simian line, sometimes the *FFF* running as above; and sometimes the *Verschmelzung* of the two sections of the *DFF* and the *FFF*.

The Result-Oriented Approach

The simian crease has been the subject of a large number of recent studies. Right from Langdon-Down (1909), Shuttlewurth (1909) and Crookshank (1924), the results relating to simian crease started pouring from numerous workers. Lestrange gave comprehensive details regarding the distribution of the Transverse Crease in Europe (1969). And several similar attempts were made to find out the effectiveness of the trait under discussion. Simian crease stood as a monarch who represents its entire subjects. This second error has again given a bad jolt to the crease sciences.

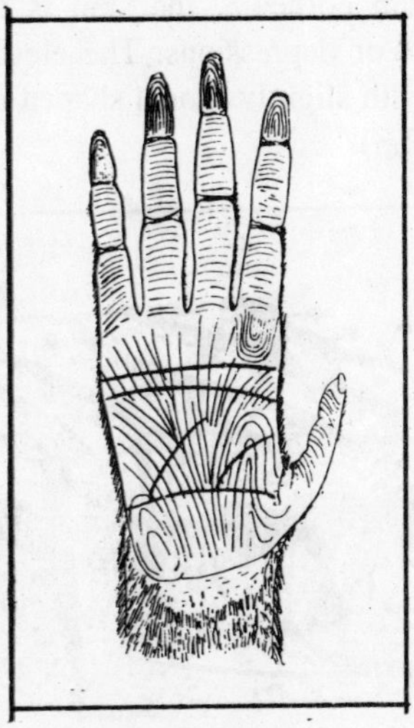

FIG. 3.2: Orang palm (after Sonntag) (*op cit.*, Sarkar)

But for simian crease, the crease has not so far been defined. The existing definition of crease or creases speaks about its type or form. There is not a single definition which refers to crease anatomy or describes its attributes or its mode of occurrence in various dermatoglyphic regions.

Crease may be defined as an area which occurs amidst dermal configurations, bears a distinct core which is devoid of dermal ridges and finds its shape and direction through ridge margin or crease border. The core of the crease finds its shape through ridge endings.

The creases make a significant appearance in their coursing through the entire region of dermatoglyphics. The creases represent the location of firmer attachment of the skin to an underlying structure. The dermal anatomy of the skin which bears ridges, furrows and creases is differently evolved to meet the functional requirements of the primate in general and man in particular.

Before discussing the morphology of creases it is imperative to describe the anatomy of the ridged skin.

There are two main layers : (1) epidermis and (2) dermis. The "epidermis" which is the protective layer consists of five layers from the surface inwards (a) the corneous, (b) the transparent, (c) the granular, (d) the Malpighian and (e) the generating layer. On the outer surface of the stratum corneum, the skin is formed into elevations separated by furrows or depressions. The elevations, called papillary ridges, are studded with slightly funnel shaped openings, better known as sweat pores (Fig. 3.3).

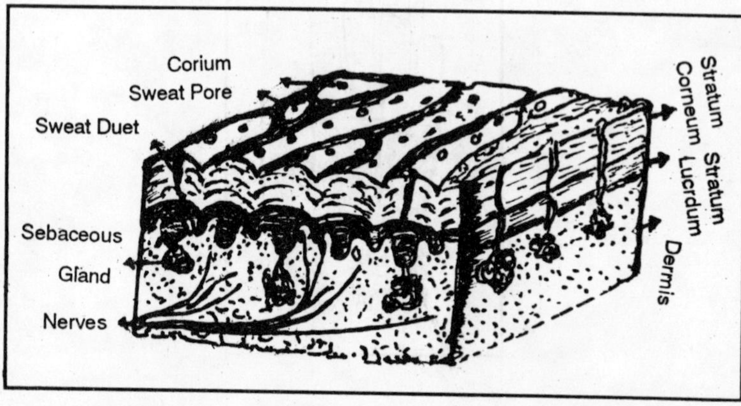

FIG. 3.3: Enlarged portion of a bulb of finger (from the book *Science of Finger Prints* by Edgar Hoover)

These ridges may be damaged temporarily through occupational activities, bruises or superficial injuries, or skin disease, age, etc., but owing to the cellular activity constantly going on in the epidermic portion, the affected skin recuperates, and the damaged ridges again assume their former appearances, as already stated, there being left no scar of the damage.

The second main layer "dermis" is composed of two layers: (a) papillary tissue and (b) the corium. These two layers are separated by an intervening network of blood and lymphatic vessels and herein are also contained sweat glands which are connected with the underlying layer.

The crease core provides firm attachment to the underlying structure, it has to differ from ridged skin and so its anatomy is much different from the ridged skin of palm and sole.

Developmental and Structural Attributes of Creases

The morphogenesis of individual crease configuration on different crease areas, if studied from an evolutionary point of view, could evolve better classificational norms which will reveal to us the various stages in crease pattern modification due to the independent course of specialization in evolution.

Sole and palm, though homologous, have varied crease distribution. A similar condition prevails in case of fingers and toes. The creases in toes like configurational patterns show striking reduction as compared to fingers.

The relative complexity of crease configuration in different regions reflect adaptative gradient for a particular crease under varied functional stresses. This argument can be best understood through the following theoretical concepts:

Considering the developmental aspect of ridges and creases, de Wilde (1979) in his theory on the development of ridge patterns stresses upon the unity concept. The author proposes that the ridge patterns of the hand must be conceived as a total system in which fingers are sub-divided afterwards (Fig. 3.4). In support of this assumption the author cites syndactylism which is generally explained by the persistence of an embryonic developmental stage. Because the unseparated fingers in syndactylism cannot lengthen independently, their ridge patterns are still continuous in a transverse direction. The total ridge system (Fig. 3.5) on the phalanges of all five fingers together is sub-divided secondarily implying that the essential course of these ridges must have been determined before the separation of the fingers in the seventh embryonic week.

When ridges end on or just before another ridge, that is discontinuous in direction, such a ridge pattern is called reduction cusp. Reduction cusp is formed because it meets two converging ridges formed at an early stage (Fig. 3.6). These cusps are numerous and are found in the hypothenar and thenar area and are also found in loop and whorl patterns. From the reduction cusps we get information about the direction of growth of the bundle and its sequence of development.

The inter-digital bundles develop from inter-digital spaces and spread into the blank area of the palm. When ulnar ridges meet inter-digital ridges the pattern formation take place.

Our sole aim of discussing de Wilde's theory is to trace the form and direction of creases and their probable relevance to thenar area of the palm. The case of thenar transformation is of much relevance to crease development.

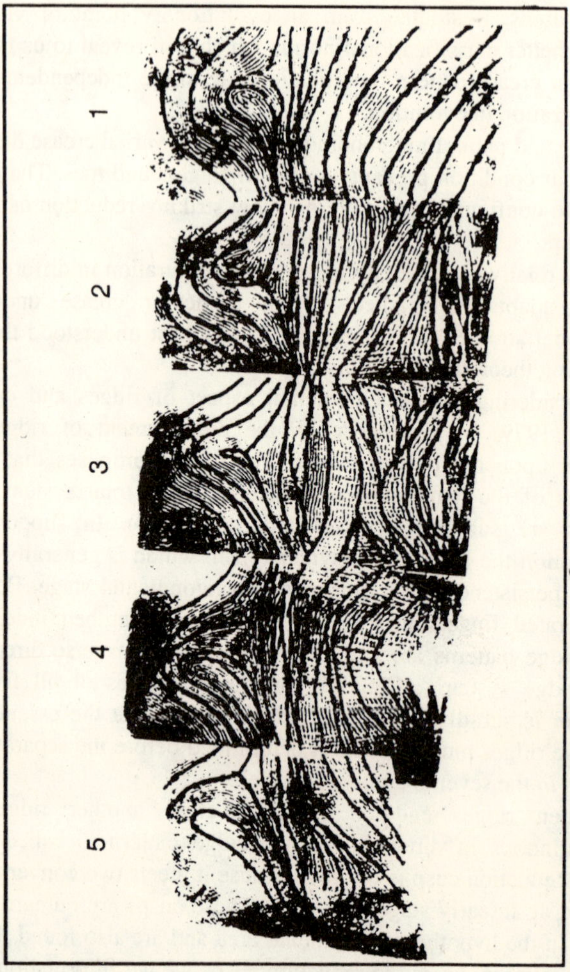

FIG. 3.4: Ridges on the middle and terminal phalanges of the left hand (after de Wilde)

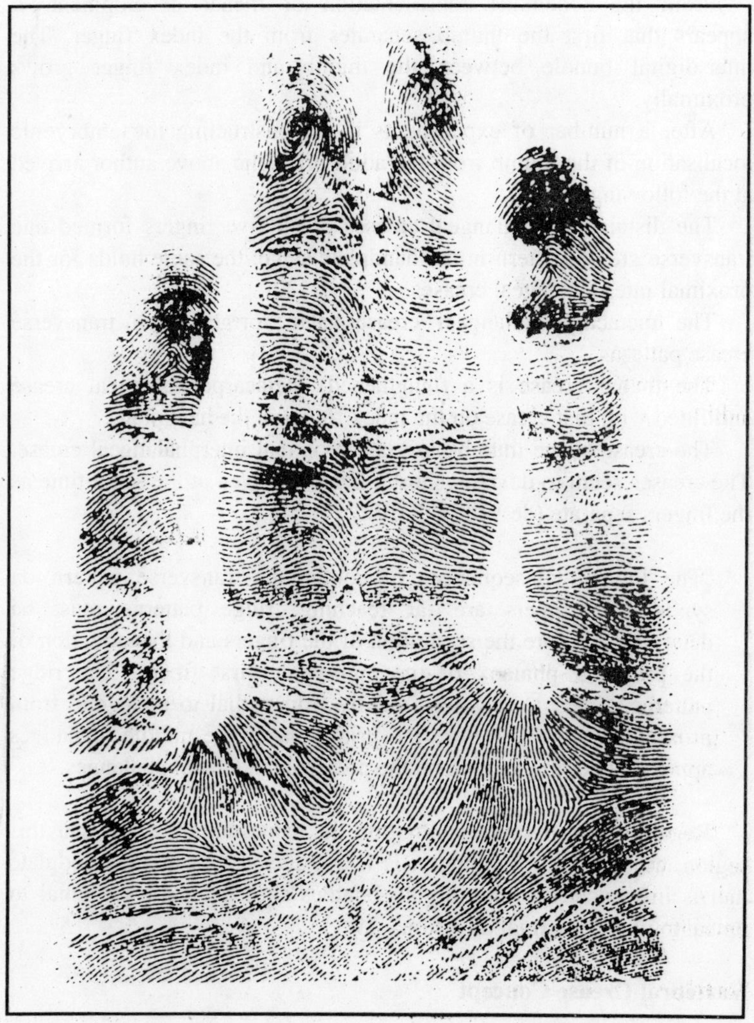

FIG. 3.5: Dermal ridges on the syndactylic fingers (after de Wilde)

Since the ridges of the middle phalanx of the index finger fit with those of the proximal phalanx of the thumb, the ridges of the basal phalanx of the thumb cross the basal crease of the thumb and are continuous with the thenar ridges. The thumb primodia are arranged parallel with those of the index finger.

From the schematic representation of thenar development, it appears that first the thumb separates from the index finger. The inter-digital bundle between the thumb and index finger grows proximally.

After a number of experiments in re-constructing the embryonic localisation of the thumb from the adult print, the above author arrived at the following theory:

The distal inter-phalangeal creases of all five fingers formed one transverse crease pattern in the handplate stage: the same holds for the proximal interphalangeal creases.

The metacarpophalangeal creases also formed such transverse crease patterns.

The thenar crease is a (lengthened) metacarpophalangeal crease and fitted with that crease on the index finger in the handplate.

The crease at the thumb-base is a proximal interphalangeal crease. The creases seem to develop shortly before or even at the same time as the fingers separate (de Wilde, 1979).

> "The logical consequences of continuous transverse pattern on syndactylic fingers are far reaching: ridge patterns must be determined before the separation of the fingers and thenarization of the proximal phalanx of the embryonic first finger. The ridge patterns appear to develop initially from radial to ulnar and from proximal to distal. Before the primordia of the middle phalanges appear, ridges are formed on the proximal and distal phalanges."

Regarding the hypothenar region the same author states that this region, according to his theory, is last inducted part of the handplate and is influenced by inter-digital bundles showing radio-proximal to apical to ulnar proximal direction.

Vertebral Crease Concept

From the above discussion it is amply clear that ridges and creases show unity at embryonic development and appear to develop initially from radial to ulnar and from proximal to distal directions under this dual stress longitudinal radial crease (vertebral crease) splits. The thenarization process makes this vertebral crease to get splitted first from the proximal end. The primary transverse creases show two splits. The direction of the splits is from radial to ulnarward and moving distalward with a greater velocity. The radial base point of the split show minimum velocity thus giving rise to transverse crease. The first proximal split show clockwise movement in the right hand palm and anti-clockwise movement in the left hand palm, keeping its distal end attached to the radial longitudinal crease thus giving birth to distal transverse crease or heart line. Similarly second large split results into proximal transverse crease or head line. These primary embryonic splits from primordial crease (vertebral crease) give rise to primary transverse split (Fig. 3.7).

The only split, which takes place on either ends of the vertebral crease and moves away from it towards ulnar side with equal distal and proximal velocity, gives rise to sagittal crease or life line. The primary creases are the result of primary splits, secondary from the secondary split and tertiary from the tertiary split.

Crease Split Theory

Creases have inherent property to get splitted. This universal splitting tendency of creases of various dermatoglyphic areas, show uniformity of split behaviour.

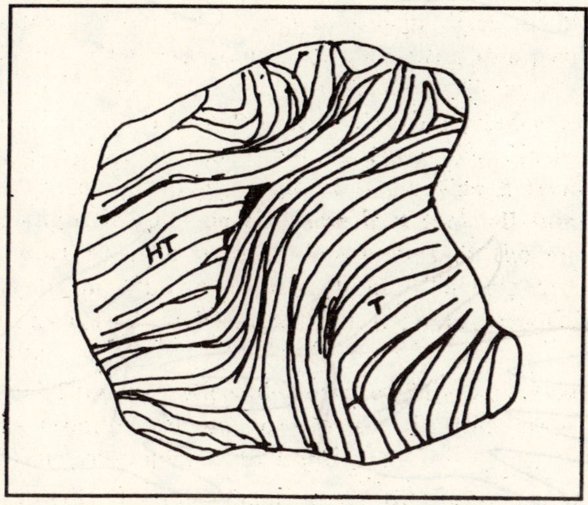

FIG. 3.6: Reduction cusps indicated by black arrows (after de Wilde)

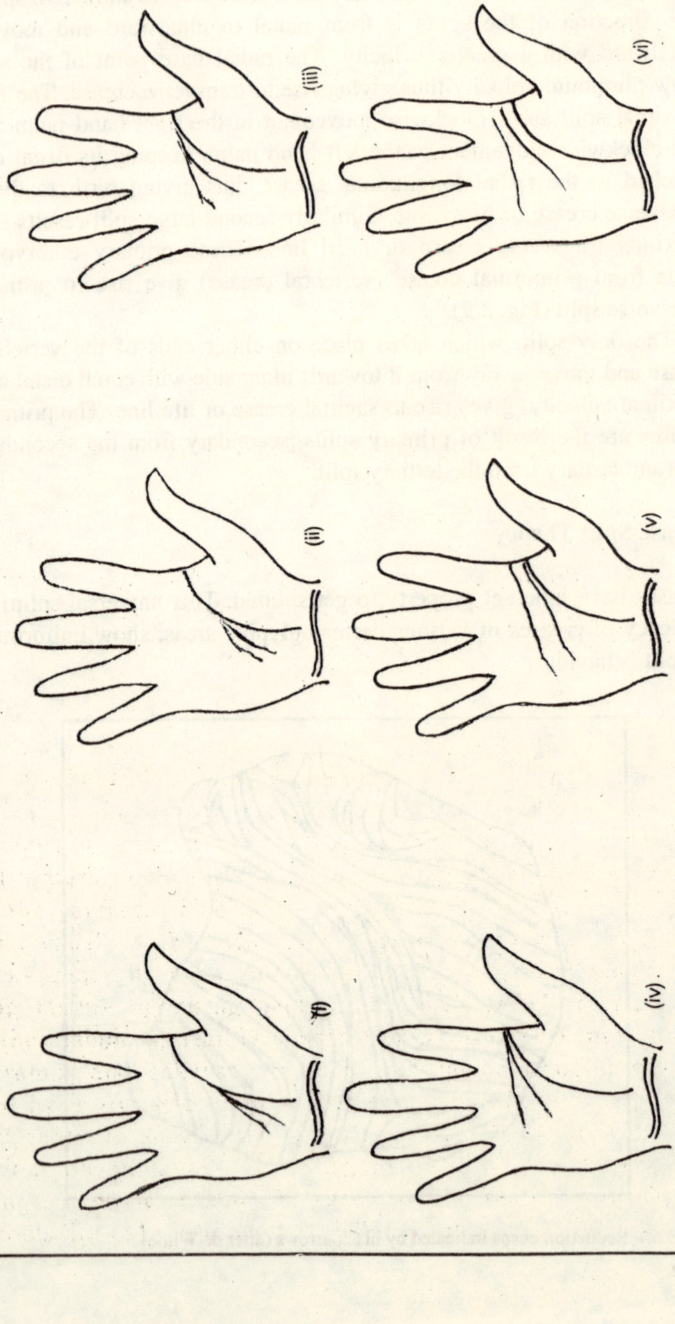

Crease split in Transverse creases

FIG. 3.7: Vertebral crease and crease split

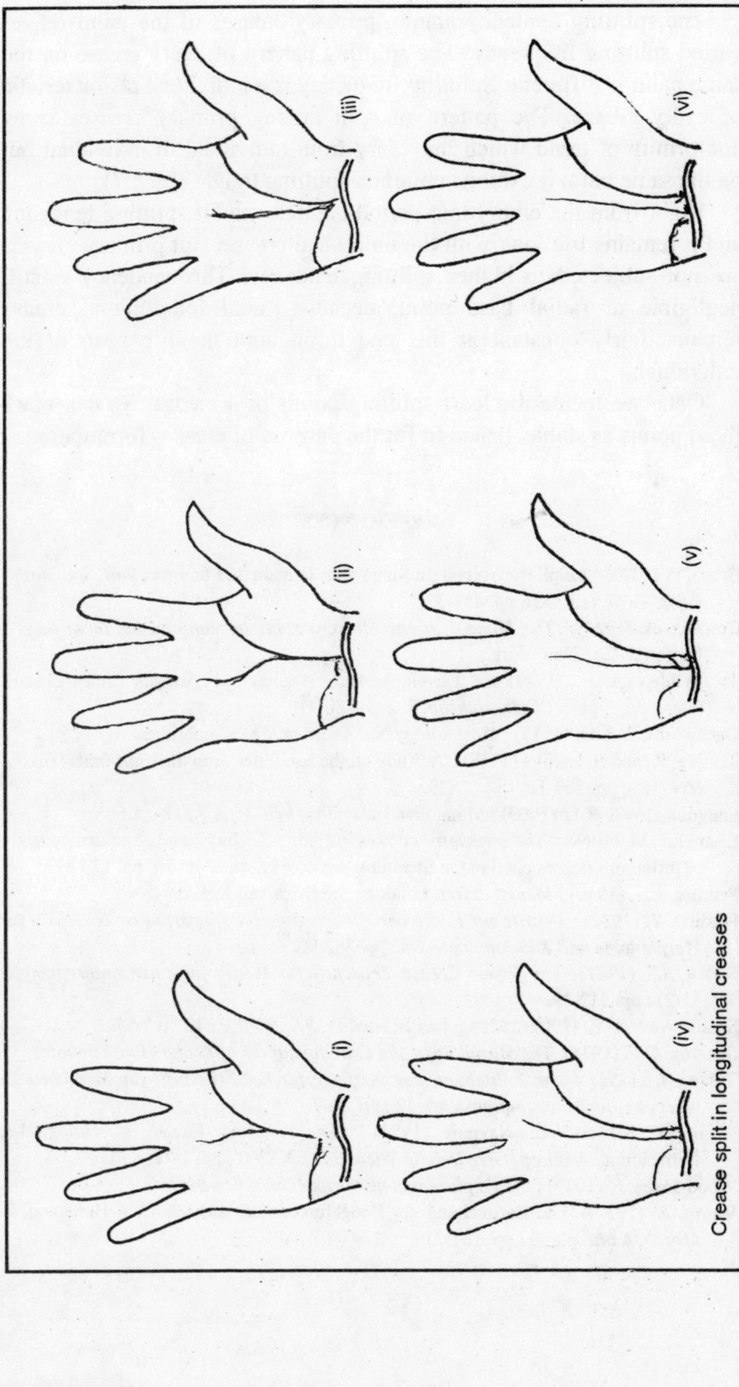

FIG. 3.7: Vertebral crease and crease split

The splitting tendency among primary creases of the palm reflect varied splitting frequency. The splitting pattern of every crease on the same palm is different. Splitting frequency is a individual characteristic of every crease. The pattern of split among primary creases show conformity of trend which may vary from individual to individual but on the same palm it exhibits common splitting trend (Fig. 3.7).

Right from the embryonic period creases exhibit splitting tendency and it remains life long with the individual crease. But primary creases are not subjected to higher splitting tendency. This tendency is still negligible at radial base point, because radial longitudinal crease remains fairly constant at this end throughout the life span of the individual.

Once we locate the least splitting points of a crease, we can mark these points as stable, hence fit for the purpose of creases formulation.

REFERENCES

Broca, P. (1877) : Le pli transversal du Singe dans la main de l'homme. *Bull. Soc. Anthr. Paris, Ze Serie*, t. XII, pp. 431-32.

Crookshank (1924) : *The Mongol in our Midst. a study of man and his three faces* - Duffon & Co., New York.

de Wilde, A.G. (1979) : Developmental Aspects of Ridges and Creases (Dermatoglyphics) *Coll. Anthrop*. 3, 2: pp. 201-10.

Duckworth, W.L.H. (1915) : *Morphology and Anthropology*, Cambridge.

Kimura, K. and S. Hagiya (1958) : A Study on the handlines of twins. *Jinruigaku Zasshi*. 66 (718) : pp. 209-15.

Langdon-Down, R.L. (1909) : Mongolian Imbecility, *Brit. Med. J.*, 12 : p. 665.

Lestrange, M. (1969) : The transverse creases in Europe — Index and comparative study of different samples cited in the literature. *Am. J. Phy. Anthrop*: 30: pp. 173-82.

Penrose, L.S. (1949) : *Mental defect*. London : Sidgwick and Jackson.

Portius, W. (1937) : *Beitrag zur Frage der Erblicheit der vierfingerfurche Zeitschrift fur Morphologie und Anthropologie*. 36 : pp. 382-90.

Sarkar, S.S. (1961) : *The Simian Crease. Zeitschrift fur Morphologie und Anthropologie*. 51(2) : pp. 212-19.

Shuttleworth, G.E. (1909) : Mongolian Imbecility. *Brit. Med. J.*, 12 : p. 665.

Sonntog, C.F. (1924): *The Morphology and Evolution of the Apes and Man*, London.

Tillner, I. (1953) : *Zur Entstehung dev vierfingerfurche. Zeitschrift fur Menscheliche verebungs und Konstitutionslehre* 32 : pp. 56-7.

Weninger, M. and L. Navratil (1957) : Die Vierfingerfurche in atiologischer Betrachtung. Anthrop. *Gesellsch. in Wien. Bd.*, LXXVII : pp. 1-21.

Wood-Jones, F. (1929) : *Man's place among the mammals*, London.

Wurth, A. (1937) : Die Entstechung der Beugefurchen der menschlichen Hohlhand. Z. *Morph. Anthrop.*, 36 : pp. 187-214.

4

MORPHOLOGY OF CREASE CONFIGURATIONS

FOR ANCIENT thinkers the greatest study of mankind was of man's biological being. The variation and adoptation of its physical form could fascinate them most. Out of several human morphological attributes, the study of palmar crease variation have aroused their interest long ago.

A crease occurs on dermatoglyphic surface, bears a base and terminal end with a distinct core and crease border. These features of the individual crease find frequent description in several books of cheiromancy. But scientific reference of above crease features are absent from the literature.

While defining crease, it has been pointed out the crease is devoid of dermal configurations and its borders are defined by ridge ending. It is the ridge character which provides shape and form to the individual crease. A crease is true crease when a core is not intercepted by dermal ridges. When certain portion of the crease core is intercepted by the ridges the crease is designated as mixed crease but in case of complete interception it is called pseudo crease.

On the basis of crease origin, it is possible to assort major creases, i.e., primary creases from secondary or tertiary form.

In this chapter we intend to deal with various crease attributes. Bali and Rawat (1980), in their paper on attributes of crease form, have systematically discussed the majority of crease features.

The creases make a significant pattern in their coursing through the entire region of dermatoglyphic. The crease represent the location of firmer attachment of the skin to an underlying structure. Its special muscles make them appear special and distinctly different from ridged skin. The dermal ridge endings at the crease borders form a furrow of a ridgeless core, running amidst the centre of the crease borders. The ridge irregularities along the crease border are expressed with localized mode of ridge formation, the ridges and furrows give shape to the creases and also to their borders.

Crease Forms

On the basis of crease anatomy we can differentiate creases into three forms. The basis of this classification is the interrelationship between crease core and ridge border of the crease. It has already been emphasised that it is the crease core which forms the major body of a crease. The size and shape of individual crease can be determined through crease core. It is imperative to observe each crease from the stand point of its core features with full care.

True Crease

Those creases whose core is free from ridge interception and whose distinct borders are made of ridge and furrow ending are called true creases (Fig. 4.1).

Pseudo Crease

When dermal ridges and furrows do not end at crease border, but instead they cross the crease core showing feable ridge feature at the core of the crease, the crease is designated as pseudo crease (Fig. 4.1). It may be noticed that the entire core of a pseudo crease shows ridge interception.

Mixed Crease

When a crease core exhibits a mixed ridged feature, i.e., certain portion of the crease bears pseudo crease character and the rest of it is of a true crease nature the crease is designated as mixed crease (Fig. 4.1). Incidence of pseudo crease is much higher among younger age-groups as compared to the older. Crease once in a life time passes through all these stages to get true crease form. In other words the gerontological crease expression is a valid feature for future investigations.

Crease Types

Age change in crease is one of the essential characters of every crease. Creases right from the embryonic development reflect dimensional and

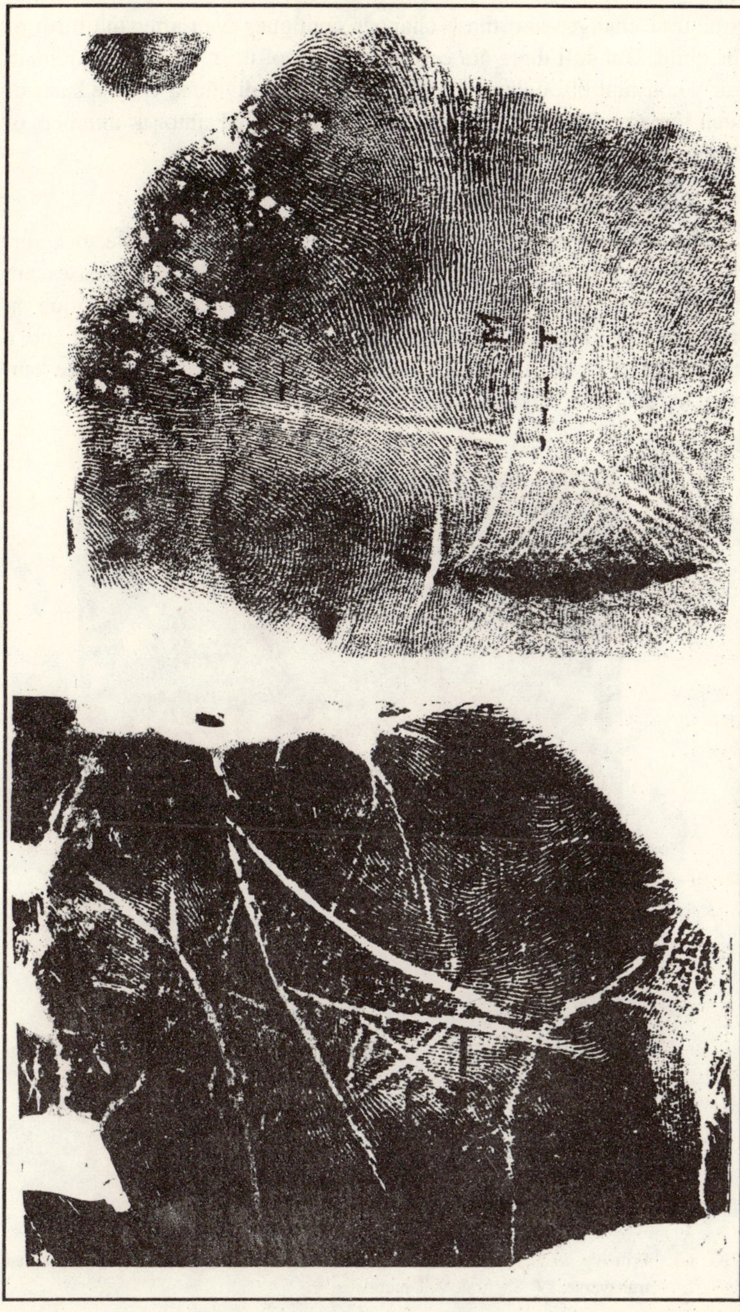

FIG. 4.1: Palm print, sole print

structural changes and these changes continue, even after the birth of the child. But still there are certain features of the crease which remain fairly constant throughout the life span of an individual. On the basis of such crease features the creases are classified into a number of categories.

Primary Creases

On the basis of crease origin and crease form it is possible to assort primary crease from secondary or tertiary type. Primary creases are embryonic in nature and are pre-ordained in their shape and position on palm or sole. Primary crease has a distinct base, terminal end and a core. The core of a primary crease determines its prominance and primary characteristics.

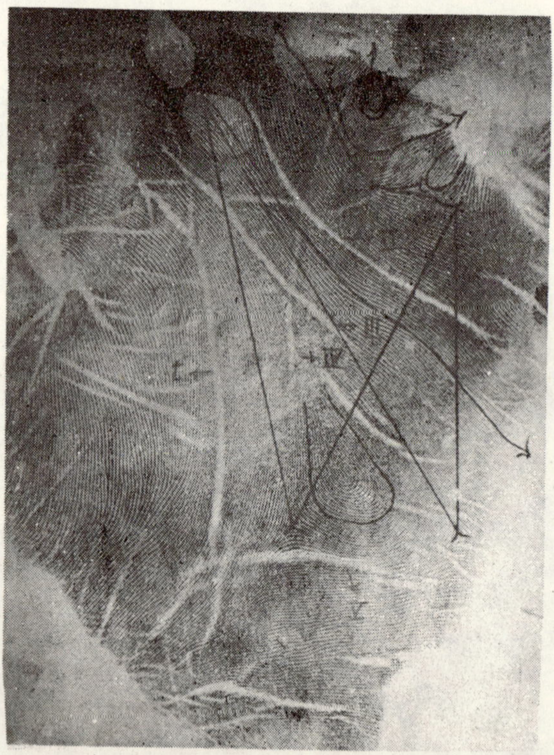

FIG. 4.2: Primary creases; I. Radial longitudinal, II. Distal transverse, III. Proximal transverse, IV Sagittal, V. Ulnar

Among palmar creases radial longitudinal crease, distal transverse crease, proximal transverse crease and ulnar crease are of primary crease type (Fig. 4.2). Primary creases of palm and sole show similarity of shape and form, while primary creases on phalanges and bracelet area have a distinct shape of their own and do not conform to primary crease definition which pertains to palm or sole.

Secondary Creases

The secondary creases are secondary manifestations of crease configuration, and they trail along with the primary creases; secondary creases, like primary creases, show fairly constant locations and well-defined base points and occur on all areas of dermatoglyphics.

The parallel lines along the sagittal crease and the line running parallel to radial longitudinal crease may be grouped under this crease category. The secondary lines or creases (called the Jupiter, the Sun and the Mercury lines in Cheiromancy) run from proximal phalangeal bases towards the proximal direction of the palm across the digits 2nd, 3rd and 4th. Apart from these lines there are line of Mars health live and girdle of Venus. (Fig. 4.3).

Similarly, secondary creases run along the primary creases of the sole (Fig. 4.4). Secondary creases on phalanges show equal status of primary crease both in terms of direction and size (Fig. 4.4).

Tertiary Crease

Tertiary creases occur on all dermatoglyphic areas. These creases do not show specific size and shape and are scattered in all directions. These creases are the result of secondary crease splits and loose connection with their parent crease (Fig. 4.4).

Minutiae

These fragmented minute crease pieces are the result of tertiary splits. Minutiaes are scattered indiscriminately in all directions and on entire dermatoglyphic areas (Fig. 4.4).

White Lines

White lines have been cited by few workers but strictly speaking these lines do not bear the crease features. These lines can be found indiscriminately scattered on palmar and plantar regions (Fig. 4.4).

FIG. 4.3: Secondary creases I. Sun line, II. Mercury line, III. Mar's line, IV. Girdle of Venus

Individual Crease Morphogenesis

It has already been emphasised that without properly observing the individual feature of each crease it is difficult to assign it to its respective category. It is after proper and complete examination that creases can be classified into various types and sub-types. If we believe that creases are biological traits then all biological attributes are also applicable to creases. We are not left with the choice to select a few and leave others. It is true that crease configurations not only appear as confusingly difficult but less stable in shape, size and location. It is,

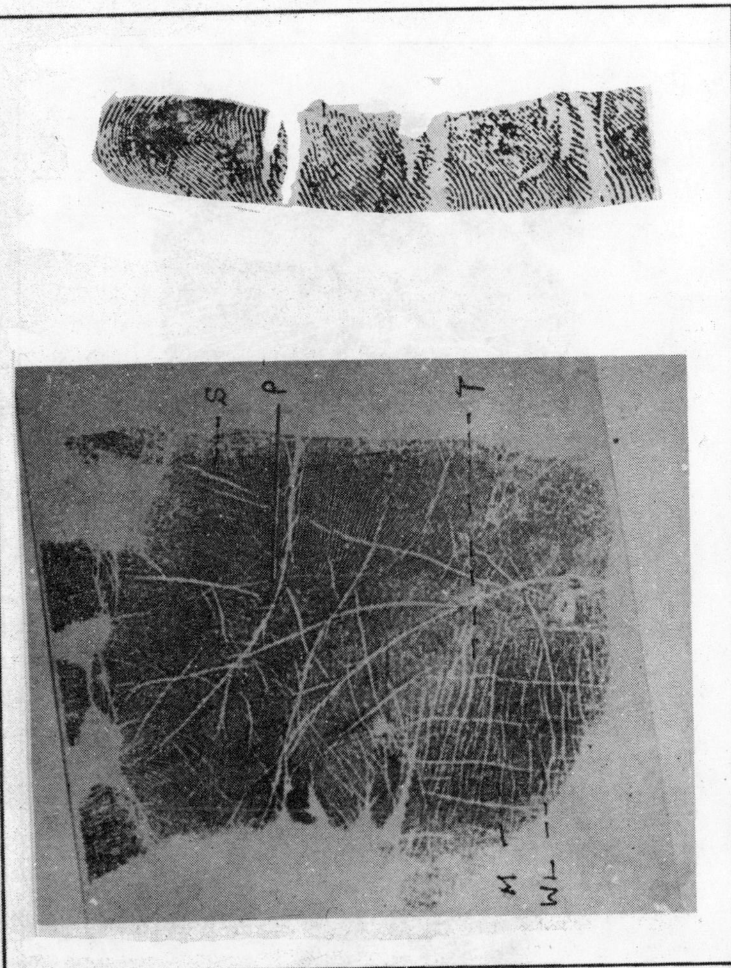

FIG. 4.4: Primary, secondary, tertiary creases - Minutiae & White lines P - Primary, S - Secondary, T - Tertiary, M - Minutiae, WL - White lines

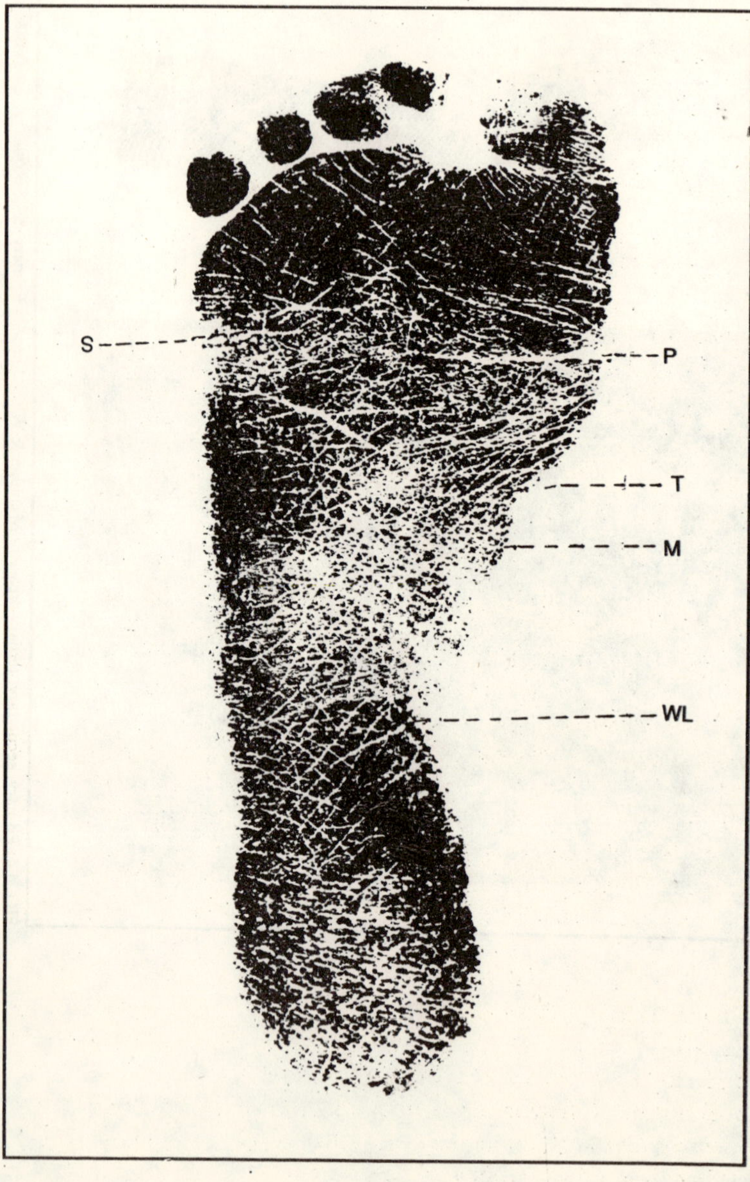

FIG. 4.4: Primary, secondary, tertiary creases - Minutiae & White lines P - Primary, S - Secondary, T - Tertiary, M - Minutiae, WL - White lines

therefore, recommended to analyse each crease from the standpoint of its following features:

Crease Core

The core of the crease determines the prominence of a particular crease. The central deeper smooth ridgeless area of the crease may be traced from its borders which provide a distinctive colour and shape to the crease. The core is, indeed, the crease itself. In other words, it is the core which makes the crease. The core of the crease takes its shape through ridge endings. The cores of primary, secondary and tertiary creases vary in size and form. The core may be smooth, uniform, dotted, uneven, broken or may have ridges in the centre. The colour of crease core varies from person to person and from crease to crease.

The skin pigmentation and pigmentation of the palm when compared with the colour of the creases show distinctive pattern of colour combinations. The inter-individual and intra-individual colour variation and the variation of crease colour among individuals show characteristic pattern in the gradient of colour pigmentation of hand, palm and crease.

The crease core may be spindle shaped, thread-type, parallel-type or beaded-type. The thread-type creases are common on palm and sole, while parallel, spindle and club type of cores occur among metaphalangeal creases. The beaded-type of core is found among bracelet creases (Fig. 4.5).

Crease Shape

The creases make a significant linear thread shape coursing through the entire dermatoglyphic regions (Fig. 4.6).

The crease, therefore, may be straight or looped. It may curve or bend at the terminal end and may show bunching at the base or may start from an enclosure or island. In case of transverse creases, the curve may get distal or proximal concavity, and in case of longitudinal creases, the concavity is towards lateral or medial side, i.e., ulnar and radial side (Fig. 4.6a).

Crease Border

Crease borders are formed by ridge endings. The splitting tendency of the borders make creases appear different from each other. The borders of the crease provide shape to the individual crease.

FIG. 4.5: Crease core, I. Main crease core, II. Terminal branching point, III. Crease border, IV. Main branch, V. Sub-branch.

The border of the crease may be straight, smooth, serrated, mixed or broken. It may be irregular and wavy (Fig. 4.5). The serrated and wavy borders are common among secondary creases. A single horizontal ridge running along the crease border may form a smooth border of a crease.

Crease Split

The splitting tendency is common among creases. Distal and proximal splitting is exhibited by transverse palmar creases, while longitudinal creases show lateral and medialward splits. In the case of plantar creases, the distal medial creases and calcar creases on the medial margin of the foot show higher incidence of splitting tendency. The phalangeal creases show distal and proximal splits.

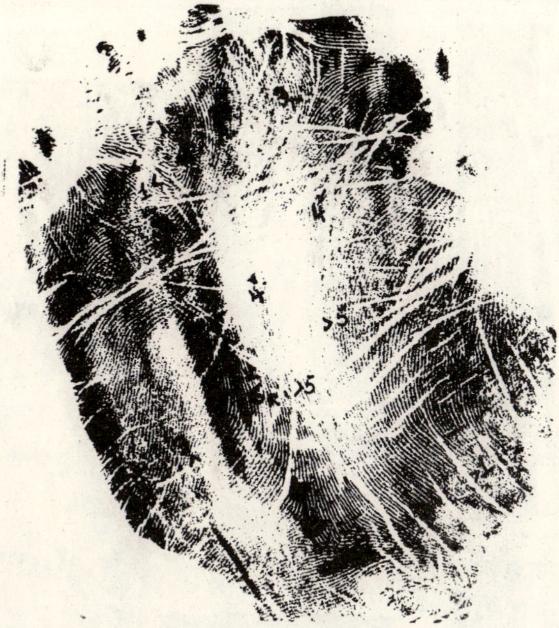

FIG. 4.6: Crease forms; 1. Straight, 2. Distal loop, 3. Distal curve, 4. Proximal curve, 5. Medial curve, 6. Lateral curve, 7. Terminal bend, 8. Bunching.

The split may be differentiated into positive and negative. The former type opens towards the terminal end and the later towards the base end. When the appositely split lines happen to be on the same side of the crease they may meet at a point. In such case the split is known as neutral split (Fig. 4.7).

The above type of crease splits in case of transverse creases may further be designated as distal or proximal positive or negative splits and in the case of longitudinal creases ulnar and radial terms may be used to specify the splitting direction of the crease. A similar nomenclature may be adopted for plantar creases. In case of phalangeal creases the incidence is more of ulnar and radial split rather than of distal or proximal split. Creases on toes also follow a similar trend.

Crease Bifurcation or Branching

The branching and splitting of a crease are two different crease attributes. The branching is the terminal division of the crease, while

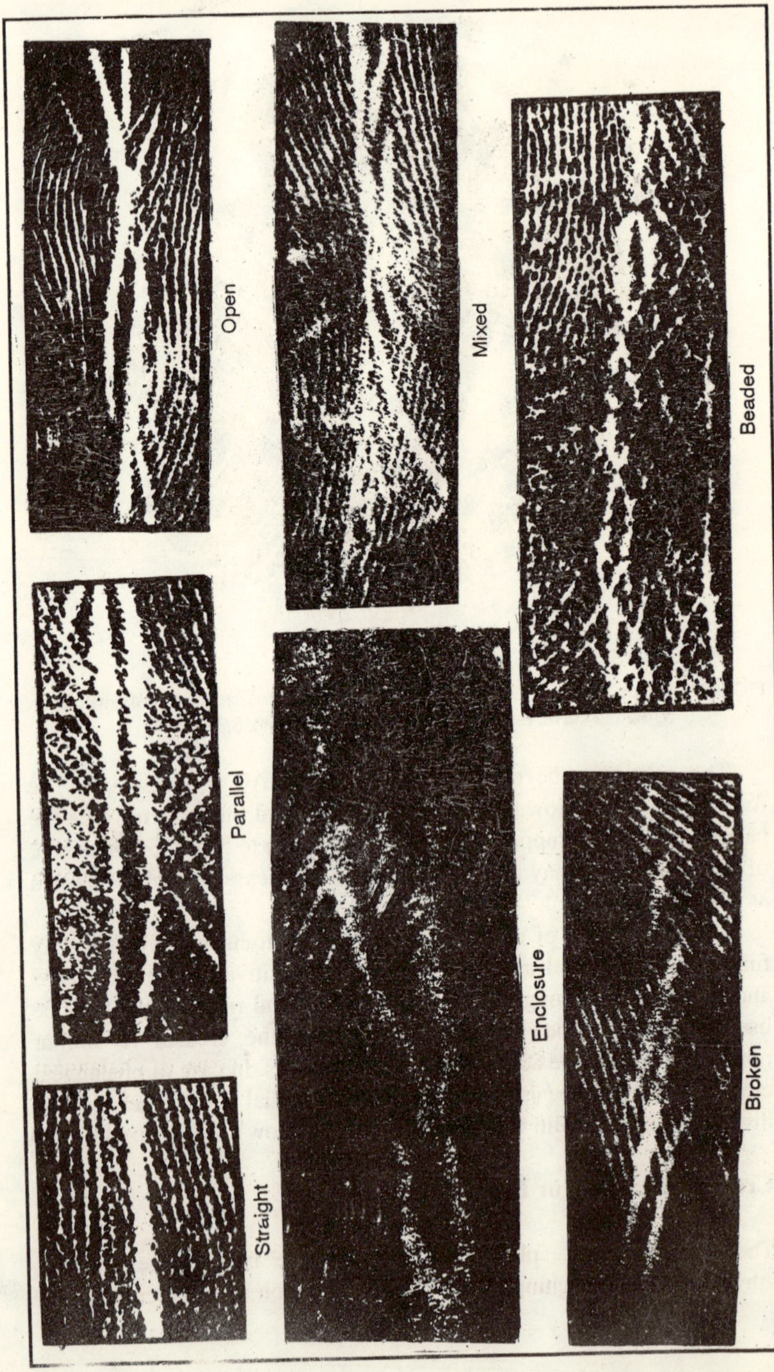

FIG. 4.6a: Crease shape

FIG. 4.7: Crease Split — I. Base end, II. Terminal end, III. Positive split, IV. Negative split, V. Neutral split.

split is a peeling off characteristic of the crease (Fig. 4.5). To differentiate main branch from sub-branch it is necessary to trace the crease core to find out its central axis. This axis is projected further and its deviation is measured. The branch exhibiting lesser deviation is called the main branch.

Relative Length Formula

The relative length formula of the primary creases of the palm measures their relative lengths. The relative lengths of radial longitudinal creases, distal and proximal transverse creases are expressed in terms of their absolute length, measured from base point to terminal end. When radial longitudinal crease is longer than the distal transverse crease and distal transverse crease is longer than proximal transverse crease, the formula is stated as R>D>P. Bali & Rawat (1980) were first to introduce this feature of the crease and have worked out the importance of the above attribute as a pre-requisite for crease formulations.

Radial Base Point

The primary creases are marked by their significant appearance both on palm and sole. Their size, their union and divergence of their terminal ends are characteristics of their own. Their emergence from a single area or point is one of the important attributes of the creases.

The radial base point shows one, two or three independent bases each for radial transverse crease, distal and proximal transverse crease. These different creases may also originate in groups from the same base or bases. The positioning of radial base point has already been discussed in Chapter 2. According to the theory of separation of the intra-digital bundles (de Wilde, 1979) it is the thumb which separates first from the index finger. After its proximal growth the area stabilizes and forms the radial base for transverse creases of the palm (Fig. 4.8). This area is designated as radial base point. In crease formulations this area play an important role.

Crease Transversality

The tendency of transversality among the primary creases take their orientation from this region of the palm.

Carpal Base Point

A similar area or point is located at the proximal end of the radial longitudinal crease (vertebral crease). This point lies just above the bracelet crease towards the thenar bulge where radial longitudinal creases join the bracelet crease. From this area (point) two more primary creases make their appearance, i.e., sagittal and ulnar crease. This point is useful for longitudinal crease formulation (Fig. 4.9).

Medial Base Point

When all the three primary creases of the sole, i.e., medial longitudinal crease, tibial transverse crease and fibular transverse crease, make a union at a point, this point is referred as "Medial base point" (Fig. 4.10). This point forms the basis for the formulation of plantar creases.

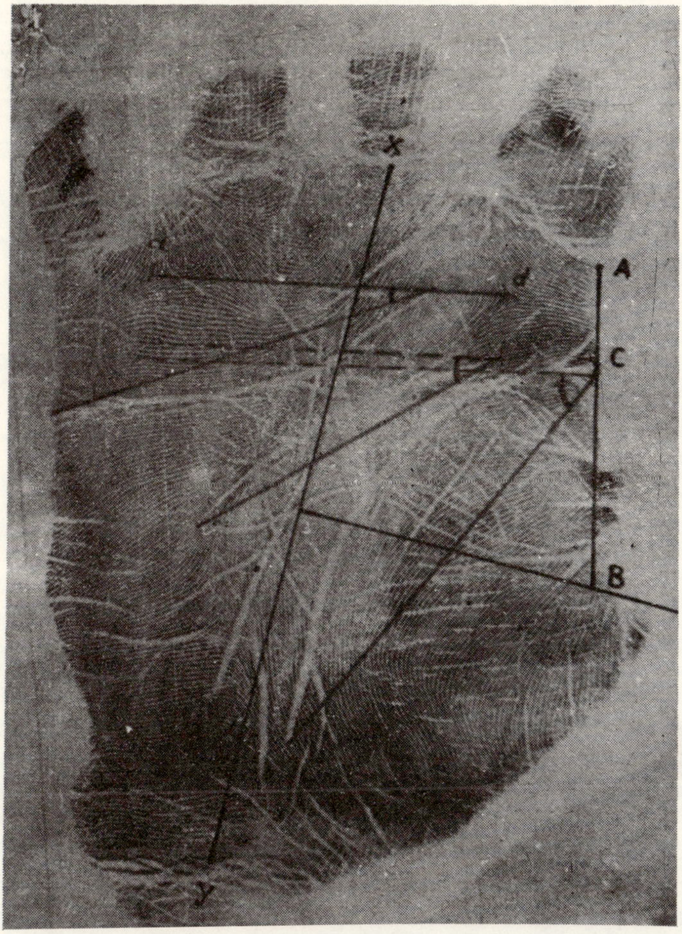

FIG. 4.8: Showing the crease transversality and position of radial base point

To conclude the above discussion it may be stated that for eliminating the possibility of genetic disunity among the various creases, it is imperative to find a common genetical factor, or factors, which controls the orientation of the creases in general. Under the independent course of their functional stress they may have taken varied directions and shape. It is through the keen observation of various crease attributes that we can sort out the most intricate problems of creases and make them worthy for biological investigations. Creases are important human morphological variables and their use in anthropological study is immense.

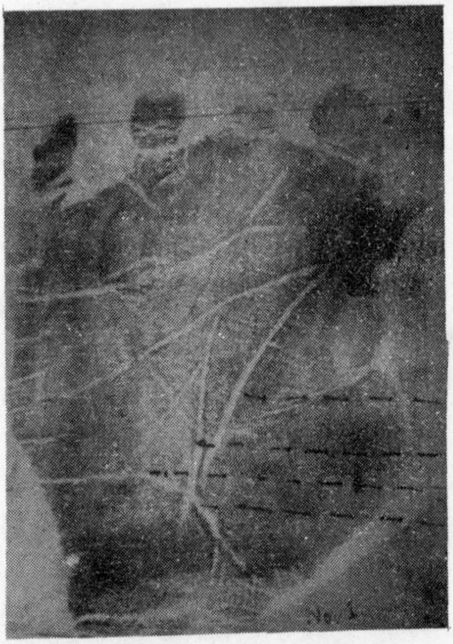

FIG. 4.9: Carpal base point

Monomorphic Hands

Volotzkoy (1936) was the first to apply the term "monomorphic" to a hand in which all digits bear the same pattern type. Bali (1964) applied monomorphism in toes and reported the incidence of pattern expression.

The application of this expression is also valid in case of phalangeal creases. Every phalangeal crease site needs independent treatment. Monomorphism in distal phalangeal crease, medial phalangeal crease and proximal or metacarpophalangeal crease can be applied separately.

In case creases of all the three sites show similarity of pattern types on their respective sites the hand may be designated as 'Absolute monomorphic' type. The probability of this type of hand is remote in phalanges but its chance of occurrence in toes is somewhat bright.

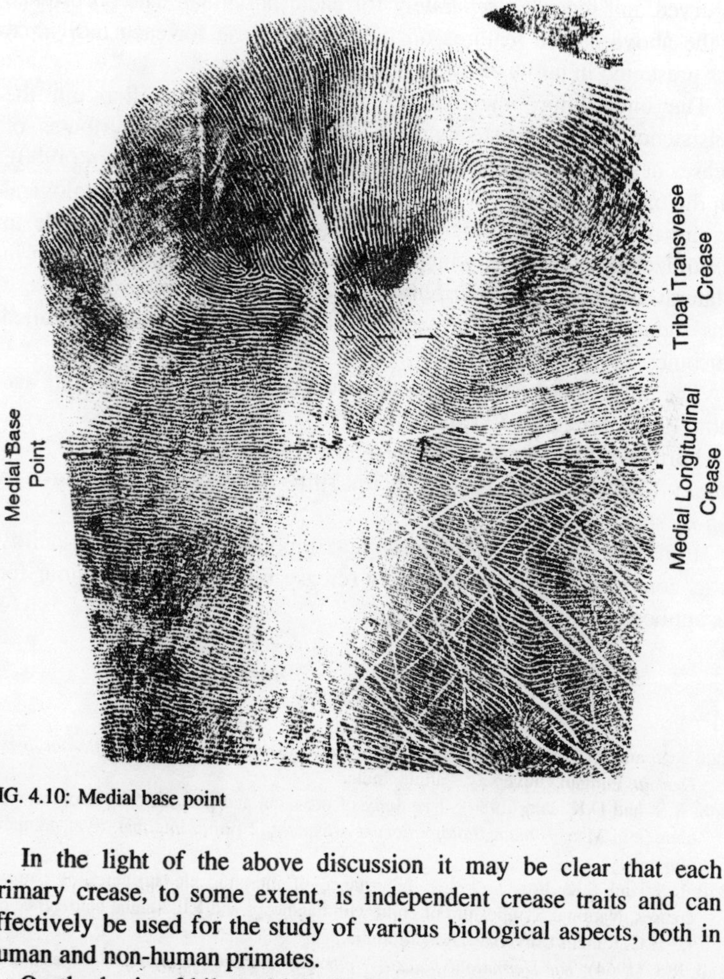

FIG. 4.10: Medial base point

In the light of the above discussion it may be clear that each primary crease, to some extent, is independent crease traits and can effectively be used for the study of various biological aspects, both in human and non-human primates.

On the basis of bilateral inked prints of either sex, numbering 106 each; (Rawat, 1983) treated all above morphological traits in details. The occurrence of various types and forms of creases in each individual was examined, counted and classified.

While dealing with the individual crease morphogenesis various types of crease cores, their shape and size were recorded. The incidence of crease split, crease bifurcation and type of crease border for every primary crease was recorded.

Relative length formula, radial and carpal base point were carefully observed and recorded separately for each individual. The occurrence of the above crease features on individual crease for each individual was presented in terms of frequencies.

The underlying objective of above work was to find out the consistency or inconsistency in occurrence of various attributes of creases as reported by Bali and Rawat (1978); Bali and Mishra (1980). On the basis of the above numerical distribution of each morphological feature of individual primary creases of the palm it was possible to scrutinize those features which followed consistency of trend both in bilateral and bi-sexual distributions. On the basis of our experience it was found that majority of these features are biologically controlled attributes.

The subsequent attempts in this direction were made by Bali and Jain (1980), Singh (1983) and Jain (1978).

Further efforts were made by Patel (1981), Chanderia (1981) and Dubey (1981) to find out the heretability of above features through family study.

It may be concluded that individual importance of crease variability is as convincing as their collective (crease formulation) behaviour for its application in anthropology.

REFERENCES

Bali, R.S. and R. Mishra (1980): Age change and crease morphogenesis, *Internat. Sym. Dermat*, Punjabi University, Patiala, India.

Bali, R.S. and D.K. Jain (1980): The study of pre-natal and post-natal Development of creases in Man. *Human Biology Recent Advances*, 2 (Proc. Intermat. Sym. Punjabi University).

Bali R.S. and S.K. Rawat (1980): Inheritance of morphogenic attributes of palmar creases. National Symposium of child with handicaps and VII Annual conference of I.S.H.G. Ranchi University, Ranchi, India.

Bali, R.S. (1964): *Toe Dermatoglyphics — Inheritance and Comparison with the Finger Ball Patterns*. Ph.D. Thesis, Delhi University, Delhi.

Chanderia, A.K. (1981): *The study of inheritance of palmar creases and crease Transversality*. M.Sc. Thesis*, Saugar University, Sagar.

De Wilde, A.G. (1979): Developmental Aspects of Ridges and Creases (Dermatoglyphics) *Coll Anthropl.*, 3, 2: pp. 201-10.

Dubey, N.M. (1981): *The study of inheritance of crease and crease surface area — Morphogenesis and their Attributes*. M.Sc. Thesis*; Saugar University, Sagar.

Jain, D.K. (1978): *Age change — Morphology of hand and palmar flexion creases among*

* The above cited M.Sc. and Ph.D. Dissertations were guided by the author.

Brahman girls. Thesis submitted in part fulfilment for the requirement of the degree of M.Sc., Saugar University, Sagar.

Patel, B.P. (1981): The study of inheritance of palmar creases and their base point positioning. M.Scs. Thesis*; Saugar University, Sagar.

Rawat, A. (1983): Study of attributes of palmar creases and phalangeal flexion crease.

Singh, N.R. (1983): A study of plantar creases among Rajputs. M.Sc. Thesis*; Saugar University, Sagar.

Volotzkoy, M.V. (1936): On the genetics of finger prints. Proceedings of the Maxim Gorky Medico-Genetical Research Institute.

5

MORPHOMETRY OF CREASES

THE PALMAR flexion creases have been on the scientific anvil for the last one century. The early simian crease-oriented work is essentially on phenotypic crease formulations and their distribution among various populations. The quantitative crease expression is yet an unexplored field.

Morphological precision in crease description is obtainable through quantitative crease expression, which, in turn, can lead to a systematic and scientific crease investigation. Crease biology does not find answers only through the system of crease formulations. The morphogenesis of creases is an essential aspect of the creases' study and demands a probe. It is true that crease formulation is an essential field, and on the basis of crease formulations we are able to study and prove the validity of various morphological variables for investigating and interpreting data on different populations. But validity of any formulation must conform to the crease biology.

In the light of the above fact the study of age change among creases is imperative and deserves our immediate attention. Along with the hand and fingers the creases also grow and conform to the growth norms. Bali and Mishra (1978) reported linear, age-wise growth of hand palm and creases among boys and girls. The subsequent study of Bali and Jain (1980) on new born infants and children ranging between one to eleven years of age further confirmed the above finding. Rai and Jain (1980) made the similar observation. Dubey (1981), Singh (1983), Patel (1981) and several others have also contributed towards this field of crease investigation.

Without the use of morphometric or quantitative crease expression it is not possible to find out the effective utility of creases in anthropology. The crease morphometry could best be interpreted in terms of crease length, crease breadth, crease depth, positioning of base point, crease transversality and crease surface area.

The quantitative crease expression (crease morphometry) relates to the individual primary creases of both palm and sole. The methodologies employed for morphometric investigation of primary creases are given as under:

Crease Length

The length of the crease is, in fact, a length of crease core which courses through the dermal configuration of palm and sole.

The absolute length of crease is the length of its entire core from base to its terminal end or point. It is simple to locate terminal point but location of base point quite often gets complicated because of bunching at crease bases.

Through the method of crease tracing (Fig. 2.7) we can overcome this problem. The absolute length of the crease is measured by an instrument named measurer (Fig. 2.9). The length can also be measured by tape, steel wire or planimeter.

Projectile Length of Crease

The projectile length measures a straight distance of a crease between terminal and its base point.

The above linear dimension of the crease can be expressed in centimetre scale (Fig. 5.1). To overcome age-change problem a more stable and reliable scale is the biological scale, i.e., ridge count scale. The ridge count scale measures the number of ridges per unit area on a related area of dermatoglyphics. Ridges contained by one centimetre are counted and these counts are used as scale. This biological scale can eliminate all probable errors caused by age change in creases.

Crease Breadth

The greatest or maximum crease breadth in the middle of the crease is the best representative breadth of a crease. But it is advisable, also, to measure maximum breadth of the crease at its base end.

The measurement can be recorded in millimetre scale or in ridge count scale.

The above cited works were conducted under the author's supervision and none of it interprets the crease length or crease breadth in terms of ridge count scale. The biological scale in fact, has not been tested as yet.

FIG. 5.1: Projectile lengths of: A-B=Distal transverse crease, C-D=Proximal transverse crease, D-E=Radial longitudinal crease.

Crease Depth

The depth of a particular crease is not easily obtainable crease dimension. Even the plastic moulds cannot provide accurate results. Through microscopic technique the crease depth is obtainable, but it is quite cumbersome to perfect this method. It is, therefore, suggested to record the depth of a crease at a point where the width of the crease is maximum simply by halving the number of ridge counts or reading in millimetre scale of crease breadth. This indirect measurement of the crease is not fully reliable.

It may be pointed out that length of a crease is the most prominent crease feature and shows consistency of trend, both in bilateral and bi-sexual variations. Apart from Bali and Mishra (1980), Bali and Jain (1980), Bali and Rawat (1980), the work of Patel (1981), Rawat (1983), Chanderia (1981) and Dubey (1981) is worth mentioning. The above crease dimensions have been employed by Bali and Jain (1980) and Singh (1983) in the study of age-change in creases of palm and sole.

The above cited crease traits have also been used to study both inter and intra-individual relationship between palmar and plantar creases.

Positioning of Base Point

All primary creases, both of palm and sole, in one form or the other, show affinity at base point resulting into union of primary creases. On palmar surface, the base points can be located adjoining the proximal and distal ends of radial longitudinal crease. The distal area falls between first and second inter-digital towards the medial or radial margin of the palm. This area shows the union between primary creases and the point is called "radial base point".

Similarly on the proximal end the primary creases meet or tend to meet at a point called carpal base point. This point lies at the root of radial longitudinal crease just above the bracelet line.

de Wilde (1979) contends that radial base area is the result of an early embryonic proximal shift of first digit and the area gets settled first as compared to the rest of the palm.

While discussing the thenarization of the palm, the above author theorises the early location of carpal base point (Fig. 4.9).

The thenarization of plantar area is not on the line of hand. Hence, there is a shift of base point towards febular side. The medial base point lies between the first and second toe but more proximally as compared to the palm. This may be due to the functional stress that the foot has undergone during the course of evolutionary changes.

The embryonic and phenotypic importance of different base points in creases has already been discussed in Chapter 2. Of late, it was realised that mere definitions of the base points are not enough information to make them viable morphometric trait. Through Ph.D. and master dissertations, extensive probe was done by several workers under author's supervision.

Under the heading "The crease morphogenesis and positioning of their radial base point", Patel (1981) investigated the quantitative shift in crease base point in different individual. The trait was studied for its heretability with the help of family data. Later investigation of this trait by Chanderia (1980), Rawat (1983) and Dubey (1981) confirmed the findings.

The positioning of the base point is an expression of relative distance between the base point C and Point A or B (Fig. 5.2). All the above three fall on a single straight line between the first and second inter-digital areas of the palm.

FIG. 5.2: Crease transversality angle;
∠a d p. proximal crease angle,
∠a d q. distal crease angle,
∠a d r. radial crease angle.
Relative base point distance, AB. lengh, AC. length, BC. length.

Point 'A' occupies a middle proximal margin of the basal phalangeal crease of index finger.

Point 'B' can be traced indirectly by drawing a straight anatomical axis of the palm by joining it at X and Y points in the middle of the third phalangeal base and mid-point of the bracelet crease or wrist. On dividing it in the middle and by projecting a perpendicular on its mid-point which joins at basal phalangeal crease of the thumb the point is marked as 'B'. The line AB necessarily cuts the base point area of the crease starting from a single or double crease bases.

The positioning of base point is an expression of relative distance between the base point C and A or B (Fig. 5.2). The positioning of base point equips us for the investigation of relative proximity shift in the base point either towards the first or the second phalanx of the palm.

The radial base point line AB and its two segments — AC and BC — are three different components or traits and their measures can usefully be employed as ethnic variables. This morphological variable shows consistency of trend among sexes and bilateralism. The trait has been studied by the author (1980) among criminals and normal individuals. The heretability of AB, AC and BC base lines has already been established by Bali and Rawat (1980). This morphological variable appears to be sensitive and its quantitative expression qualifies it as an effective investigational tool in anthropology.

In the case of carpal base point and plantar medial base point, the basal areas can be investigated on the similar line as adopted in case of radial base point line.

Crease Transversality

In Chapter 2 we have discussed in detail the de Wilde's phalangeal unity theory and the author's vertebral creases concept as well as the crease split theory. Because of differential embryonic velocity in primary crease development, the transverse palmar creases show variation in the transversality angles of distal and proximal transverse creases of the palm. This embryonic crease attribute shows crease relation with the palm especially with a, t, d tri-radii.

We have first to establish the biological transverse axis of the palm, i.e., 'a' and 'd' axis. This axis is obtained by joining tri-radiis 'a' and 'd' of the palm. By drawing parallel lines from base points of three major creases of the palm, i.e., radial longitudinal crease, distal transverse crease and proximal transverse crease we get transverse axis. By joining the base of a crease to its terminal point an angle is formed at the base point of each crease. These angles represent the transversality of above three creases (Fig. 5.2).

By joining the 'a' and 't' tri-radii and by projecting it to 'n' point we can achieve three angles for ulnar expression of crease transversality. The above transversality angles are radial expression of crease transversality.

The heretability of crease transversality was first established by

Chanderia (1981). In his master's dissertation, he tested the above trait for bi-manual and bi-sexual trends. The subsequent work of Patel (1981), Dubey (1981), Rai (1980) and Rawat (1983) established the credential of crease transversality in anthropology. Bali and Rawat (1980) independently arrived at the similar results.

The transversality angle of distal transverse crease show minimum bi-sexual variation as compared to radial longitudinal and proximal transverse creases. A significant bilateral difference has been reported in the case of radial longitudinal crease transversality but proximal transverse crease shows nominal difference.

From the ethnic stand-point the above traits have not so far been studied. The criminal application of the trait indicates significant association, especially in case of radial longitudinal crease transversality.

Crease Surface Area

In the previous Chapter we have discussed in detail, the morphology of crease core besides showing the various types of crease cores. The present discussion deals with the quantitative interpretation of crease core, i.e., measuring the surface area of each crease. This quantitative dimensional expression of cores of primary creases releases another important parameter for anthropological investigations. The intra-individual variation of each crease can best be studied through crease surface area. For the study of crease biology the utility of crease surface areas is immense. It is highly sensitive crease feature and its application in the study on crease growth has already been realised. The crease surface area is an area of a crease core measured in centimetres, on ridge counts and on cell counts scale. The area can be measured with the help of planimeter (Fig. 2.8). Bali and Jain (1980) were first to use this instrument for measuring the surfaces of crease cores.

The three different scales, adopted for quantitative expression of crease surface area, show the level of precision and micro-sensitivity for recording the change in crease core. The crease surface area, in millimetre scale, is directly recorded by the instrument. By tracing the boundary of a particular crease we can measure its surface area. The level of accuracy can be enhanced, if tracing needle is moved slowly and carefully. Biological or ridge count scale first measures the area in centimetres with the help of planimeter and then this scale is converted into ridge counts, which relates a crease core to the count of ridges contained in one centimetre. This biological scale is more sensitive and minimises the age change influence on surface areas of the creases.

The microscopic scale, again, is a biological scale but it can trace the micro-vibrations in the increment of crease surface area. Having measured the total surface area of a crease, we can convert it into a micro-unit to calculate the number of crease cells occupied by the micro-unit of the crease core. This unit bears a microscopic precision. We can find out the smaller terminal segments of a crease, showing brisk cellular activity and cellular growth at a particular point of the crease ages.

The application of ridge count scale and cellular count scale has not been verified. The existing work on crease surface area is carried out only in centimetre scale. Bali and Jain (1983), Patel (1981), Rawat (1983) and Rawat and Bali (1980) studied crease surface area of the palmar creases. Singh (1983) applied this technique of measuring surface area in plantar creases. Mishra and Bali (1979) were first to report their work on crease surface area.

Dubey (1981) investigated the trait from inheritence stand-point. Besides the collective behaviour, the crease shows individual characteristics. Most of these crease characteristics are heritable. The crease surface area is a major crease attribute and its inheritance is of much importance.

The study of crease surface area among new borns was reported by Bali and Jain (1983). Their subsequent work on children of either sex ranging between one and eleven-year age shows the age-wise increment level of the trait under discussion. The above authors also applied this technique in the study of crease embryology (1980). The incidence of crease surface area in normal and abnormal populations reflects genetical basis and their sex and bilateral characters confirm the ethnic validity of the trait and subsequently its importance in anthropology.

REFERENCES

Bali, R.S. and R. Mishra (1978): The study of morphological change in hand, palm and palmar flexion creases of one to eleven years old boys and girls. Xth Internat. Congr. Anthrop. & Ethno. Sciences, New Delhi, India.

Bali, R.S. and R. Mishra (1980): Age change and crease morphogenesis. *Internat. Sym. Dermat.* Punjabi University, Patiala, India.

Bali, R.S. and D.K. Jain (1983): The study of pre-natal and post-natal Development of creases in Man. *Human Biology Recent Advances,* 2 (Proc. Internat. Sym. Punjabi University).

Bali, R.S. and S.K. Rawat (1980): Inheritance of morphogenic attributes of palmar creases. *National Symposium on Child with Handicap and VII Annual Conference of I.S.H.G.* Ranchi University, Ranchi. India.

Chanderia A.K. (1981): The study of inheritance of palmar creases and crease transversality. M.Sc Thesis. Saugar University, Sagar.

de Wilde, A.G. (1979): Developmental Aspects of Ridges and Creases (Dermatoglyphics) *Coll. Anthropl.*; 3, 2: pp. 201-10.

Dubey, N.M. (1981): The study of inheritance of crease and crease surface area — Morphogenesis and their Attributes. M.Sc. Thesis, Saugar University, Sagar.

Mishra, R. (1979): Inheritance and methodological study of plantar creases. Thesis submitted in part fulfilment for the requirements of the degree of Ph.D., University of Saugar, Sagar.

Patel, B.P. (1981): The study of inheritance of palmar creases and their base point positioning. M.Sc. Thesis, Saugar University, Sagar.

Rawat, S.K. and R.S. Bali (1980): Morphogenesis of crease among murderers. *National Sym. on Child with Handicap and VII Annual Conference of I.S.H.G.*, Ranchi University, Ranchi, India.

Rawat, A. (1983): Study of attributes of palmar creases and phalangeal flexion crease. M.Sc. Thesis, Saugar University, Sagar.

Rai, A.K. (1980): Intra-individual relationship between palmar creases — Dermatoglyphics of newborn. M.Sc. Thesis, Saugar University, Sagar.

Rai, A.K. and D.K. Jain (1980): *Age change and crease morphology*, Madhya Pradesh Vigyan Academy, Jabalapur (M.P.).

Singh, N.R. (1983): A study of plantar creases among Rajputs. M.Sc. Thesis, Saugar University, Sagar.

6

CREASE EMBRYOLOGY

THAT THE palmar creases develop between second and third embryonal month, and are independent of the functional results of flexing of hand was established by Wurth (1937). Schaeuble (1933) related embryonal development of creases with the development of inter-digital pads. Blümel and Poll (1928) and Patten (1953) made their observations on epidermal ridges and flexion creases of the embryos. Schenk and Patzer (1959), on the basis of close embryonal sequence of development between hands and feet, assumed that plantar creases, like palmar creases, are formed between the embryonal pads. Dar, Schmidt and Nitowsky (1977) observed an association between interrupted transverse creases and intra-uterine methadone exposure. Usher, et al., (1966) utilized plantar crease appearance for determining the gestation age of the foetus. Schawman and Alter (1976) confirmed the findings of above authors.

The differentiation of epidermal ridges and creases can be traced from sixth to seventh week of the foetal development, when the epidermis is thin and smooth and volar pads show their first appearance. At this stage the paddle-like hand indicates the position of five digits. At the close of the second month, when the foetus is about 2.5 cm in length, the pads or bulges become rounded and localized. These round bulges become prominent and individualized (Fig. 6.1). In the 13th week the foetus shows regression in pads expressing a phenomenon of recapitulation.

The delayed embryonic development in case of foot lags behind from the developmental sequences of the hand. The hand and foot being homologous show similarity of developmental trends. But due to differential evolutionary stresses the foot shows variation of form and shape.

Whether epidermal ridge differentiation is influenced by external pressure as suggested by Cummins and Midlo (1961) or by in-growth of digital nerve and blood sinus as suggested by Bonnevie (1927) is still not clear. Bonnevie stresses the cushioning as pre-disposing factor in the development of ridge pattern mechanism. Cummins and Midlo, emphasises localization of growth activity which results into irregularities in ridges. The volar surfaces possess the inherent capacity to develop ridges, but dispositions of these ridges are related to differential stimuli of growth agent – Dermatoglyphics – being differentiated in their final form during the third and fourth foetal months, remain stable throughout the life span of an individual.

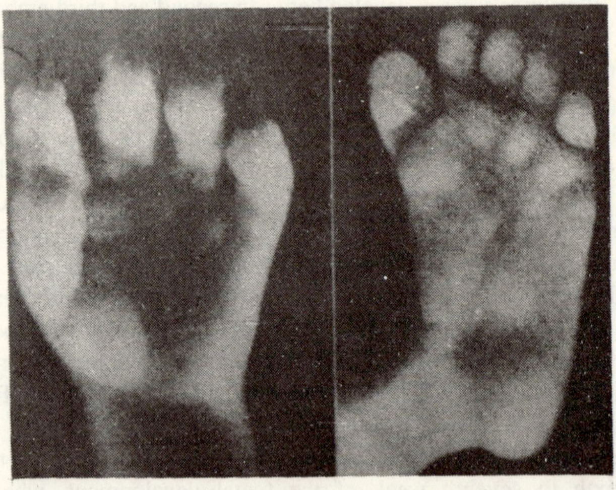

FIG. 6.1: Hand of a human foetus and foot of another specimen (from Cummins and Midlo, 1961)

Creases and dermatoglyphics are topographical associates but both are independent components of the palm or sole. The embryonic developmental sequences of creases conform very closely with dermatoglyphic. But for their origin and terminal orientation creases show the element of age change throughout the life of an individual. The change is more obvious in secondary and tertiary creases.

The base point fixation of primary creases of palm as well as of sole is of embryonic nature and their orientation in shape and size is pre-ordain manifestation of localised activity of volar pads.

Schaeuble (1933) states that the development of the palmar creases is directly related to the development of the inter-digital pads. The arrangements of the crease be related to the specific growth of the skin, the pads and papillary system of the palm. The above discussion, in the light of de Wilde's theory "Developmental aspects of ridges and creases" (1979), finds answers for several developmental sequences of creases.

de Wilde derives much of his logic from syndactylism. He concludes that ridge pattern of the hand must be conceived as a total system in which the fingers are sub-divided afterwards. The ridges and creases appear first and then digital separation takes place thus showing common embryonal sharing stage of creases forms. Primary creases must have been determined earlier to the pad development stage of the foetus [de Wilde (1979)].

It could be observed from figure that in syndactylism phalangeal crease pattern shows unity of crease form and finger exhibits this unity to the level of a transverse crease.

Keeping in view the above facts we can derive from de Wilde's theory that it is the pre-existent continuity which, on lengthening of phalanges, gets disturbed and induced the changes in the creases.

On the embryonic stages of development the phalanges sub-divide later to crease formation. In the 7th embryonic week the appearance of notches between the rays indicates the places of future fingers. The ridges and creases must have been determined just before or at the same time that the finger manifested themselves in the radial part.

Reduction cusps and bundles, together, work to form a pattern. They are numerous in the hypothenar and thenar areas, and are also found near tri-radii and in loop and whorl patterns. The reduction cusps direct the growth of bundles thus providing seat for creases.

Creases, in fact, are a result of interaction between ridges and blank palmar areas.

As compared to plantar creases, the thenar transformation process is more intense in palmar creases. This developmental feature provides a more distinctive identity to the base points of primary creases in the palm as compared to the plantar creases. In the reconstruction of the embryonic localization of the thumb from the adult prints, de Wilde arrived at the following theory:

1. The distal inter-phalangeal creases of all 5 fingers formed one transverse crease pattern in the hand plate stage; the same holds for the proximal interphalangeal creases.
2. The metacarpophalangeal creases formed such a transverse crease pattern too.

3. The thenar crease is a (lengthened) metacarpophalangeal crease and fitted with that crease on the index finger in the hand-plate stage.
4. The crease at the thumb-base is a proximal inter-phalangeal crease.

The phalangeal creases seem to develop shortly before or even at the same time as the fingers separate. The unequal length of the middle phalanges as demarcated by the creases influences the course and width between the ridges. The ridge patterns appear to develop initially from radial to ulnar and from proximal to distal.

The hypothenar region is that last inducted part of the hand plate which in turn explains the ulnar and radial orientation of the creases. It also provides answer for distal crease split and logic of giving base point character to creases at radial, instead of ulnar, margin.

The crease embryology has also been studied by Wurth (1937), Blümel and Poll (1928), Schenk & Patzer (1959), Usher, et al. (1966) and Nakiela (1972). Büchi (1954) asserts that the creases on the palm appear to be dependent on the interplay of quite a number of genetically developmental processes. Any change in one of the genes involved or any environmental disturbance in one of the reaction chains may cause a change in the crease picture. The development of the single transverse furrow in particular seems to be favoured when the harmony of normal palmar growth is interfered with. The simian crease is most frequent on the right hands of men and least frequent on left hands of women. This sexual and right/left difference might be ascribed to epistatic influences of sex and symmetry/asymmetry genes or to environmental influences intrinsic to embryo itself.

Apart from noting the appearance of creases on various dermatoglyphic regions at embryonic stage it is imperative to interpret each crease in terms of its various features or attributes; such as crease core, bifurcation, crease border, crease direction and their splitting tendency, etc. All those parameters of creases which have been discussed in Chapter 5 are valid tools for embryonic crease interpretation.

From the above standpoint, the study of crease morphology of foetuses by Bali and Jain (1983) provides sufficient details to probe individual creases of the foetus and their embryonic status in terms of their developmental stages.

Crease morphology of foetuses ranging between foetal age of three to nine months was investigated by the above authors.

It was reported by the above authors that its radial longitudinal crease is the most marked crease as compared to other creases of the palm. It appears between two-and-a-half to three months of foetal age. The other primary creases follow little late and take time to get set on the palm. These primary creases are distal and proximal transverse creases. Secondary creases show late appearance.

On the fourth month of their foetal age all the three primary creases find their firm bases and terminal orientation. The sagittal longitudinal crease may show its early appearance or it may appear after birth. From our data the sagittal crease makes its appearance on fifth foetal month. It is incomplete but in seventh month it attains a distinctive feature of its own. Along with these creases white lines or skin folds due to shrinkage also make their appearance. They are not creases in the real sense of the term.

The crease proliferation in seven to eight months old foetuses shows stable crease character. Lunar crease and ulnar crease sometimes make their appearance. Tertiary creases show rapid growth when the foetus is fully grown.

The relative increase of hand, palm and creases is dealt in the proceeding Chapter on ethnocity of crease variability.

The bilateral palm and sole prints were appropriated for embryological interpretations of creases.

The interpretation of data on foetal creases is on the similar lines as adapted by Bali and Jain (1983). The investigation on the foetal data was carried out in terms of following crease features; crease length, crease breadth, crease depth, crease surface area, crease transversality and positioning of crease base point.

For determining primary creases from secondary and tertiary creases, the observation on crease core, crease borders, base and terminal crease points, crease bifurcation and crease split is essential.

A unique feature of rapid declination of crease increase is exhibited by foetuses ranging between six to eight months. In radial longitudinal crease this feature shows dextral tendency. Transverse creases show linear increase of crease length between six and eight months. The trend is also maintained by other features of the crease, i.e., crease breadth, crease depth, etc.

Crease surface area and positioning of 'base point' exhibits a similar trend of age change among foetuses.

Crease splits and bifurcation is a late manifestation of embryonal development. Primary creases are represented by three to four months old foetuses, while secondary and tertiary crease proliferation begins after eight and nine months.

The embryonal study on positioning of 'base point' reveals that the basis of crease formulations given by the author in this text is of embryonal nature, because the principal criteria used for the formulation of palmar and plantar creases is pivoted on 'base points'.

The age change and morphology of palmar creases show change of size but basic feature of crease origin remains stable from early foetal age to the full life span on an individual.

The embryological details of dermatoglyphic traits have fully been studied by several workers. The work on crease embryology is not only scant but provides meagre embryological details concerning crease morphology.

A short review of crease embryology as given above shows that creases are embryonic in nature and appear along with the dermatoglyphic traits. Their relation with volar pads is definite but crease-wise expression is missing. The primary creases bear pre-ordained shape and size and their orientation is also embryonic in nature. Secondary creases are often feably marked but sometimes they may attain a prominent shape. Tertiary creases and white lines or minutiae are secondary manifestation of crease formation.

The characteristic features of crease border, crease bifurcation, direction and its splitting tendency need a closer scrutiny for assigning a particular crease to its category, i.e., primary, secondary or tertiary crease types.

Bali and Jain (1983) examined foetuses from the standpoint of crease morphology. The foetuses were collected from various hospitals. Their exact age determination was not much reliable so as to consider weekwise changes as a general rule. The authors have, therefore, adopted ages of the foetuses in months. The details are listed as under:

To study the embryonic development of creases, the data on 24 foetuses, ranging between foetal age of three to nine months was taken. It has been observed that out of all palmar flexion creases, it is the radial longitudinal crease which makes its first appearance between two-and-a-half to three months. The Radial longitudinal crease is the most marked as compared to other types of palmar creases. The secondary creases are not marked at this foetal age. Among primary creases only three creases make their first appearance in the foetal age of three months. These creases are radial longitudinal, proximal transverse and distal transverse. The palmar creases of four months old foetuses show the above three creases with firm bases as compared with three months old foetuses. The sagittal longitudinal crease makes its first appearance in five months old foetus, while the same crease in seven months old foetus show distinct shape of its own. Along with the development of these creases, the pseudo creases or skin folds, due to shrinking of skin, make their appearance. These folds are not interrupted by dermal ridges of the palm. The crease proliferations between seven to eight months old foetuses do not show substantial differences but for the emergence of lunar lines or formation of ulnar creases. Apart from the primary creases several secondary creases also make their appearance directly or from the primary creases during eight months of foetus. Tertiary creases show rapid growth during eight to ninth months, old foetuses. The crease morphology of new born and nine months old foetuses show greater agreement both in term of its qualitative and quantitative expressions.

The relative increase of palm and radial longitudinal crease length among three to nine months old foetuses show linear trend of increase both in palm and radial longitudinal crease.

It could be seen from Fig. 6.2 and Table 6.1 that there is a slight deviation in the linear trend of growth of the palm and of radial longitudinal crease among various foetal ages.

The most striking trend in the increase of palmar length is exhibited by foetuses ranging between six to eight months. During this period the increasing tendency in the palm length abruptly stops or shows rapid declination, a unique feature of crease development. An agreement to the above trend is also offered by radial longitudinal crease which stops to grow in length, between six to eight months old foetuses. This feature shows dextral tendencies.

TABLE 6.1: Palm length and radial longitudinal crease length of foetuses

Age groups	Right Hand				Left Hand			
	Palm length		Crease length		Palm length		Crease Length	
(Mon-ths)	Mean (cm)	S.D.	Mean (cm)	S.D.	Mean (cm)	S.D.	Mean (cm)	S.D.
3	0.89	±0.031	0.70	±0.000	0.88	±0.031	0.70	±0.000
4	1.28	±0.216	1.13	±0.051	1.36	±0.212	1.16	±0.052
5	1.71	±0.170	1.50	±0.082	1.66	±0.132	1.46	±0.082
6	2.63	±0.220	2.00	±0.126	2.65	±0.190	1.80	±0.185
7	2.74	±0.240	2.10	±0.185	2.80	±0.215	2.00	±0.195
8	2.92	±0.245	2.10	±0.224	2.90	±0.230	2.00	±0.235
9	3.20	±0.290	3.00	±0.270	3.15	±0.290	3.00	±0.270

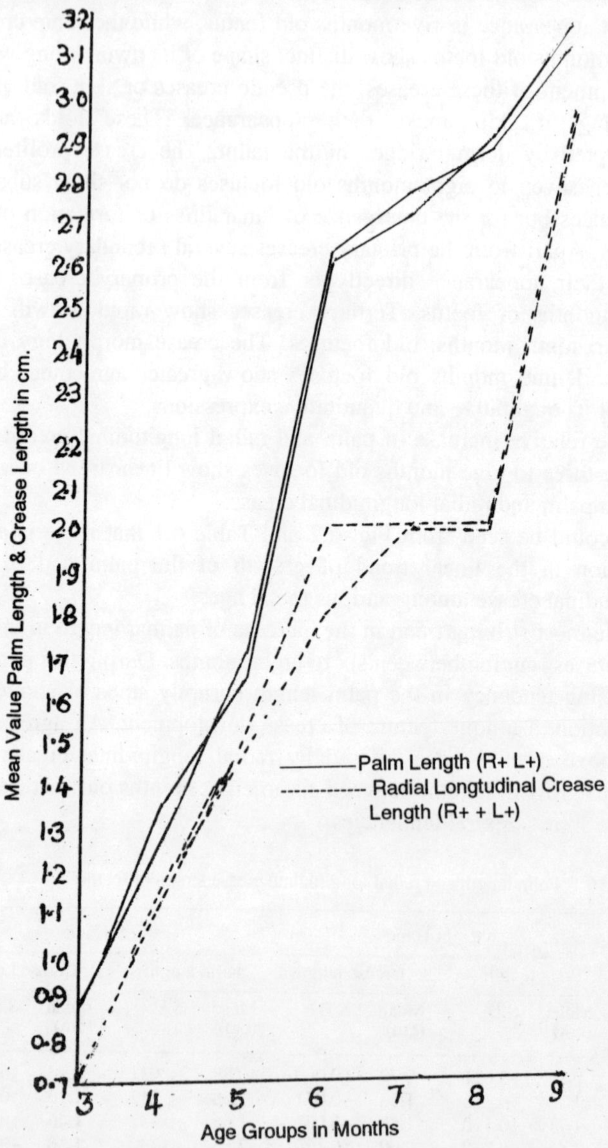

FIG. 6.2:Palm length and radial longitudinal crease length of foetuses

TABLE 6.2: Palm breadth, proximal transverse crease length and distal transverse crease length of foetuses

Age groups (Months)	Right Hand						Left Hand					
	Palm breadth		Proximal transverse crease length		Distal transverse crease length		Palm breadth		Proximal transverse crease length		Distal transverse crease length	
	Mean (cm)	S.D.	Mean (cm)	S.D.	Mean (cm)	S.D.	Mean (cm)	S.D.	Mean (cm)	S.D.	Mean (cm)	S.D.
3	0.69	±0.044	0.45	±0.000	0.50	±0.000	0.68	±0.031	0.40	±0.000	0.50	±0.000
4	1.12	±0.164	0.76	±0.040	0.93	±0.040	1.10	±0.311	0.76	±0.040	0.96	±0.040
5	1.53	±0.134	0.86	±0.075	1.11	±0.080	1.52	±0.122	0.90	±0.070	1.11	±0.080
6	2.36	±0.195	1.50	±0.120	1.70	±0.160	2.36	±0.190	1.50	±0.130	1.90	±0.150
7	2.36	±0.210	1.50	±0.170	2.00	±0.170	2.36	±0.210	1.50	±0.170	2.00	±0.170
8	2.65	±0.210	1.50	±0.230	2.00	±0.200	2.63	±0.210	1.60	±0.200	2.00	±0.190
9	2.80	±0.265	2.70	±0.280	2.40	±0.280	2.70	±0.230	2.60	±0.310	2.50	±0.280

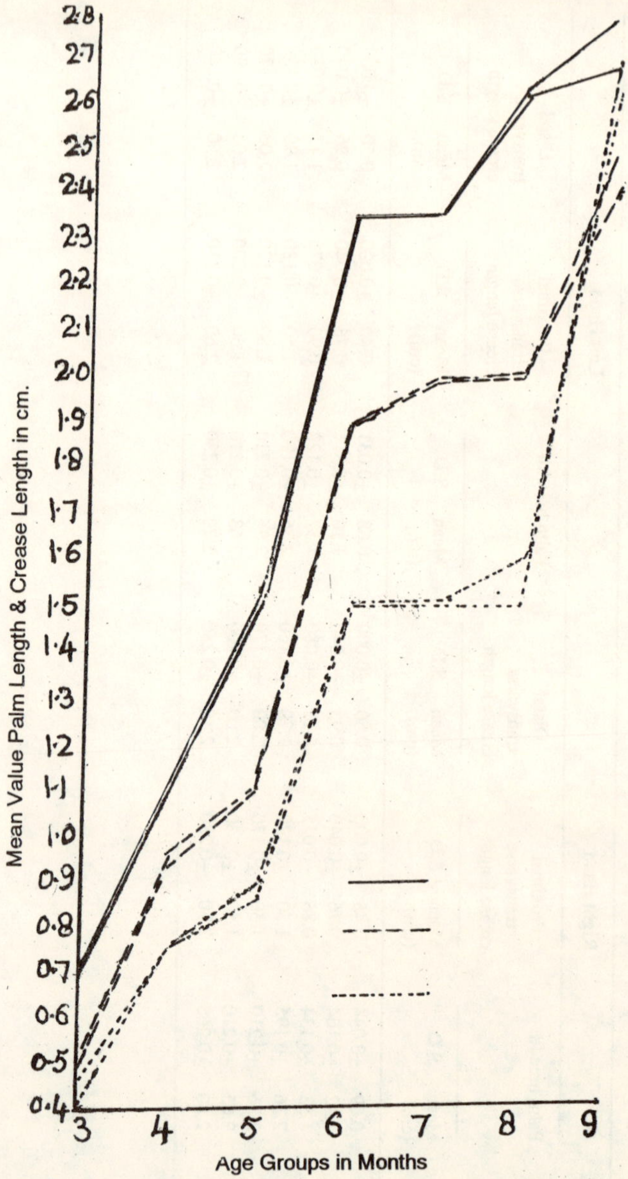

FIG. 6.3: Palm breadth, proximal and distal transverse creases' length of foetuses

The differential increase in length of palm as well as of longitudinal crease among foetuses, ranging between three to nine months, show periods of their rapid, slow or zero growth.

Considering the relative growth of proximal and distal transverse creases with breadth, it is noticed that the increase in palm breadth is associated with the increase in length of transverse crease.

The longitudinal and transverse growth of the palm shows linear trend of increase. The same trend is maintained by transverse and longitudinal creases.

It is interesting to note (Fig. 6.3 and Table 6.2) that the rapidly growing palm suddenly slows down and stops to grow between six to eight months old male foetuses. It may further be pointed out that the zero growth among transverse creases as well as longitudinal creases finds its rythmic increase with the increase of palm's length. The zero growth trend shows bilateralism which is more prominent in right hands as compared to the left.

REFERENCES

Bali, R.S. and D.K. Jain (1983): The study of pre-natal and post-natal development of creases in man. *Proceeding Internat. Sym. Dermato.* Punjabi University, Patiala, India.

Blümel, P.; H. Poll (1928): *Fingerliniemuster und geistige Norm Medizinische Klinik 24*, pp. 1428-30.

Bonnevie, K. (1927): *Die ersten Entwicklungsstadien der papillarmuster der menschlichen Finger ballen. Nyt Mag F. Nuturv*, Vol. 65 pp. 19-56.

Büchi, E.C. (1954): The Simian Crease in India. *Bulletin of the Indian Department of Anthropology* 3(1) : pp. 39-49.

Cummins, H. and C. Midlo (1961): *Finger prints, palms and soles: An introduction to dermatoglyphics*. New York: Dover.

Dar, H., R. Schmidt, and H.M. Nitowsky (1977): Palmar crease variants and their clinical significance: A study of newborns at risk. *Pediat. Res.* 11 : pp. 103-08.

de Wilde, A.G. (1979): Developmental Aspects of Ridges and Creases (Dermatoglyphics) *Coll. Anthropol*: 3, pp. 201-10.

Nakiela, J. (1972): Flexion furrows of the feet in poles. *Folio Morphol. (Warsz.)*, 31 : p. 301.

Patten, B.M. (1953): *Human embryology*, Blakistan, New York, p. 19.

Schaeuble, J. (1933): Die Entstehung der palmaren digitalen Triradien. Ein Beitrag Zur Entwicklung der Hautleistenzuge der distalen Palma, *Zeitschrift fur Morphologie and Anthropologie*. 31(3): pp. 403-38.

Schawman, B. and M. Alter (1976): *Dermatoglyphics in medical disorders*. Springer-Verlag, New York, pp. 118-22.

Schenk, H. and H. Patzer (1959): Das Fussfurchenbild des Neugeborenen, *Kinderarztliche Praxis* 27(4) : pp. 169-73.

Usher, R., F. McLean and K.E. Scott (1966): Judgment of foetal age. II. Clinical significance of gestational age and an objective method for its assessment. *Pediatr. Clin. North Am.*, 13 : p. 835.

Wurth, A. (1937): Die Entstehung der Beugefurchen der menschlichen Hohlhand. *Z. Morph. Anthrop.*, 36 : pp. 187-214.

7

CREASE VARIATION IN PRIMATES

AMONG PRIMATES the friction skin and flexion creases are functional adaptations for grasping and locomotion and are shaped after volar pads of palmar and plantar surfaces. Gyenis and Hera (1971) studied creases of primates in relation to the volar pads.

The simian crease has been subjected to a large number of studies and the fact about its being truly simian needs to be admitted. "The simian crease has been defined variably by various authorities since its first mention by Langdon-Down, and it being termed "Mongolian or Orangoid" by Crookshank. In the present study, from few available figures of the anthropoid palms, it has been shown that there are two to three transverse palmar flexure lines, running across the palm from the radial to the ulnar end and that there are variations within the same anthropoid ape (Sarkar, 1961).

Crookshank studied simian lines in anthropoid apes and monkeys and found it only in orangutan. A similar findings of Duckworth (1915), Sonntag (1924) and Wood-Jones (1929) revealed that the palm of the apes is characterized by one or more transverse lines. Except simian creases a comparative study of palmar, plantar and phalangeal creases is not available and needs to be attempted.

The relationship between dermal ridges and creases as given by Okajima (1978) in macaque specimen explains the affect of creases on dark groove lines as ". . . grooves are affected under the flexion creases, usually becoming elongated and expanded or losing their linear construction, as if there were an inter-actional or situational relationship between the ridges and the creases. This is available on the palm at the transverse crease, the longitudinal crease, the thenar crease, the crease of the distal margin of the proximal, hypothenar eminence and the distal inter-phalangeal creases." The characteristic of creases and dermal ridges can best be observed by Okajima's method of chemical treatment of the epidermis.

The transverse creases on macaque palm show wide variation in traversing the palm. The irregular construction of grooves under the transverse crease stops at the longitudinal crease. Such constructions are absent in the shallow fold extending from the terminal into the radial side of the longitudinal crease. The author cites Penrose (1973) to stress his findings that the simian crease in the hands of sub-human primates is a product of the fusion of two transverse creases.

The above-mentioned author's precise examination for macaque specimens is a valuable finding in creases, and so has been incorporated in the present text with minimum change of expression.

The work on simian creases by Langdon-Down (1909), Shuttle Worth (1909), Wurth (1937), Portius (1937), Tillner (1953) and Weninger and Navratil (1957), show simian crease relation to certain abnormalities in human populations.

The depressed parathenar area is slow loris is seen as ridgeless flexion furrows, while rest of the area is complete with ridge configurations. This condition varies in different primates (Cummins and Midlo, 1961). The ridgeless furrows of flexion are, in fact, the creases or their precursors.

In most of the monkeys, apes and men, continuous configurations of ridges on palm and sole are found except flexion furrows which are devoid of ridges.

Okajima (1978) in his new technique magnifies both crease and dermal ridge features of non-human primates having melanin on their palms and soles. By treating these areas chemically the prominance of volar pads and the dark groove lines in loris, monkeys, baboons and chimpanzees, makes the task of crease observation more efficient.

Using the present technique, other characteristics of dermal ridges: furrow, papillar, sweat ducts, etc., can be observed in more natural situation than possible with other methods.

By virtue of his new technique, Okajima describes the crease anatomy in relation to ridges in non-human primates as below:

> "The relationship between dermal ridges and creases in macaque specimens: the dark groove lines have various appearances under the flexion and secondary creases. Their structures are not essentially affected under the secondary creases (Fig. 7.1). On the other hand, grooves are affected under the flexion creases, usually becoming elongated and expanded or losing their linear construction, as if there were an inter-actional or situational relationship between the ridges and the creases."

FIG. 7.1: Ridge relation with creases (after Okajima)

The work is done on non-human primates and exclusively on dermatoglyphics. But his chalk and tape method for lifting the print of non-human primates is applicable to creases also (1978).

While tracing the evolutionary thread of ridge configurations, Whipple (1904) finds ridges as modified scales. Each scale is associated with one hair, or a hair group, and sweat gland. In the evolution of friction skin the hair disappears, and scales aggregate into ridges.

Cummins and Midlo (1961) cite transitional areas between the junction of dermatoglyphic and unspecialised skin of the palm and sole as relic of phylogeny.

Based on pad distribution the topography of dermatoglyphic regions of palm and sole finds its phylogenetic interpretation. The plan of pads is correlated with the topography of configurational area. The subsequent influence of these pad constellations provides orientation to creases on palm and sole via velocity and degree of pad expressions and depressions under differential growth stimuli.

In addition to the seven pads there are two smaller and four accessary pads adjunct to distal areas of the palm. Three central pads, both in palm and sole, cover the distal margin of parathenar area (Fig. 7.2).

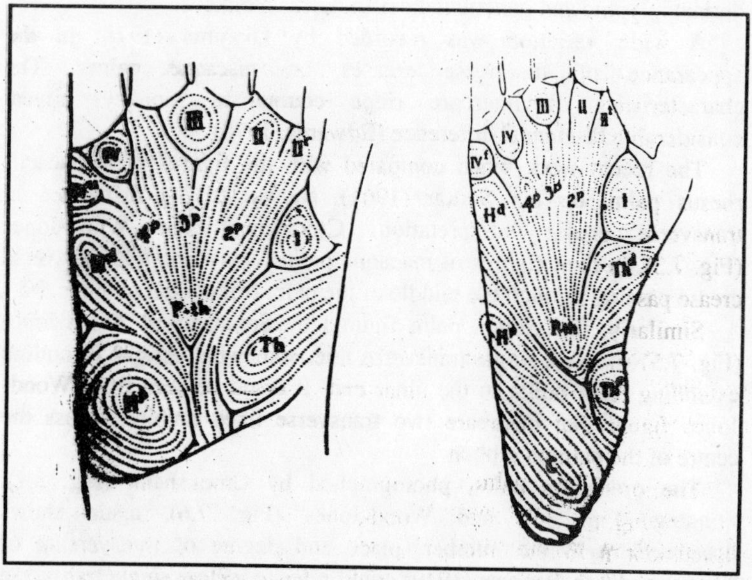

FIG. 7.2: Morphological plan of palm and sole showing pads of monkey (after Cummins and Midlo)

The study of phenotypic variation in flexion creases of non-human primates, in the absence of any definitive and reliable crease formulation, appears a formidable problem. The inseparable sampling of dermatoglyphics from creases should encourage the work on creases but it is not so, the reason being simple that creases are not age stable and the number of formulations and workers is almost the same. On these grounds creases have failed to find firm base in anthropology.

Nonetheless, a number of studies dealing with non-human primates are at hand. It may be because Broca (1877) introduced creases in anthropology with reference to single transverse crease (simian crease) as a primitive trait. The subsequent investigations of simian creases were extended to non-human primates to establish the simian character of the line.

The maximum work on creases is cited along with dermatoglyphics because of their close topographical association. Crease variation in primates is, in fact, the variational study of dermatoglyphics.

The morphology of palmar dermatoglyphics of monkeys has been summerised by Midlo and Cummins (1942), Biegert (1961) and Cummins and Midlo (1961). Edwards (1978) compared dermatoglyphic and genetic indices in rhesus monkeys.

A wide variation was recorded by Okajima (1978) in the appearance of transverse creases on macaque palms. The characteristics of intercore ridge counts in monkeys reveal considerable bi-manual difference (Edwards, 1978).

The recent work when compared with the figures of a macacus rhesus palm, *op cit.* Sarkar (1961), shows striking difference in transverse crease interpretation. Crookshank and Wood-Jones (Fig. 7.3), in their figures of macaque palms, show a single transverse crease passing through the middle of the palm from radial to ulnar end.

Similarly, the gibbon palm figured by Sonntag and Wood-Jones (Fig. 7.5) shows a single transverse line, somewhat oblique in outline extending from radial to the ulnar end. It could be seen from Wood-Jones figure that there are two transverse lines running across the centre of the palm in gibbon.

The orangutan palm, photographed by Crookshank (Fig. 3.1), Sonntag (Fig. 3.2) and Wood-Jones (Fig. 7.6), again shows disagreement in the number, place and degree of transversing of transverse lines. Penrose (1949) could refer to a clear single transverse line as simian crease while dealing with Mongolian imbecile. It is not simple to find such typical cases in orangutan palms. The variation of number in transverse lines is a much frequent trend of orang's palms.

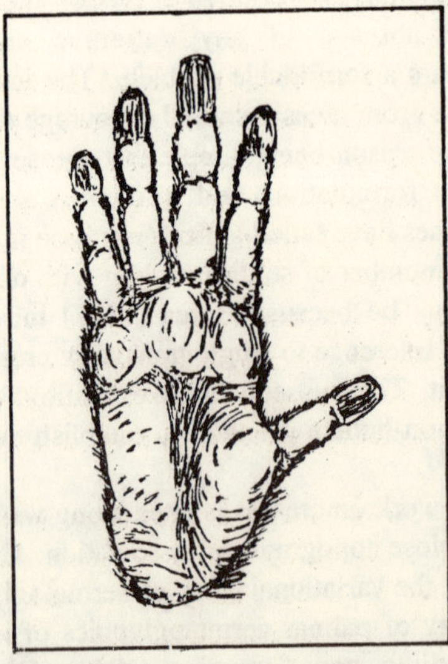

FIG. 7.3: Macaque palm (after Wood-Jones) (*op cit* Sarkar)

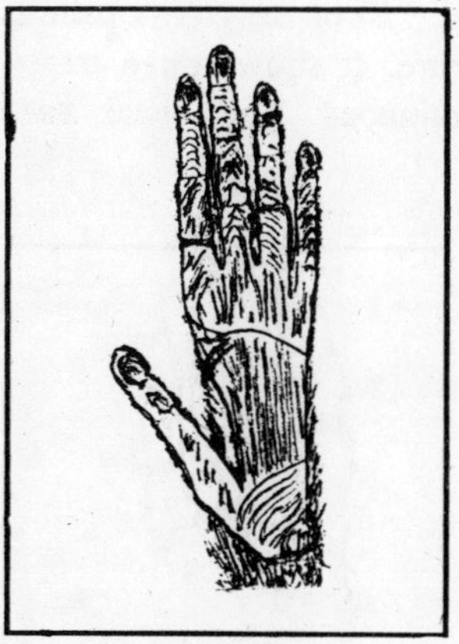

FIG. 7.4: Bornean Gibbon palm (after Sonntag)

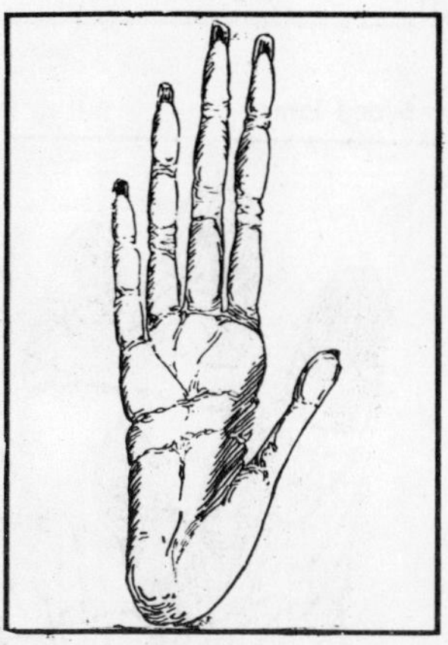

FIG. 7.5: Gibbon palm (after Wood-Jones)

The figures of gorilla's hand, showing transverse creases on its palm, are after Duckworth (1915), Sonntag (1924) and Wood-Jones (1929).

Duckworth's figure of a young gorilla palm (Fig. 7.7) shows four transverse lines at the centre of the palm. The proximal one appears to be the largest, but broken up into two segments, one large and one small. The distal transverse line is represented by a large fragment at the centre of the palm.

Sonntag figure (Fig. 7.8) of the gorilla palm is somewhat different from Duckworth's figure. It shows three transverse lines in which proximal line is continuous. The distal transverse line is also continuous.

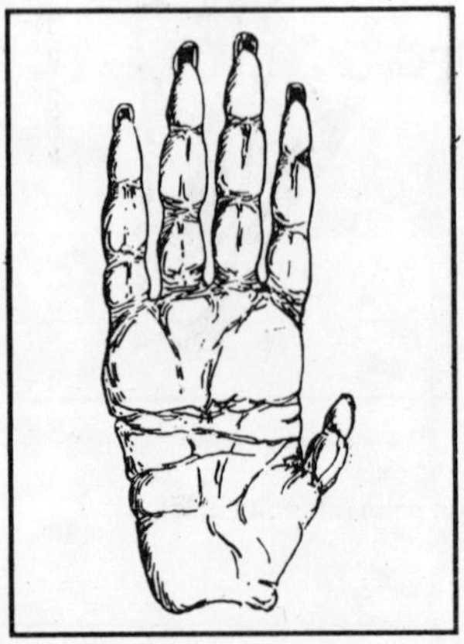

FIG. 7.6: Orang palm (after Wood-Jones)

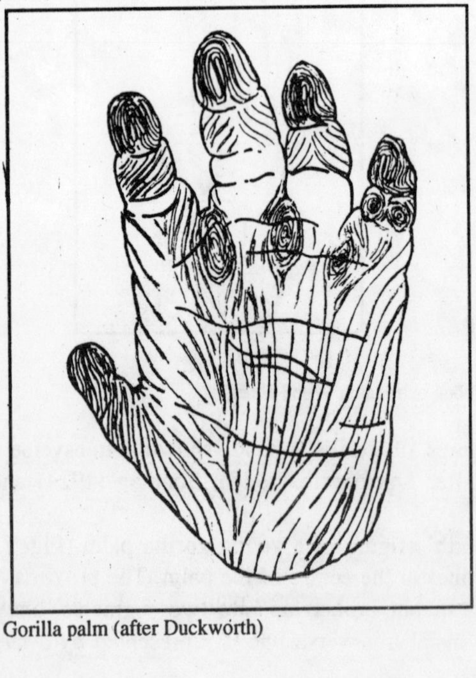

FIG. 7.7: Young Gorilla palm (after Duckworth)

The gorilla palm figured by Wood-Jones (Fig. 7.9) shows continuous line from the ulnar to the radial end of the centre of the palm. The proximal line is also continuous.

Chimpanzee palm, figured by Sonntag (Fig. 7.10) and Wood-Jones (Fig. 7.11), shows discrepancy in transverse lines with respect to their distal shift in the former figure.

The main objective of the above description is to impress upon the readers the prevalent myth like early notions with regard to simian creases.

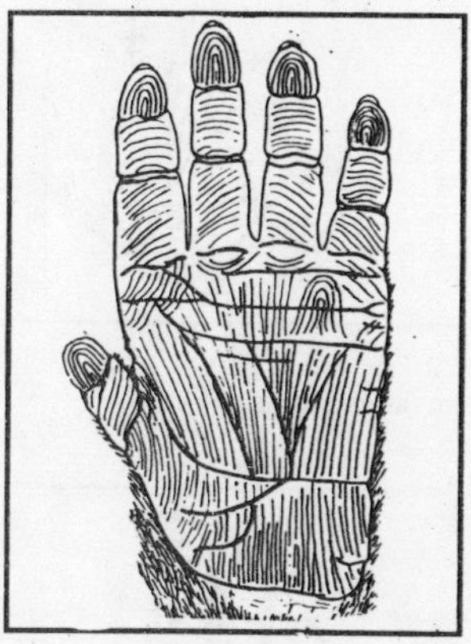

FIG. 7.8: Gorilla palm (after Sonntag)

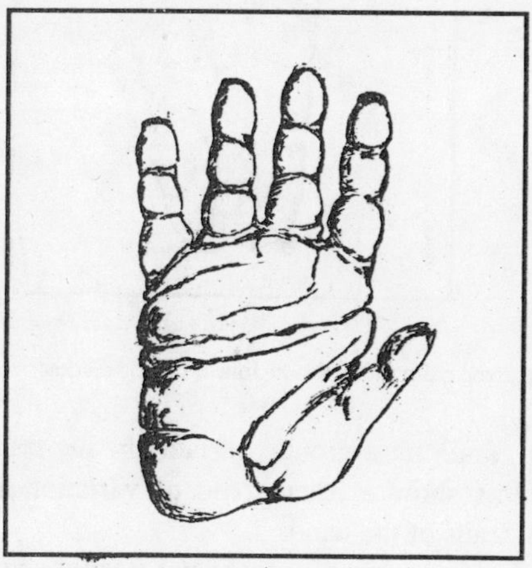

FIG. 7.9: Gorilla palm (after Wood-Jones)

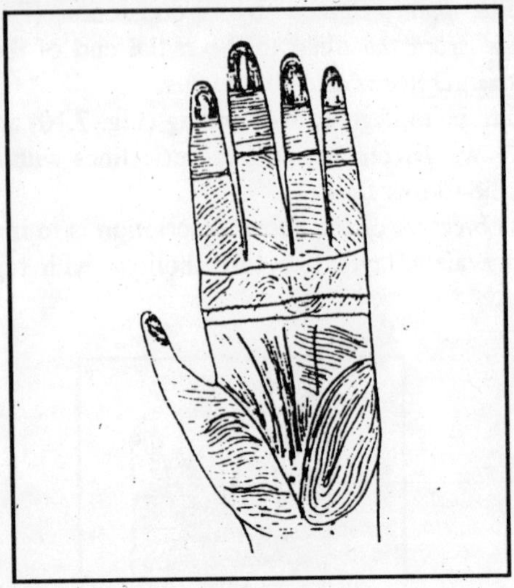

FIG. 7.10: Chimpanzee palm (after Sonntag)

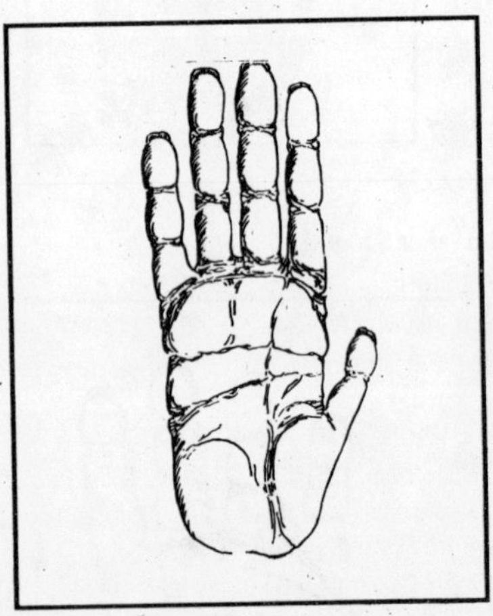

FIG. 7.11: Chimpanzee palm (after Wood-Jones) (*op cit.* Sarkar)

The inter and intra-group variations in transverse lines of anthropoid palms show a usual trend of variation as found in other morphological traits of the hand.

The firm simian crease concept is not a valid scientific expression, otherwise multi-simian crease formulations would not have been the result. It is the simian crease fixation which has hampered the natural growth of crease science.

REFERENCES

Biegert, J. (1961): *Volarhaut der Hande und Fusse. primatologia* 1 (suppl. 2) pp. 4-326.

Broca, P. (1877): Le pli transversal du Singe dons Le main de l'homme. *Bull. Soc. Paris, Ze Serie* t XII. pp. 431-32.

Cummins, H. and C. Midlo (1961): *Finger prints, palms and soles. An introduction to dermatoglyphics.* New York: Dover.

Duckworth, W.L.H. (1915): *Morphology and Anthropology*, Cambridge.

Edwards, C.R. (1978): A Chalk and Tape method for lifting the palm prints of non-human Primates. *Dermatoglyphics. An Introductional Perspective.* Moutan Publishers, Paris.

Gyenis, G. and G. Hera (1971): Investigation of the hand creases in the random sample of subjects in Baranya Province of South Hungary. *Anthropological Kozlemenyek* (Budapest) 15(1) : pp. 29-47.

Langdon-Down, R.L. (1909): Mongolian Imbecility. *Brit. Med. J.*, pp. 12-65.

Midlo, C. and H. Cummins (1942): Palmar and plantar dermatoglyphics in primates. *American Anatomical Memoirs* 20 : pp. 1-98.

Okajima, M. (1978): A new technique for examining Primate dermatoglyphics. *Dermatoglyphics: An Introductional Perspective.* Moutan Publishers, Paris.

Penrose, L.S. (1949): *Mental Defect.* London: Sidgwick and Jackson.

Penrose, L.S. (1973): *Finger Prints and Palmistry.* Lancet 1(7814) pp. 1239-42.

Portius, W. (1937): Beitrag zur Frage der Erblichkeit der vier (fingerfurche) *Zeitschrift fur Morphologie und Anthropologie.* 36 : pp. 382-90.

Sarkar, S.S. (1961): The Simian crease. *Zeitschrift fur Morphologie und Anthropologie.* 51(2) : pp. 212-19.

Shuttle Worth, G.E. (1909): Mongolian Imbecility. *Brit. Med. J.*, 12 : p. 665.

Sonntag, C.F. (1924): *The morphology and evolution of the Apes and man*, London.

Tillner, I. (1953): Zur Entstehung der Vierfingerfurche. *Zeitschrift fur Menschliche Vererbungs und Konstitutionslehre* 32: pp. 56-7.

Weninger, M. and L. Navratil (1957): Die Vierfingerfurche in atiologischer Betrachtung. *Anthrop. Gesellsch. in Wien. Bd.*, LXXVII : pp. 1-21.

Whipple, I. (1904): The ventral surface of the mammalian chiridium, with special *Morphologie und Anthropologie* 7: pp. 261-368.

Wood-Jones, F. (1929): *Man's place among the mammals*, London.

Wurth, A. (1937): Die Entstehung der Beugefurchen der menschlichen Hohlhand. *Z. Morph. Anthrop.*, 36 : pp. 187-214.

8

SYMMETRY AND OTHER ASPECTS OF SPECIAL MORPHOLOGY

HAVING CONSIDERED the various aspects of crease morphology and crease morphometry it is now amply clear that studies on crease biology have virtually been ignored. There can be several reasons for showing lack of interest towards this field of crease anthropology.

The foremost reason is the misconception among the workers that crease formulation/classification is the ultimate goal for understanding and applying creases in the study of human variation. To them it is the final measure for the interpretation of creases as morphological variable. This approach has restricted the natural growth of the field with the result that creases have remained underutilized for anthropological investigations.

The crease study was bracketed with simian crease or sydney line and creases other than these types were ignored thus hampering their integrated development.

Another deceptive notion, that creases and dermal ridges are totally independent from each other, is not true. In fact, the dermal ridges provide space to creases and the crease gets its shape, form or size through these ridges only. Every crease is the manifestation of ridge action or, in other words, creases split ridges and furrow to create space for attaining their shape. The area which is devoid of ridges and furrows forms a crease, thereby showing closer interaction between creases and dermatoglyphics. For becoming a true crease it has to pass through pseudo and mixed crease stages of crease development.

Instead of having an integrated approach, the creases on palm, sole, phalanges or toes have been treated in isolation thus depriving them of common biological approach. Creases, like any other biological variable, respond to genetic, nutritional and environmental influences to a certain extent.

Age Change in Creases

For better understanding of crease biology, age change in creases needs to be fully investigated.

The study of morphological change in hand, palm and palmar flexion creases of one to eleven years old boys and girls was undertaken by Bali and Mishra (1978).

The measurements of hand, palm and creases were taken by spreading caliper. For taking breadth and length of the hand the standard anthropometric techniques were used.

The palm breadth was taken directly by using the above caliper. The same caliper was used for measuring palmar prints. On the anatomical axis the most distal and most proximal points of palmar surface were measured for palmar length, and the breadth was measured as the maximum distance at right angle to the anatomical axis toward ulnar and radial margin of the palm.

The palmar prints of the same individual were lifted by inking method. A special stress was laid to get printed the entire margin of the palm. The measurement on palmar print was compared with the direct measurement taken on the palm of the subject.

Each primary crease of the palm was measured and compared with the measurements of palm and hand. The longitudinal creases were compared with the length of palm and hand while hand breadth and palm breadth were related to transverse palmar creases.

There exists a positive relationship of age change between creases, palm and hand. The age-wise rhythm of increment in creases show full agreement of increase of hand and palm.

A subsequent attempt on a similar line was again made by these authors (1983) by increasing the sample size and confirmed the early findings.

Bali and Jain (1983), in their study of pre-natal and post-natal developments of creases, established the early reported trends of growth in creases, palms and hands. The cross-sectional data of foetuses and children of five years were appropriated for the above study.

It may be pointed out that the study on creases was not restricted to length only but other crease features were also incorporated.

Crease Morphology of Children (one to five years)

The relative increase of length of palm and radial longitudinal crease among children ranging between one to five years age-groups show linear increase (Fig. 8.1). The increase in the length of the palm is almost uniform with a slight increase of steep between two to three years.

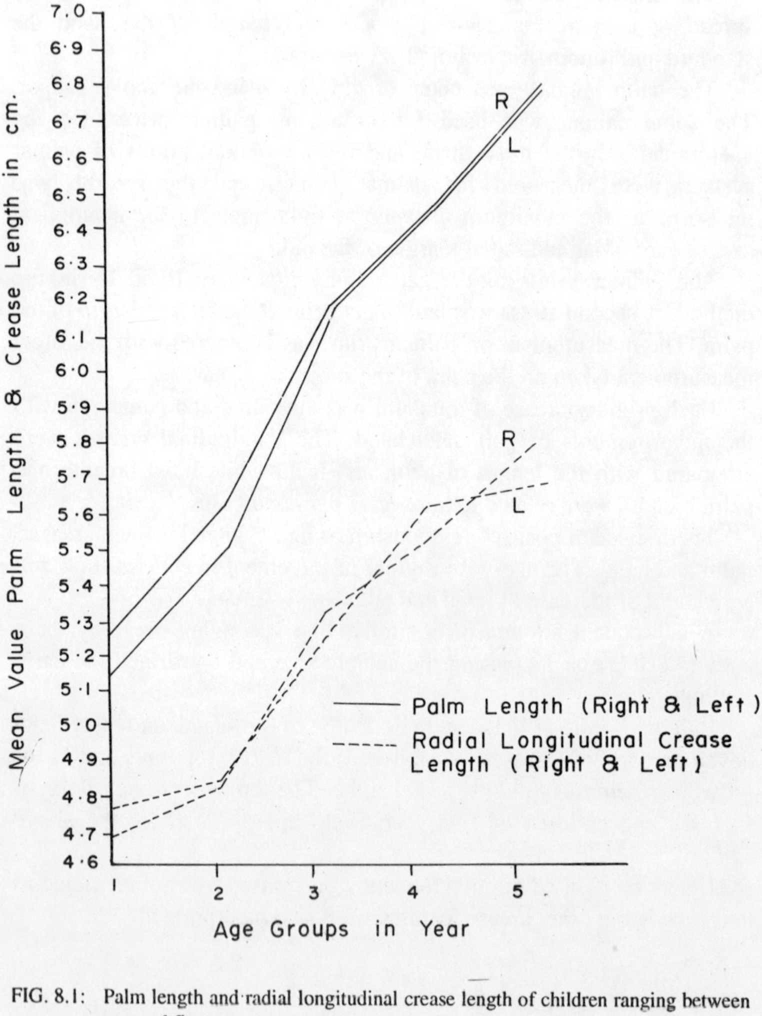

FIG. 8.1: Palm length and radial longitudinal crease length of children ranging between one and five years

TABLE 8.1: Palm length and radial longitudinal crease length of children ranging between one and five years

Age groups Years	Right Hand				Left Hand			
	Palm length		Radial longitudinal crease length		Palm length		Radial longitudinal crease length	
	Mean (cm)	S.D.	Mean (cm)	S.D.	Mean (cm)	S.D.	Mean (cm)	S.D.
1	5.27	±0.343	4.68	±0.448	5.15	±0.281	4.76	±0.409
2	5.62	±0.254	4.81	±0.597	5.49	±0.359	4.83	±0.428
3	6.20	±0.360	5.31	±0.500	6.19	±0.256	5.24	±0.464
4	6.50	±0.481	5.52	±0.664	6.48	±0.423	5.62	±0.575
5	6.85	±0.492	5.79	±0.584	6.83	±0.409	5.68	±0.509

The increase in the length of radial longitudinal crease is slow between one to two years and this rise is rapid between two to three years age-group. From two to five years the curve takes the linear direction as indicated by palm length.

A similar trend of linear increase is also indicated by the palm breadth. As compared to the increase of the palm breadth the increases in the length of proximal transverse crease is slow at the age of one year but the increase is rapid between two to three years of age and four to five years old boys show linear-wise increase, as exhibited by palm breadth.

Considering the age-wise increase of distal transverse crease, it could be seen (Fig. 8.2) that one to two years age group shows a nominal increase in the left hand, while the right hand crease shows minimum increase of length. The boys ranging between the age-group, two to three years, show a steep rise in the length of distal transverse crease, which takes a linear course of increase between three to five years.

The differential trend of increase is more pronounced in the distal transverse crease as compared to the proximal transverse crease which is least marked in palm breadth (Table 8.2, Fig. 8.2).

The crease surface area of an individual crease may be defined as an area which occupies the total square centimetre space on dermatoglyphic surface. The crease surface area is the total length into total breadth of a particular crease.

The area is measured by a special instrument called planimeter

(Fig. 2.8). The pointed needle is revolved around the crease which is transmitted to the graduated wheel fitted with vernier. The surface area covered by needle is read in mm scale.

It could be seen from the Table 8.3 that surface area of longitudinal transverse crease among one to five years old boys shows linear trend of increase in both the hands (Fig. 8.3).

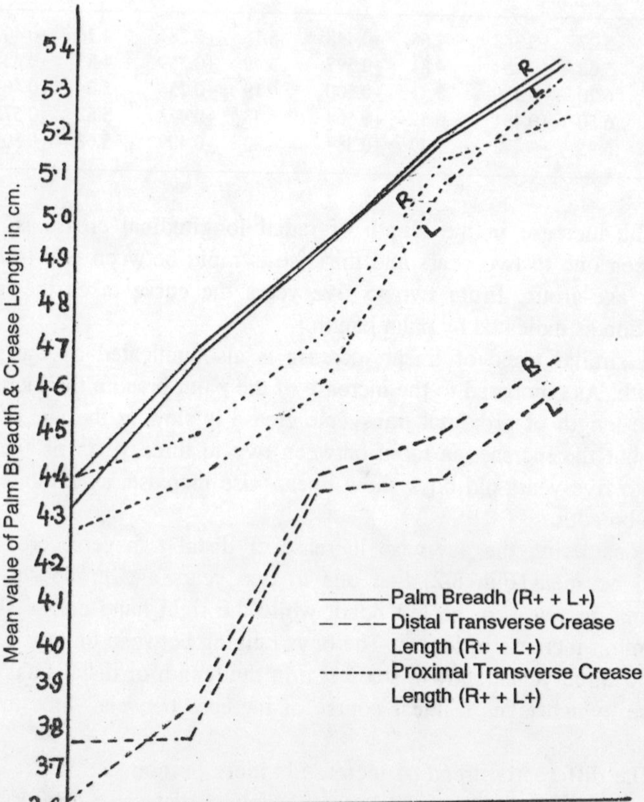

FIG. 8.2: Palm breadth, proximal and distal transverse creases' length of children ranging from one to five years

TABLE 8.2: Palm breadth, proximal and distal transverse crease length of children ranging between one and five years

Age Groups Years	Right Hand						Left Hand					
	Palm breadth		Proximal transverse crease length		Distal transverse crease length		Palm breadth		Proximal transverse crease length		Distal transverse crease length	
	Mean (cm)	S.D.	Mean (cm)	S.D.	Mean (cm)	S.D.	Mean (cm)	S.D.	Mean (cm)	S.D.	Mean (cm)	S.D.
1	4.38	±0.359	4.38	±0.294	3.75	±0.248	4.31	±0.277	4.25	±0.638	3.62	±0.225
2	4.68	±0.270	4.48	±0.555	3.76	±0.367	4.65	±0.260	4.38	±0.526	3.84	±0.480
3	4.92	±0.296	4.71	±0.424	4.38	±0.450	4.92	±0.256	4.58	±0.367	4.34	±0.514
4	4.19	±0.320	5.13	±0.591	4.47	±0.718	5.18	±0.277	5.07	±0.626	4.37	±0.402
5	5.38	±0.260	5.24	±0.532	4.66	±0.313	5.36	±0.268	5.33	±0.712	4.59	±0.538

TABLE 8.2a: Occurrence of plantar creases in relation to anatomical axix

Sex	Creases main types	Creases in Tribal side				Creases in Fibular side			
		Right foot		Left foot		Right foot		Left foot	
		Ab.	Pc.	Ab.	Pc.	Ab.	Pc.	Ab.	Pc.
Male	SMBC	77	59.23	74	56.92	8	15.09	8	13.90
Female	SMBC	50	43.47	58	47.15	11	14.66	9	12.50
Male	DMBC	52	40.00	53	40.76	44	87.01	17	81.03
Female	DMBC	63	54.78	64	52.03	62	82.66	62	86.11
Male	TMBC	1	0.76	3	2.30	1	1.88	3	5.17
Female	TMBC	2	1.73	1	0.81	2	2.66	1	1.38
Total Male		130	99.99	130	99.98	53	99.99	58	99.99
Female		115	99.98	123	99.99	75	99.98	72	99.99

A similar trend of increase in crease surface area is exhibited by proximal transverse and distal transverse creases of both right and left hands.

The crease surface area is further interpreted in terms of ridge count, i.e., the total ridges per square centimetre. This scale gives the relationship of increase which is directly proportional to the increase between two ridges and the crease surface area, in terms of ridge count expression, the relative increase of crease and inter-ridge distance with respect to age-change is noticed.

It could be seen from Table 8.4 that the age-wise increase in crease is synchronized by the increase in inter-ridge distance, which is expressed by ridge counts occupied per unit area of the palm. The biological importance of this crease expression appears to be of great value.

The crease surface area is further interpreted in terms of cell counts. This expression is highly sensitive and could best be expressed with the aid of planimeter.

Another important feature of the crease is its relation to the point of origin (radial base point) with respect to its distance between lower margin of basal inter-digital crease of the index finger and upper or distal margin of the radial longitudinal crease at its root on radial base point.

This relationship of crease origin is given in Table 8.5. It could be seen that instead of increase, the area under study shows a striking dip. This is, perhaps, the only trait which shows retrogression in the growth of dimensional change. This feature has strongly been interpreted as a proof for the split theory of palmar crease, which forms the basis of crease formulation (Bali, 1980).

Anatomical Axis and Distribution of Phalangeal Crease Patterns

Many structural features are correlated with reference to the anatomical axis, such as longer persistence of pre-natal webbing (Schultz, 1924) and syndactylism in second and third toes. In relation to the anatomical axis, Bali (1973) made observation on the patterns distribution. Syndactyl and zygodactily on III and IV digits of the hand were also referred to anatomical axis. The distribution of digital hair has a direct bearing on the anatomical axis (Cummins and Midlo, 1961).

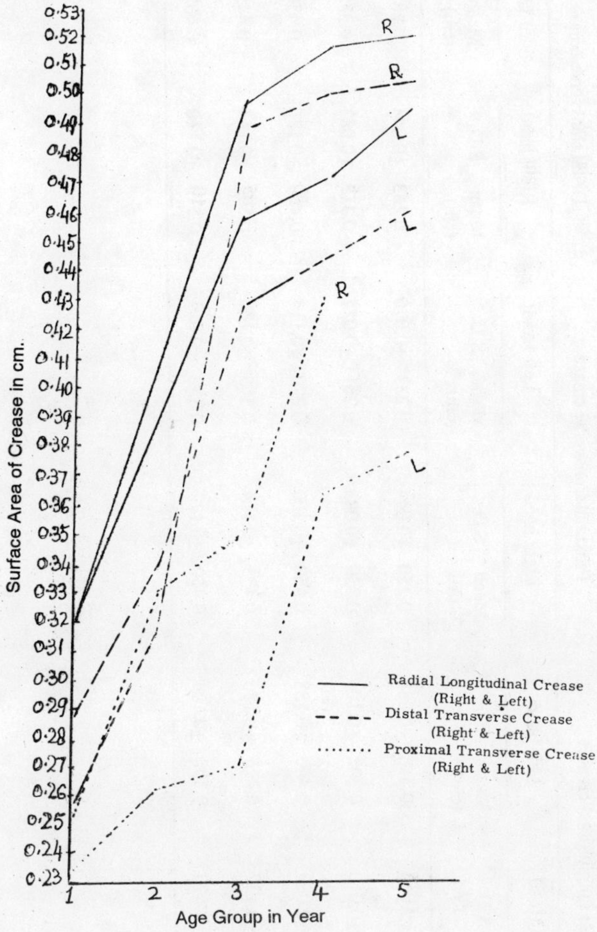

FIG. 8.3: Surface area of palmar creases of children ranging between one and five years

TABLE 8.3: Age change in surface area of palmar creases of children ranging between one and five years

Age Groups Years	Radial longitudinal creases				Proximal transverse crease				Distal transverse crease			
	Right Hand		Left hand		Right hand		Left hand		Right hand		Left hand	
	Mean (cm)	S.D.	Mean (cm)	S.D.	Mean (cm)	S.D.	Mean (cm)	S.D.	Mean (cm)	S.D.	Mean (cm)	S.D.
1	0.316	±0.063	0.316	±0.083	0.250	±0.044	0.233	±0.070	0.253	±0.044	0.283	±0.310
2	0.407	±0.070	0.392	±0.104	0.330	±0.083	0.261	±0.077	0.315	±0.083	0.338	±0.104
3	0.500	±0.089	0.460	±0.158	0.550	±0.100	0.270	±0.114	0.490	±0.126	0.430	±0.144
4	0.520	±0.137	0.475	±0.130	0.435	±0.154	0.365	±0.130	0.505	±0.141	0.445	±0.137
5	0.525	±0.070	0.500	±0.104	0.460	±0.122	0.380	±0.054	0.510	±0.140	0.465	±0.109

TABLE 8.3a: Distribution of isopedal individual

Plantar Crease Type	Male		Female		Total		Grand Total	
	Ab.Fr.	Pc.	Ab.Fr.	Pc.	Ab.Fr.	Pc.	Ab.Fr.	Pc.
SMBC	69	62.72	41	32.27	110	99.99	110	53.39
DMBC	38	40.00	57	60.00	95	100.00	95	46.11
TMBC	—	—	1	100.00	1	100.00	1	0.48
							206	99.98

TABLE 8.4: Ridge counts' square in per centimetre area of palm of children ranging between one and five years

Age Groups	Right hand		Left hand	
Years	Mean (cm)	S.D.	Mean (cm)	S.D.
1	1000.00	±113.79	1026.00	± 96.78
2	809.00	±135.16	785.00	± 65.02
3	729.00	± 73.99	718.00	± 77.11
4	658.00	± 93.22	663.00	± 84.68
5	605.00	±117.33	602.00	±104.39

TABLE 8.5: Crease origin and radial distance of children ranging between one and five years

Age Groups	Right hand		Left hand	
Years	Mean (cm)	S.D.	Mean (cm)	S.D.
1	1.12	±0.126	1.08	±0.141
2	0.99	±0.109	0.95	±0.164
3	1.19	±0.164	1.14	±0.189
4	1.32	±0.181	1.29	±0.184
5	1.47	±0.202	1.38	±0.238

In the present context the phalangeal crease patterns are being related to the anatomical axis. The distal phalangeal crease patterns show nominal variation but crease patterns, especially feather type, show ulnar trend in their distribution at basal phalangeal crease. Enclosure, open and boat shaped patterns are more common on the ulnar side of the anatomical axis, i.e., on III, IV and V digits at their medial phalangeal crease sites.

The symmetrical and asymmetrical expressions of palmar flexion creases are rather unconventional type of problems and ordinarily evade solution.

Symmetry of Palmar Creases

To denote the incidence of symmetrical or asymmetrical occurrence of palmar flexion crease, as based upon right/left combinations, it is worthwhile to consider the contributions of the authors who have worked on the symmetry of dermatoglyphic traits.

Henck et al. (1933) talks of 'Assymetrie' of homologous finger pairs. Cummins and Midlo (1927) attempted this problem on the line of Kirchmair (1935). Mayer-Heydenhagen (1934) worked on concordance and homologous symmetry concept. Weinand (1935) uses the term 'Kombination' to denote right/left distribution of palmar traits. Verschuer (1957) uses the term *Konkordang-Diskordanz* for symmetrical/asymmetrical occurrence of dermatoglyphic traits. Sharma restricts to R/L combination. Renes (1946) on the basis of R/L combinations worked on symmetrical and asymmetrical occurrences on papillary patterns. Later Kumbanani applied Rene's method. Datta (1964) studied the symmetry of plantar main line. Bali (1964) applied Rene's system of symmetrical and asymmetrical occurrences on finger patterns (1968) and also toe patterns (1965).

In the case of palmar flexion creases very few references are available to express right and left differences. The bilateral difference of crease types have been stated by several workers. Bilaterical symmetry of creases find references, but, in the true sense of the word, we can cite the work of Iagolnitzer (1980) and of the present author.

Iagolnitzer (1980) gave a new concept of pseudo-axial symmetry in palmar flexion creases. The deep insight of the above author on this specific problem of pseudo-axial crease symmetry has revealed a valuable clue for the interpretation of crease relation with other palmar components.

'The dactyloglyphic distributional structure demonstrating clusters, I, II and III-IV-V has suggested a relationship with palmar flexion creases and a pseudo-axis of symmetry for the radial longitudinal and the distal transverse creases. This symmetry has been extended to the pair made of the proximal transverse crease and the middle finger crease' (Fig. 8.4).

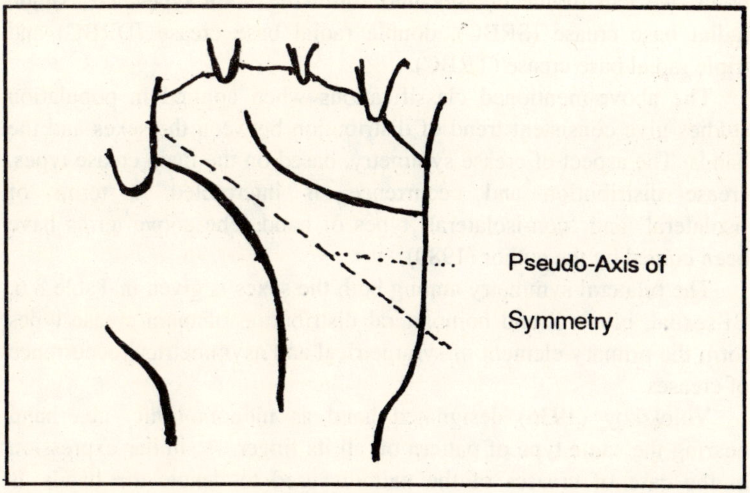

FIG. 8.4: Pseudo-axis (after Iagolnitzer 1983)

According to Iagolnitzer the pseudo-axis symmetry forms two clusters I and III-IV-V. The clusters are characterized by the high ridge counts observed on finger I and finger IV, while finger II exhibits low ridge count showing a symmetrical mode of distribution.

Similarly the radial longitudinal crease and distal transverse creases may be seen as symmetrical to an axis running approximately from the base of second digit to the centre of hypothenar, the axis being called 'pseudo-axis'.

The author believes that pseudo-axial symmetry in the palmar flexion creases will lead to structural understanding of the whole crease system of the palm. The above quoted authors' approach is exclusively on the three-fold crease classification.

The expression of symmetrical and asymmetrical occurrences of creases in terms of their classificatory status was first introduced by Sharma and Bali (1980). The palmar crease classification of Bali and Chaube (1971), Eswaraiah (1977) and the subsequent revision of the above two crease formulations, given by the author in Chapter 9, form the basis of our present discussion on symmetry.

The study is based on bilateral ink prints of either sex numbering a hundred each. Both transverse and longitudinal crease forms have been considered. Each classificatory system has its independent criteria, i.e., radial and carpal base points. On the basis of crease origin from this point, we can divide creases into following main types, i.e., single radial base crease (SRBC), double radial base crease (DRBC) and triple radial base crease (TRBC).

The above-mentioned classifications when applied in population studies give consistent trend of distribution between the sexes and the hands. The aspect of crease symmetry, based on the main crease types, crease distribution and occurrence, is interpreted in terms of 'isolateral' and 'non-isolateral' types of hand. The above terms have been coined by the author (1980).

The bilateral symmetry among both the sexes is given in Table 8.6. Bi-sexual, bilateral and homolateral distribution of main crease types form the primary element of symmetrical and asymmetrical occurrence of creases.

Volotzkoy (1936) designated hand as monomorphic, i.e., hand bearing the same type of pattern on all its finger. A similar expression in the case of creases of the palm is used to denote the hands as 'isolateral', i.e., showing the same type of crease pattern in both the hands and if the condition is absent the hands are designated as non-isolaterals. The isolateral hands show striking bi-sexual variation (Table 8.7).

The second situation is the occurrence of three similar crease types on both hands, i.e., a similarity between transverse palmar creases and longitudinal palmar creases. This situation is nearer to the isolateralism of the crease expression. It could be seen from (Tables 8.8 & 8.8a) that only few columns of the tables are represented by various combinations of radial and corpal base point crease types.

TABLE 8.6: Bimanual distribution of creases

Main	Crease Types	Male (%)		Female (%)	
		Rt	Lt	Rt	Lt
Transverse crease	SRBC	6	6	2	7
	DRBC	87	86	66	72
	TRBC	7	8	32	21
	Total	100	100	100	100
Longitudinal crease	SCBC	41	55	49	62
	DCBC	59	45	50	37
	TCBC	—	—	1	1
	Total	100	100	100	100

TABLE 8.7: Frequency distribution of isolateral hands

Main crease types	Distribution hand types			
	Rt hand	Lt hand	Male (%)	Female (%)
Transverse crease	SRBC	SRBC	2	—
Longitudinal crease	SCBC	SCBC		
Transverse crease	DRBC	DRBC	31	14
Longitudinal crease	DCBC	DCBC		
Transverse crease	TRBC	TRBC	—	—
Longitudinal crease	TCBC	TCBC		
Total	Isolateral hands		33	14
	Non-isolateral hands		67	86
	TOTAL	:	100	100

TABLE 8.8: Distribution of three same crease patterns

Crease form	Rt	Lt	Male (%)	Female (%)
T. Crease	SRBC	SRBC	1	1
L. Crease	SCBC	DCBC		
T. Crease	SRBC	SRBC		
L. Crease	SCBC	TCBC	—	—
	Total	:	1	1
T. Crease	DRBC	SRBC	19	14
L. Crease	DCBC	SCBC		
T. Crease	DRBC	DRBC		
L. Crease	DCBC	TCBC	—	—
T. Crease	DRBC	SRBC	—	2
L. Crease	SCBC	DCBC		
T. Crease	DRBC	TRBC	—	1
L. Crease	DCBC	DCBC		
	Total	:	19	17
T. Crease	TRBC	TRBC	—	—
L. Crease	TCBC	SCBC		
T. Crease	TRBC	TRBC	—	—
L. Crease	TCBC	DCBC		

TABLE 8.8a: Distribution of three same crease patterns

Crease form	Lt	Rt	Male (%)	Female (%)
T. Crease	SRBC	SRBC	—	—
L. Crease	SCBC	DCBC		
T. Crease	SRBC	SRBC		
L. Crease	SCBC	TCBC	—	—
T. Crease	SRBC	DRBC	—	2
L. Crease	SCBC	SCBC		
	Total	:	—	2
T. Crease	DRBC	DRBC	7	8
L. Crease	DCBC	SCBC		
T. Crease	DRBC	DRBC	—	2
L. Crease	DCBC	TCBC		
T. Crease	DRBC	SRBC	2	—
L. Crease	DCBC	DCBC		
	Total	:	9	10
T. Crease	TRBC	TRBC	—	—
L. Crease	TCBC	SCBC		
T. Crease	TRBC	TRBC	—	—
L. Crease	TCBC	DCBC		

The occurrence of symmetrical and asymmetrical combinations is listed in Table 8.9 out of nine probable combinations two combinations i.e., SRBC and TRBC, show their conspicuous absence.

TABLE 8.9: Combinations of symmetrical and asymmetrical occurrence of crease types

T. Crease L. Crease Combinations	Male (%)		Females (%)	
	Rt	Lt	Rt	Lt
SCBC × SRBC	4	4	1	3
SCBC × DRBC	2	2	1	4
SCBC × TRBC	—	—	—	—
DCBC × SRBC	34	46	32	44
DCBC × DRBC	53	40	33	27
DCBC × TRBC	—	—	1	1
TCBC × SRBC	3	5	16	15
TCBC × DRBC	4	3	16	6
TCBC × TRBC	—	—	—	—
Total :	100	100	100	100

The individual with two symmetrical and one asymmetrical crease types shows bi-sexual variation. The incidence is high in males (Table 8.10) while, occurrence of two asymmetrical and one symmetrical combination shows higher incidence in females.

TABLE 8.10: R/L combinations of symmetrical and asymmetrical occurrence of creases

Group	T. Creases	L. Creases	Frequency (%)	
			Male	Female
2sym. + 0Asym	Sym.	Sym.	67.0	44.0
1sym. + 1Asym	Sym.	Asym.	28.0	33.0
	Asym.	Sym.	3.0	12.0
0sym. + 2Asym.	Asym.	Asym.	2.0	11.0
		Total :	100	100

Anatomical Axis and Mode of Plantar Crease type Distribution

Mishra (1979) correlated plantar creases with reference to the anatomical axis and found the anomaly in the distribution of crease types in foot. The Tibial and Fibular distribution of plantar creases with reference to anatomical axis show anomaly. The scope and limitation for explaining the higher concentration of crease types towards the Tibial side can best be explained in terms of anatomical axis.

The Tibial incidence of the single medial base crease (R+59.23, L+56.92) in males and in females (R+43.47, L+47.15) shows Tibial side dominance of the anatomical axis. This is true of both feet and of both sexes (Table 8.2a).

The Tibial incidence of double medial base crease and triple medial base crease in either sex shows lesser Tibial shift as compared with single medial base crease.

Isopedal Feet

It is an old expression used by Volotzkoy (1936) for distribution of dermatoglyphic patterns in hand. Mishra (1979) used this term in plantar creases to express the similarity of creases on the feet of an individual. Distribution of isopedal individual is given in Table 8.3a.

Bali et al. (1980) used this expression in palmar creases, under the term 'isolateral' and 'non-isolateral'.

The Intra-Individual Relationship Between Palmar and Plantar Creases

While discussing the genetic inter-correlation between finger and toe patterns, Bali (1968) speaks about the genetic interdependence and differential effect of the independent courses of evolutionary specialization as the factors responsible for the change in the above two dermatoglyphic areas.

There seems to be a general agreement that dermatoglyphic areas of foot and hand agree closely with the developmental sequences of the embryo. Davenport (1933) has ably discussed the growth of human foot and suggests that the factors that activate control and development of the terminal segments of the appendages are probably the same and both hand and foot grow together and increase with age.

"The morphology of the sole according to Cummins & Midlo (1943), follows closely with that of the palm and may be interpreted in the same way. It holds true for fingers and toes also. Newman (1936) and Bali (1968) has already given some correlation between the finger and the toe dermatoglyphic of the same individual."

Because foot shows a departure from the hand, both in shape and function, it is, therefore, showing the deviation, both in creases and dermatoglyphic configurations. The relationship between palmar and plantar creases does not show convincing association. Perhaps, it is due to the divergent and functional evolutionary stresses which has caused deviation between palmar and plantar creases. This deviation subsequently is expressed through the crease formulation. It could be seen from Table 8.6 that frequency relationship between double radial base crease of palm and double medial base crease of sole show inverse relationship. The frequency of triple radial base crease in palm is much higher as compared with sole.

Considering the intra-individual relationship between palmar and plantar creases it could be seen from Table 8.5 that incidence of double radial base crease in palms and single medial base crease in soles is higher.

The homolateral intra-individual relationship between palm and sole shows higher incidence of single radial base crease in the palm while lesser incidence of single medial base crease is observed in sole.

The homolateral crease relationship between palm and sole of the same individual shows similar trend in the incidence of single and double base creases.

The bitrolateral crease variation shows higher incidence of single medial base crease in the sole whereas in the palm, the incidence of double radial base crease is very high. The relationship between the same type of crease of hand and palm shows disconcordant.

Seasonal Influence on Creases

The environmental stress on human body is natural and its subsequent role in shaping pre- and post-natal phenotypic traits is well known fact. Rai (1978), in her comprehensive probe with reference to dermatoglyphic and crease features, arrived at the conclusion that out of palmar and phalangeal creases it is the bracelet crease which shows seasonal rhythm (summer, rainy, winter). The data on both sexes for each season was appropriated to the tune of nine hundred individuals.

Creases in Relation to Syndactyly and Polydactyly

The occurrence of developmental abnormalities like syndactyly and polydactyly in relation to crease alignment is of biological interest.

Bali et al. (1989) studied the above abnormalities in relation to palmar creases (Transverse & Longitudinal) and also phalangeal creases with the help of a control population.

The deviation was observed in case of phalangeal creases while among longitudinal palmar creases the observed difference between control and abnormal individuals was nominal.

REFERENCES

Bali, R.S. (1964): Toe Dermatoglyphics-Inheritance and comparison with the Finger ball patterns. Ph.D. Thesis, Delhi University, Delhi.

Bali, R.S. (1965): Finger Dermatoglyphic Study of Kashmiri Muslims. *Madhya Bharati*, 14-16, pp. 104-10.

Bali, R.S. (1968): Genetic inter-correlation between finger and toe patterns. *Zeitschrift fur Morphologie and Anthropologie* 59(3): pp. 244-72.

Bali, R.S. (1973): Correlation study between palmar creases. Schizophrenia, Leprosy and Tuberculosis: IXth Internat. Congr. Anthrop. & Ethno. Sciences. Chicago, U.S.A.

Bali, R.S. (1983): Inheritance of phalangeal flexion creases, Human Biology Recent Advances, (*Proc. Internat. Sym.*, Punjabi University).

Bali, R.S. et al. (1983): Intra-Individual relationship between palmar creases and plantar creases. Human Biology Recent Advances, (*Proc. Internat. Sym.* Punjabi University).

Bali, R.S. and R. Mishra (1978): The study of morphological change in hand, palm and palmar flexion creases of one to eleven years old boys and girls. Xth Internat. Congr. Anthrop. & Ethno. Sciences, New Delhi, India.

Bali, R.S. and R. Mishra (1980): Age change and crease morphogenesis. *Internat. Sym. Dermat.* Punjabi University, Patiala, India.

Bali, R.S. and Ramesh Chaube (1971): On the formulation of palmar creases. *Z. Morph. Anthrop.*, 63: p. 121.

Bali, R.S. and D.K. Jain (1983): The study of pre-natal and post-natal Development of creases in Man. Human Biology Recent Advances 2 (*Proc. Internat, Sym.* Punjabi University).

Bali, R.S., S. Koley, K. Bannerjee and S. Bannerjee (1989): The study of Syndactyly and Polydactyly in Relation to phalangeal creases. Internat Conf. on Progress and Trends in Dermatoglyphic Research, Calcutta.

Bali, R.S., S. Koley, K. Bannerjee and S. Bannerjee (1989): Transverse and longitudinal creases in Relation to syndactyly and polydactyly. Internat Conf. on Progress and Trends in Dermatoglyphic Research, Calcutta.

Cummins, H. and C. Midlo (1927): Dermatoglyphics in Jews. *American Journal of Physical Anthropology*, 10: pp. 91-113.

Cummins, H. and C. Midlo (1943): *Finger prints, palms and Soles: An introduction to dermatoglyphics*. Philadelphia, Blakiston.

Cummins, H. and C. Midlo (1961): *Finger prints, Palms and Soles: An introduction to dermatoglyphics*. New York, Dover.

Datta, P.K. (1964): The symmetry of the plantar main-life formula in an Indian population. *Acta Geneticae Medicae et Gemellologiae*, 13(3): pp. 305-12.

Davenport, C.B. (1933): The growth of Human foot. *Am. J. Phys. Anthrop.*, 17: pp. 167ff.

Eswaraiah, G. (1977a): Palmar flexion creases of Muslims and their symmetrical occurrence (R/L Combination), Indian Anthropologist.

Henck, K.O. (1933): *Contribuciones al estudio de la antropologie Chilena. III. La disposicion de las crestas papilares de las falangitas en los indigenas de la provincia de Cautin. Boletin de la sociedad de Biologia de Concepcion* (Chile) 7: pp. 35-60.

Iagolnitzer, E.R. and J. Iagolnitzer (1983): Pseudo Symmetry in the Palmar Flexion Crease System. Human Biology Recent Advances, 2 (*Proc. Int. Sym.* Punjabi University).

Kirchmair, M. (1935): *Der Fingerabdruck im Dienste der Rassen und Konstitutionsforschung Munchener Medizinische Wochenschrift* 82(1): pp. 529-31.

Meyer-Heydenhagen, G. (1934): Zur Erbbiologie der Papillarleisten der Handflache. *Zeitschrift fur Induktive Abstammungs und Vererbungslebre* 67: pp. 302-05.

Mishra, R. (1979): *Inheritance and methodological study of plantar creases.* Thesis submitted in part fulfilment for the requirements of the degree of PH.D., University of Saugar, Sagar.

Newman, M.T. (1936): A comparative study of finger prints and toe prints, *Human Biology*, 8(4): pp. 531-52.

Renes, R.C. (1946): Symmetrical and asymmetrical occurrence of papillary patterns. *American Journal of Physical Anthropology*, 4(2): pp. 169-91.

Sharma, A. (1960): Symmetry of four palmar main lines collectively and of modal types in the Burmn Series. *The Anthropologist*, 7(1-2): 21-31.

Sharma, A.N. and R.S. Bali (1980): The Occurrence of Symmetrical and Asymmetrical Palmar Creases: Human Biology Recent Advances 2(*Proc. Int. Sym.* Punjabi University, Patiala.

Schultz, A.H. (1937): Foetal growth and development of the rhesus monkey. *Contributions to Embryology* (Carnegie Institute) 26: pp. 71-97.

Verschuer, O.V. (1957): Die biologischen Grundlagen der menschlichen Mehrlingsforschung. *Zeits. f. ind. Abst. und Vererbungsl*, pp. 147-205.

Volotzkoy, M.V. (1936a): Dactyloscopic graphs and formulae. *Anthropologicbeskii Zburnal (Moskva)* 4: pp. 428-37.

Weinand, H. (1935): Familienuntersuchungen uber der Hautleistenverlauf der Hand-flache. *Zeitschrift fur Morphologie und Anthropologie* 36: pp. 418-42.

PART II

METHODS AND DESCRIPTION OF PALMAR, PLANTAR, PHALANGEAL AND BRACELET CREASES

PART II

METHODS AND DESCRIPTION OF PALMAR, PLANTAR, PHALANGEAL AND BRACELET CREASES

9

PALMAR FLEXION CREASES

PALMAR FLEXION creases, though not the components of dermatoglyphics, are usually associated with the dermal configurations of the palm. The simian crease (*Affenfurche* or *vierfingerfurche*) has been the subject of a large number of recent studies. Among the palmar creases much emphasis has been laid on the study of simian crease.

Human creases or creases of non-human primates, like other biological aspects, could also have attracted the attention of biologists other than the anthropologists if treated under single classification. In the absence of a single standardized formulation system the proliferation of multi-crease formulations have rapidly increased. In spite of the fact that creases for the last one century are under scientific consideration for want of an appropriate system of crease classification, the search is still on.

The palmar, plantar, phalangeal, toe and bracelet creases have characteristic features of their own but all these creases conform to a common definition of crease and possess all important crease attributes which are essential for crease identity.

The creases are divided into primary, secondary and tertiary types. The formulation of creases is exclusively based on primary creases. To accommodate various configuration type of creases, several systems of crease classification from time to time were devised. The most ancient system is that of palmists.

The simian-crease-oriented system of palmar crease formulation dominated the screen for quite a long time and the exact description of what may be included under the term simian crease has been tried by several workers.

Formulations of Simian Creases

Broca (1877) introduced a single transverse line in anthropology. Shuttleworth (1909) studied this principal fold in Mangolian

Imbecility, Langdon-Down (1909) showed two transverse lines. Crookshank (1924) termed these principal lines as 'Mangolian' or orangoid as one transverse line, instead of a distinct line of heart (DFF) and head (FFF).

Pöch (1925) was first to give crease classifications. He treated both transverse and longitudinal creases of the palm in terms of formulas. Later Lasinski and Urbanowicz (1960) showed the importance of these formulas in ethnic study. They noted the significance of formula 1 × 2.3 among Polish males and compared it with other population (Fig. 9.1a).

Schaeuble's (1933) embryonic interrelation of creases with inter-digital pads serves a guideline for crease classification.

Portius (1937) classified the simian creases for the first time into four types: i.e. one transitional, two incomplete (ii & iii) and one complete (iv) (Fig. 9.1). He concluded that the trait must be recessive as in many cases of simian creases, the parents of subjects do not show any sign of this characteristic.

Tillner (1953-55) thought the simian crease to be originated from *Verschmelzung* or *Fortsetzung*, between the relevant section of distal and proximal transverse crease. He classified the typical simian crease as separate type I from a transitional type II.

Büchi (1954), the author, made five categories of simian creases. The 'O' category is free from any trace of simian crease. 'I' is a transitional type II, III and IV are incomplete types, while V is a complete simian crease (Fig. 9.2).

His types III and IV were an addition to the classification of the previous workers. In the course of his study the author stresses the role of genetic and embryonal factors for the development of simian or other crease types.

Weninger and Navratil (1957) gave four categories of simian creases; Ia, Ib, IIa and IIb. (Fig. 9.3). The above authors classified type I as the typical simian crease and type II as the transitional one.

Kimura and Hagiya's (1958) classification is essentially of radial longitudinal crease and incorporated it with the proximal transverse crease. They realized the importance of the radial longitudinal crease and incorporated it with the proximal transverse crease to give five probable types. On the basis of their relative position at the point of origin the authors made five types or categories: opened, meeting, crossing, sub-close and closed (Fig. 9.4).

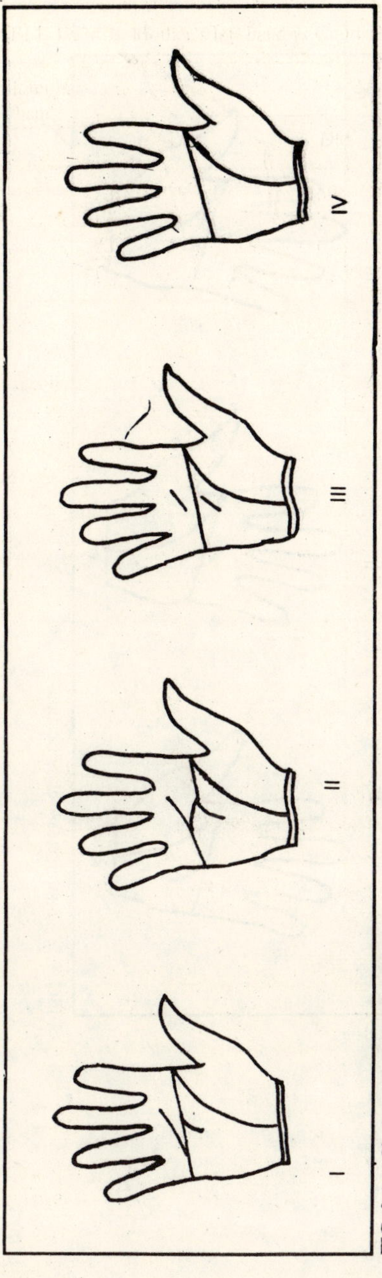

FIG. 9.1: Simian crease classification

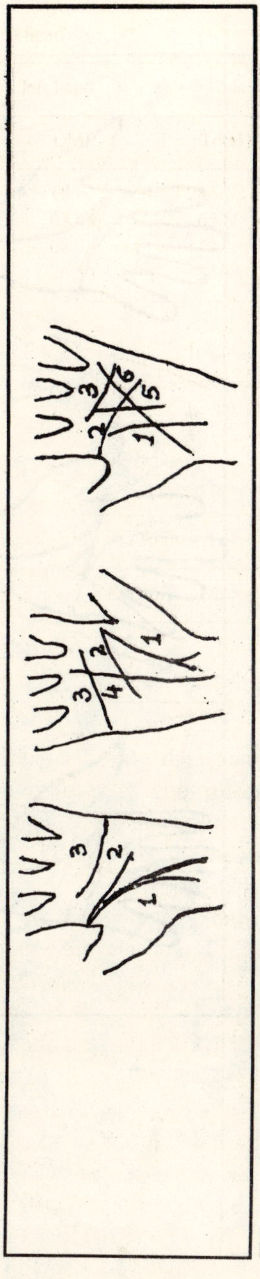

FIG. 9.1a: Non-simian: Palmar crease formulation

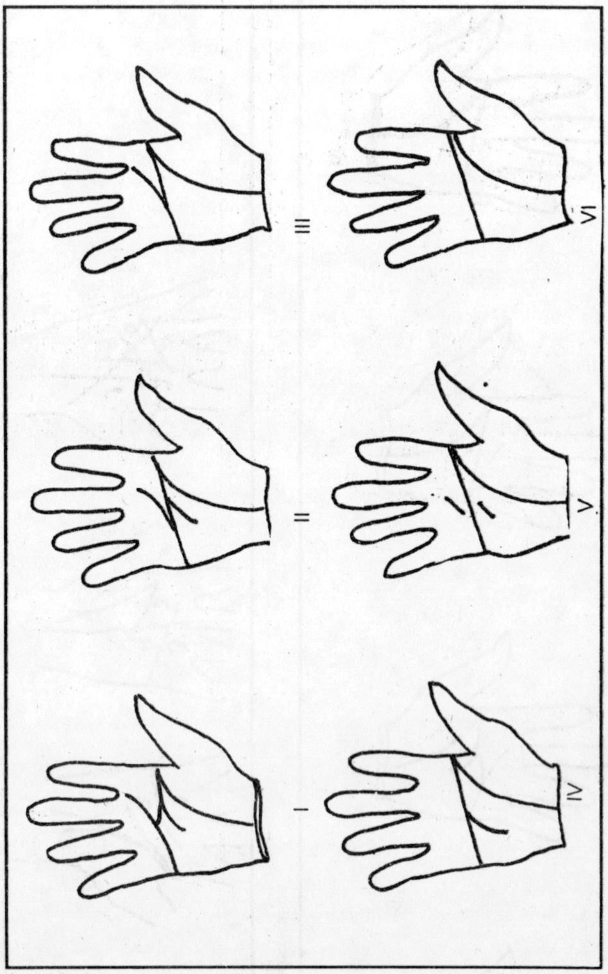

FIG. 9.2: Simian crease classification

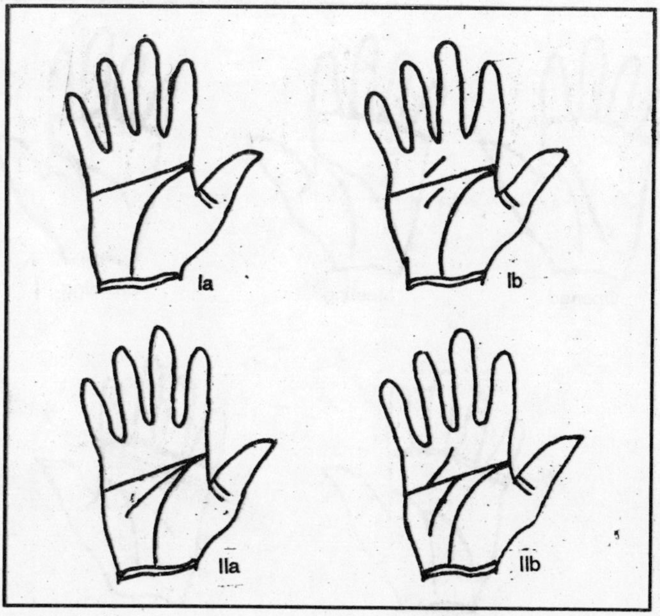

FIG. 9.3: Simian crease classification (Weninger & Navratil, 1957)

Leiber (1960), the author, proposed three theoretical sets (A, B and AB) of crease combinations, between distal transverse crease, proximal transverse crease and radial longitudinal crease. Each set comprises 36 types (Fig. 9.5 a,b,c). Gyenis and Hera (1971) made use of Leiber's system of crease classification. Although the system is complex, it is comprehensive enough to accommodate all crease types in its fold. The genetic unity between the above three sets is yet to be established.

Kimura (1968) classified all the transverse creases into five groups from A to E, including nine types, as the complete type and five groups from 'a' to 'e' (including seven types) as the incomplete type (Fig. 9.6). In his study of palmar creases in Ainus, the author has given the incidence of simian creases both complete and incomplete types and also non-simian crease types.

Besides this, his work on 'M' figure in Ainus population is based on the classification of Kimura and Hagiya (1958).

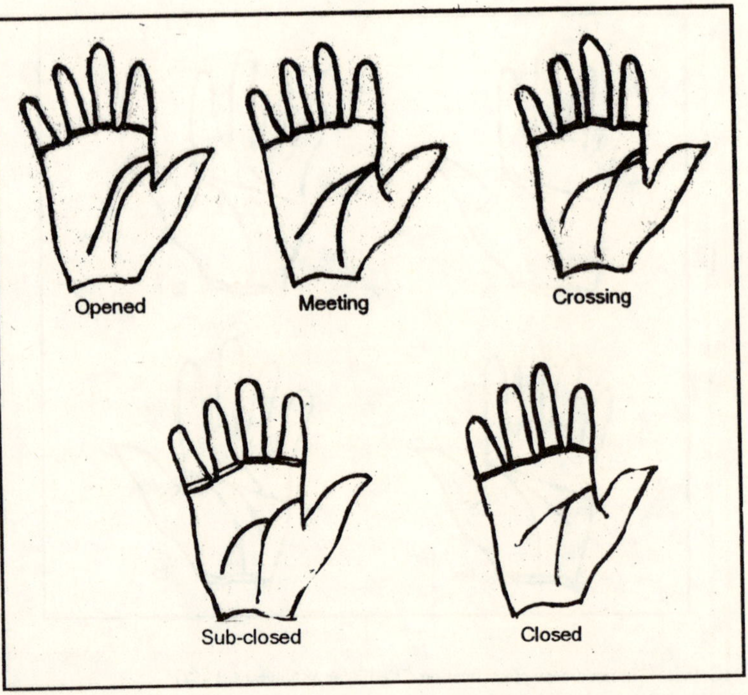

FIG. 9.4: Palmar crease formulation (Kimura & Hagiya, 1958)

Lestrange (1969a), incorporated eleven types of transverse creases into her classification. The author made three categories: (1) the hand flexion creases, (2) normal configurations and (3) typical transverse crease; and included 3→ 2⁺ f, 2→ + 3⁺ f and 3t variations into her classification (Fig. 9.7).

Loeffler (1969) divided the palmar creases into three groups — 1. Major creases, 2. Minor creases and 3. Secondary creases.

Mavalwala (1958) opines that phenotypic variation of flexion creases is not as complex as finger print patterns but the types most commonly observed on the human palm can be sub-divided into many types. The classification given in (Fig. 9.8) is being used at the University of Toronto, (Mavalwala, 1971).

The simian and sydney creases classification of Shaha and Dermat (1980) is just another addition in the list of palmar crease classification (Fig. 9.9).

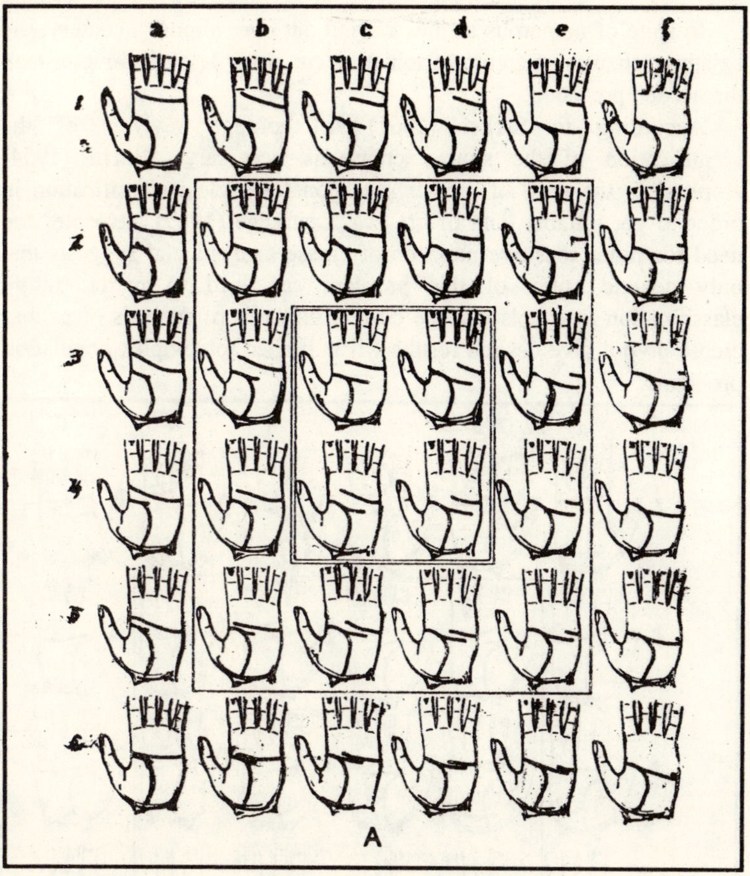

FIG. 9.5 (A): Palmar crease classification (Leiber, 1960)

Bhanu (1972) by inserting the terms 'vestigial bi-crease' (11) and 'complementary vestigial distal crease' (10), further complicated the system of simian crease classification (Fig. 9.10).

Dar, et al. (1977) developed a system of palmar crease classification which distinguishes 55 types of creases. The system is represented by four main groups (Fig. 9.11); normal variant, simian crease and its variant, sydney line and its variant and another group or normal variants which do not fit into the other groups.

Out of the above crease classifications only four are non-simian type while the rest of the classifications are simian crease oriented.

In spite of numerous studies carried out over almost a century, the existing schemes of crease formulation are either less sensitive or lack the needed precision.

According to Sarkar (1961) 'a thorough revision of the identification of the simian crease is necessary'. Büchi (1954) emphasises the need of greater precision for a clear classification in order to get reliable data of creases. Lestrange (1969) advocates the need for more sensitive methods of crease analysis and suggests that only genetic study of this problem can lead to partial future classification and feels that the current methods of analysis of palmar crease do not give desired results when applied to complex population problems.

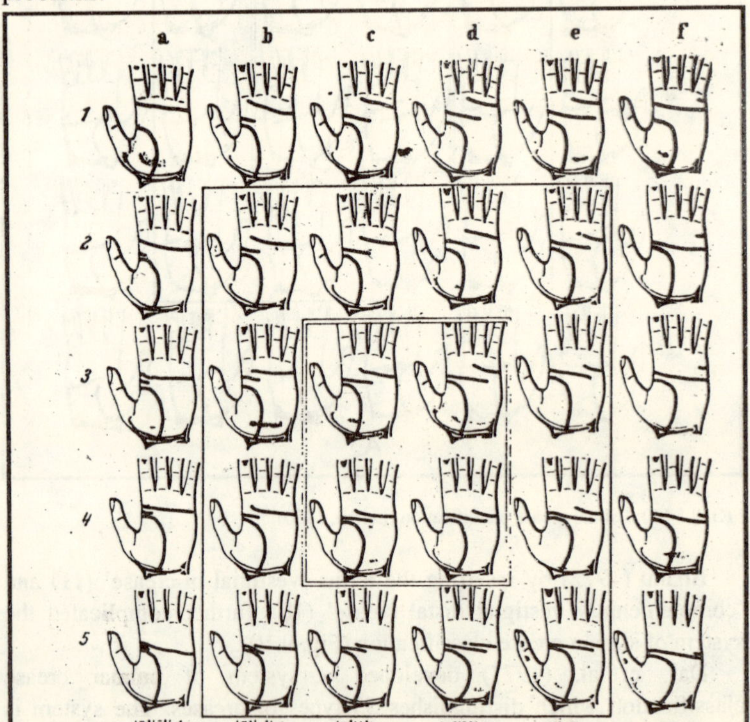

FIG. 9.5(B): Palmar crease classification

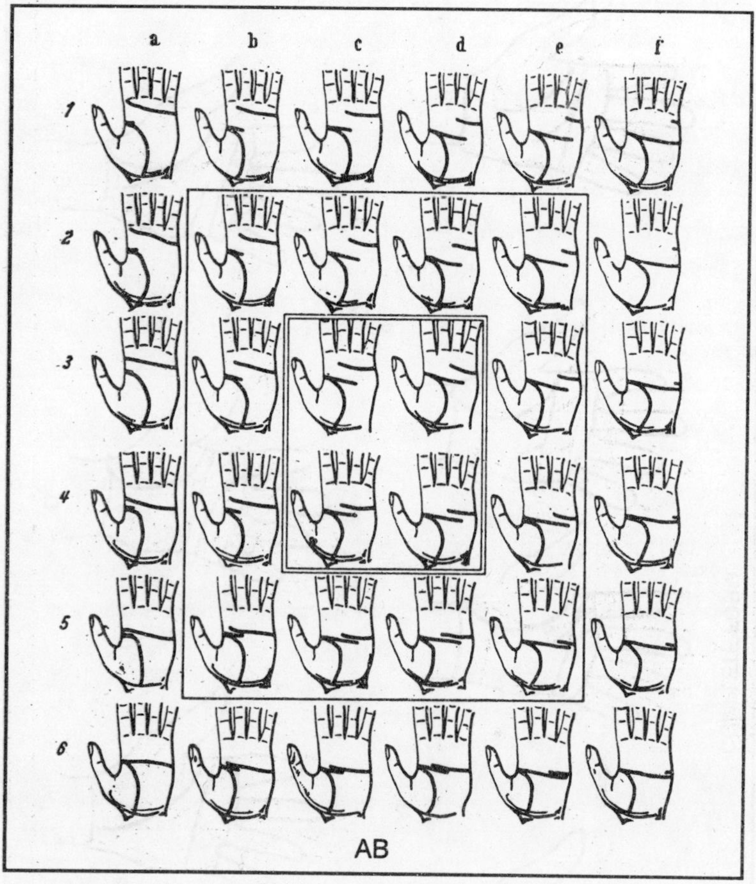

FIG. 9.5AB: Palmar crease classification (Leiber, 1960)

Fisher (1949) advocates the genetic basis of classification of creases while Wurth (1937), Patten (1953) and Dar, *et al.* (1977) emphasise embryonic consideration in crease formulation (1954).

Büchi's (1954) epistatic and de Wilde's (1954) penetrance hypothesis have been of lesser value towards the solution of crease formulation.

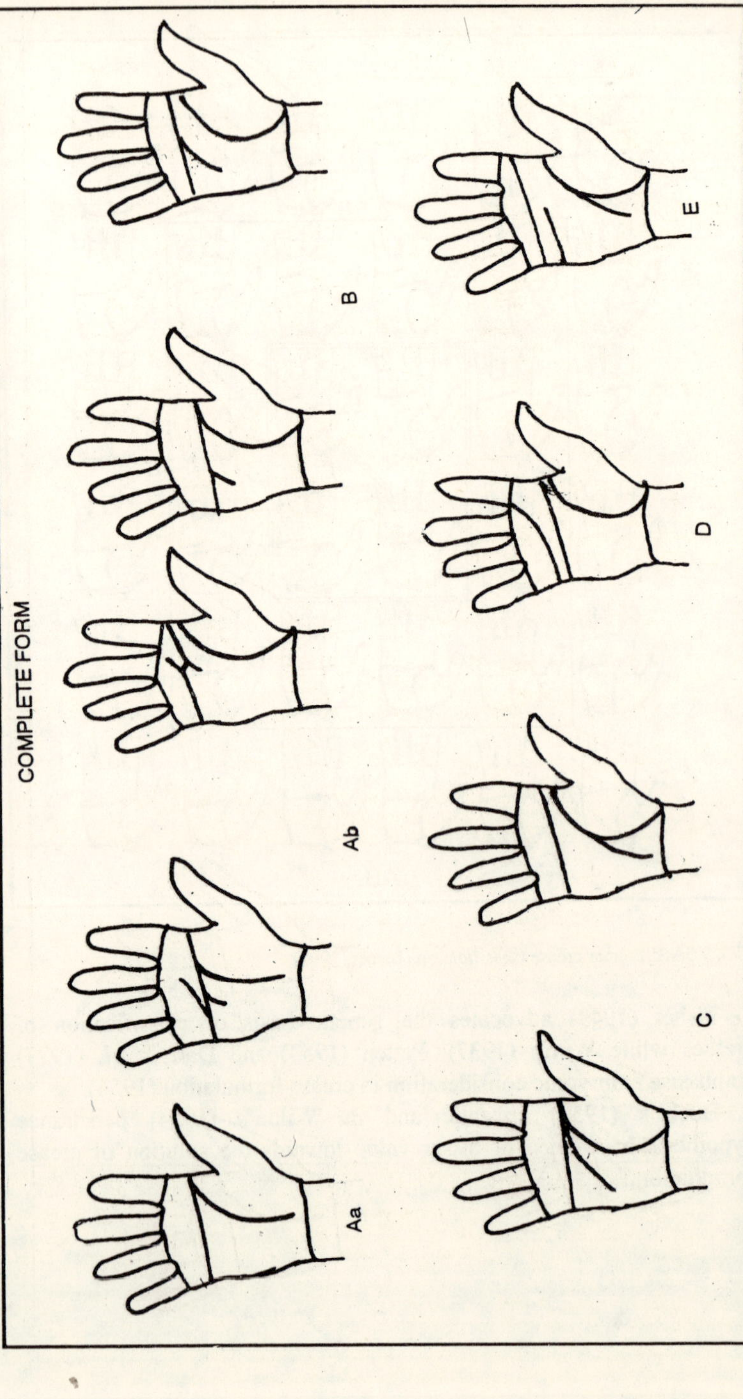

FIG. 9.6: Simian crease classification

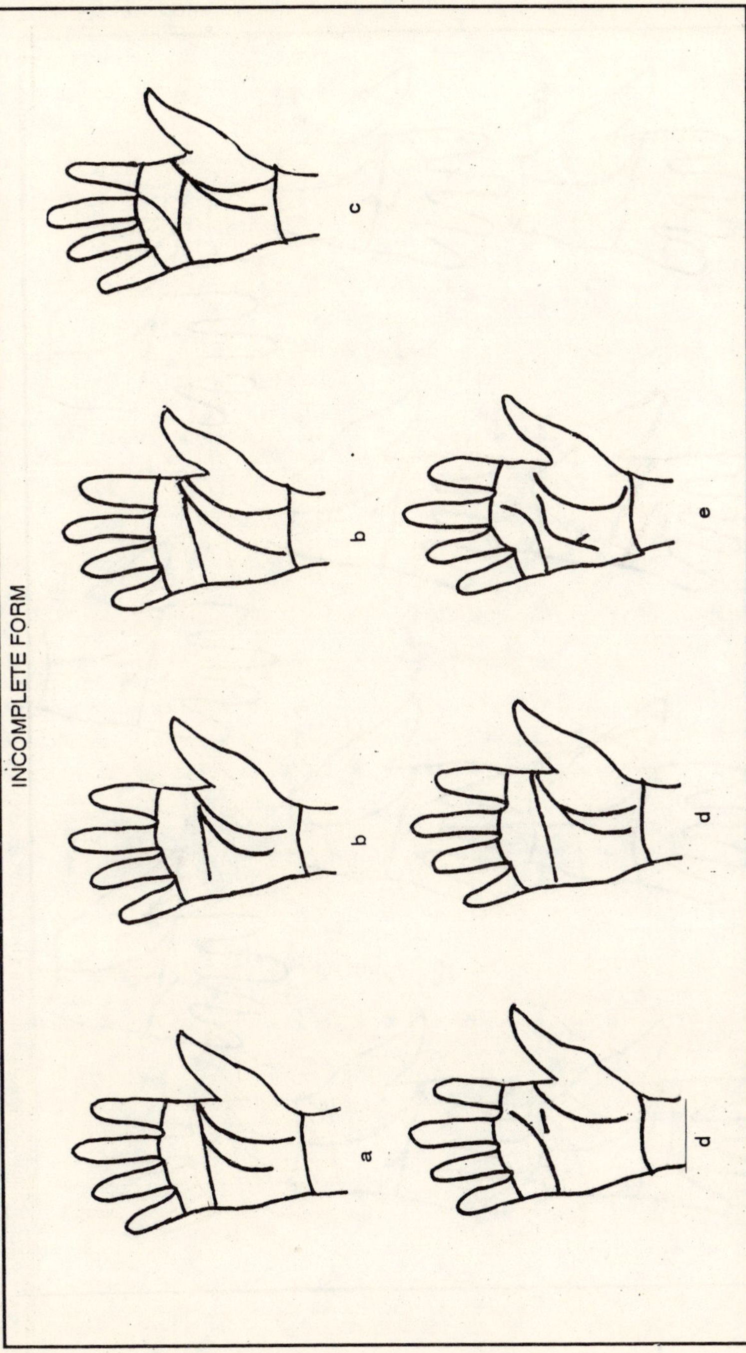

FIG. 9.6: Simian crease classification

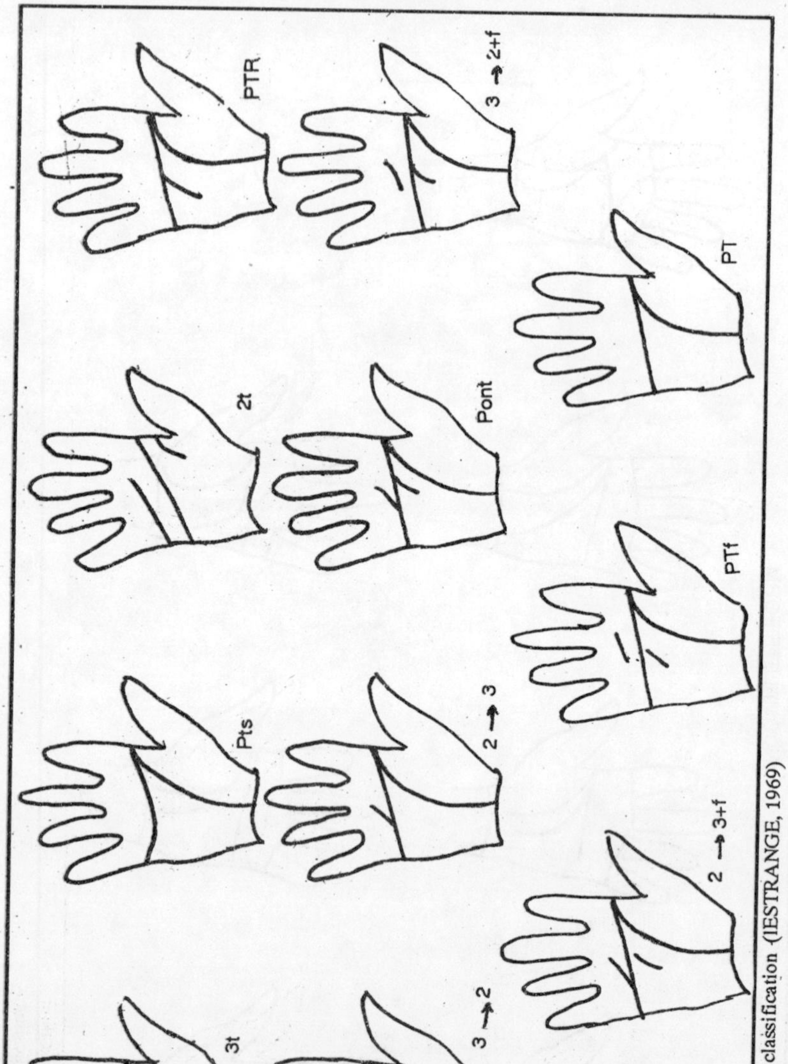

FIG. 9.7: Simian crease classification (IESTRANGE, 1969)

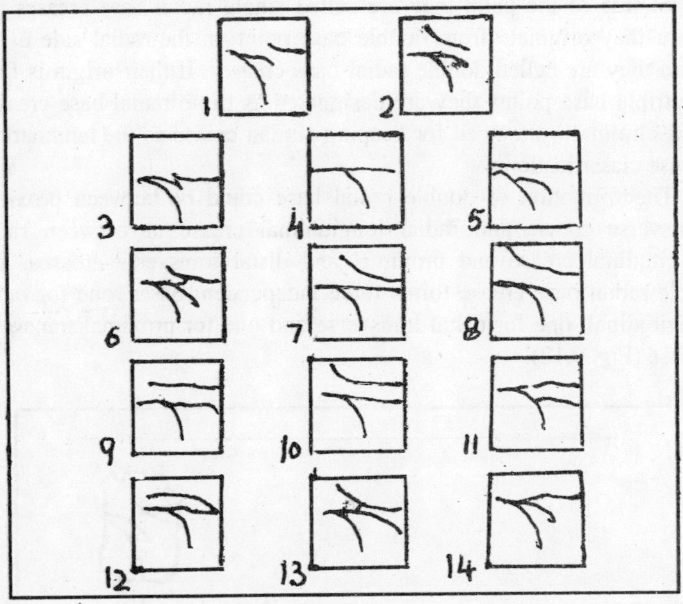

FIG. 9.8: Types of transverse flexion creases (Mavalwala, 1971)

Transverse Crease Formulation

Bali and Chaube (1971) advocate for a fresh approach and plead that most of the existing methods are simian crease oriented and their subsequent influence appear to have hampered the growth of new methods of crease classifications.

An attempt was made by the above authors to settle this much argued problem through fresh approach of treating the radial margin, i.e., an area between first and second digits of the palm as pro-mordial for classification of the palmar flexion creases. On the basis of this trait the palmar creases were classified into three main categories.

Single radial base crease (SRBC)
Double radial base crease (DRBC)
Triple radial base crease (TRBC)

This three-fold classification signifies the base point of crease origin, that is, when creases originate from a single base point on the radial side of the palm they are called single radial base creases and when they originate from double base point on the radial side of the palm they are called double radial base creases. If their origin is from the triple base points they are designated as triple radial base creases. This eliminates the need for keeping simian crease as the landmark of crease classification.

The formation of double radial base could be between proximal transverse crease and radial longitudinal crease or between radial longitudinal crease and proximal and distal transverse creases. The triple radial base crease forms three independent bases, one for radial longitudinal, one for distal transverse and one for proximal transverse crease (Fig. 9.12).

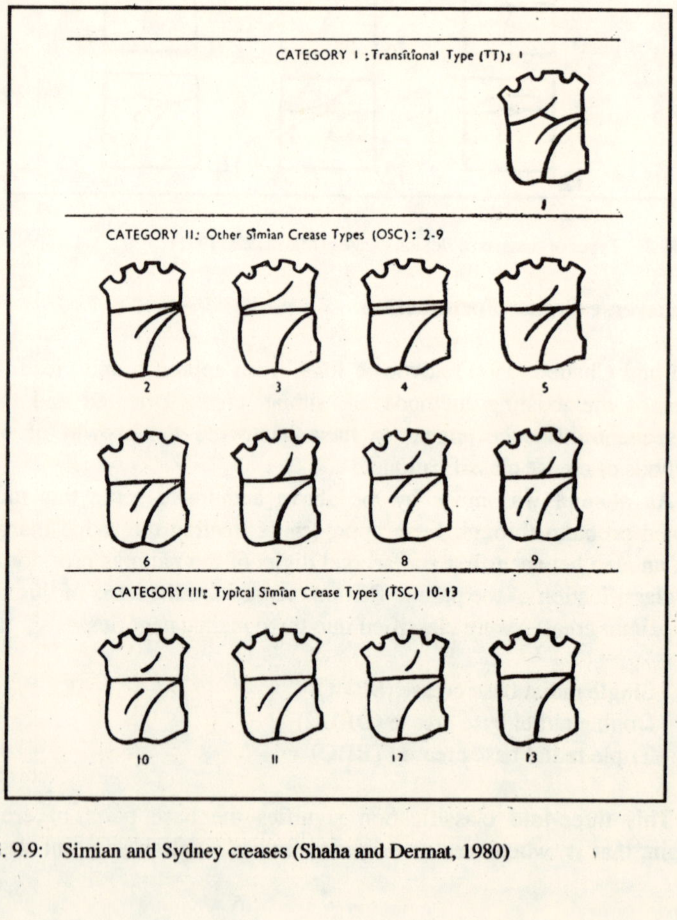

FIG. 9.9: Simian and Sydney creases (Shaha and Dermat, 1980)

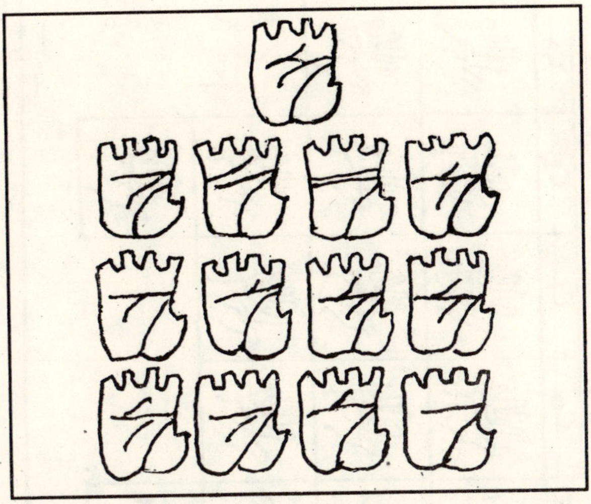

FIG. 9.10: Simian crease classification (Bhanu, 1972)

The proposed method corresponds closely to the existing methods of classification and most of the transitional types could easily be re-arranged according to the proposed method. The various types and sub-types of creases, already classified by Portius, Büchi, Kimura and others can logically be fitted into the present scheme of classification.

The finer classification of the main types, i.e., Single radial base, Double radial base and Triple radial base crease types, is classified on the basis of crease splits. If the split is radial-ward, starting from the ulnar end, the sub-type could be numbered according to the position of the splitting point (Fig. 9.13) with regard to the digits of the hand. For instance, if the split is in the region of digit, V, IV, III, II, or at the radial base point, adjoining to the digit I (thumb), the creases could be classified into S_1, S_2, S_3 types, respectively. According to the above definition all the transitional types could be arranged with regard to their position of split, starting from ulnar to radial side. Double radial base creases have also been sub-divided into further sub-types (Fig. 9.14). The sub-types of triple radial base crease has not been found in the present data (Fig. 9.15).

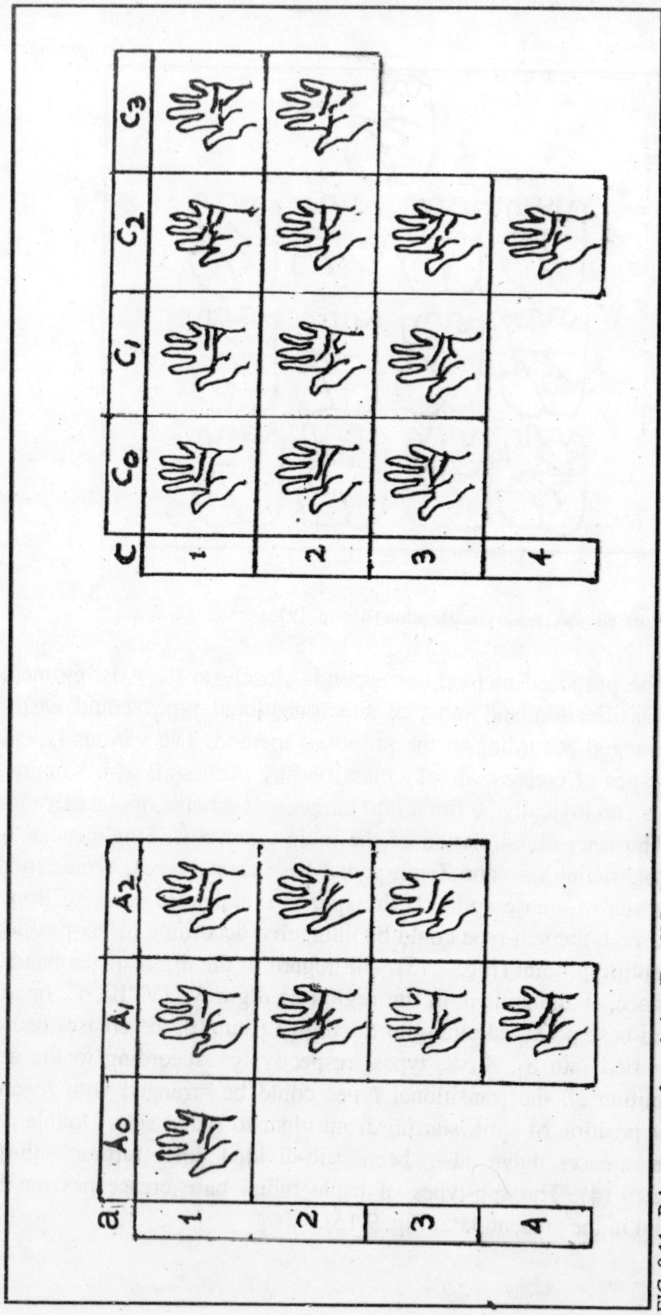

FIG. 9.11: Palmar crease formulation (Dar, H.R. Schmidt and Nitowsky (1977))

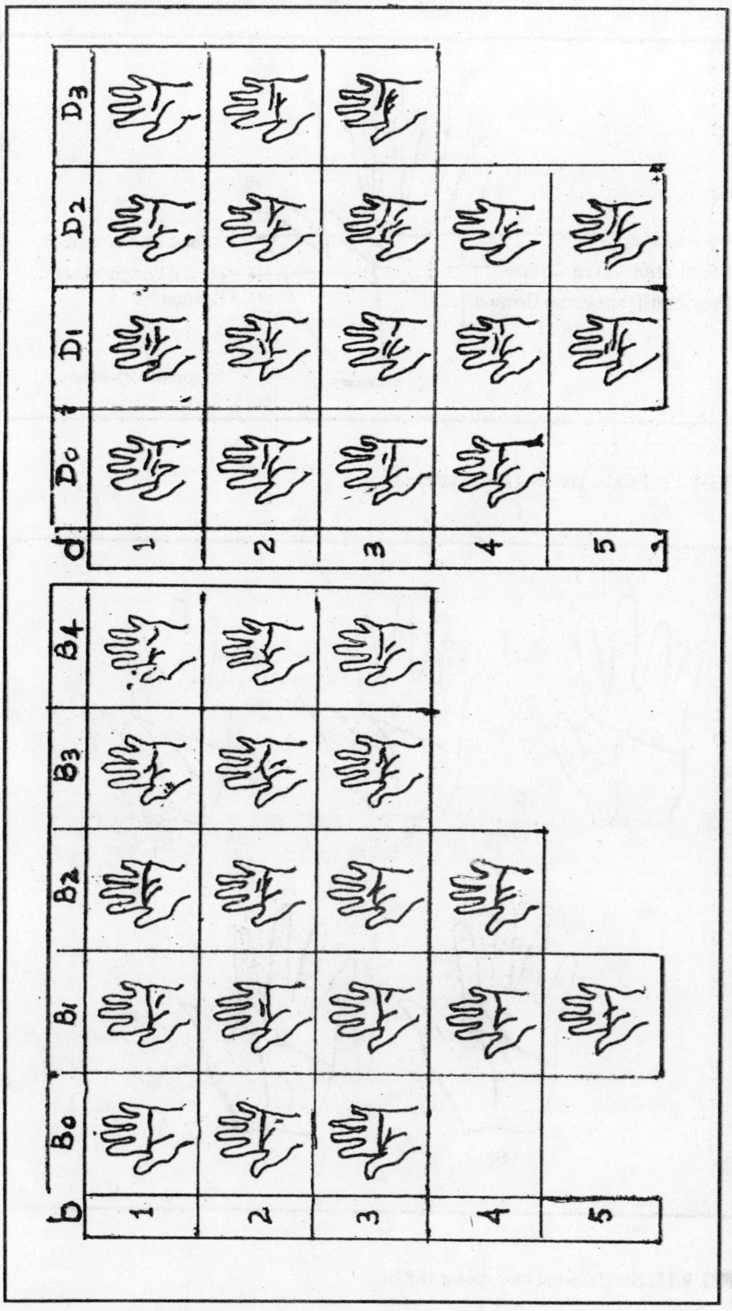

FIG. 9.11: Palmar crease formulation (Dar, H.R. Schmidt and Nitowsky (1977))

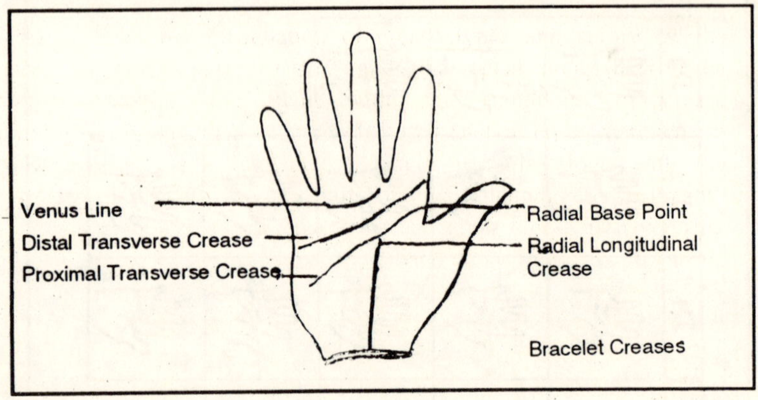

FIG. 9.12: Palmar creases (Transverse)

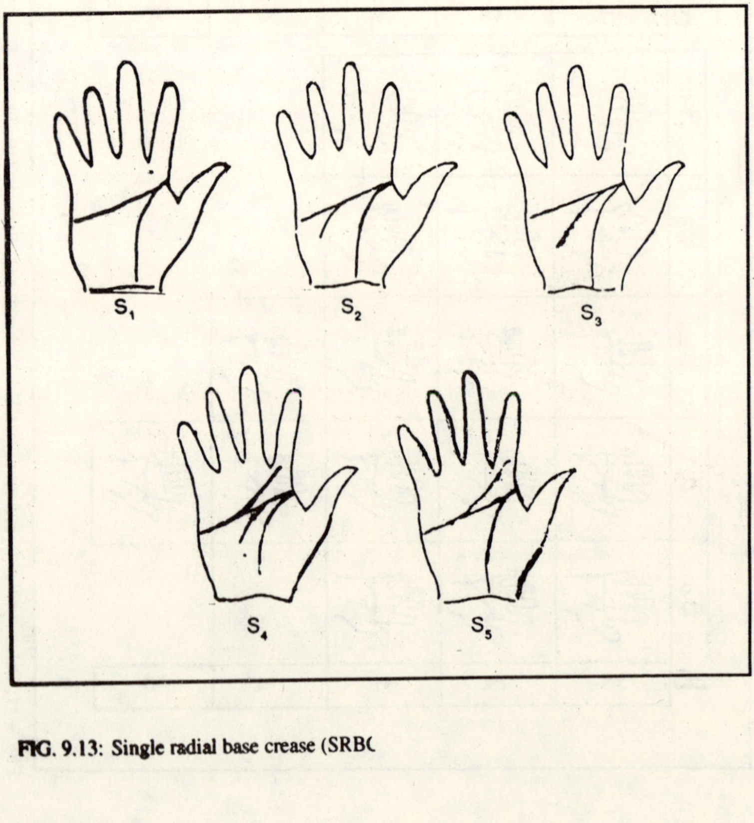

FIG. 9.13: Single radial base crease (SRBC

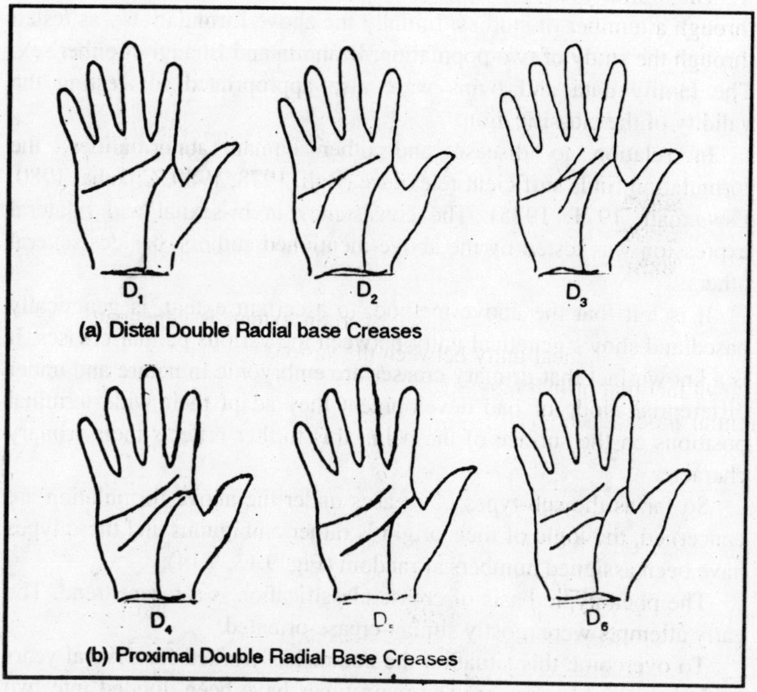

FIG. 9.14: Double radial base crease (DRBC)
(a) Distal double radial base crease
(b) Proximal double radial base crease

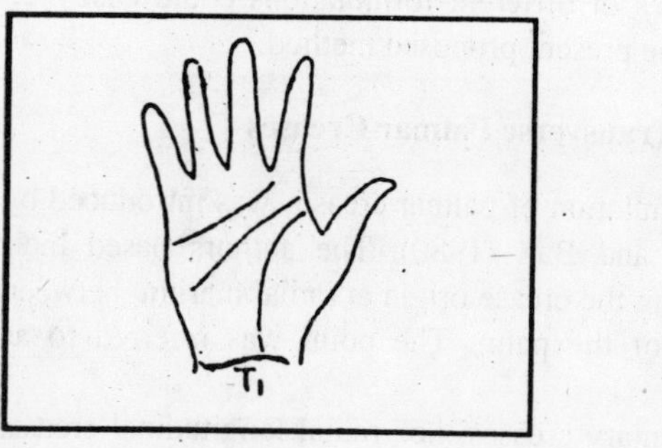

FIG. 9.15: Triple radial base crease (TRBC)

The validity of the above method of classification was tested through a number of studies. Initially the above formulation was tested through the study of two population; Brahmin and Bhangi of either sex. The family data and twins were also appropriated for testing the validity of the classification.

In relation to disease and other human abnormalities, the formulation finds sufficient relevance (Bali, 1978, 1980, Chaube, 1980, Eswaraiah, 1971, 1975). The consistency in bi-sexual and bilateral expression was tested by the above-mentioned authors, besides several others.

It is felt that the above method, to a certain extent, is genetically based and shows genetical unity between the various palmar creases. It is a known fact that primary creases are embryonic in nature and under differential mode of pad development they adapt their wide terminal positions on the surface of the palm, this further reflects their primary character.

So far as the sub-types of creases under the above-formulation are concerned, the logic of their origin is rather ambiguous and these types have been assigned numbers at random (Fig. 9.13, 9.14).

The phenotypic basis of crease classification is a recent trend. The early attempts were mostly simian-crease-oriented.

To overcome this situation the author has worked for several years to find the viable answer. The main types have been divided into two different categories for better sensitivity and precision. The sub-types have been assigned their biological or anatomical positions.

The revised method corresponds closely to the existing methods of crease classifications of Bali and Chaube (1971) and most of the transitional types of creases of different formulations could easily be re-arranged according to the present proposed method.

Revised Formulation of Transverse Palmar Creases

A new element in the formulation of palmar creases was introduced by Bali and Chaube (1971) and Bali (1980). The authors based their classification on positioning the crease origin at radial margin, between first and second fingers of the palm. The point was referred to as 'radial base point'.

When all the three primary creases, i.e., radial longitudinal crease, proximal transverse crease and distal transverse crease, emerge from a single point, the creases are designated as single radial base crease. When the above three creases form two independent bases, the crease

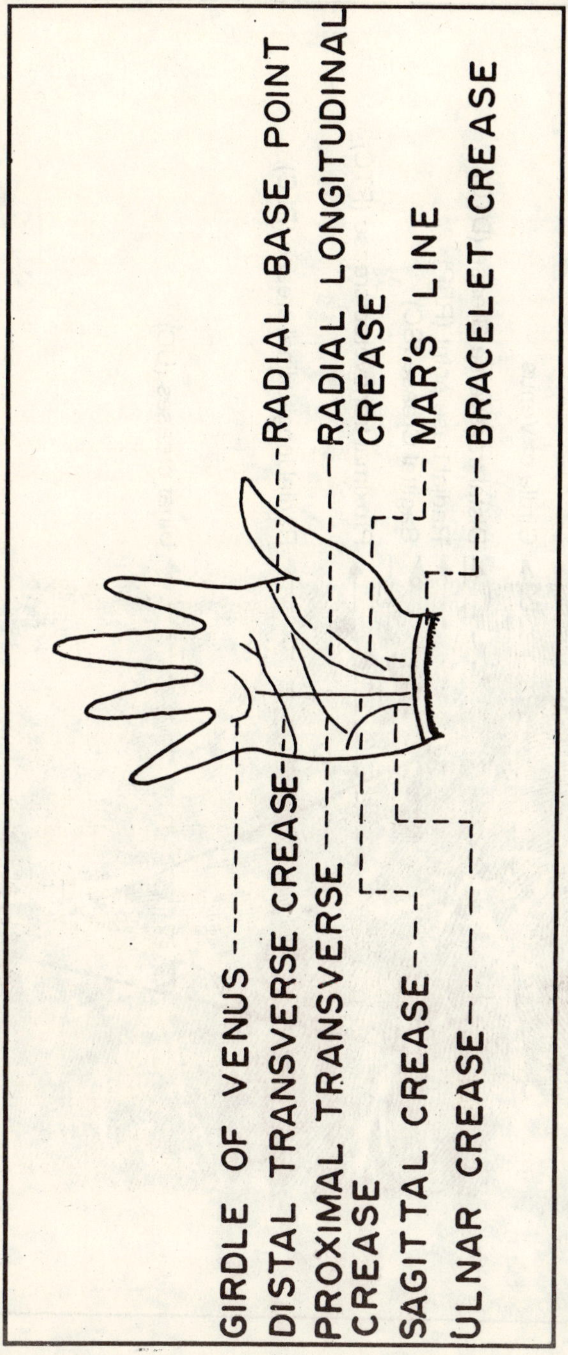

FIG. 9.16: Palmar creases

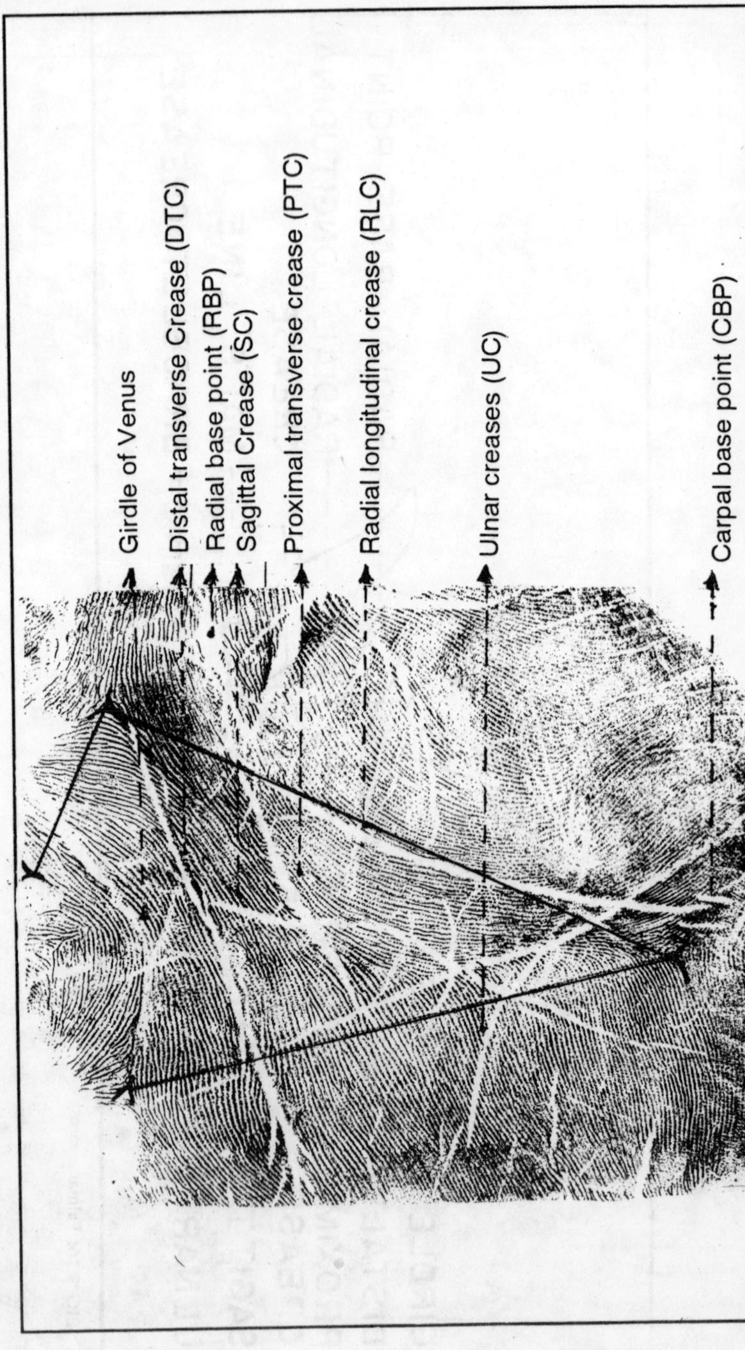

FIG. 9.16: (a) (LH) Palmar creases

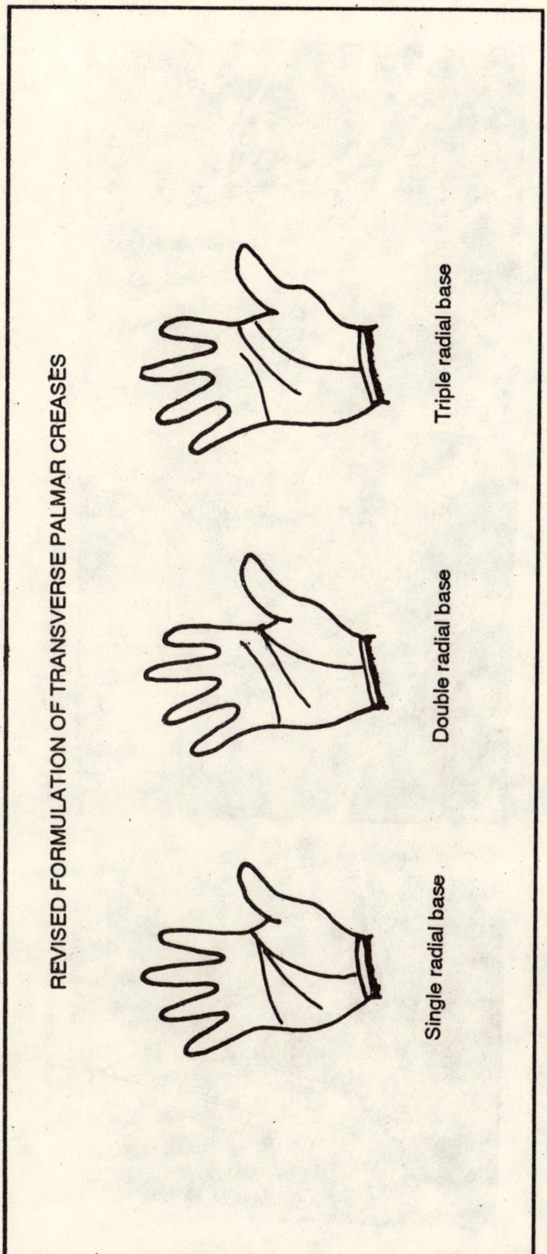

FIG. 9.16: (i) Major crease types

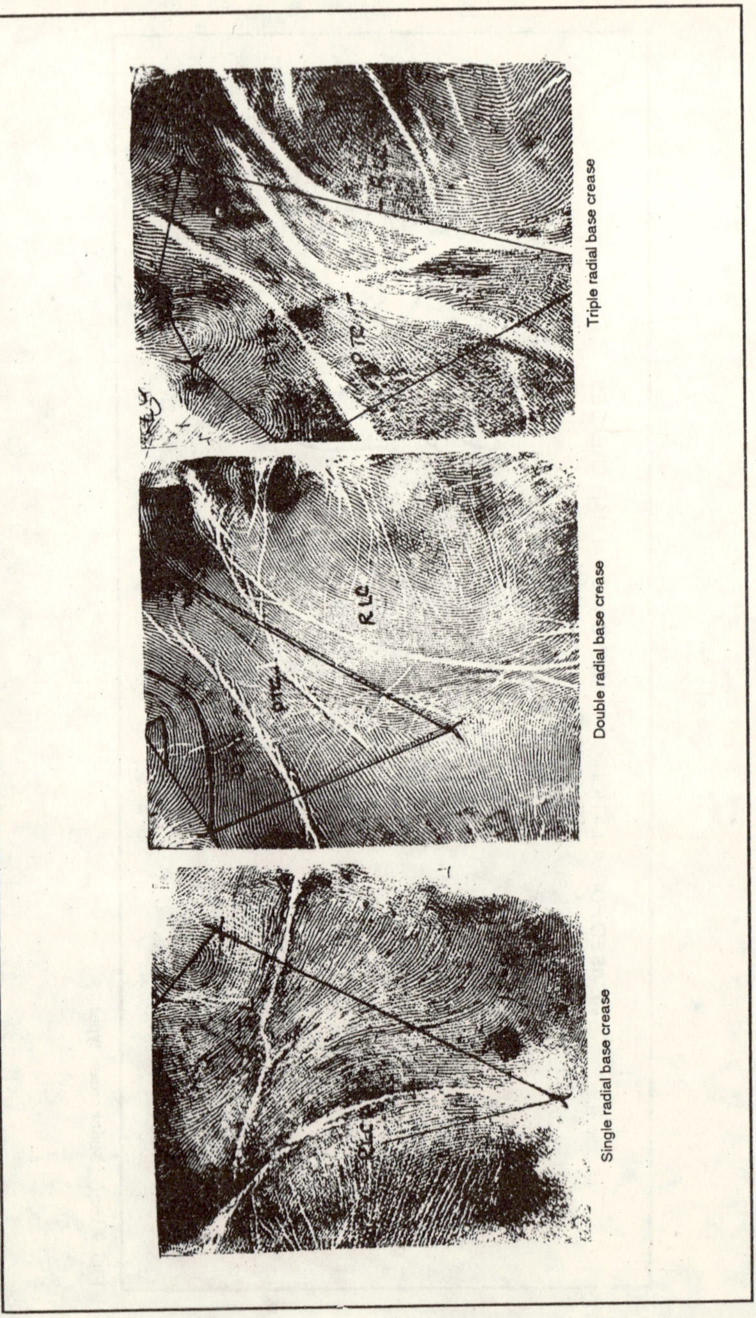

FIG. 9.16: (a) (i) Major crease types

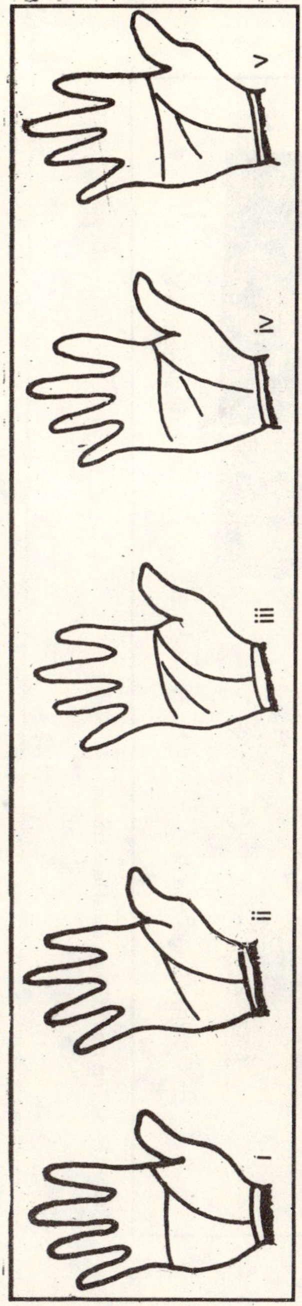

FIG. 9.17: True type of single radial base creases

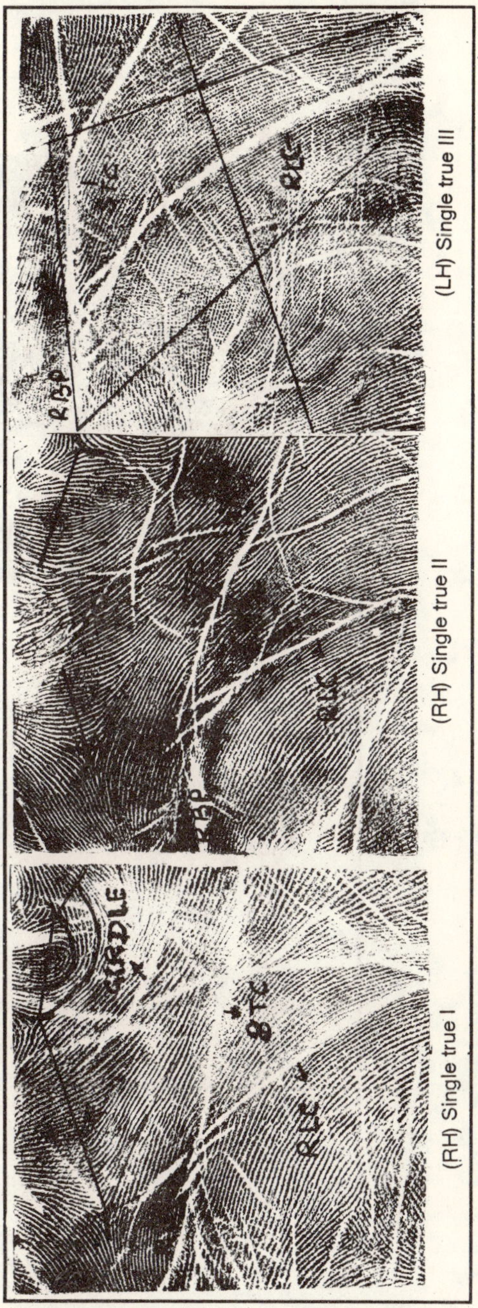

FIG. 9.17:-(a) True type of single radial base creases

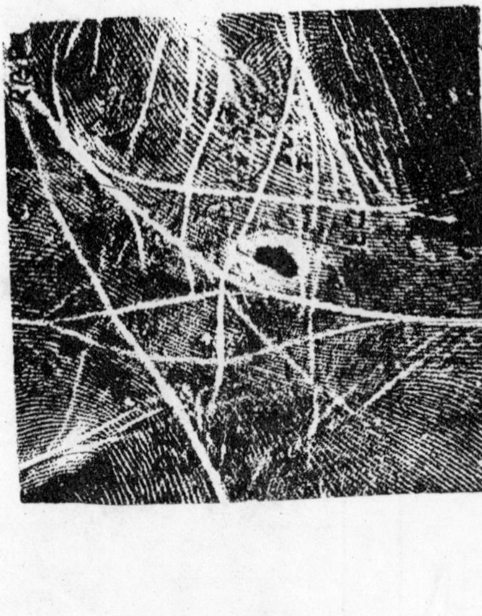

(LH) Single true V

(RH) Single true IV

FIG. 9.17: (a) True type of single radial base creases

is called double radial base crease. The formation of double radial base could be between proximal transverse crease and radial longitudinal crease or between radial longitudinal crease and proximal and distal transverse creases. The triple radial base crease forms three independent bases, one for radial longitudinal, one for distal transverse and one for proximal transverse crease (Fig. 9.16).

When the bases of the above four types of creases are firm, direct and clear-cut, the creases are categorised as 'true types' Fig. 9.17 and 9.17(a). When the union at the radial base point is not direct and clear-cut the creases are grouped as 'transitional types'. The transitional creases make indirect union through a branch or branches, emerging either from radial longitudinal, proximal transverse or distal transverse creases at the radial base point. When the branch emerges from radial longitudinal crease, the crease is designated as 'radial transitional type', when it emerges from proximal transverse crease, the crease is called 'proximal transitional type' and when the branch is from the distal transverse crease, the crease is called 'distal transitional type' and when, instead of one, there is mixed type of union, the crease is called 'mixed transitional type' (Fig. 9.18 and 9.18(a)).

When a primary crease shows a distal or proximal split to make a union between two creases at a particular digital area, the crease accordingly is classified into II, III, IV or V sub-types of true or transitional types of double radial base creases (Fig. 9.19 and 9.19(a); Fig. 9.20 and 9.20(a)). On a similar basis triple radial creases are classified (Fig. 9.21 and 9.21(a))

Formulation of Longitudinal Palmar Creases

Eswaraiah (1977) was first to introduce longitudinal set of palmar crease as a separate group. The above-quoted author has tested the longitudinal crease types in his study, 'palmar creases and diseases'. His formulation was based on a similar criteria as giver by Bali and Chaube (1971). Instead of radial base point he chose carpal base point. His classification is as under:

The palmar longitudinal creases or carpal creases, namely, the radial longitudinal crease (the palmist's 'Line of Life'), the sagittal crease (the 'Fate Line') and ulnar crease (the 'Mercury line') emerge from the carpal region of the palm, i.e., carpal base point, their point of origin (Fig. 9.22). On the basis of this point of origin, the palmar creases could be classified into three main categories:

Single carpal base crease (SCBC)
Double carpal base crease (DCBC)

Triple carpal base crease (TCBC)

This three-fold classification signifies the base point of crease origin. When creases originate from single base point on the carpal side they are called single carpal base creases; when they originate from double base points on the carpal side they are called double carpal base creases and when they originate from the triple base points they are called triple carpal base creases.

The single carpal base crease (SCBC) could be further classified into four types (Fig. 9.23):

1. Single carpal base crease (Single): It is marked by the presence of radial longitudinal crease only.
2. Single carpal base crease (Sagittal): This is a condition when the sagittal crease joins radial longitudinal crease or base.
3. Single carpal base crease (Ulnar): This is a condition when the ulnar crease joins the radial longitudinal crease proximally or distally to form a single base.
4. Single carpal base crease (Complete): This is a condition when the sagittal crease and the ulnar crease meet at the base point or proximally form a single base along with the radial longitudinal crease.

Double carpal base creases are divided into five sub-types (Fig. 9.24):

1. Double carpal base crease (Sagittal): The radial longitudinal crease from two separate base points with the sagittal crease in the absence of ulnar crease.
2. Double carpal base crease (Ulnar): The radial longitudinal crease and ulnar crease form two bases in the absence of the sagittal crease.
3. Double carpal base crease (Radial Sagittal): In this condition, the sagittal crease joins the radial longitudinal crease while the ulnar crease forms a separate base.
4. Double carpal base crease (Sagittal Ulnar): This is a condition when the sagittal crease joins the ulnar crease and forms a base, while the radial longitudinal crease has an individual base point.
5. Double carpal base crease (Radial Ulnar): In this case, the ulnar crease joins the radial longitudinal crease while the sagittal crease forms a separate base.

The sub-types of triple carpal base crease (T) have not been found in the present data (Fig. 9.25).

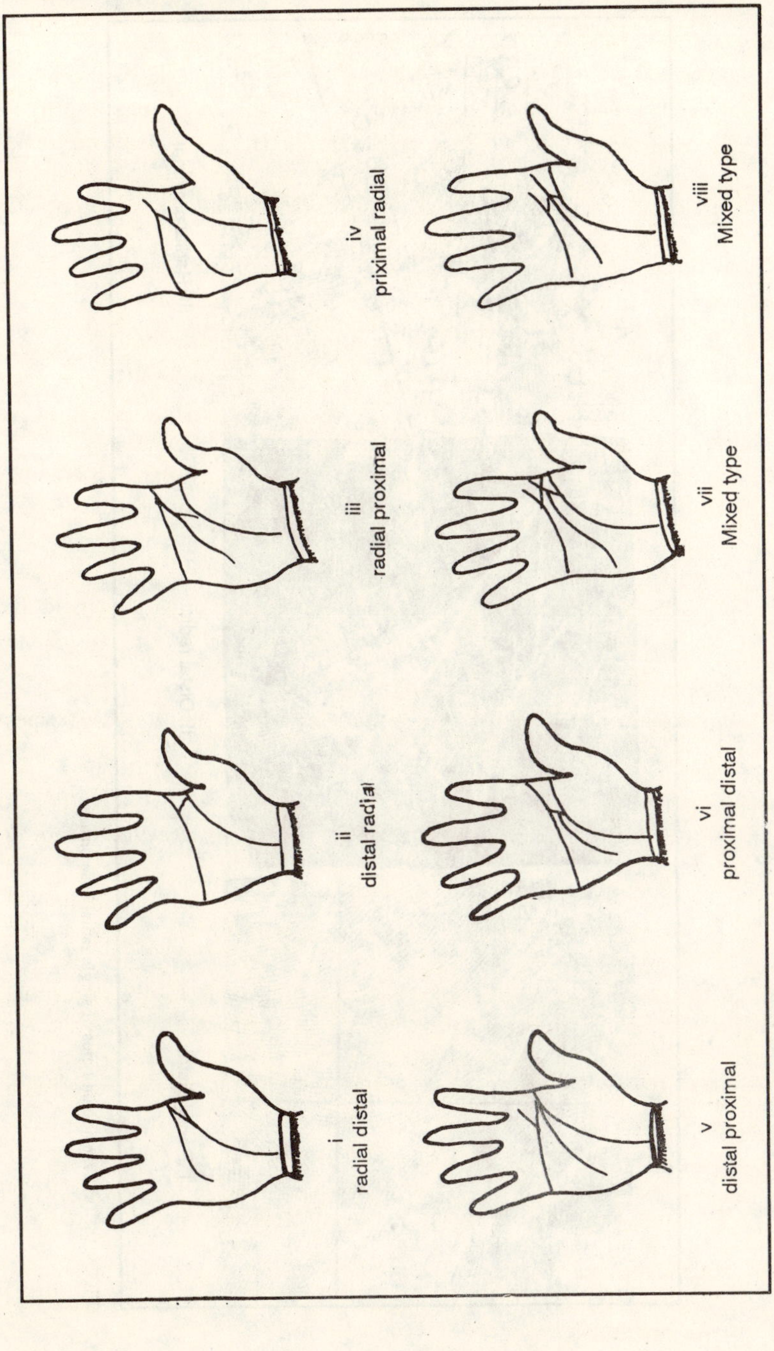

FIG. 9.18: Transverse palmar creases

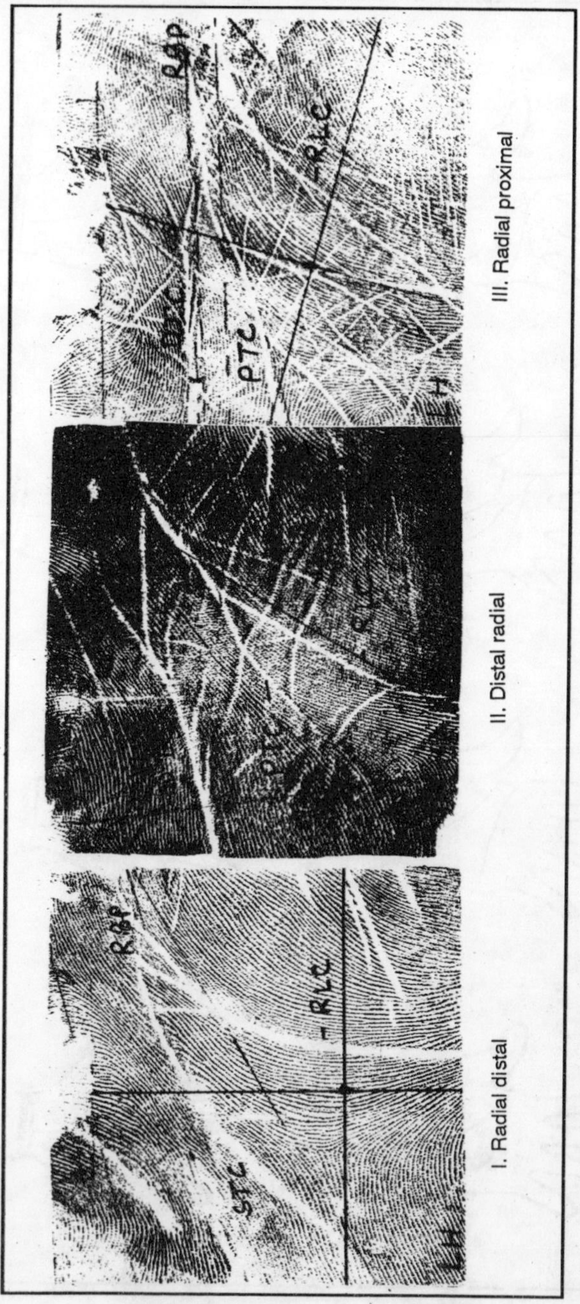

FIG. 9.18: (a) Transitional types of single radial base creases

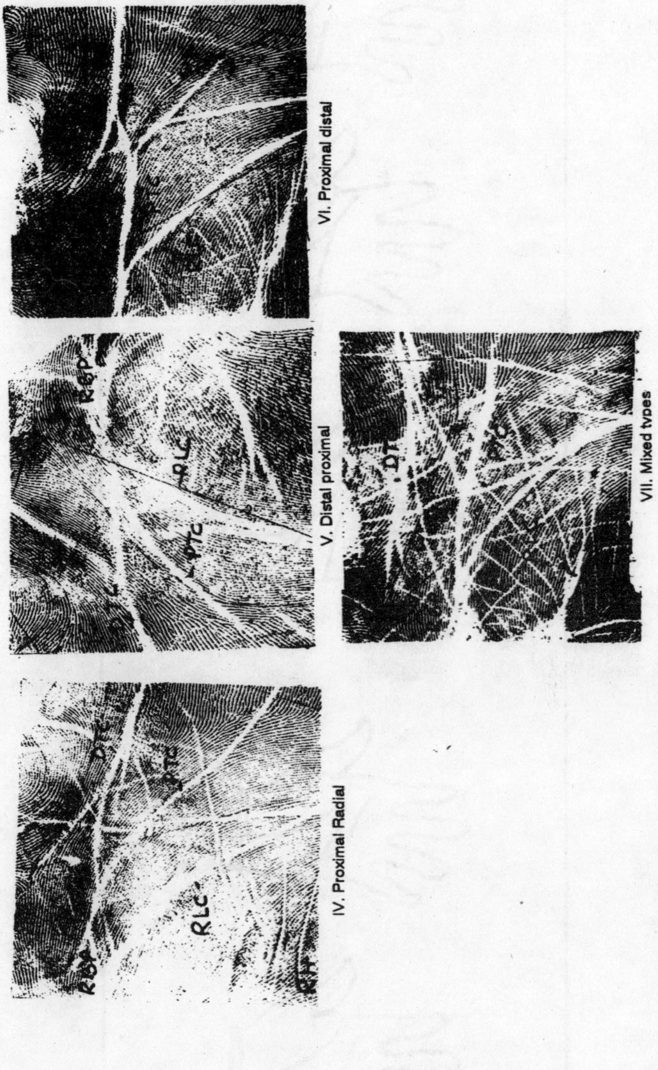

FIG. 9.18: (a) Transitional types of single radial base creases

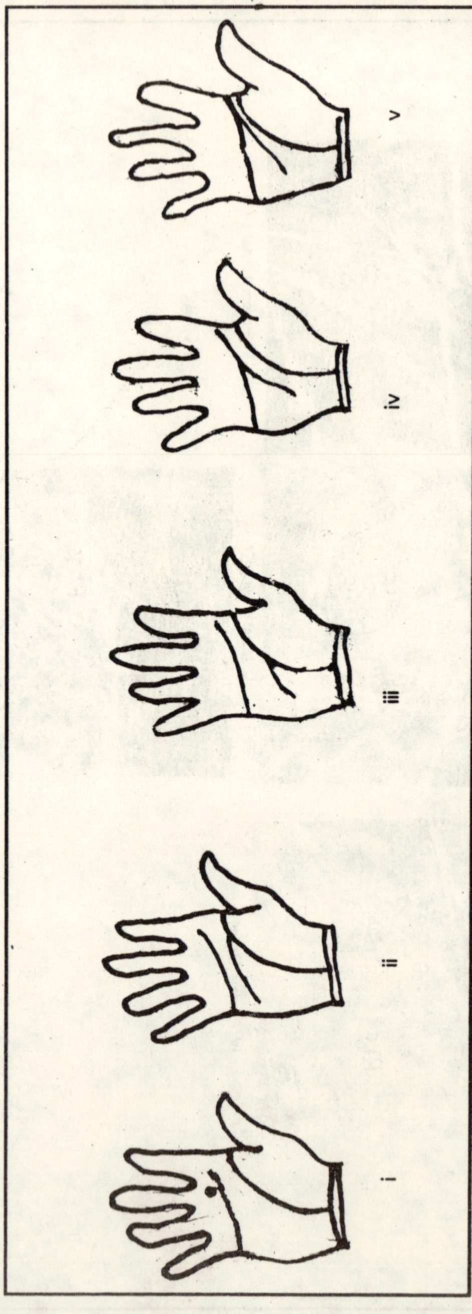

FIG. 9.19: True types of double radial base creases

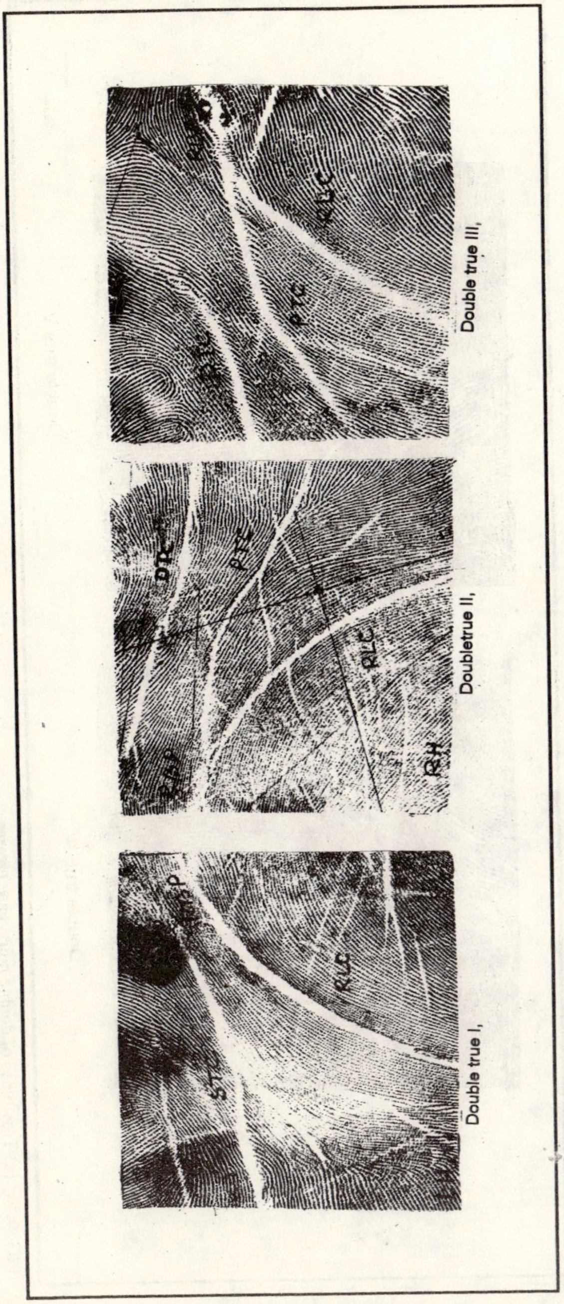

FIG. 9.19: (a) True types of double radial base creases

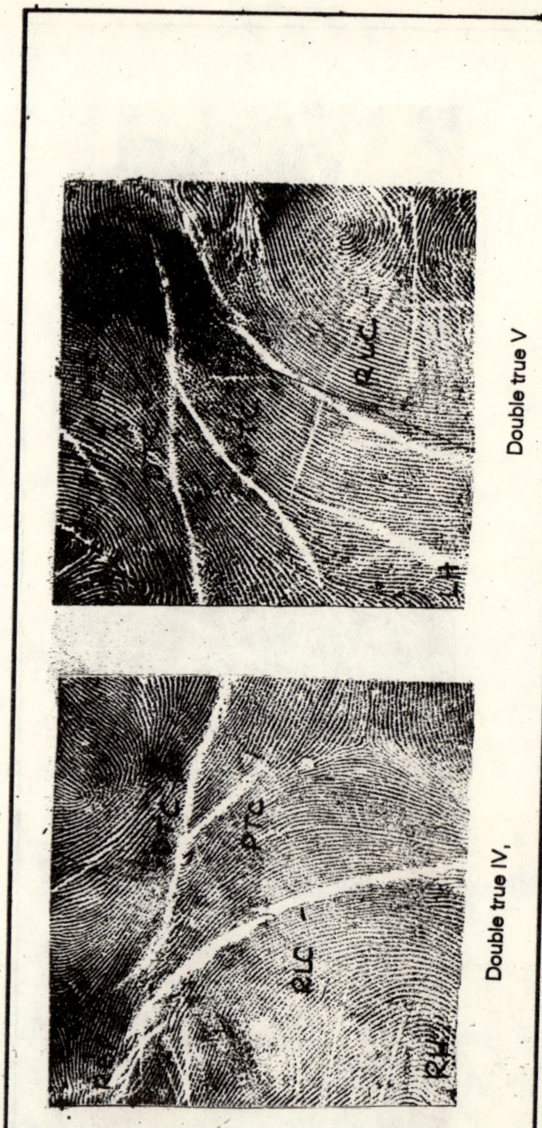

FIG. 9.19: (a) True types of double radial base creases

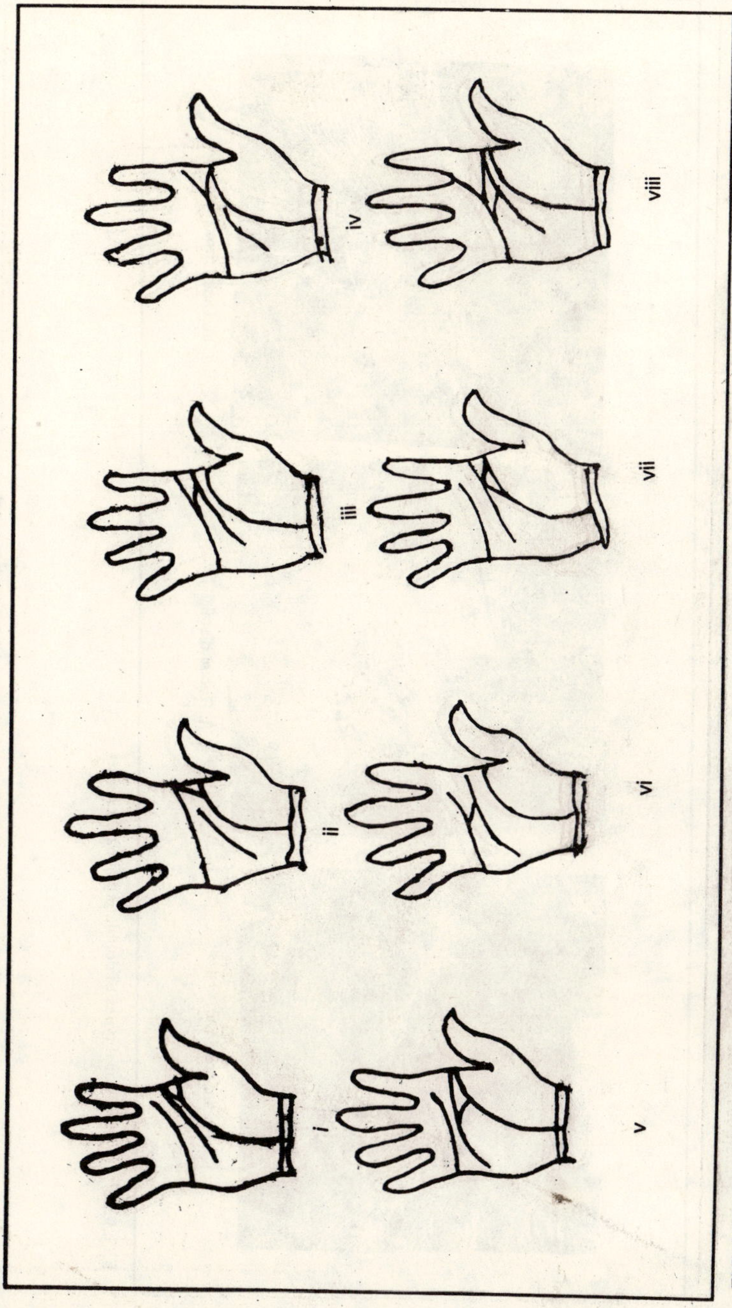

FIG. 9.20: Transitional types of double radial base creases
i. radial proximal, ii. radial distal, iii. distal proximal, iv. distal radial, v. proximal radial, vi. proximal distal, vii & viii. mixed types

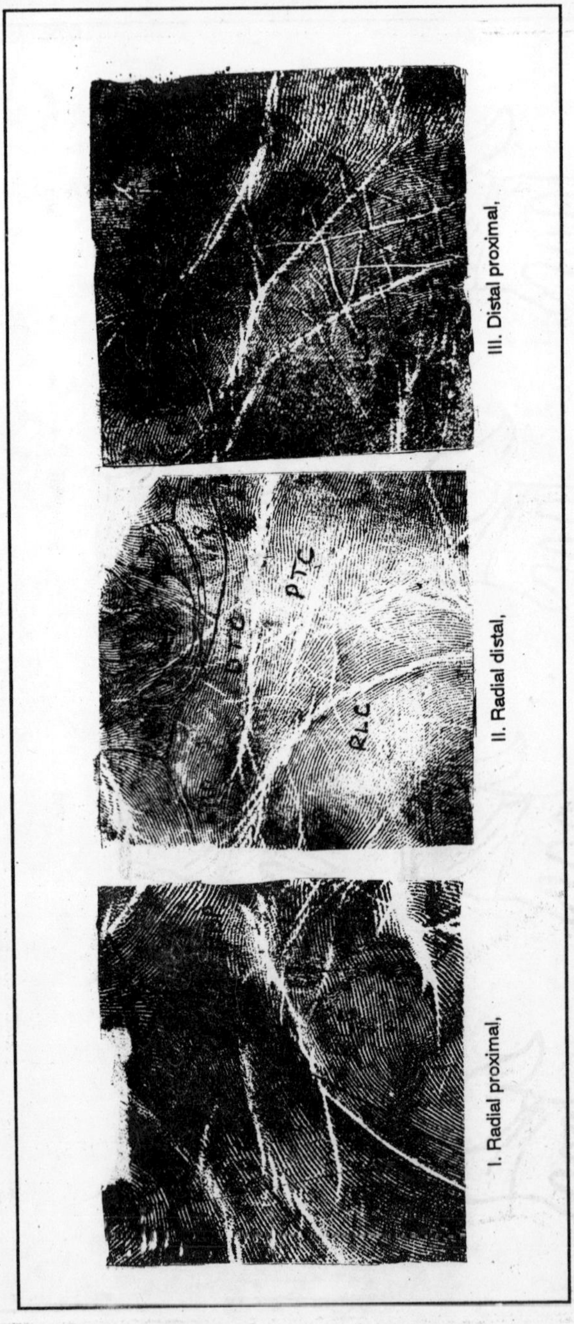

FIG. 9.20: (a) Transitional types of double radial base creases

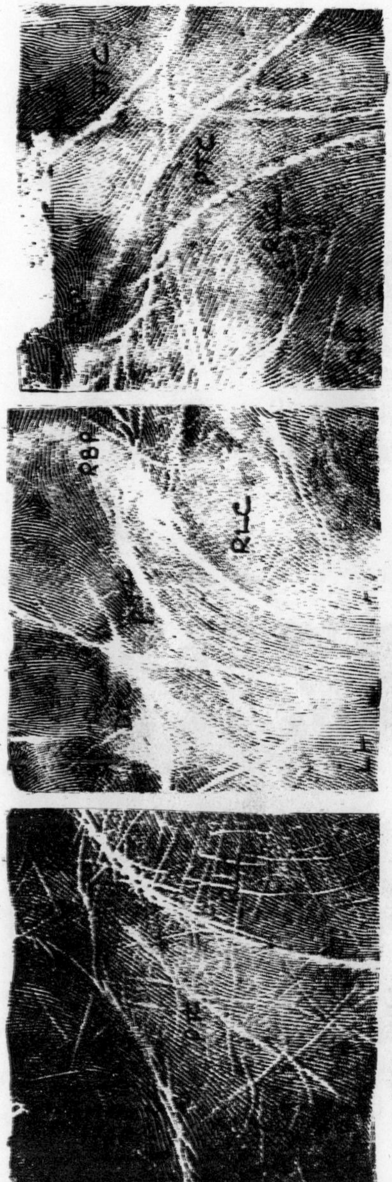

IV Distal radial, V. Proximal radial, VI. Proximal distal,

FIG. 9.20: (a) Transitional types of double radial base creases

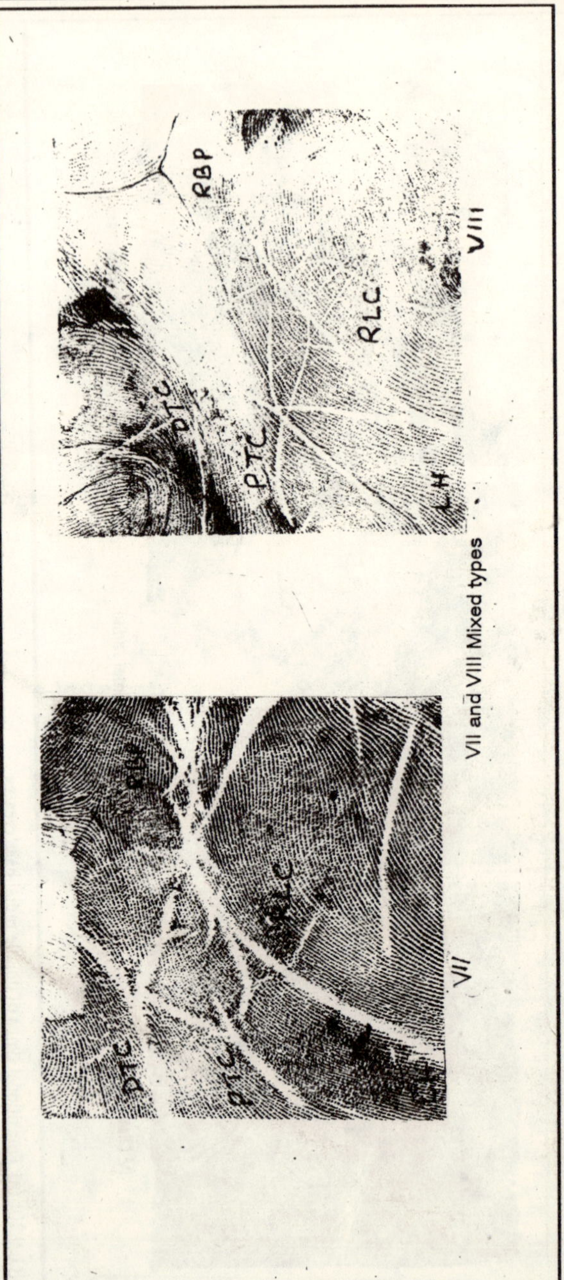

FIG. 9.20: (a) Transitional types of double radial base creases

Revised Formulation of Longitudinal Palmar Creases

Three primary longitudinal creases are : Radial longitudinal creases, sagittal crease (fate-line) and ulnar crease (Fig. 9.26). These creases emerge from the carpal or proximal area adjacent to bracelet crease. On the basis of their union at 'carpal base point', the longitudinal creases are classified into 'single carpal base' creases. There are True and Transitional types of carpal base creases. The definition for true and transitional types remains the same as stated above (Fig. 9.17 (a)).

The number of true type of single, double and triple carpal base creases are four, five and one, respectively (Fig. 9.27 and 9.27(a)). True longitudinal single carpal base creases are of four types Fig. 9.28 and 9.28(a). The transitional types, which make indirect union between their bases by branching, show the same number as exhibited by true type of crease (Fig. 9.23). The nomenclature follows the same pattern as in the case of transverse palmar creases see Fig. 9.29 and 9.29(a).

True types of double carpal base creases are represented by four sub-types (Fig. 9.30 and 9.30(a)).

The transitional types of double longitudinal or carpal base creases show union through branches of the primary longitudinal creases which are given under Fig. 9.31 and 9.31(a).

The longitudinal palmar creases do not show frequent sub-types but system of sub-types remains essentially the same as described in case of transverse palmar creases (Fig. 9.22).

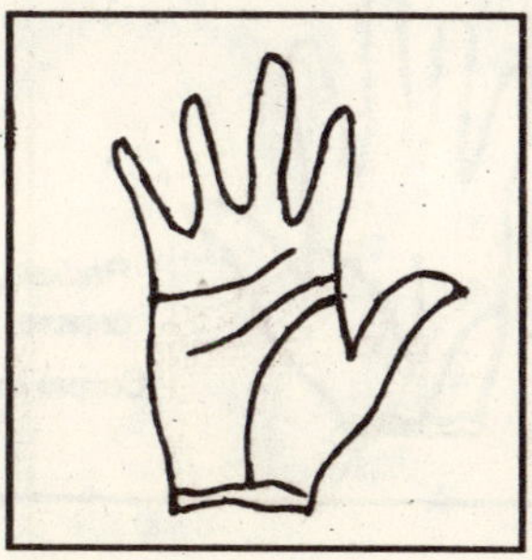

FIG. 9.21: Triple radial base crease

Validity of the Formulation

The formulation of both transverse as well as longitudinal palmar creases has been tested for validity through the study of inheritance among families, twins and on the basis of frequencies among different populations. In relation to diseases and other human abnormalities, the formulation finds sufficient relevance.

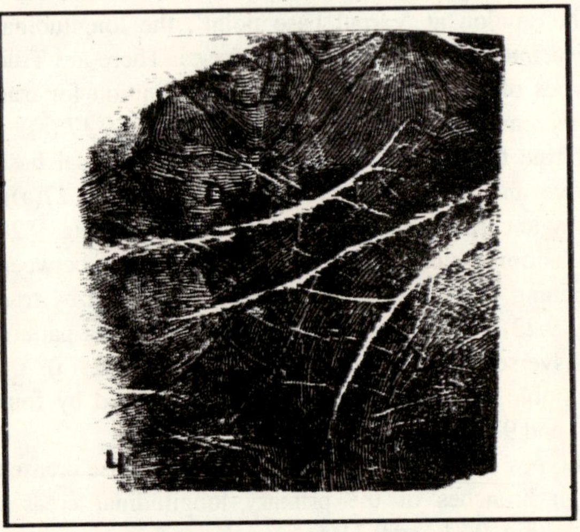

FIG. 9.21 (a): Triple radial base crease

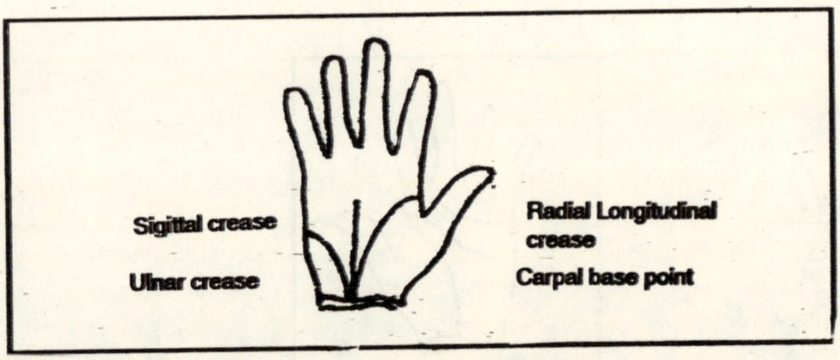

FIG. 9.22: Longitudinal palmar creases

The consistency in bi-sexual and bi-manual expression of creases in various populations has been tested by Bali and Chaube (1971), Bali (1978, 1980), Chaube (1976, 1980) and Eswaraiah (1971, 1975).

The relationship of creases to the anatomical axis and their symmetrical and asymmetrical occurrences show a similar consistency as has been exhibited by dermatoglyphic traits (Bali *et al.*, 1980).

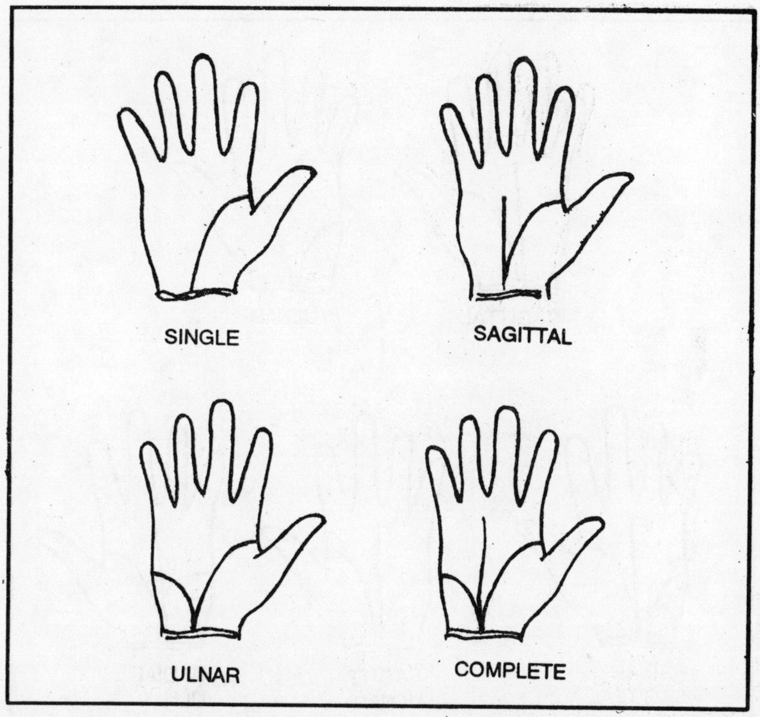

FIG. 9.23: Single carpal base creases

The inheritance of palmar creases has been studied by Bali and Chaube (1971), Chaube (1971, 1976), Mishra (1979), 1980) and Bali (1978, 1980). The above-mentioned authors made similar observations on twins to establish heritability of palmar creases. The palmar crease methodologies given by the author are also tenable in twin diagnosis.

The relationship of creases with diseases and other disorders has been tested by Bali (1971, 1971b, 1973), Eswaraiah (1975, 1977, 1978), Bali and Eswaraiah (1971), Chaube (1980) and others. Bali and Sharma (1980) and Rawat (1980) applied the above crease methodology in a study of delinquents and criminals.

The above work emphasises that crease morphogenesis make creases a viable phenotypic variable.

The longitudinal palmar creases do not show frequent sub-types but the system of sub-typing remains essentially the same as described in case of transverse palmar creases (Fig. 9.22).

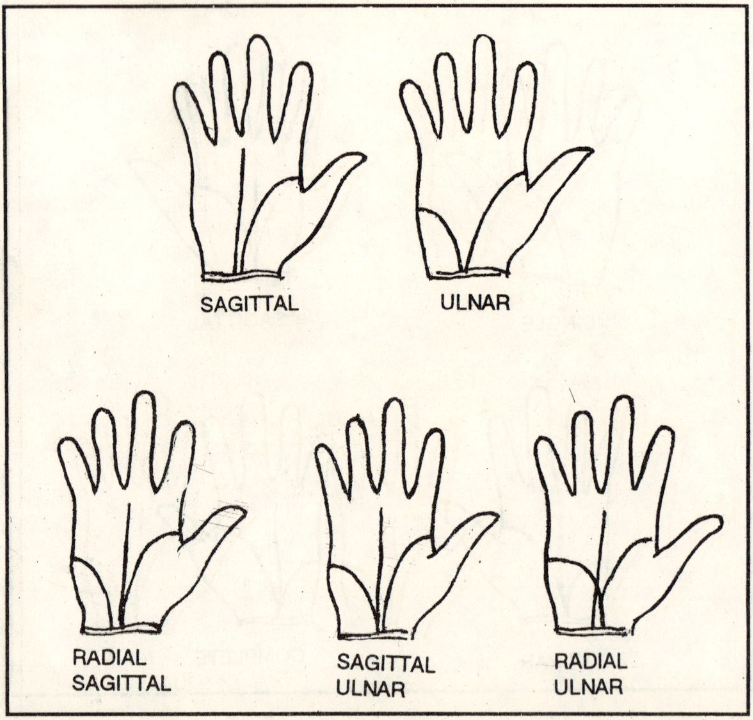

FIG. 9.24: Double carpal base creases

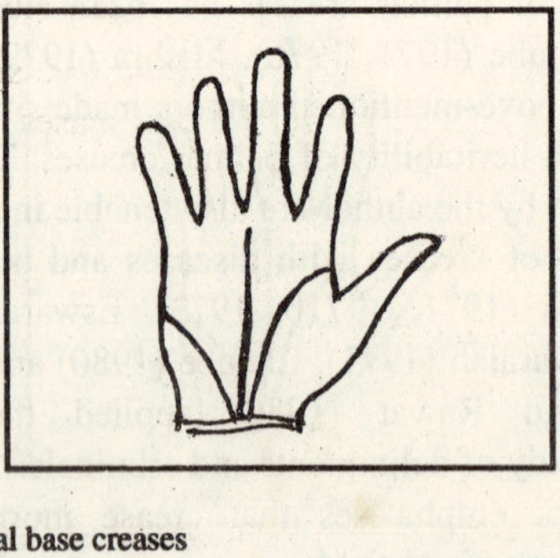

FIG. 9.25: Triple carpal base creases

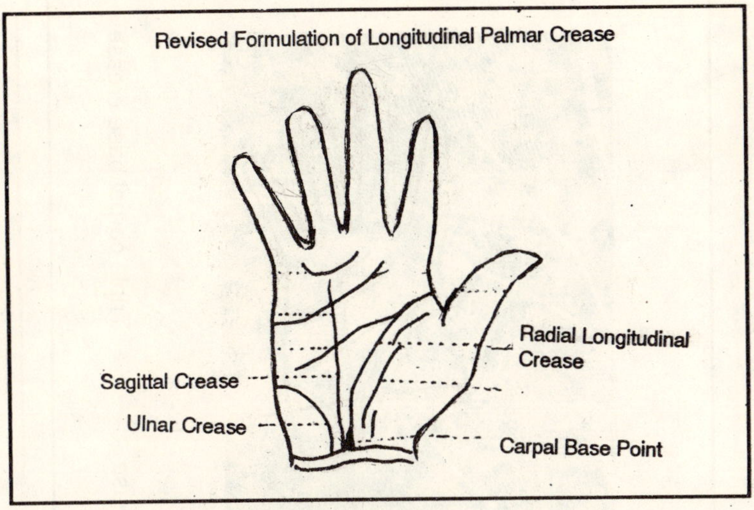

FIG. 9.26: Longitudinal palmar creases

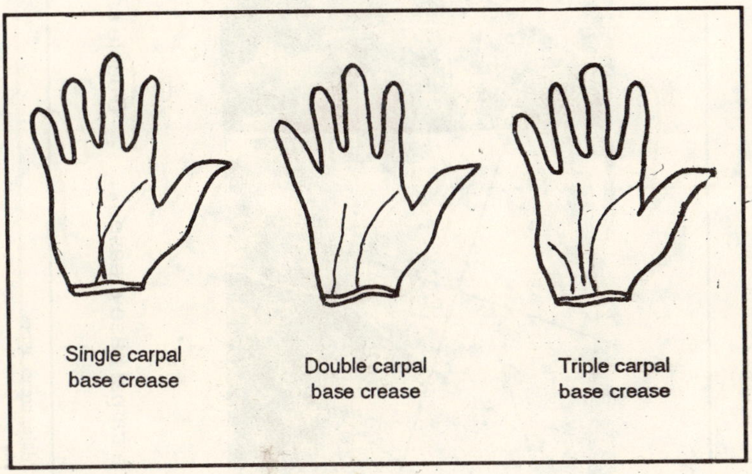

FIG. 9.27: Major crease types

FIG. 9.27: (a) Major crease types

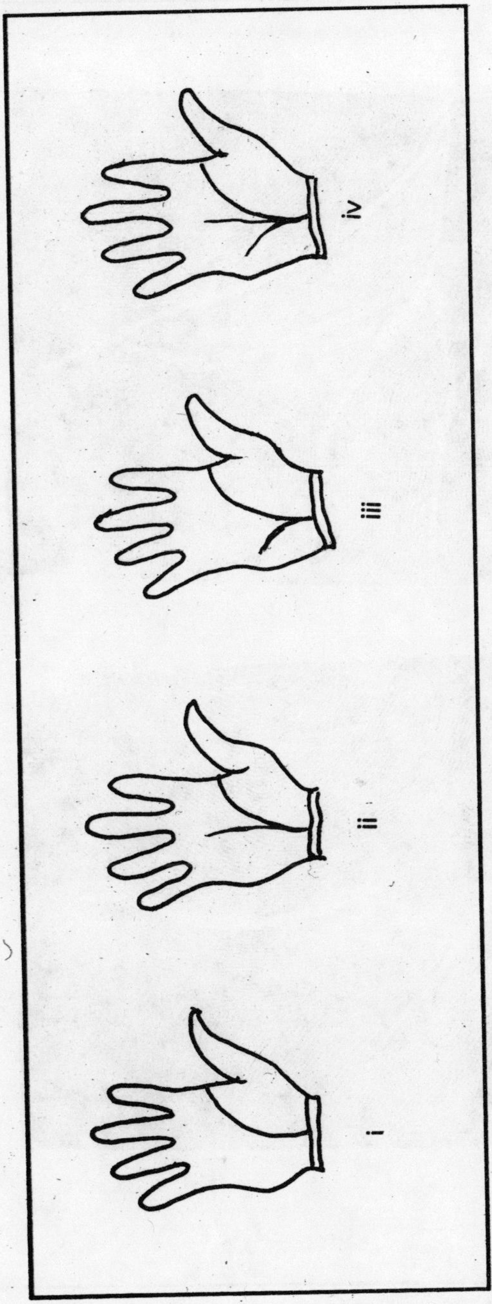

FIG. 9.28: True types of single carpal base creases

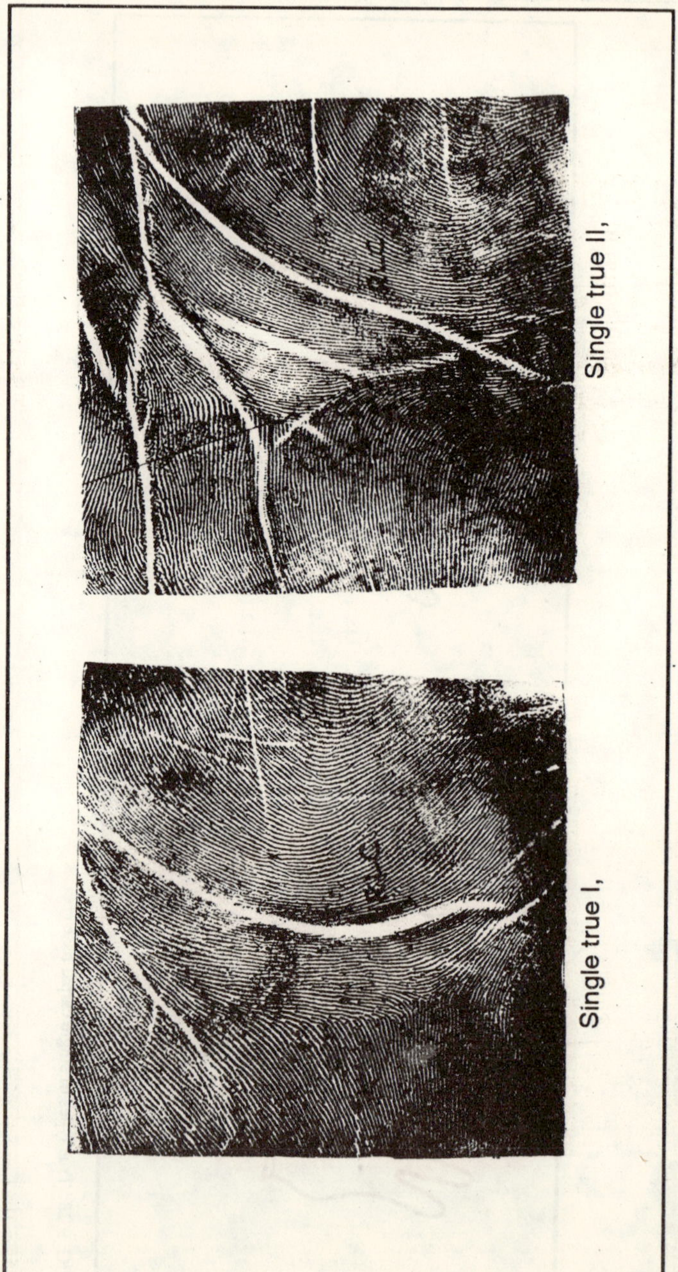

FIG. 9.28: (a) True types of single carpal base creases

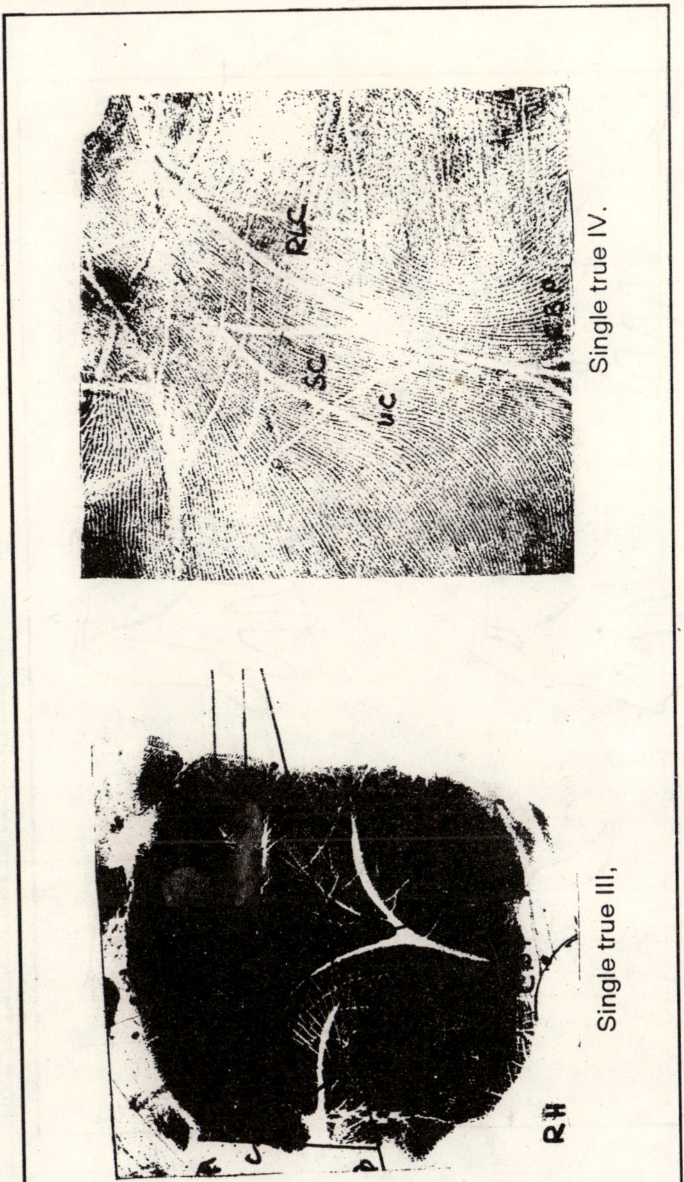

FIG. 9.28: (a) True types of single carpal base creases

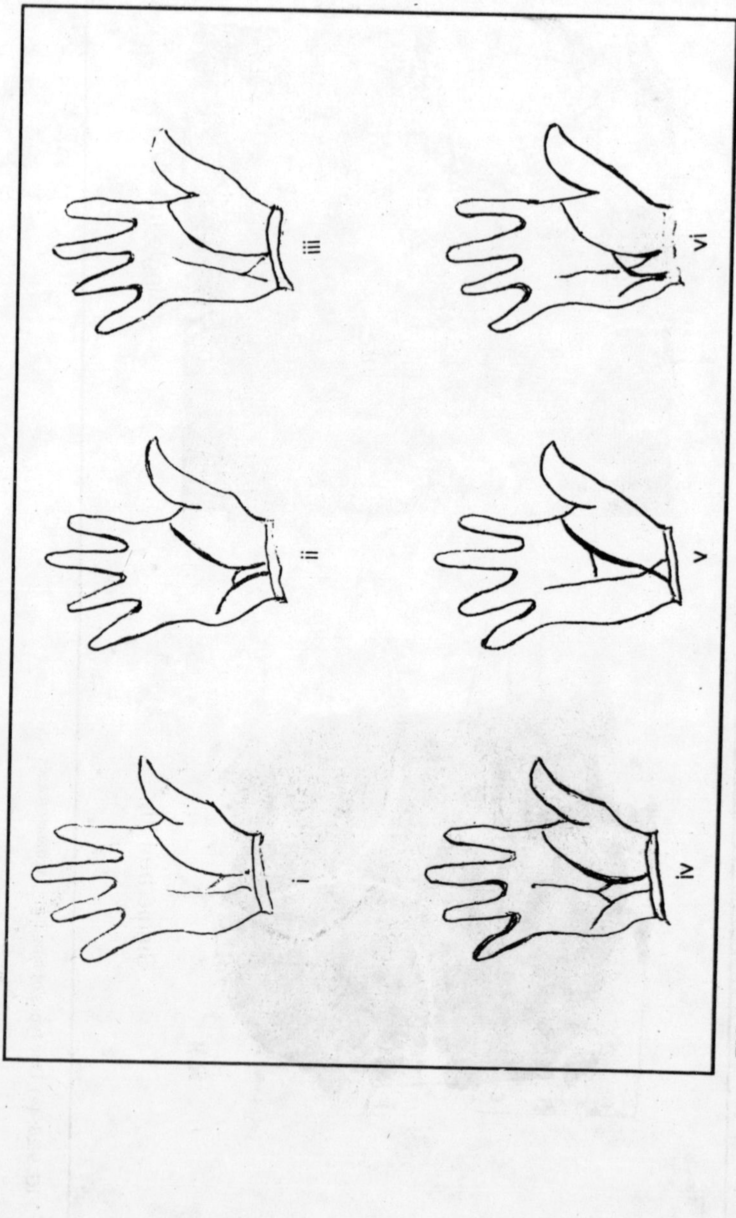

FIG. 9.29: Transitional types of single carpal base creases
i. Radial Sagittal, ii. Radial Ulna, iii. Sagittal Radial, iv. Sagittal Ulnar, v and vi Mixed types

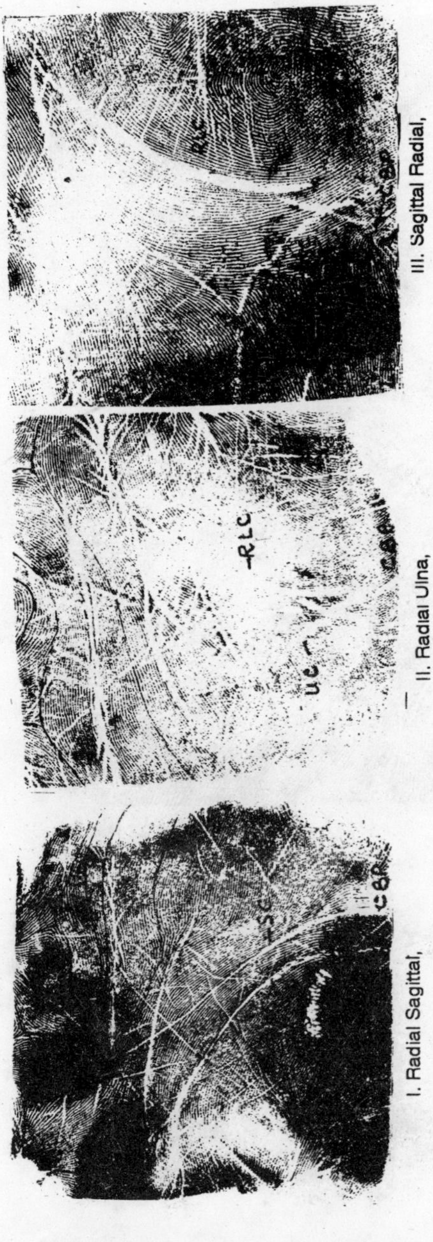

FIG. 9.29: (a) Transitional types of single base creases

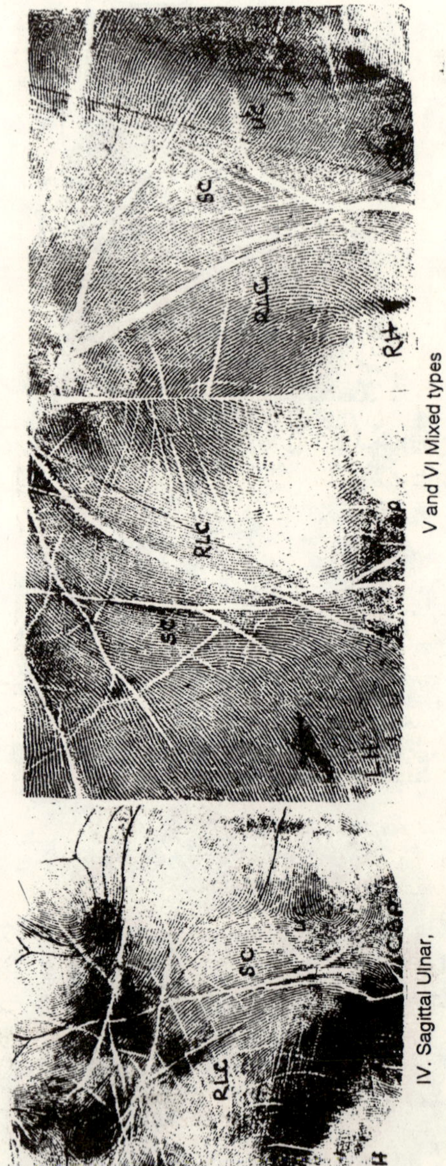

FIG. 9.29: (a) Transitional types of single base creases

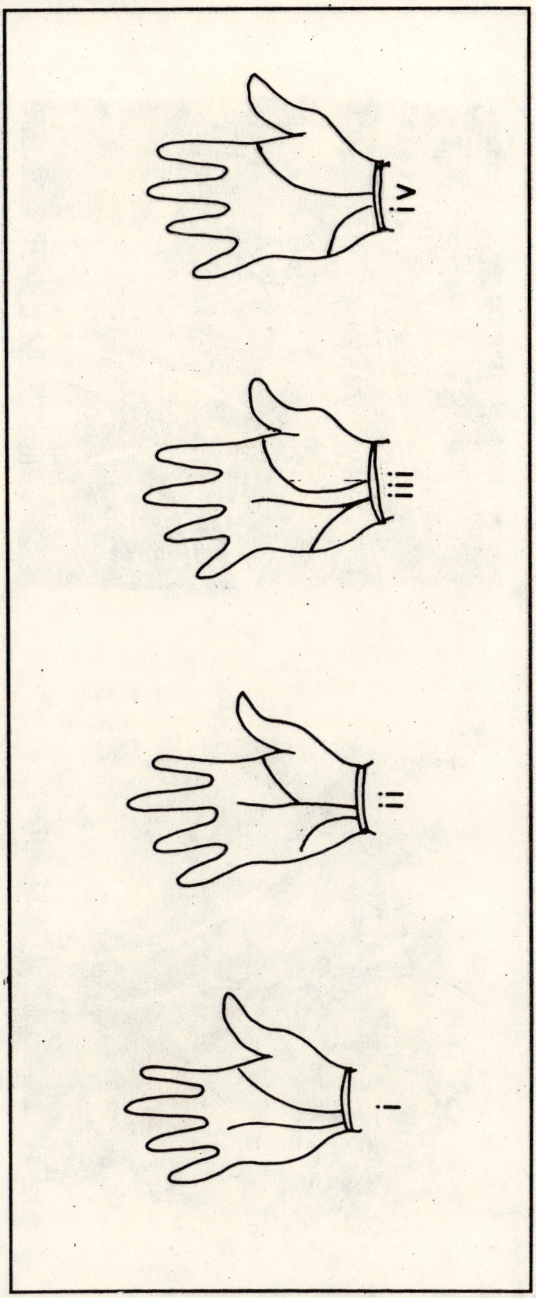

FIG. 9.30: True types of double carpal base creases

Double true I,

Double true II,

FIG. 9.30: (a) True types of double carpal base creases

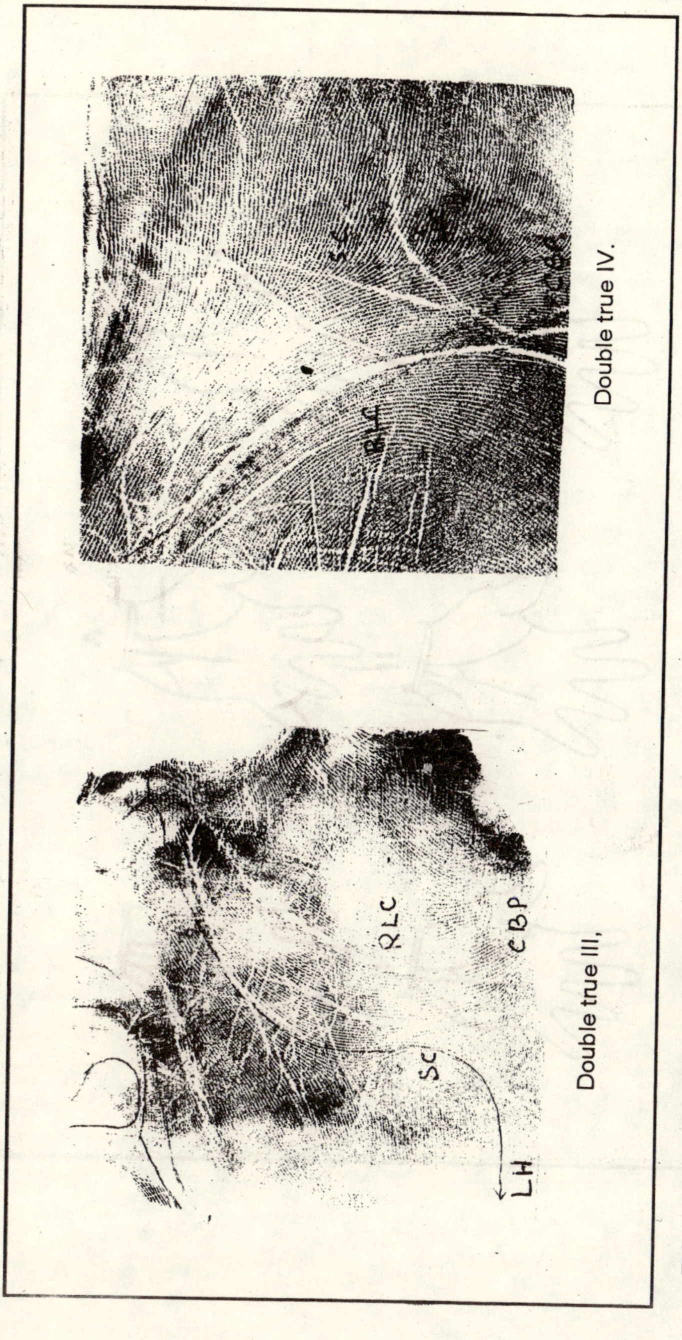

FIG. 9.30: (a) True types of double carpal base creases

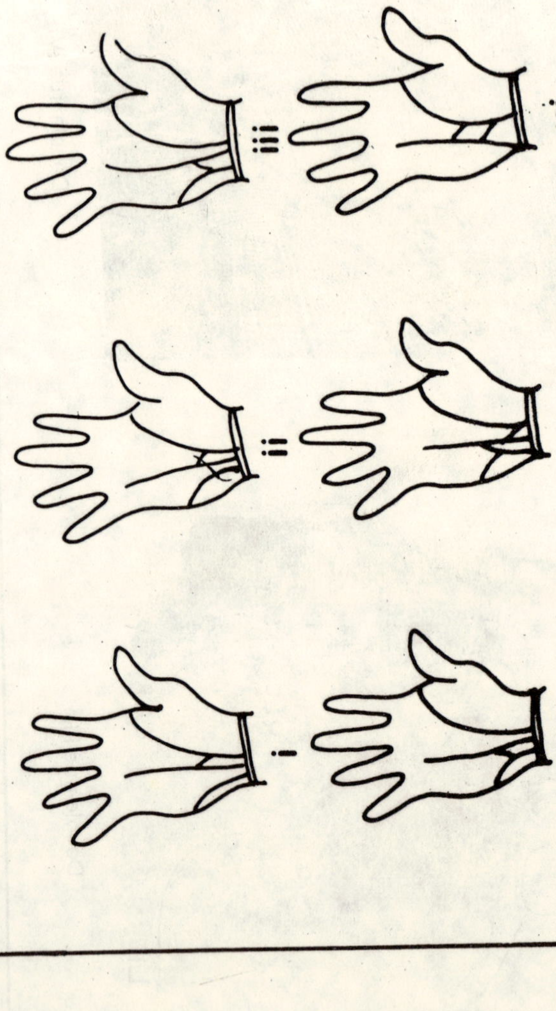

FIG. 9.31: Transitional types of double carpal base creases
i. radial sagital, ii. sagital radial, iii. sagital ulnar, iv. ulnar sagital, v & vi. mix type

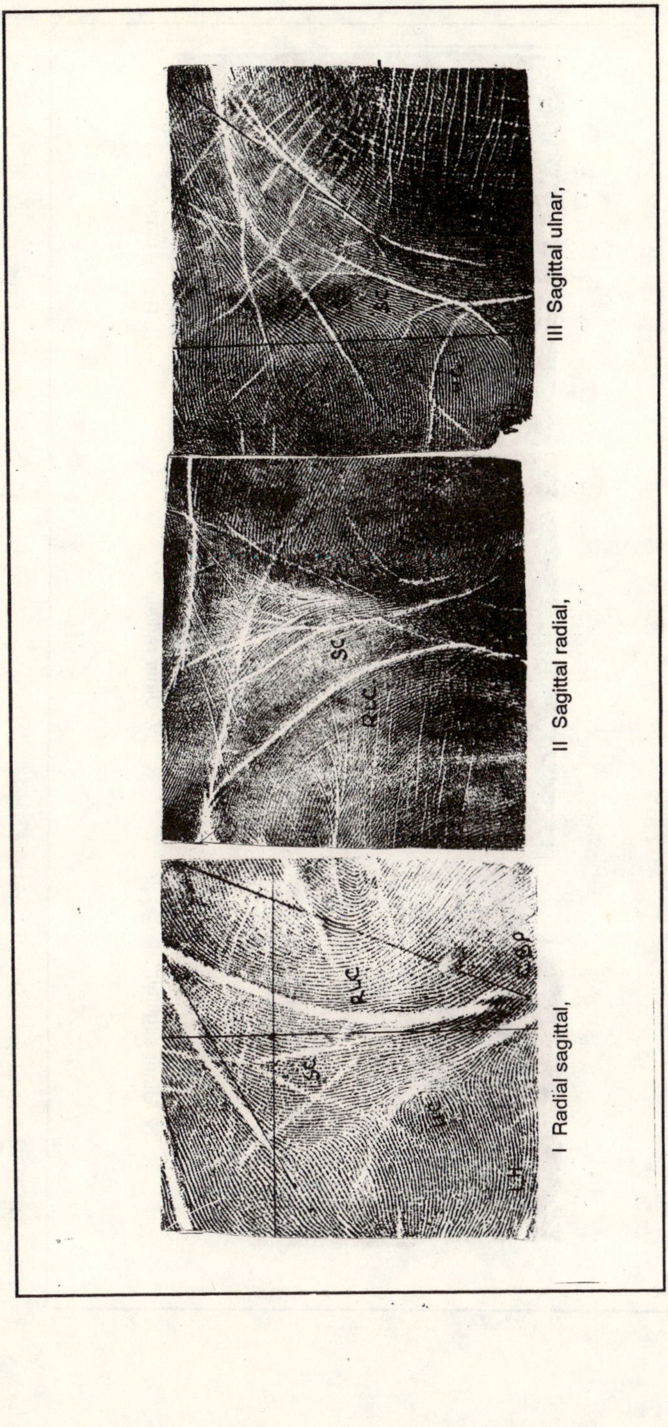

FIG. 9.31: (a) Transitional types of double carpal base creases

VI Radial ulnar.

V Ulnar radial,

IV Ulnar sagital,

FIG. 9.31: (a) Transitional types of double carpal base creases

Definition and Origin of Base Point

The vertebral crease concept has already been discussed in Chapter 3 along with de Wilde's theory of embryonal unity and crease split theory of the author.

Under the above theoretical concepts it is logical to believe that radial longitudinal crease (vertebral crease) could find splits, both at the radial and at the carpal ends. The radial split gave the origin to radial base point and the carpal split gave the origin to carpal base point at their respective ends. Once a crease splits from vertebral crease its detachment is from a point and not line. Therefore, the word 'point' has been adopted instead of other expressions.

On the basis of above points, two sets of palmar creases were recognized as a separate unit. It is true that vertebral crease (radial longitudinal crease) is the common factor for transverse and longitudinal palmar crease formulations.

In the light of the above hypothesis the author worked on various probable adjustment of creases given by different workers under different formulations to adopt them in the present frame. The revised longitudinal crease formulation is more sensitive and elaborate.

In order to explain all creases of the palm on a similar criteria of formulation it was necessary to revise the above formulation on the basis of transverse crease formulation into true and transitional forms.

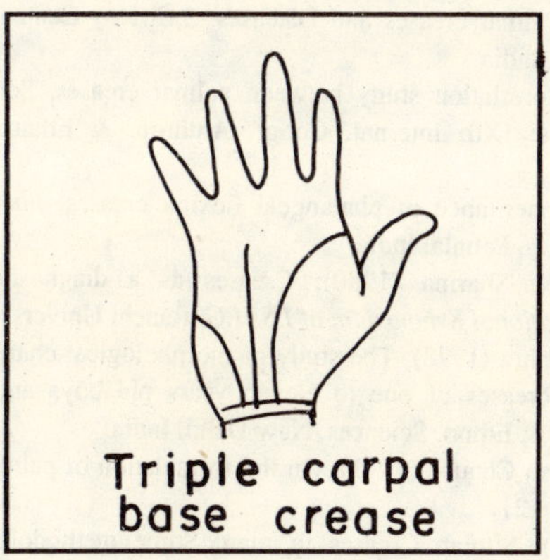

FIG. 9.32: Longitudinal palmar creases

FIG. 9.32(a): Triple-carpal base crease

REFERENCES

Bali, R.S. (1971a): Palmar creases and Schizophrenia. *Internat. Sym. Hum. Genet.* Andhra University, Waltair, India.

Bali, R.S. (1971b): Palmar creases and Diseases. S.C. Roy Centenary Celebration held in Ranchi, Bihar, India.

Bali, R.S. (1973): Correlation study between palmar creases, Schizophrenia, Leprosy and Tuberculosis: IXth Internat. Congr. Anthrop. & Ethno. Sciences, Chicago, U.S.A.

Bali, R.S. (1980): Inheritance of phalangeal flexion creases. *Internat. Sym. Dermato.* Punjabi University, Patiala, India.

Bali, R.S. and A.N. Sharma (1980): Creases as a diagnostic tool for personal identification. *National Symposium of I.S.H.G.* Ranchi University, Ranchi, India.

Bali, R.S. and R. Mishra (1978): The study of morphological change in hand, palm and palmar flexion creases of one to eleven years old boys and girls. Xth Internat. Congr. Anthrop. & Ethno. Sciences, New Delhi, India.

Bali, R.S. and Ramesh Chaube (1971): On the formulation of palmar creases. *Z. Morph. Anthrop.*, 63 : p. 121.

Bhanu, V.V. (1972): Simian Creases in man: Some methodological considerations. *Journal of Human Evolution*, 2: pp. 153-60.

Broca, P. (1877): Le pli transversal du Singe dans la main de l'homme. *Bull. Soc. Anthr*, Paris, Ze Serie, T. XII, pp. 431-32.

Büchi, E.C. (1954): The Simian Crease in India. *Bulletin of the Indian Department of Anthropology*. 3(1): pp. 39-49.

Chaube, R. (1971): The study of palmar flexion creases — Inheritance and Correlation with schizophrenic patients. Thesis submitted in fulfilment of the requirements for the degree of Ph.D., Saugar University, Sagar.

Chaube, R. (1980): *Palmar Creases and Criminality* (In press).

Crookshank (1924): *The Mongol in our Midst, a study of man and his three faces*, Duffon & Co., New York.

Cummins, H. and C. Midlo (1961): *Finger Prints, Palms and Soles: An Introduction to Dermatoglyphics*, New York, Dover.

Dar, H.; R. Schmidt and H.M. Nitowsky (1977): Palmar crease variants and their clinical significance: A study of new borns at risk. *Pediat. Res.* 11: pp. 103-08.

Eswaraiah, G. (1977): Palmar creases and diseases. Thesis submitted in fulfilment of the requirement for the degree of Ph.D., Saugar University, Sagar.

Eswaraiah, G. (1978): Palmar prints and schizophrenia. *Indian J. Psychiat.* 20: pp. 347-53.

Fischer, E. (1949): Bemerkung uber die vierfingerfurche. *Zeitschrift fur Morphologie und Anthropologie*. 41: pp. 268-74.

Gyenis, G. (1975): Dermatoglyphics of three Hungarian populations. *American Journal of Physical Anthropology* 45(2): pp. 229-32.

Gyenis, G. and G. Hera (1971): Investigation of the hand creases in the random sample of subjects in Baranya Province of South Hungary. *Anthropologiai Kozlemenyek* (Budapest) 15(1): pp. 29-47.

Kimura, K. (1968): A study of palmar creases in Ainus. *Jinruigaku Zasshi*. 76: pp. 60-74.

Kimura, K. and S. Hagiya (1958): A study on the handlines of twins, *Jinruigaku Zasshi*. 66 (718): pp. 209-15.

Langdon-Down, R.S. (1909): Mongolian Imbecility, *Brit. Med. J.*, 12: p. 665.

Lasinski, W. and M. Urbanowicz (1960): The system of skin furrows on the human palm. *Folia Morphologica* 11: pp. 115-24 (in Polish).

Leiber, B. (1960): Zur systematik und klinischen Bedentung des menschlichen Handfurch-enbildes. *Z menschl. vererb. u. Konstitution slehre*. 35. pp. 205-32.

Lestrange, M.De (1969a): The transverse crease in Europe — index and comparative study of different samples cited in the literature. *American Journal of Physical Anthropology*: 30: pp. 173-82.

Lestrange, M.De. (1969b): A propos des plis de flexion de la paume: classification et rapports entre 'l'es different types decrits. *Bulletin et memoires de la societe d' Anthropologie de Paris* 5(12): pp. 251-67.

Loeffler, L. (1969): Papillarleistren und Hautfurchensystem, in *Human genetik Enkurzes Handbuch in funt Banden* Edited by P.E. Becker, 1-2: pp. 205-408.

Loeffler, L. (1969): *Spezielle Morphologie und Indizwert der Befunde bei personnenmit chromosomalen Aberrationen. Haut leisten und Krankbeiten*, p. 105.

Mavalwala, J. (1971): The heredity of dermatoglyphic traits in non-human primates and man; in *Comparative Genetics in Monkeys, Apes, and Man* ed. by B. Charelli, 43-63. London: Academic Press.

Mishra, R. (1979): Inheritance and methodological study of plantar creases. Thesis submitted in part fulfilment for the requirements of the degree of Ph.D., University of Saugar, Sagar.

Mishra R. (1980): Inheritance of palmar creases. *Internat. Sym. Dermato.* Punjabi University, Patiala, India.

Patten, B.M. (1953): *Human embryology*, Blakistan, New York, 19.

Plato, C.C. (1970): Polymorphism of the c. line of palmar dermatoglyphics with a new classification of the c. line terminations, *American Journal of Physical Anthropology*, 33(3): pp. 413-19.

Plato, C.C. (1970): Dermatoglyphics and flexion crease of the Cypriots. *American Journal of Physical Anthropology*, 33(3): pp. 421-27.

Pöch, H. (1925): Uber Handlinien. *Mitteilungen der Anthropologischen gesellschaft in Wien* 55; pp. 133-59.

Portius, W. (1937): Beitrag zur Frage der Erblichkeit der vierfingerfurche. *Zeitschrift fur Morphologie und Anthropologie* 36: pp. 382-90.

Rawat, S.K. (1980): The study of palmar creases and palmar dermatoglyphics of murderers. *Internat. Sym. Dermato.* Punjabi University, Patiala, India.

Safia (1987): Study of twins and Reliability of creases in twin zygosity diagnosis. Ph.D. Thesis, Saugar University, Sagar.

Shaha and Dermat (1980): *Population Genetics.*

Sarkar, S.S. (1961): The Simian Crease. *Zeitschrift fur Morphologie und Anthropologie.* 51(2): pp. 212-19.

Schaeuble, J. (1933): Die Entstehung der palmaren digitalen Triradien. Ein Beitrag Zur Entwicklung der Hautleistenzuge der distalen palma. *Zeitschrift fur Morphologie and Anthropologie.* 31(3) pp. 403-38.

Shuttleworth, G.E. (1909): Mongolian Imbecility. *Brit. Med. J.*, 12: p. 1665.

Tillner, I. (1953): Zur Entstehung der vierfingerfurche. *Zeitschrift fur mensch liche Verer bungs und Konstitutions lehre* 32: pp. 56-7.

Tillner, I. (1956): Die vierfingerfurche in Beziehung zum verlaug der Handleisten. *Anthrop. Anzeiger*, 22: pp. 260-76.

Weninger, M. and L. Navratil (1957): Die Vierfingerfurche in atiologischer Betrachtung. *Anthrop. Gesellsch. in Wien.* Bd., LXXVII: pp. 1-21.

Würth, A. (1937): Die Entstehung der Beugejurchen der menschllichen Mohlhand. *Z. Morph. Anthrop.* 36: pp. 187-214.

10

PLANTAR CREASE FORMULATIONS

THE HUMAN foot has practically lost the power of grasping and is appropriated for entirely different function, other than hand or foot of non-human primates. Therefore, human sole may be showing departure both in expression of creases and dermal ridges as compared to the palm. Cummins (1935) explains this in terms of conversion; one type of pattern having transformed into another through re-arrangement of the component ridges. A similar trend is noticed among creases also. This view of pattern reduction in sole and toes is held by Kollmann (1983) and Bonnevie (1927). Functional aspect of toes and fingers can be responsible for the contour formation in toes and fingers. Newman (1936), Bali (1964) showed positive association between finger and toe patterns.

Féré (1900) proposes the 'Pressure theory' and contends that areas where greatest pressure is exerted do not indicate pattern form. He cites the heel, as example in the foot, where due to exertion of greatest pressure pattern never appears. Hepburn (1895) gave a 'Friction theory' for ridge expression.

Newman attributes to the delayed embryonic process as one of the factors to cause suppression of pattern expression in case of toes as compared to fingers. While supporting Newman (1936), Bali (1968) states: 'that both dermatoglyphic regions may be controlled by a common set of factors or factor but independent courses of specialization in evolution may have caused the differential trend of pattern reduction in toes and fingers'.

In case of plantar region the delayed embryonic processes and functional modifications might have been responsible for reduction of the patterns as compared to palmar surface.

Formulations of Plantar Creases

The functional dimorphism between hands and feet which are homologous parts is extreme. Being homologous their association is natural and, like dermatoglyphic traits, they require a common basis of crease interpretation. There is a marked difference between palmar and plantar surfaces. The variation in dermal configuration of palm and sole finds some association but in case of creases the degree of diversification is much.

Plantar surface shows two major categories of creases occurring in distal area, i.e., thenar distal and hypothenar distal and the other category of plantar creases is found proximal to calcar, i.e., hypothenar proximal and thenar proximal areas.

The present plantar crease formulation deals with the above two categories separately. On the sole, there can be no crease, one crease or several creases. Such a situation is not seen in the palm. In view of this, some deviation in the pattern of the meeting of the creases is expected. Moreover, the shift in anatomical axis is a unique feature of the human foot. Generally, on the calcar area, the creases are absent, while on proximal hypothenar they are rare.

The crease configurations on sole of the new born babies show higher incidence especially in abnormal babies as compared with adult sole. (Lynn and Murray (1978). The human sole in relation to non-human primates shows greater departure both in shape and function.

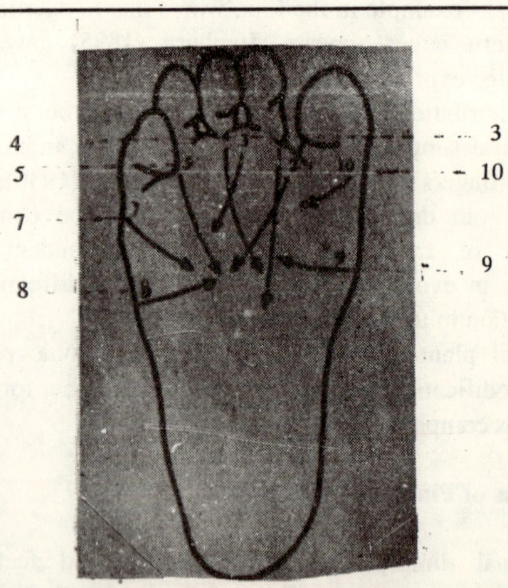

Schematic Drawing of the Main Plantar Creases in a New Born

FIG. 10.1: Plantar crease classification (Schenk et al., 1959)

Under the medial and lateral stresses the greater toe and thenar area attained alignment and the result was reduction of first and second inter-digital area. Under the distal elongation and radio-ulnar squeeze, the base point of plantar creases acquired its position proximally, just on the line of anatomical axis towards its medial side.

The shift of base point is not in terms of location but also in terms of crease origin. In foot, creases show union at this point often emerging from distal, lateral or medial margins of the sole.

Schenk et al. (1959) proposed a morphologic scheme of the plantar crease classification. The author traced nine major creases of new-born infants originating under the second toe, between first and second toes, between second and third toes, under the third and between fourth and fifth toes, and named them 1, 2, 3, 4 and 5, respectively. The creases 8 and 9 are transverse creases and originate from tibial and fibular borders of the sole, respectively. The schematic drawing of the main plantar creases of the new-born is given in Fig. 10.1.

The transverse union between creases 8 and 9 of the sole was interpreted by Hirsch as a simian crease feature.

Nekiela (1972) divided the foot into several horizontal areas and designated transverse and plantar creases as crease 1 and crease 2. Crease 1 originates from the medial border below the thenar eminence of the greater toe, while crease 2 starts from the medial border of the foot at the boundary between the heel and arch and runs obliquely towards the lateral side. These creases were observed double and even triple or quadruple (Fig. 10.2).

Penrose op. cit. and Alter (1976) reported the clinical significance of Sandal crease, a crease running longitudinally between first and second toes.

On the formulation of plantar crease, Bali and Mishra (1978) adopted the criteria of 'base point', given by Bali and Chaube (1971) in palmar crease formulation.

Anatomically the human sole may be divided into eight different regions (Fig. 10.3a). The hallucal thenar and hypothenar categories of plantar creases could be called medial longitudinal, sagittal longitudinal, lateral longitudinal, tibial transverse and fibular transverse creases (Fig. 10.3b).

The proximal thenar and hypothenar regions show a calcar crease which is placed most proximally and may or may not be present. It is the calcar crease which gives the basis for classifying proximal hypothenar and thenar group of creases.

FLEXION CREASES

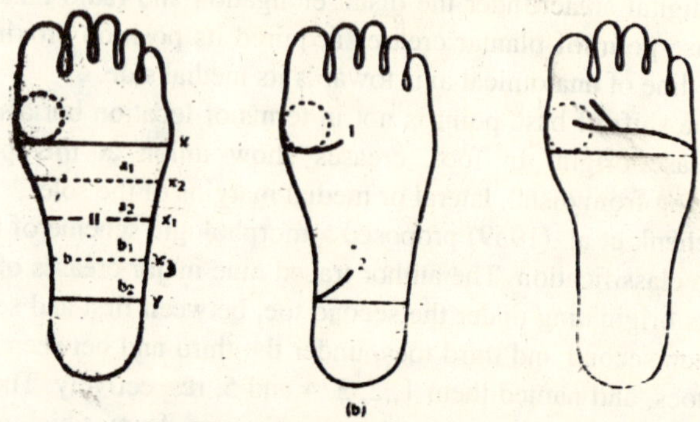

Schematic Drawing of the Most Frequent Sole Creases

FIG. 10.2: Plantar crease classification (Nekiela, 1972)

Classification of Plantar Creases

The proposed plantar crease formulation is based on the union of three main creases, i.e., medial longitudinal crease, tibial distal transverse crease and fibular distal transverse crease. The human sole in relation to non-human primates show great departure both in shape and function.

On the basis of this trait, the plantar creases can be classified into three main categories (also see Fig. 10.4a, b & c):

(a) Single Medial Base Crease (SMBC)
(b) Double Medial Base Crease (DMBC)
(c) Triple Medial Base Crease (TMBC)

The three-fold (SDT) classification signifies the union point and origin of the crease. The creases originating from second inter-digital, most distal thenar medial point and most distal hypothenar lateral point tend to meet at the distal medial base point.

When the union of these three creases at distal medial base point is observed, the creases are classified as single medial base crease (Fig. 10.4a), when union is between any two of the above type of

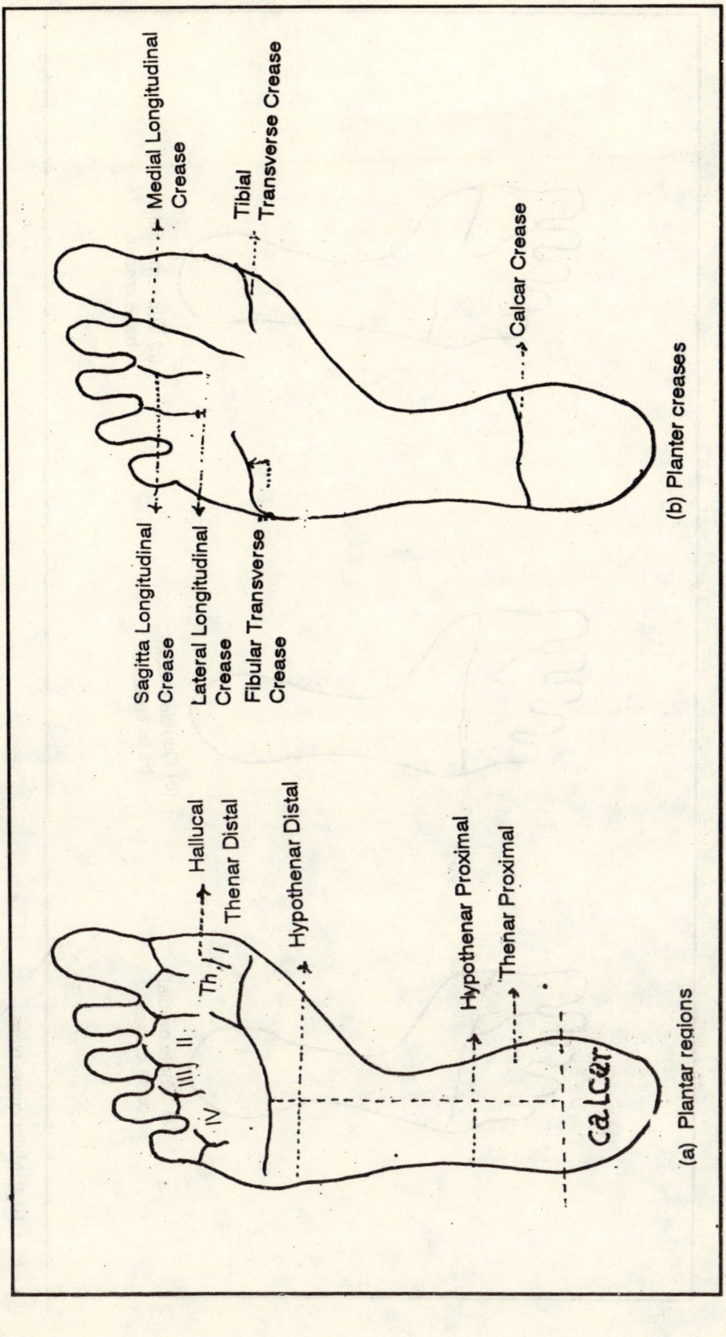

(a) Plantar regions

(b) Planter creases

FIG. 10.3: (a) Plantar regions and (b) Plantar creases

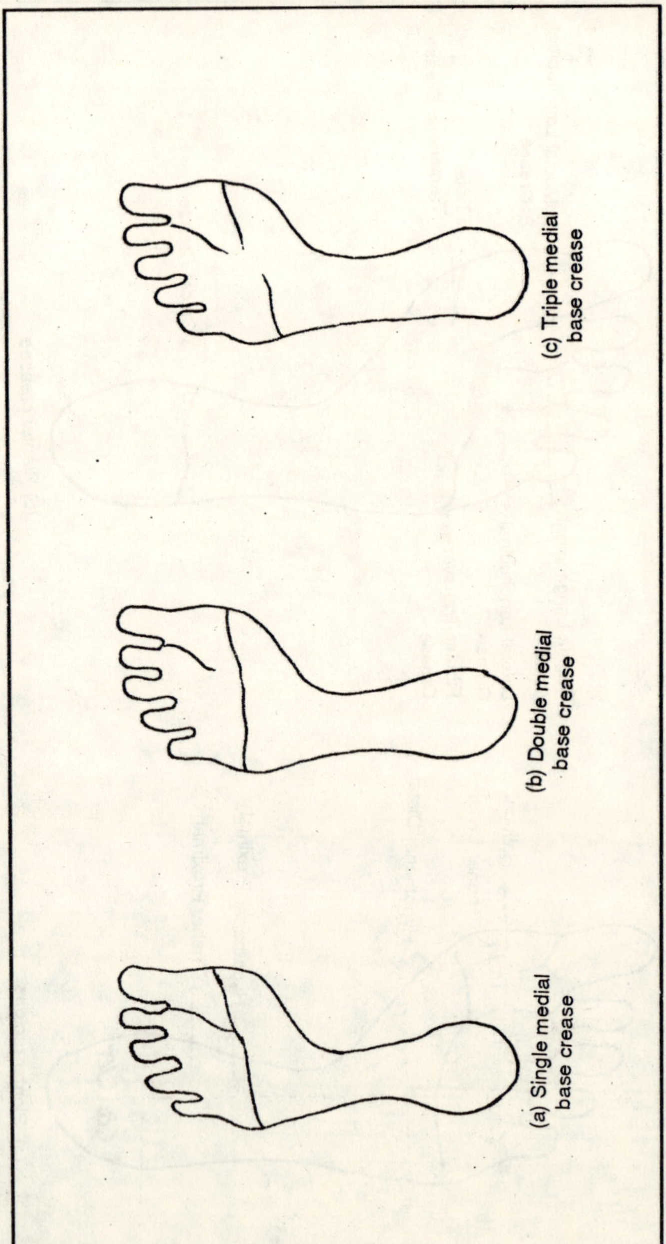

FIG. 10.4: Major crease types

creases, they are classified as double medial base creases (Fig. 10.4b), and when they fail to meet, they are named as triple medial base crease (Fig. 10.4c).

Apart from the above classification, the plantar areas show Zero type of creases, i.e., when the creases are absent and distal hallucal creases are present as mentioned above.

The three main types of plantar creases can further be sub-divided into various sub-types. The criteria of crease sub-division are based on the creases direction and their relative length at a point or points.

The sub-types of single medial base creases can be treated under two headings, i.e., simple single and single sub-types (Fig. 10.5a, b).

The simple single sub-type of single medial base creases from a single base, and all the three creases are present. Single medial base creases of the above main types do not have either of two types meeting at a single point, i.e., having medial, fibular medial and tibial medial sub-types.

The finer classification of the first and the second categories is based on the relative length of the creases (Fig. 10.5a).

(i) The simple single medial base crease forms a crease tri-radius with equal arms.
(ii) The simple single fibular base crease forms the tri-radius with the fibular transverse crease having maximum relative length and forms base at the fibular end.
(iii) The simple single tibial base crease originates from the tribal side and moves towards the medial point forming a tri-radius with the fibular transverse crease.

The second category of single base creases failed to form the tri-radius, but the union point of two creases with the dominant length of medial, tibial and fibular creases helps to designate the sub-types of the above category. It may also be pointed out that a crease characteristic of forming a firm base has been taken into consideration. A firm base crease denotes the relative width and depth of a crease at a particular point in relation to other creases (Fig. 10.5b).

(i) A single medial tibial crease shows the firm base at medial point or joins with the tibial crease.
(ii) A single medial fibular crease forms a firm point at fibular and joins with the medial crease.
(iii) Similarly, single tibial medial crease forms a firm point at tibial base and joins with the medial creases.

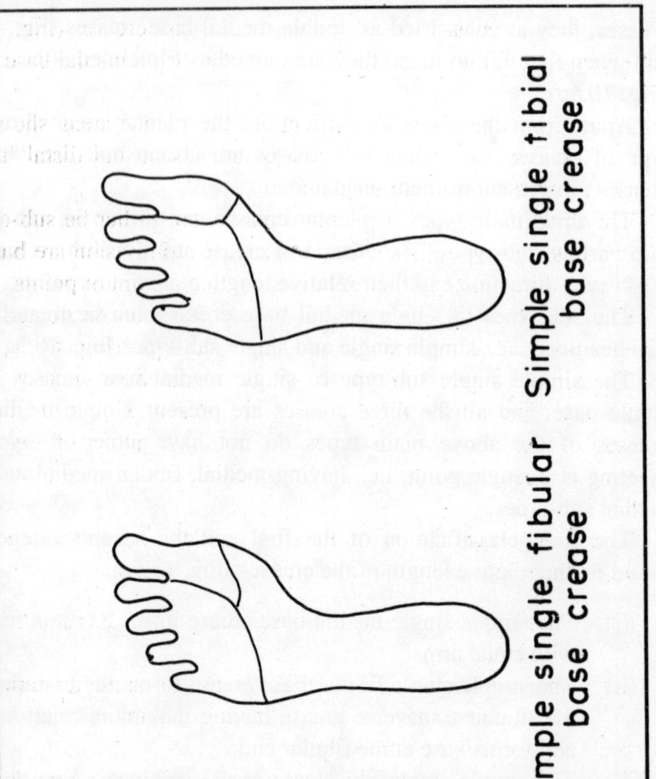

FIG. 10.5: Single medial base creases

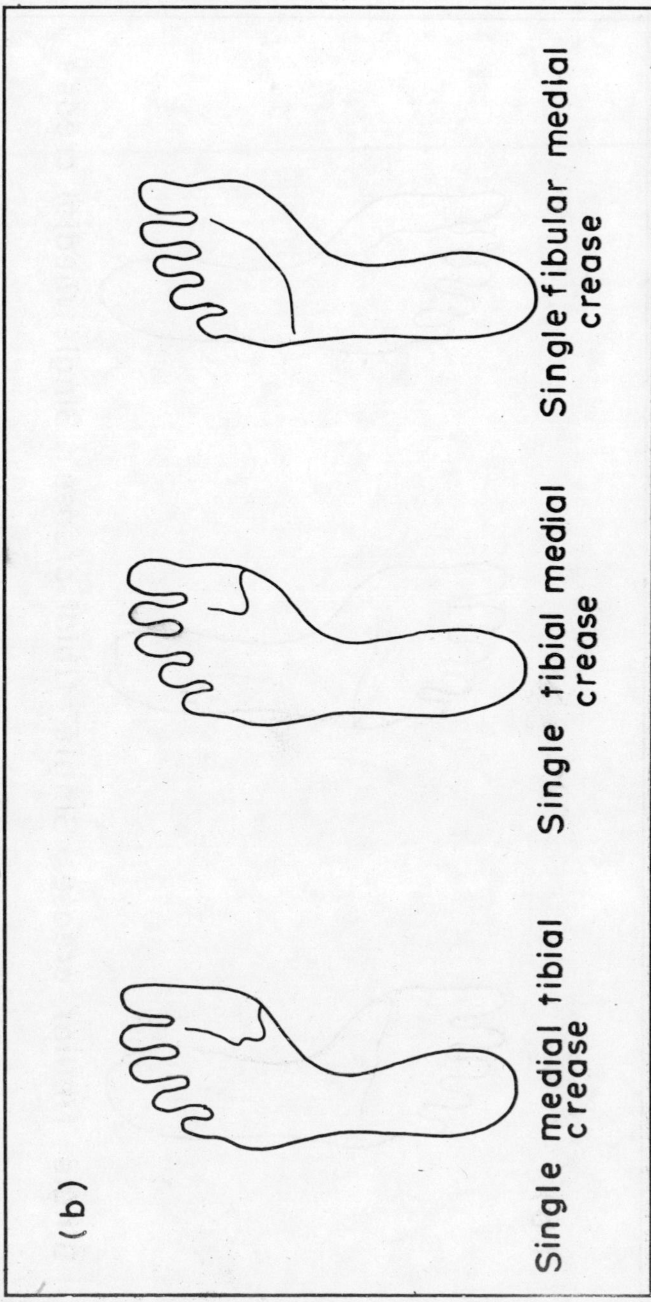

FIG. 10.5: Single medial base creases

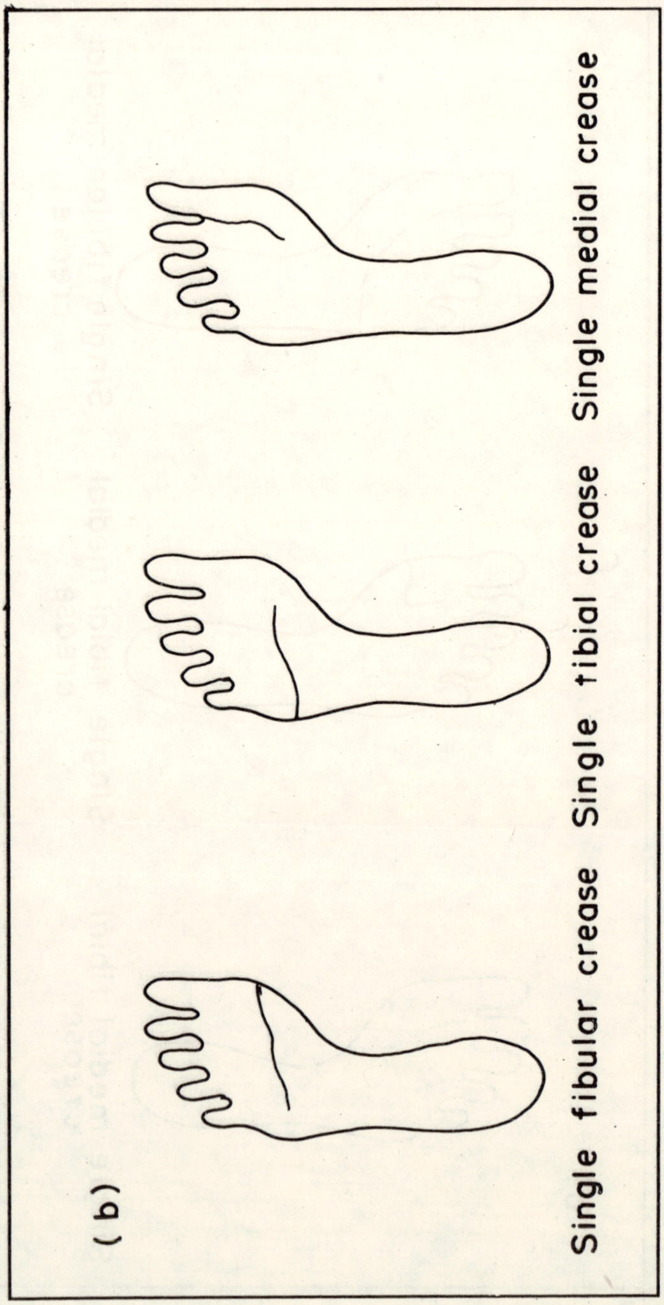

FIG. 10.5: Single medial base creases

(iv) Single fibular medial crease forms the firm point at fibular base and joins with the medial crease.

(v) Single medial crease fails to meet any tibial or fibular crease, but forms a firm point at medial base and runs along the longitudinal axis of the foot.

(vi) Single tibial crease runs transversely from tibial to fibular base. This crease shows firm base at tibial end.

(vii) Similarly, the single fibular crease runs transversely from fibular to tibial end and shows firm base at the fibular end.

The sub-types of the double medial base crease show different length and firm bases. The double medial base creases form eight sub-types on the basis of above criteria (Fig. 10.6).

(i) Double medial base creases form two separate ends. When the medial base crease shows greater relative length and form bases, the creases are called double medial base creases.

(ii) Double tibial base crease shows the firm base at tibial side and joins with the medial crease, while fibular end of the fibular crease does not join with the above creases.

(iii) Double fibular base crease shows a firm base at the fibular side and joins with the medial crease, and the end of the tibial crease is free.

(iv) Double medial tibial crease shows firm base and greater relative length of the medial crease while tibial crease makes a separate end.

(v) Double medial fibular crease may also be defined in a similar way.

(vi) Double tibial fibular crease shows firm base and relative length of the tibial crease, while fibular crease shows lesser relative length.

(vii) Double fibular tibial crease shows the greater relative length and firm base of the fibular crease while tibial crease is feeble.

(viii) Double tibial medial crease shows a greater relative length and firm base in relation to the medial base crease.

The sub-types of triple medial base creases are characterised on the basis of the crease length and their relative firm bases (Fig. 10.7).

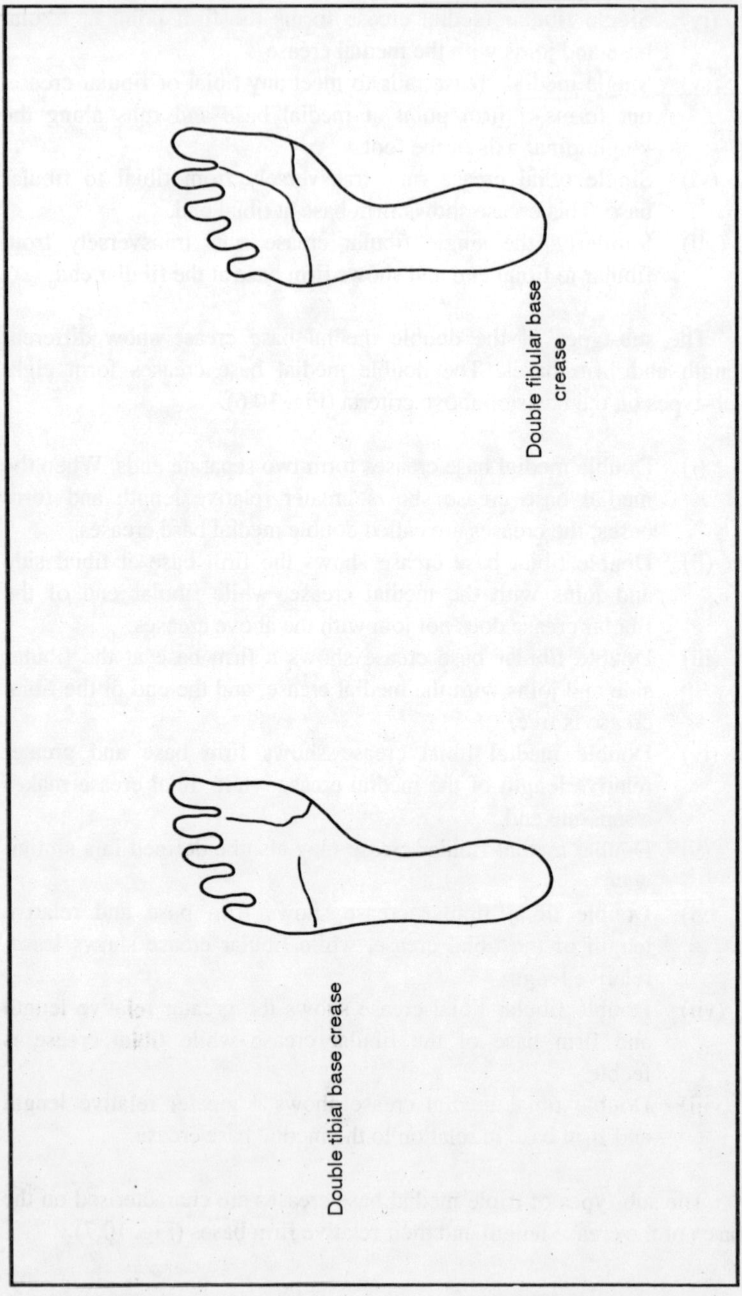

FIG. 10.6: Double medial base creases

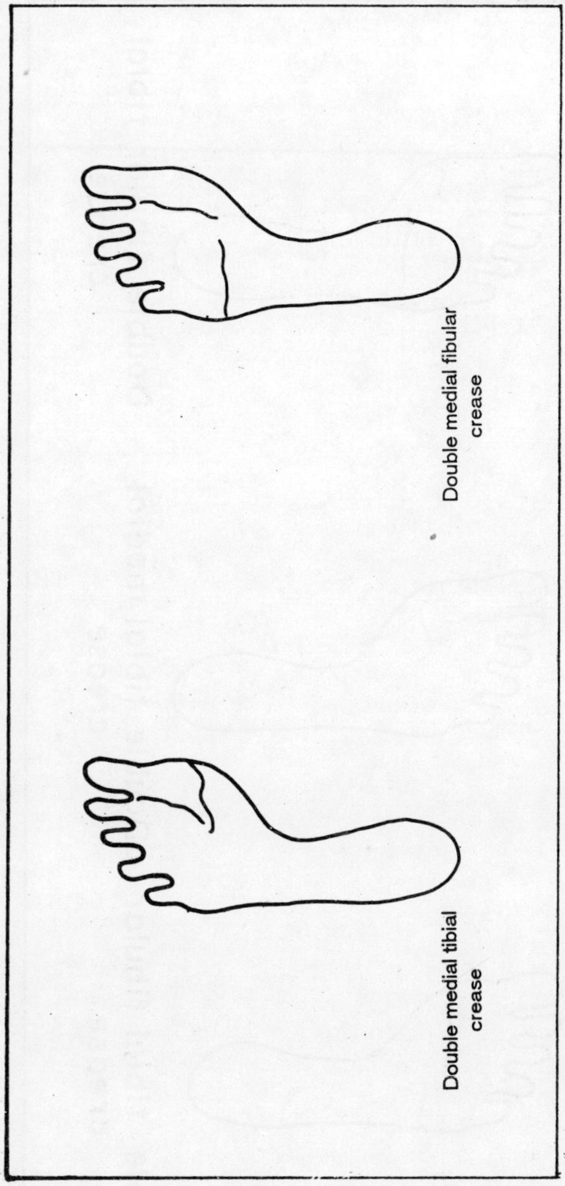

FIG. 10.6: Double medial base creases

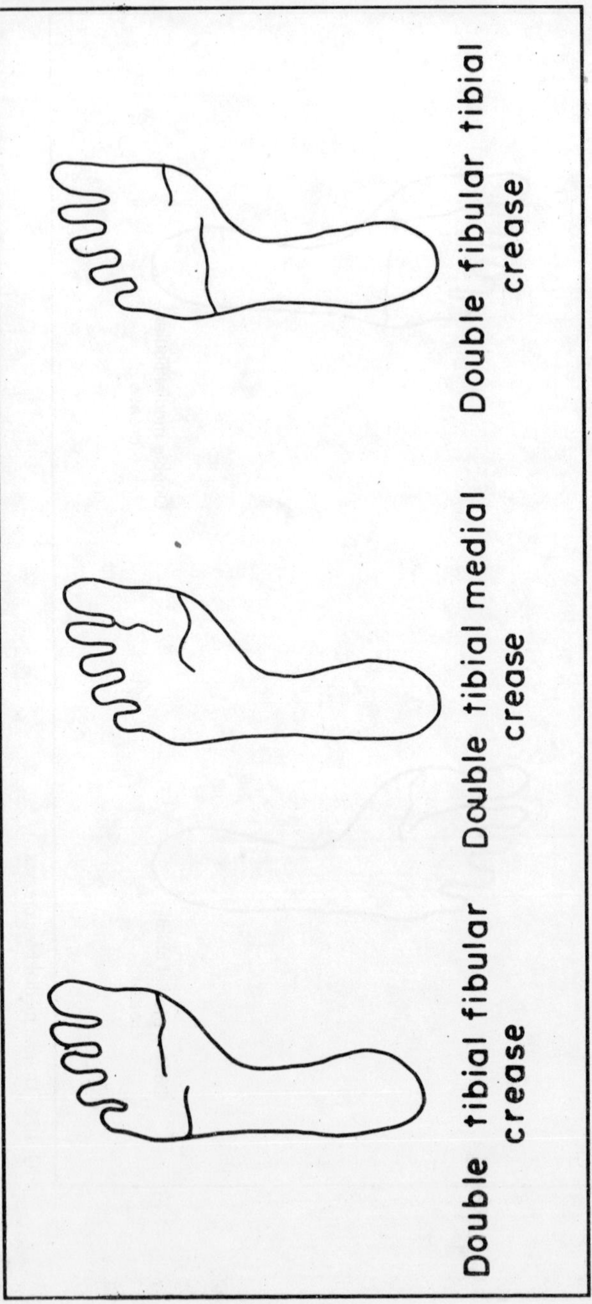

FIG. 10.6: Double medial base creases

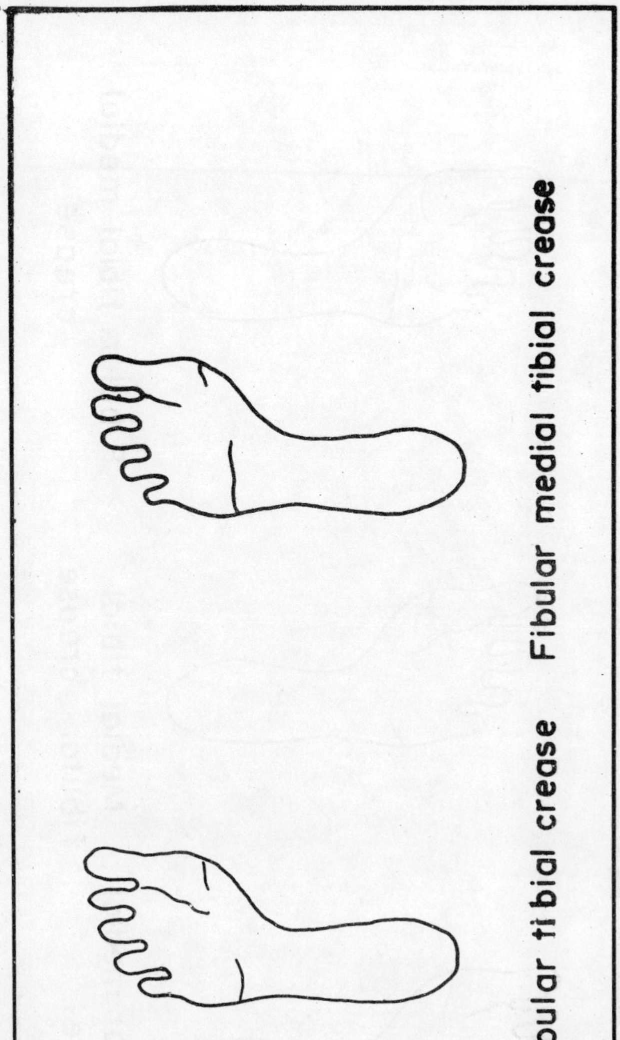

FIG. 10.7: Triple medial base creases

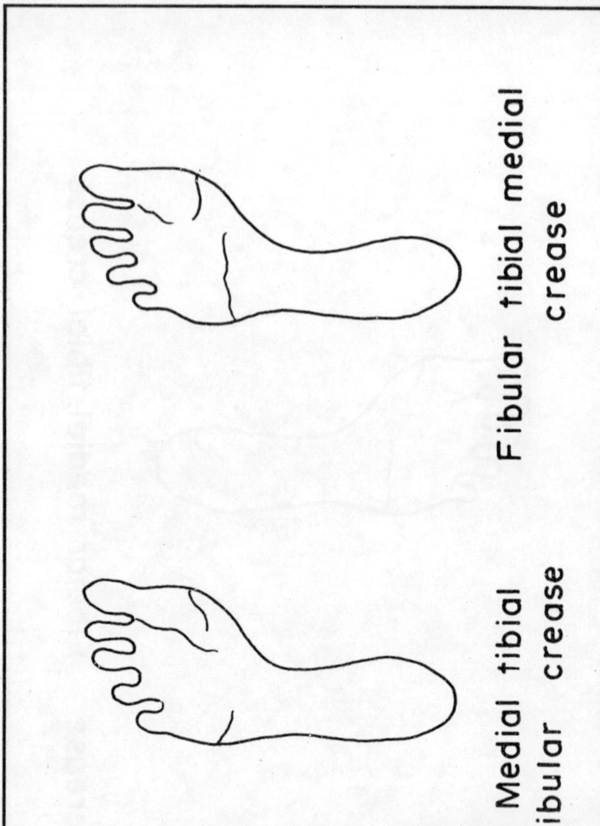

FIG. 10.7: Triple medial base creases

(i) Medial fibular tibial crease shows relative length and firm base of medial creases in relation to the fibular crease, while tibial crease shows the best developed features.

(ii) Fibular medial tibial crease shows the highest relative length and firm base of fibular crease in relation to the medial crease which subsequently shows greater length as compared to tibial crease.

(iii) Length of tibial crease in relation to fibular crease is more and relative length of the fibular crease to medial crease is more in tibial fibular medial crease.

(iv) The medial tibial fibular crease shows the greatest length and firm base of medial crease in relation to tibial and fibular creases, respectively.

(v) Fibular tibial medial crease shows the greatest length of fibular crease while medial crease shows the minimum length.

Revised Formulation of Distal Thenar and Hypothenar Creases

The plantar creases show greater obscurity of forms as compared to palmar creases; nonetheless their conformity of origin and termination warrant a common basis of formulation.

From the above point of view, Bali and Mishra formulated plantar creases into single, double and triple medial base point crease types.

When all the three primary creases, i.e., medial longitudinal, tibial transverse and fibular transverse creases, make a union at a point, which is referred as 'Medial base point' the creases are designated as single medial base point creases. The union may be between any two creases or a single crease may also be formulated into single medial base point category (Fig. 10.8a).

When the union of above creases is firm, direct and clear cut the creases are grouped as True types. When union is indirect or feeble the creases are grouped as transitional types (Fig. 10.8b). The sub-typing of transitional forms is based on length and prominence of the crease (Fig. 10.9a).

The double medial base creases make two clear cut bases of the above three primary creases, i.e., the union between medial longitudinal crease and fibular transverse crease, medial longitudinal crease and tibial transverse crease or the union between fibular and tibial transverse crease (Fig. 10.9).

When the union is indirect and is linked through branches the crease is designated as transitional type (Fig. 10.8a, 10.9a) and other types having direct union are called true types (Fig. 10.9b). Triple medial base creases form three independent bases and are sub-divided according to their relative length and prominence. The longest and most prominent crease is named first and is followed by the second longest crease (Fig. 10.10 and 10.10a).

Formulation of Calcar or Proximal Thenar and Hypothenar Creases

A single or double, complete or incomplete, crease on the most proximal thenar and hypothenar regions runs transversally and demarcates the heel from the rest of the sole. Proximal to the calcar crease, no crease has been noticed so far.

Immediately distal to the calcar crease on its medial and lateral margins run a group of creases. The group running from medial to calcar base towards the hypothenar distal region of the sole is called fibular open type.

Another group of creases takes its root from the lateral calcar base and runs towards the thenar distal region of the sole is called tibial open type. When both the groups are present on the same sole, they often make a tented appearance and are called close type (Fig. 10.11a).

When the above three types of creases emerge from the calcar crease, which may be complete or incomplete, the creases are called calcar tibial open type, calcar fibular open type and calcar close or tented type. The calcar tibial type opens towards the tibial, and calcar fibular type towards the fibular sides. The calcar close meets in the middle (Fig. 10.11b).

Quite often a crease or creases may run longitudinally to the axis of the foot and cut a crease or creases, either on tibial or fibular side; such creases are secondary in nature and are not considered for formulation purposes.

Validity of the Formulation

Distal thenar, hypothenar and calcar creases are formulated on the basis of their phenotypic features. The morphogenesis of plantar creases reflects their utility as a morphological variable. The plantar crease variability among populations suggests that the trait is genetically governed.

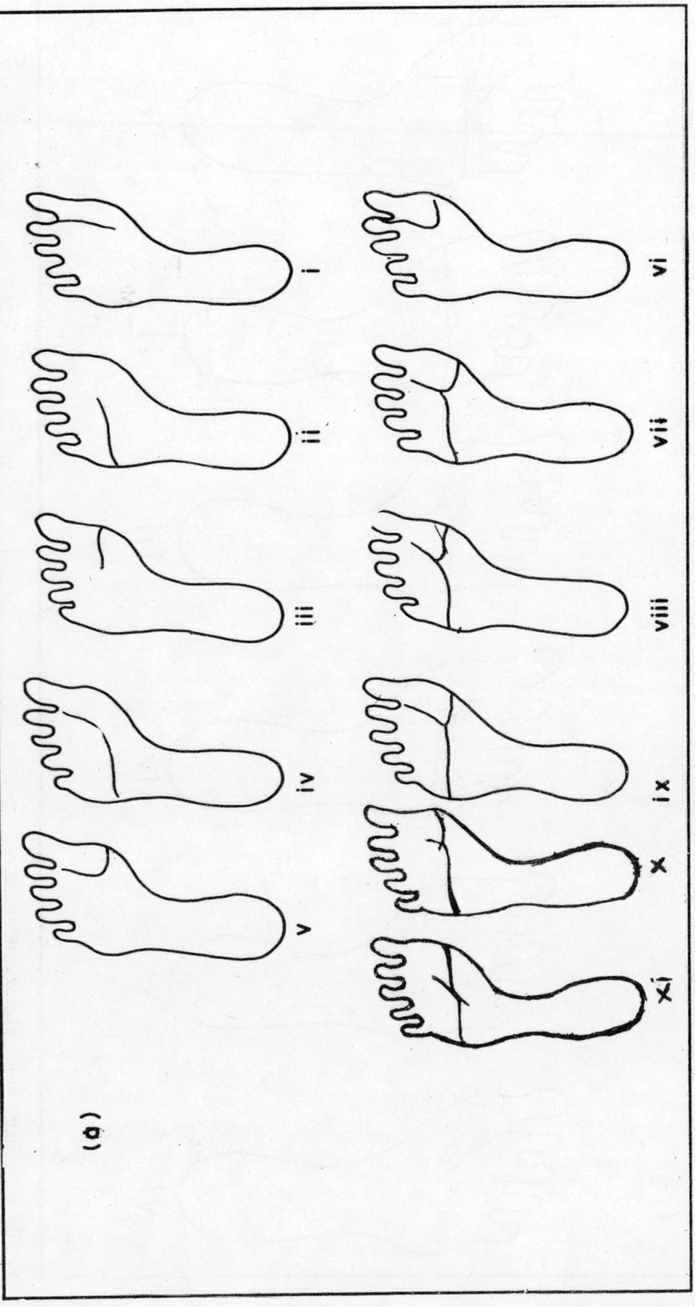

FIG. 10.8: Single medial plantar base creases
True Types: i. Single medial, ii. Single tibial, iii. Single fibular, iv. Single fibular medial, v. Single tibial medial, vi. Single medial tibial, vii. Simple single tibial, viii. Simple single fibular, ix. Simple single medial, x. Simple single fibular, xi. Simple single tibial

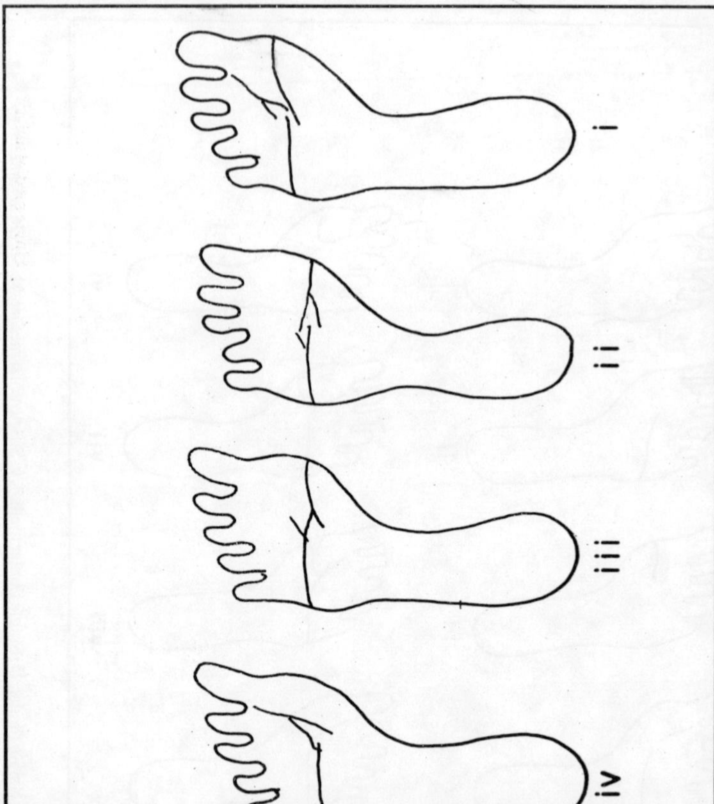

FIG. 10.8: Single medial plantar base creases
Transitional Types: i. Mix type, ii. Tibial fibular, iii. Fibular tibial, iv. Medial fibular, v. Medial tibial, vi. Tibial medial

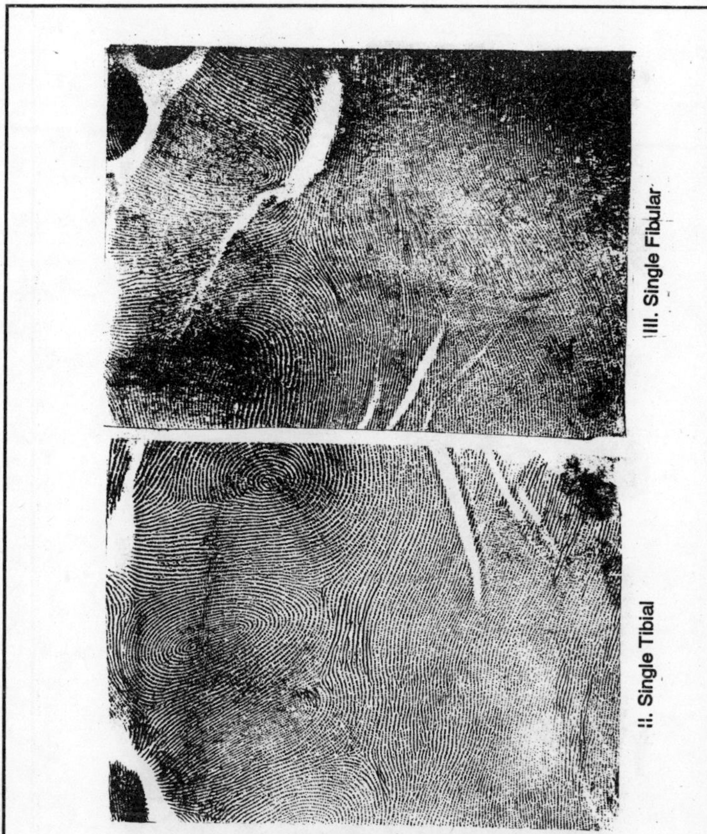

FIG. 10.8: (a) True types of single medial plantar creases

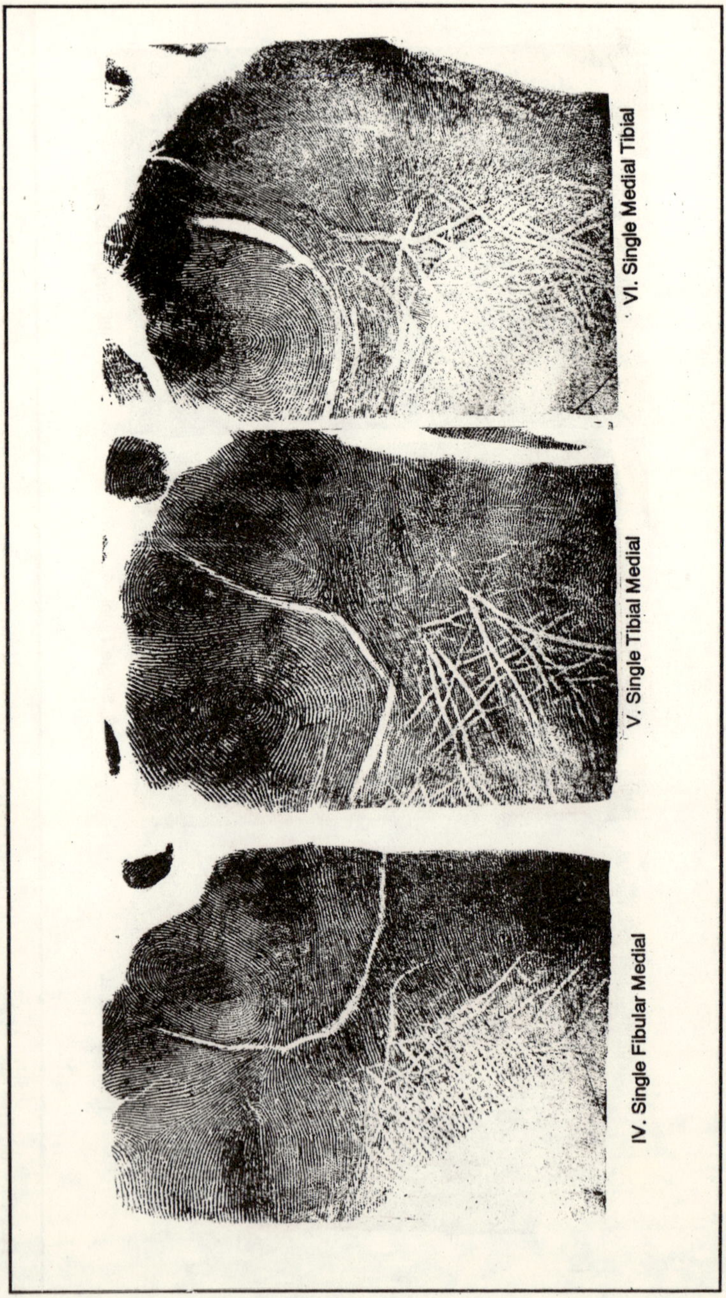

FIG. 10.8: (a) True types of single medial plantar creases

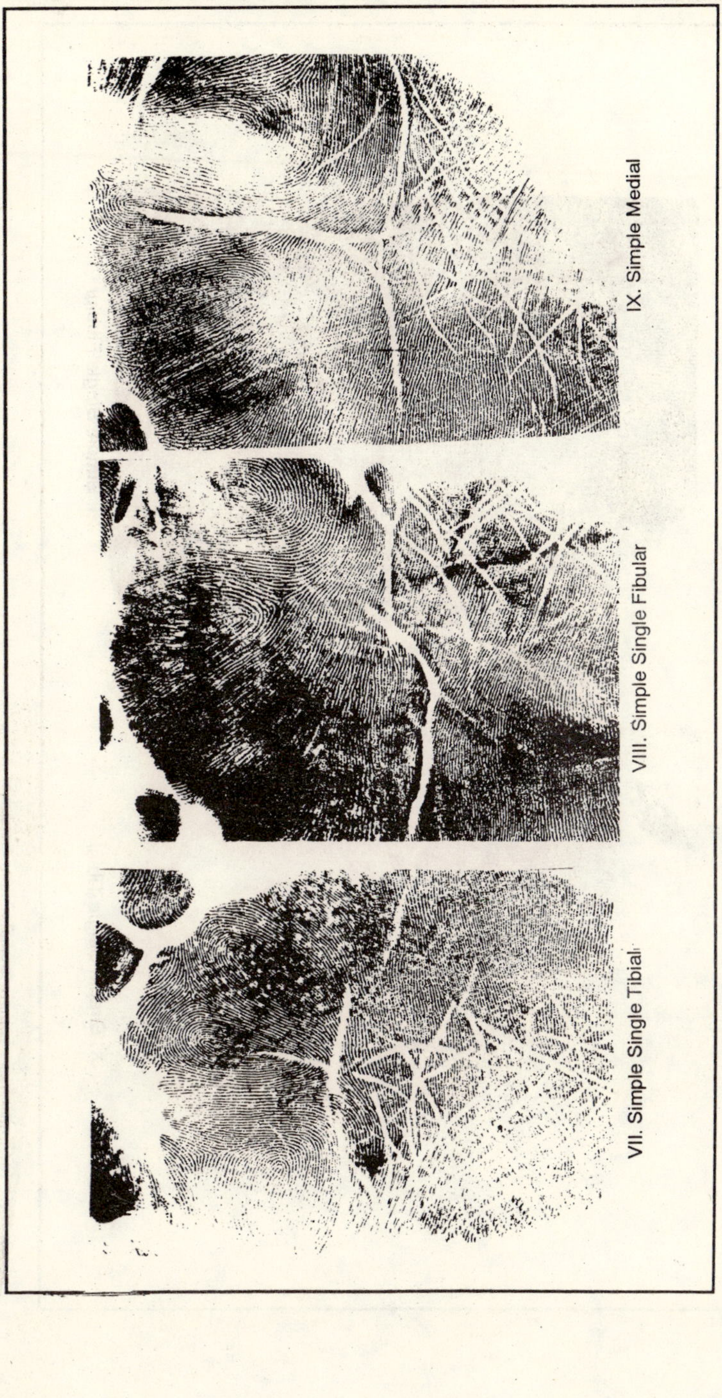

FIG. 10.8: (a) True types of single medial plantar creases

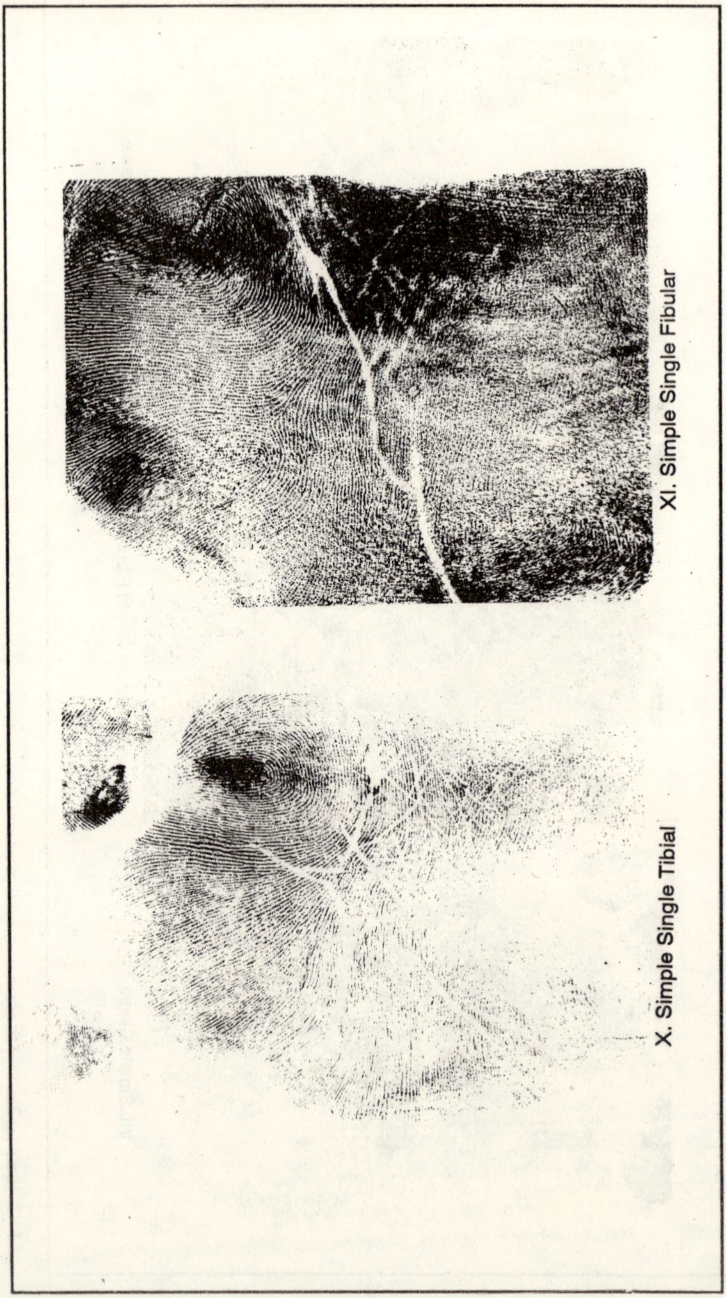

FIG. 10.8: (a) True types of single medial plantar creases
Note: The most prominent crease is named first and the least prominents named lost of all

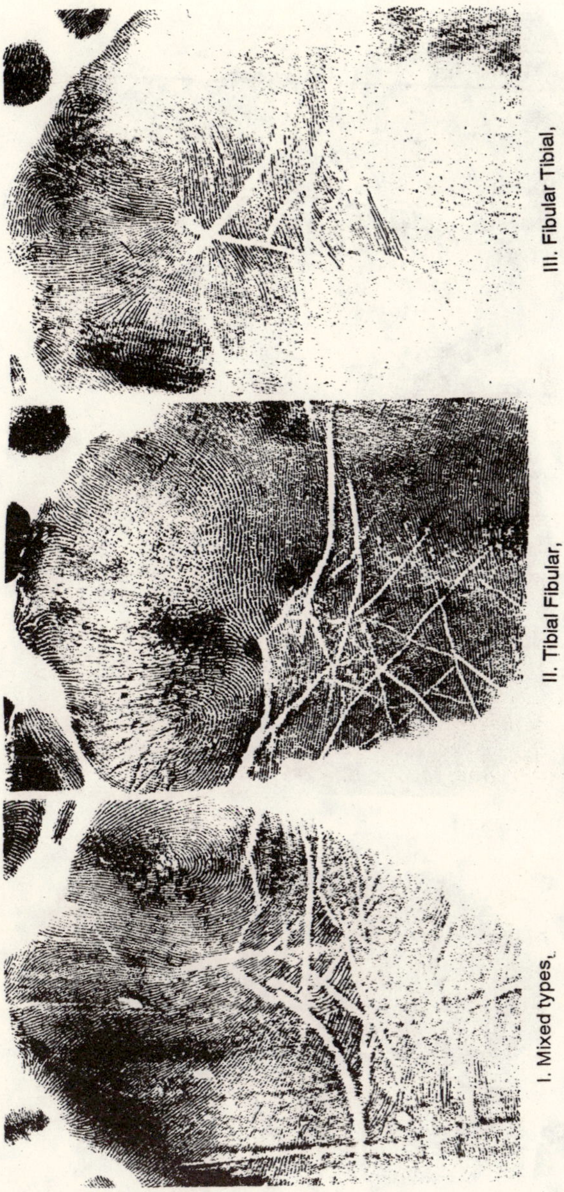

FIG. 10.8: (b) Transitional types: Single medial plantar base crease

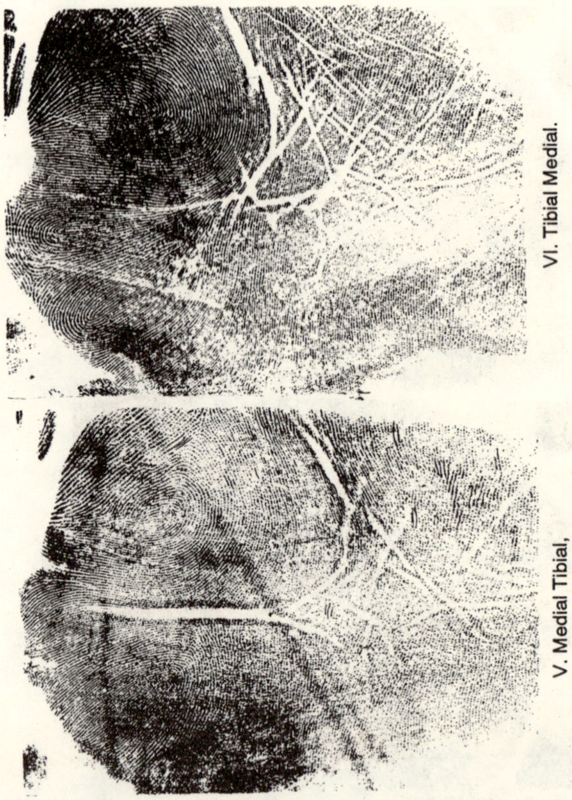

FIG. 10.8: (b) Transitional types: Single medial plantar base crease

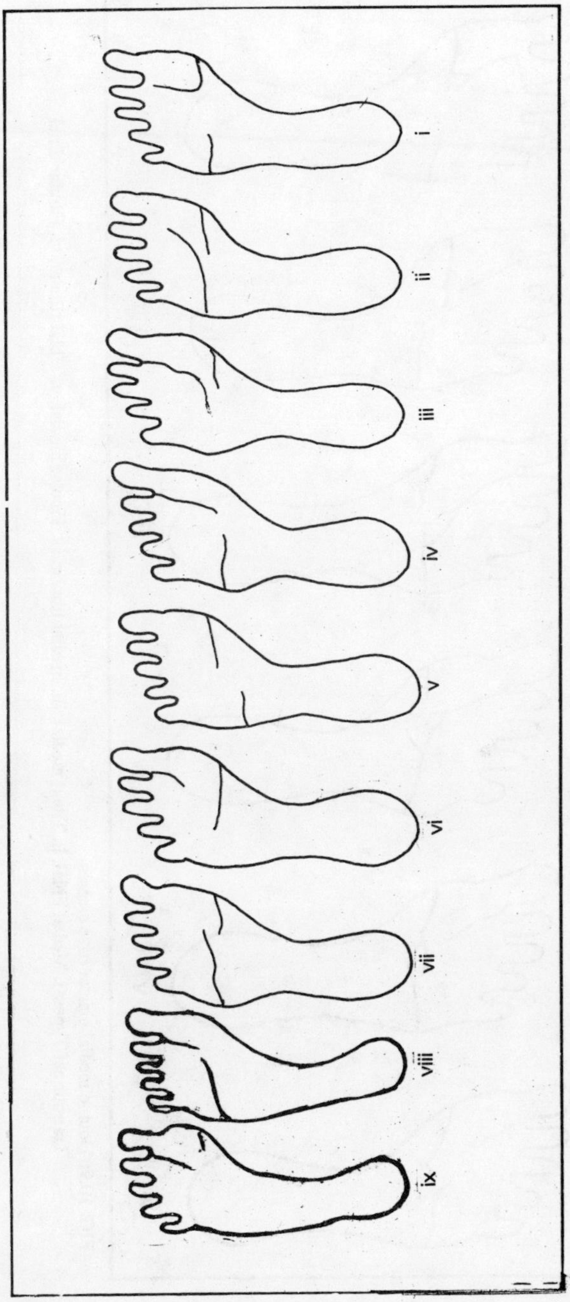

FIG. 10.9: Double medial plantar base creases

True Types: i. Double tibial, ii. Double fibular, iii. Double medial, iv. Double medial fibular, v. Double tibial fibular, vi. Double tibial medial, vii. Double fibular tibial, viii. Fibular medial, ix. Medial fibular

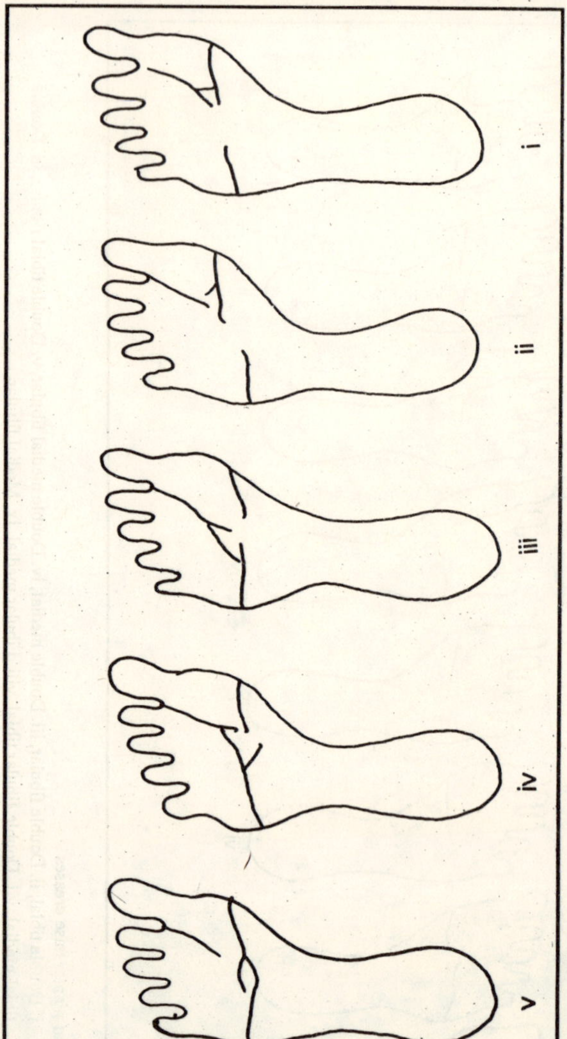

FIG. 10.9: Double medial plantar base creases
Transitional Types: i. Medial tibial, ii. Tibial medial, iii. Medial fibular, iv. Fibular medial, v. Tibial fibular, vi. Fibular tibial

FIG. 10.9: (a) True types: Double medial plantar base creases

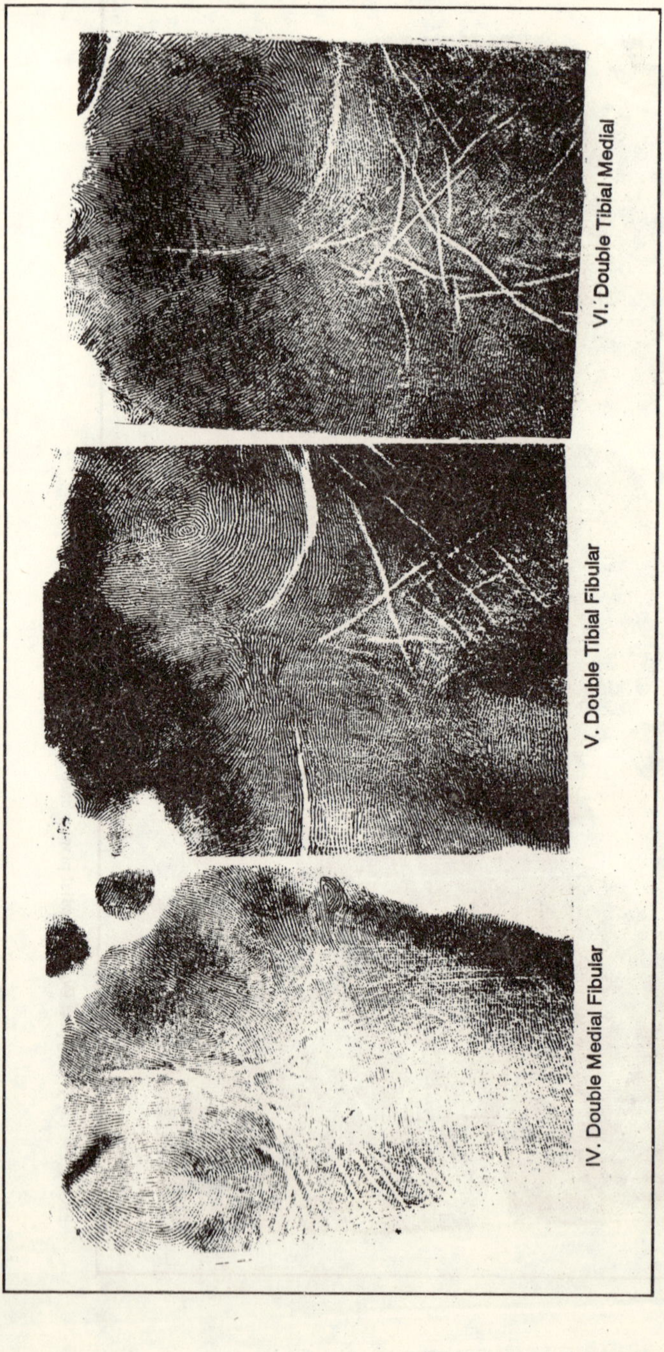

FIG. 10.9: (a) True types: Double medial plantar base creases

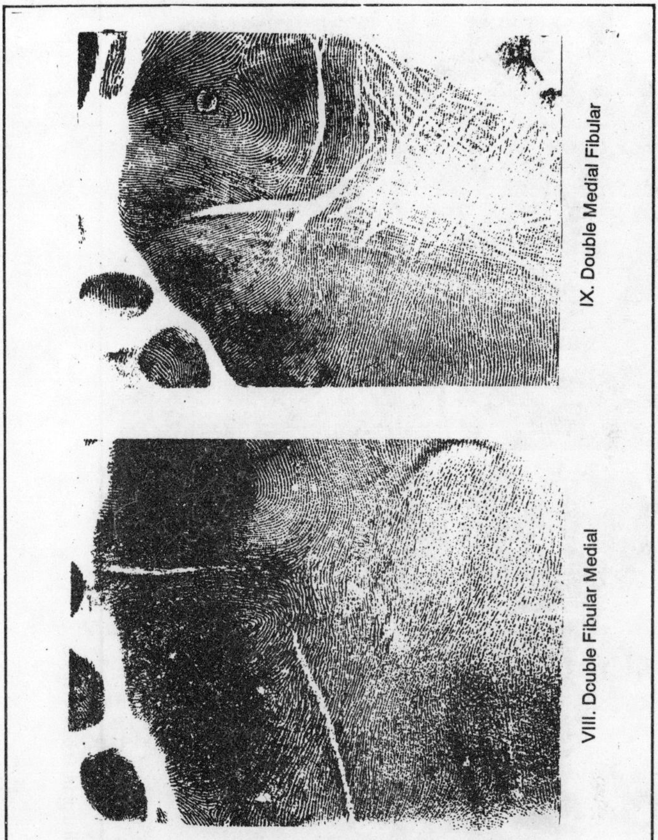

FIG. 10.9: (a) True types: Double medial plantar base creases

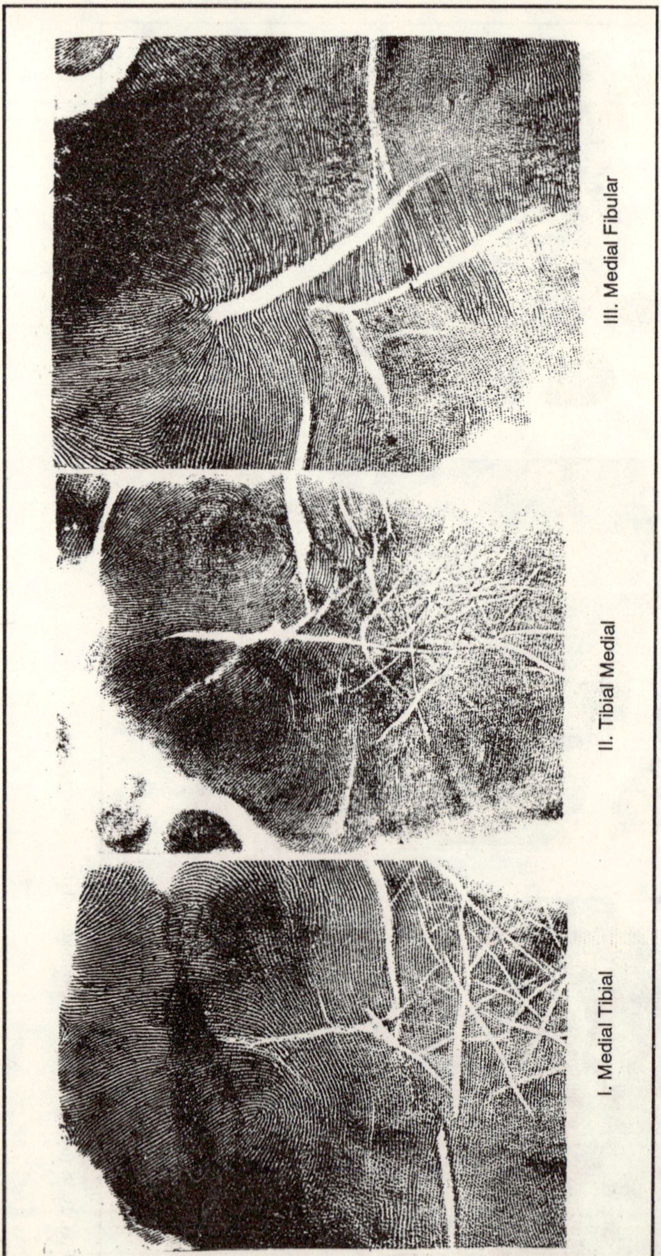

FIG. 10.9: (b) Transitional types: Double medial plantar base creases

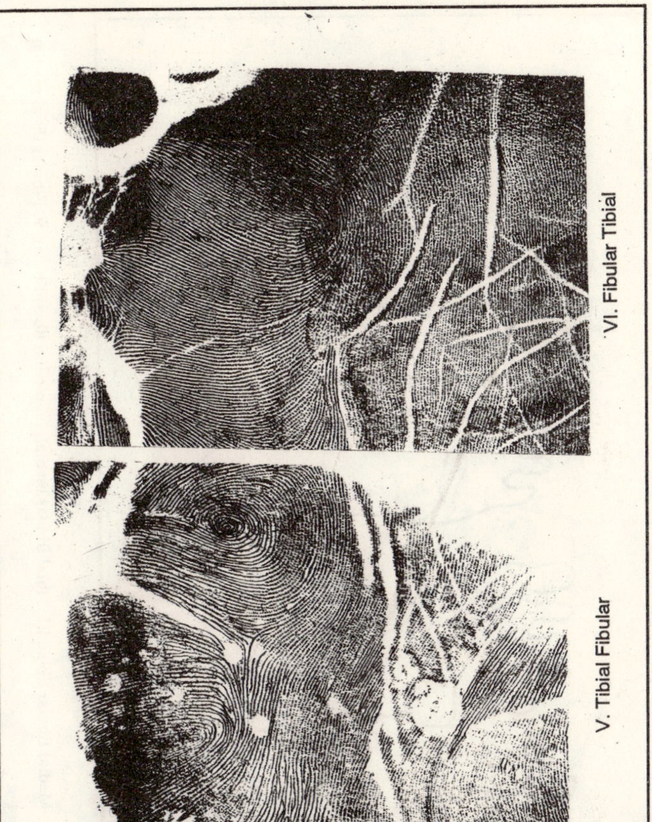

FIG. 10.9: (b) Transitional types: Double medial plantar base creases

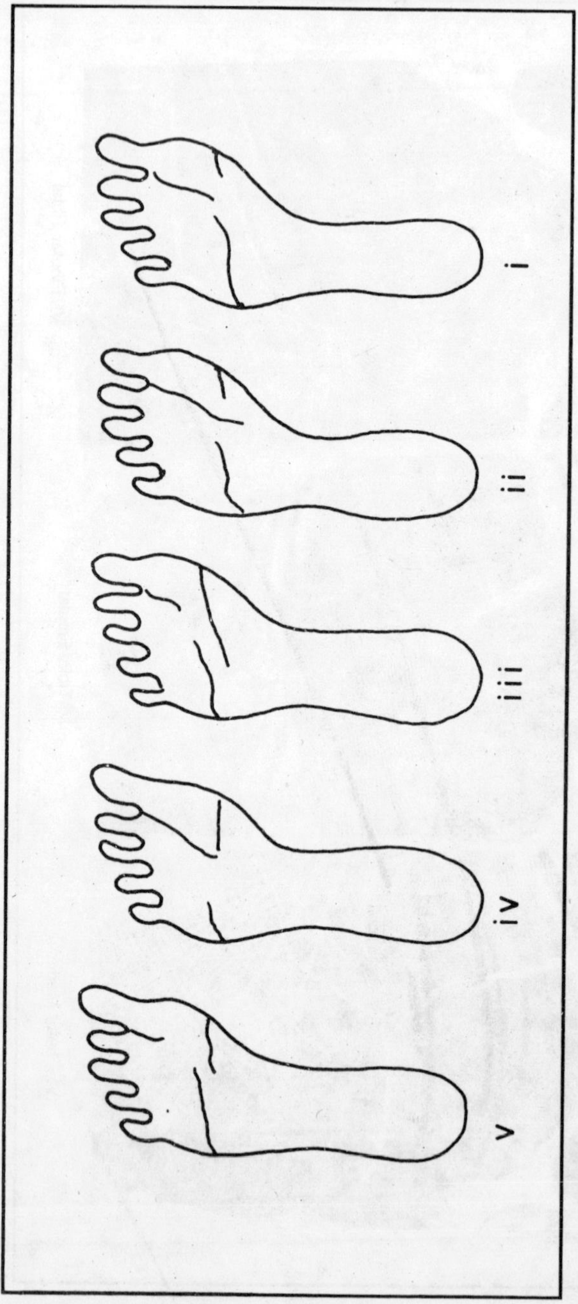

FIG. 10.10: Triple medial plantar base creases
Triple Types: i. Fibular medial tibial, ii. Medial fibular tibial, iii. Tibial fibular medial, iv. medial tibial fibular, v. Fibular tibial medial

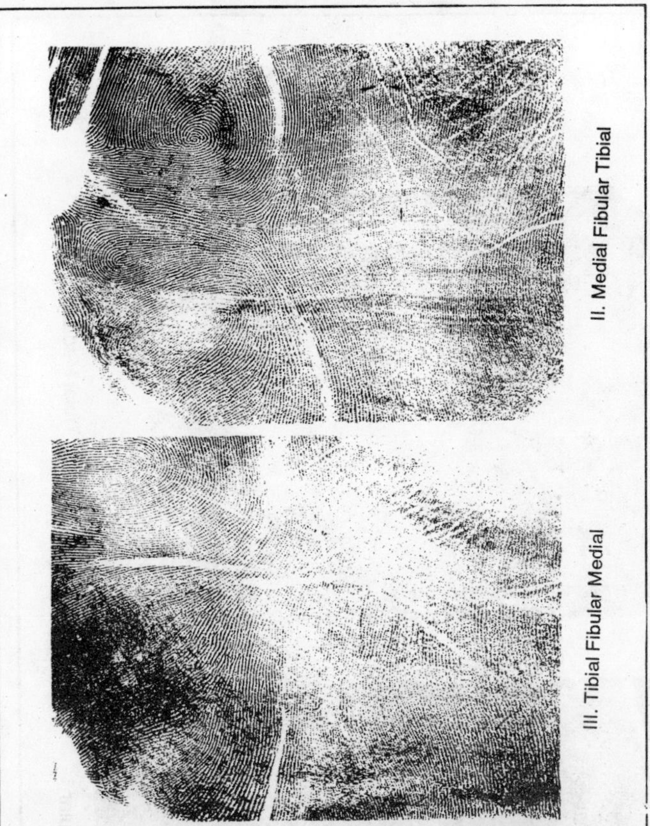

FIG. 10.10: (a) Triple medial plantar

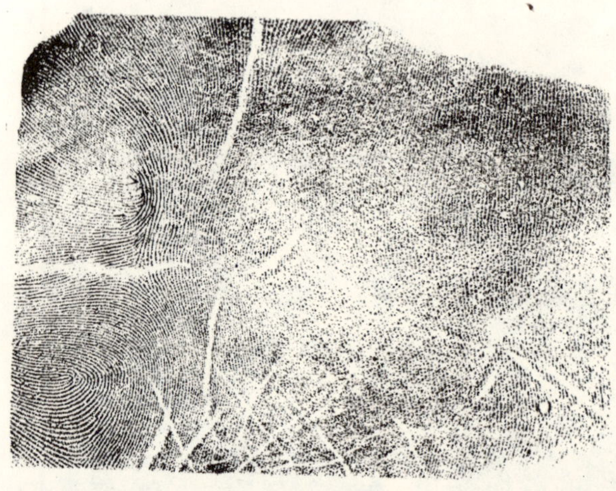

FIG. 10.10: (a) Triple medial plantar

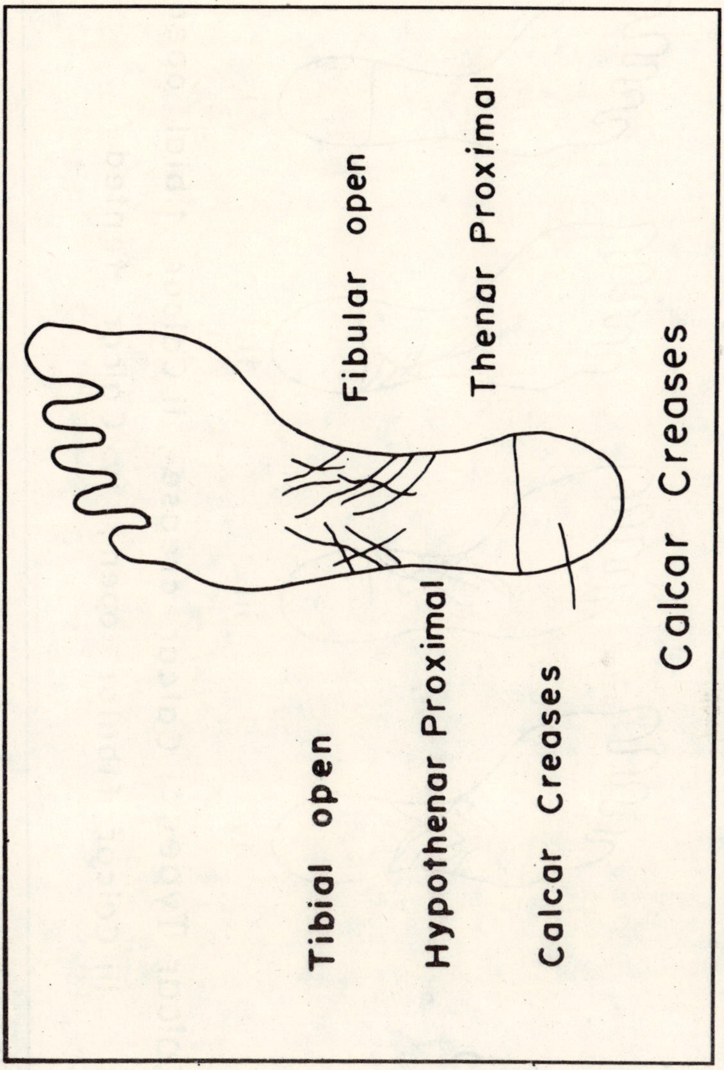

FIG. 10.11: Formulation of calcar creases

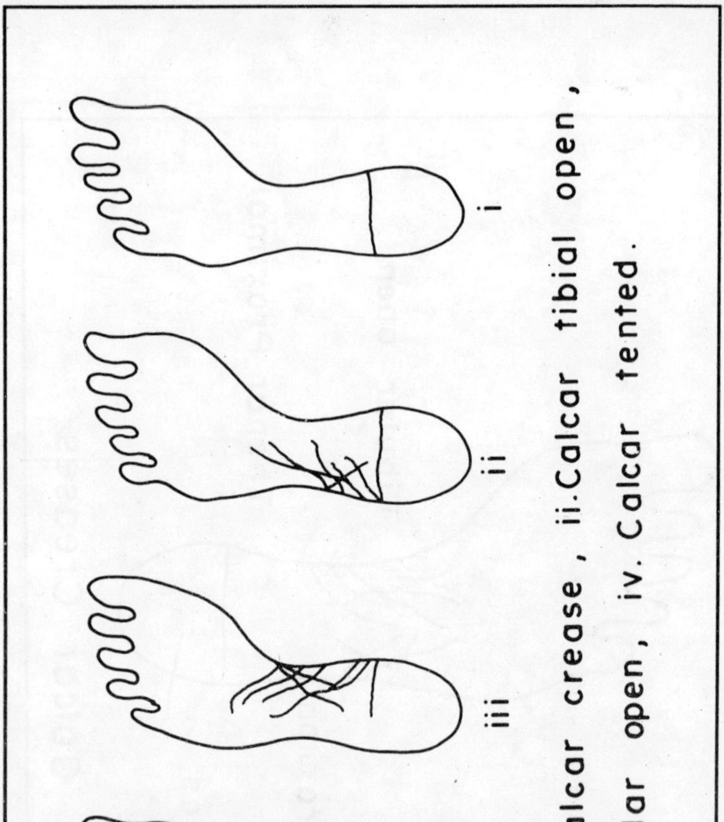

FIG. 10.11: Formulation of calcar creases

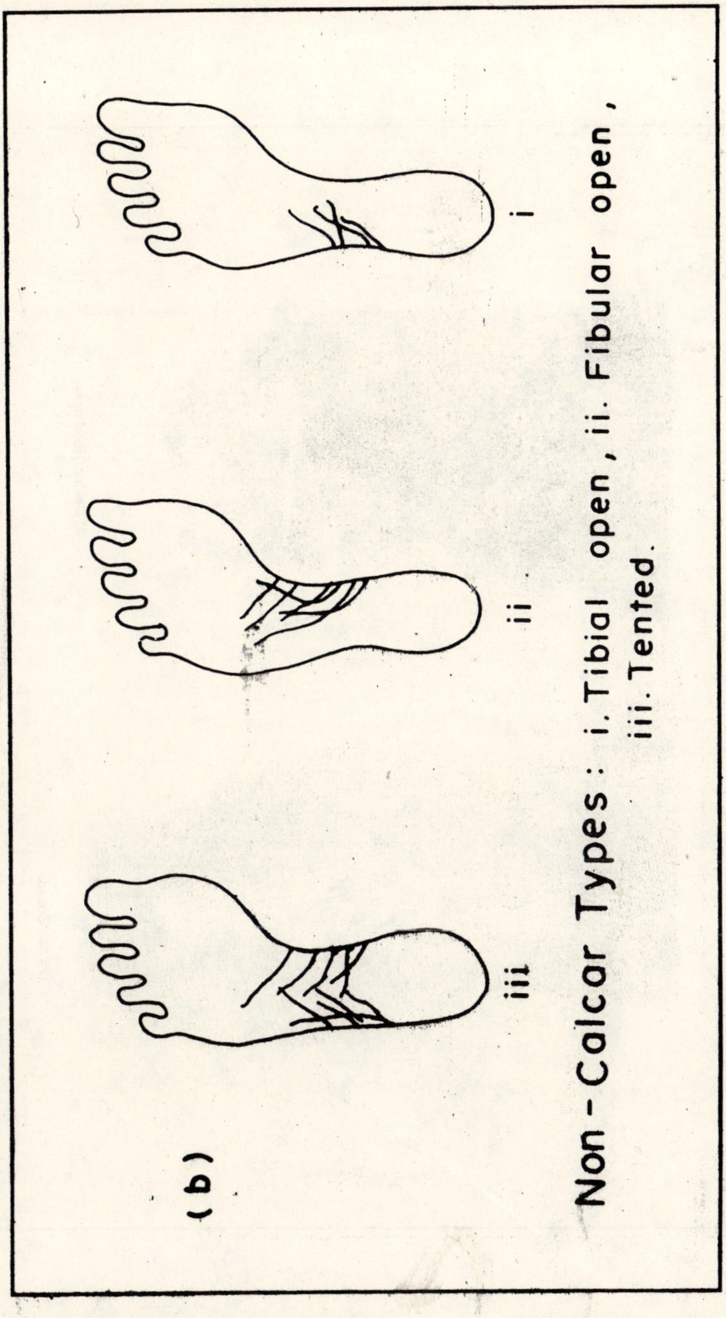

FIG. 10.11: Formulation of calcar creases

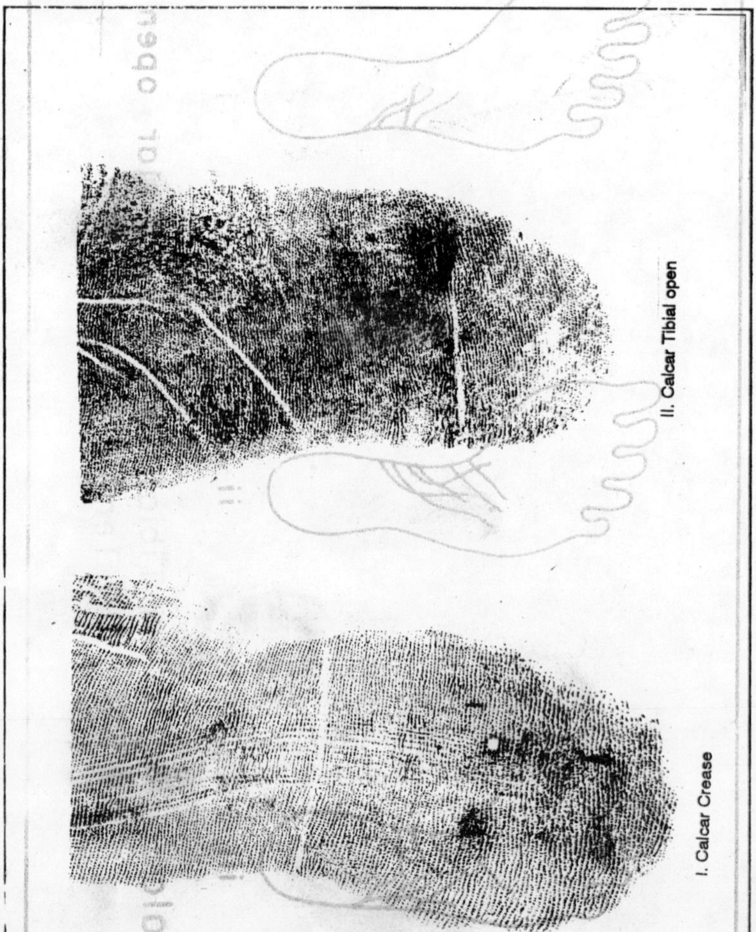

FIG. 10.11: (a) Calcar plantar creases

FIG. 10.11: (a) Calcar plantar creases

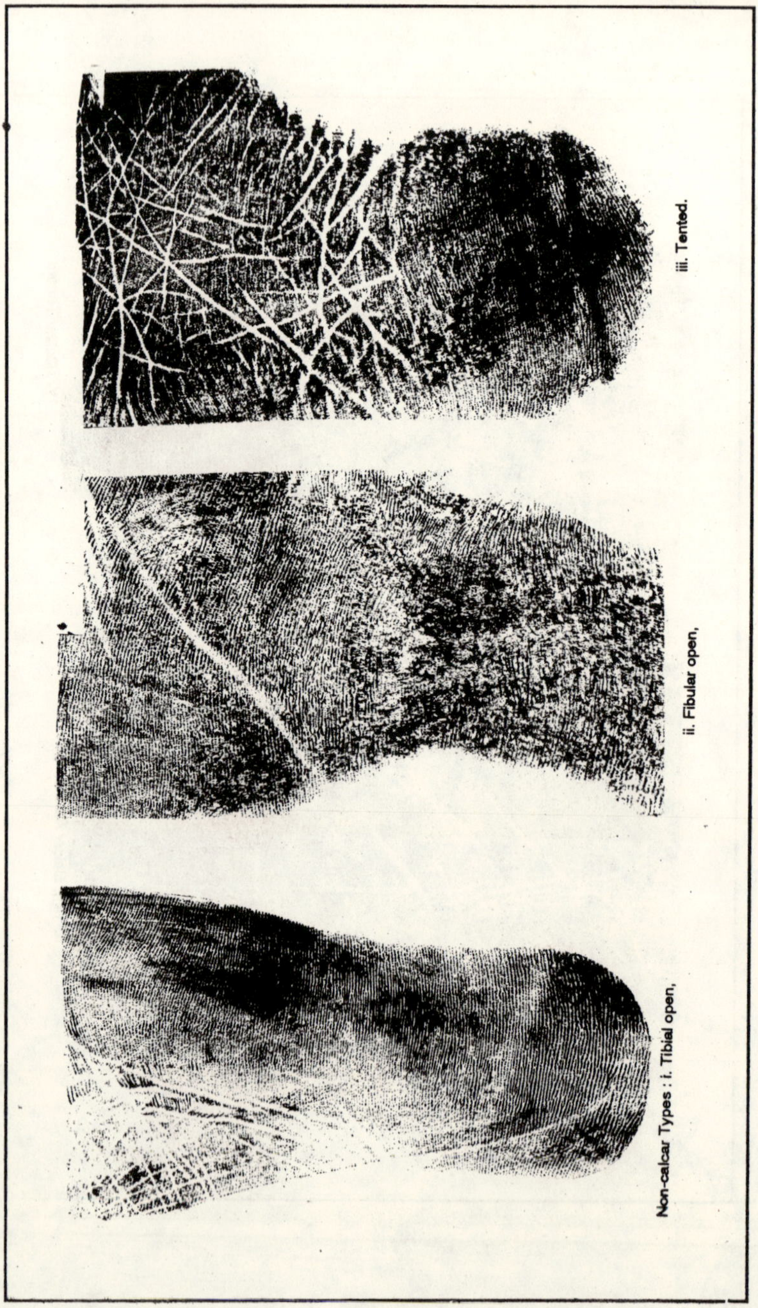

FIG. 10.11: (a) Calcar plantar creases

The bi-sexual and bi-manual distributions of plantar creases show consistency of variation among different populations.

The study of plantar crease inheritance in families and twins has been established by Bali and Mishra (1978) and Mishra (1979). Bali et al. (1980) have made observations on intra-individual relationship between palmar and plantar creases.

Plantar creases need to be studied more extensively. The evidences in favour of plantar crease formulation are convincing and warrant a probe to test their utility in the study of diseases and other anthropological parameters.

REFERENCES

Bali, R.S. (1964): Toe dermatoglyphics — Inheritance and comparison with the finger ball patterns. Ph.D. Thesis, Delhi University, Delhi.

Bali, R.S. (1968): Genetic inter-correlation between finger and toe patterns. *Zeit. schrift for Morphologie und Anthropologie* 59(3), pp. 244-72.

Bali, R.S. and R. Mishra (1978): The plantar creases and their formulation, Xth internat. Congr. Anthrop. & Ethno. Sciences, New Delhi, India.

Bali, R.S. and Ramesh Chaube (1971): On the formulation of palmar creases. *Z. Morph. Anthrop.*, 63: p. 121.

Bali, R.S. et al. (1980): On the formulation of calcar plantar creases. National Symposium on child with handicap and VII Annual Conference of I.S.H.G., Ranchi University, Ranchi, India.

Bonnevie, K. (1927): Die ersten Entwick lungsstadicn der papillarmuster der menschlichen Finger ballen. *Nyt Mag f. Nuturv*, 65. pp. 10-56.

Cummins, H. (1935): Morphology of the palmar hypothenar dermatoglyphic in man. *Human Biology* 7(1): pp. 1-23.

Cummins, H. (1935a): Dermatoglyphics in Eskimos from Point Barrow, *American Journal of Physical Anthropology* 20(1): pp. 13-7.

Féré, C. (1900a): Les lines papillaires de la plante du pied. *Journal de l' Anatomic et de la physiologie* 36: pp. 602-18.

Hepburn, D. (1895): The papillary ridges on the hands and feet of monkeys and men. *Scientific Transactions of the Royal Society of Dublin*, 5: pp. 525-38.

Hirsch, W. (1977): "Dermatoglyphics and Creases in their relationship to clinical syndromes. A diagnostic criterion" In *Dermatoglyphics: An International Perspective*, Edited by J. Mavalwala. World Anthropology. The Hague: Mouton.

Kollmann, A. (1983): *Der Tastapparat der Hand der menscblichen Rassen und der Affen*. Hamburg: Leopold Voss.

Lynn, R. and J. Murray (1978): *An Inkless Method of Recording Dermal Ridges. An Introductional Perspective*, Moultan Publication, Paris.

Mishra, R. (1979): Inheritance and methodological study of plantar creases. Thesis submitted in part fulfilment for the requirements of the degree of Ph.D. University of Saugar, Sagar.

Nekiela, J. (1972): Flexion furrows of the feet in Poles. *Folia Morphot. (Warswaz)* 31: 301.

Newman, M.T. (1936): A comparative study of finger prints and toe prints, *Human Biology* 8(4): pp. 531-52.

Schenk, H. and H Patzer (1959): *Das Fussfurchenbild des Neugeborenen. Kinderarztliche Praxis* 27(4): pp. 169-73.

11

FORMULATION OF BRACELET CREASES

A SOLITARY publication of Chaube and Bali (1976) was the landmark of first scientific interpretation of bracelet creases, a least explored field among creases.

In the strict sense, bracelet creases are not confined to dermatoglyphics and cease to qualify as creases. On the proximal fringes of palmar dermatoglyphics, the distal bracelet crease embraces dermal ridges on its distal border and extends between stylion and radial points. This crease is most prominent and is characterised by the presence of distinct islets, thus giving a beaded appearance to the crease. The parallel or transverse lines show a splitting tendency which is more frequent in medial and proximal bracelet crease. The bracelet creases on the pronation side are prominent and merge towards the radial and the ulnar side. Chaube and Bali (1976) and Chaube (1971) have made pioneer contribution on bracelet creases.

The adaptative and nutritional standard of an individual bears a casual relationship between bracelet crease and adipose tissues (Chaube and Bali, 1976). The lines are well-marked among healthy and fatty individuals. Among women the lines are more distinct than among men.

The formulation of the bracelet creases is based on their position approximating towards the graphic region of the palm or towards the most proximal area of the palm. The crease which is closer to the proximal rigid skin of the palm on its supination side is classified as distal bracelet crease (D), and the crease which falls towards the most proximal side is classified as proximal bracelet crease (P) and the other falling in-between these two creases is termed medial bracelet crease (M). But, besides these three basic bracelet creases, there may be several more creases imperfectly dividing the wrist either from the ulnar or from the radial side of the arm and are classified accordingly. Sometimes four to five bracelet creases are found on a single bracelet area. Such types of creases are categorized into the group of the proximal bracelet crease.

The bracelet creases are often confused with the pseudo creases or folds, which generally reflect the epidermal thickness of the wrist. But after careful observation, a distinct bead formation can be noticed. These small islets or beads are the characteristic feature of the true bracelet creases.

The bracelet creases have been classified into (I) Complete and (II) Incomplete groups of (a) distal bracelet crease, (b) medial bracelet crease and (c) proximal bracelet crease.

I. A complete bracelet crease runs either from stylion or from radial point, completely dividing the bracelet area transversely into two halves, when the palm is held in supination position. In pronation position, the creases appear to merge with the skin of the wrist quite often indistinctly.

II. Incomplete bracelet creases show a tendency towards completion from the radial to the ulnar side and vice versa, and are designated by 'u' and 'r' accordingly.

Since the distal bracelet crease has quite often been found complete and falls closer to the distal area of the forearm, as if it is a component of glaphic skin, the nomenclature of creases is based on their relationship to the forearm rather than to the palm.

The medial bracelet crease follows the pattern of distal bracelet crease, completely or incompletely. In other words, number is always designated as medial, while most proximal, i.e., number three or four, is classed as proximal bracelet creases. If number three or four (Fig. 11.1) are complete, the proximal creases are referred to as P and P_1, respectively. The basic requisite of all true bracelet creases is to possess a bead or beads in the shape of islets of parallel lines meeting each other at certain places.

On the basis of the above definition, all groups and sub-groups of bracelet creases are explained separately as under:

Main groups:

Distal Bracelet Crease (D)

It is the distal-most or first bracelet crease, approximating towards the glaphic skin of the palm. This crease is quite often complete (Fig. 11.2).

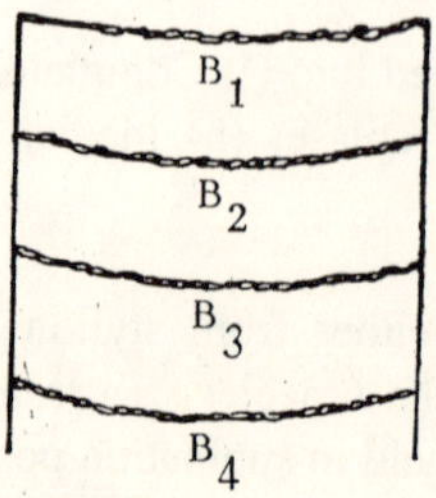

FIG. 11.1: Bracelet creases

Medial Bracelet Crease (DM)

The second bracelet crease falls in-between the proximal and distal bracelet creases, and is termed the medial bracelet crease (Fig. 11.3).

Proximal Bracelet Crease (DMP)

It is the third or fourth bracelet crease situated most proximally and is designated by P or P_1, if complete (Fig. 11.2).

All the three groups of creases have a genetic unity and, thus, are classified in relation to each other. When the distal bracelet crease is complete, it is denoted by 'D' and other incomplete creases are classified under this group. If the distal bracelet crease (D) and the medial bracelet crease (M) are complete and other creases are incomplete and show a tendency towards their completion, they are classified as medial bracelet crease or DM group. When the proximal bracelet crease (P) or creases, if complete, along with the distal bracelet crease (D) and show the tendency towards their completion, the group is designated as proximal bracelet crease (DMP). It does not matter whether the medial bracelet crease is complete or not.

The above mentioned three major groups have further been

classified into finer types.

Sub-types of Main Groups

Sub-types of distal bracelet crease or group D – Group D of bracelet crease is further divided into seven sub-types (Fig. 11.2).

1. Sub-type D – This sub-type is represented by a single complete distal bracelet crease.
2. Sub-type Dmu – A distal bracelet crease accompanied by a medial bracelet crease running towards the radial side from the ulnar side falls under this sub-type. In this type the proximal bracelet crease or creases are absent.
3. Sub-type Dmr – A complete distal bracelet crease along with incomplete medial bracelet crease tending towards the ulnar

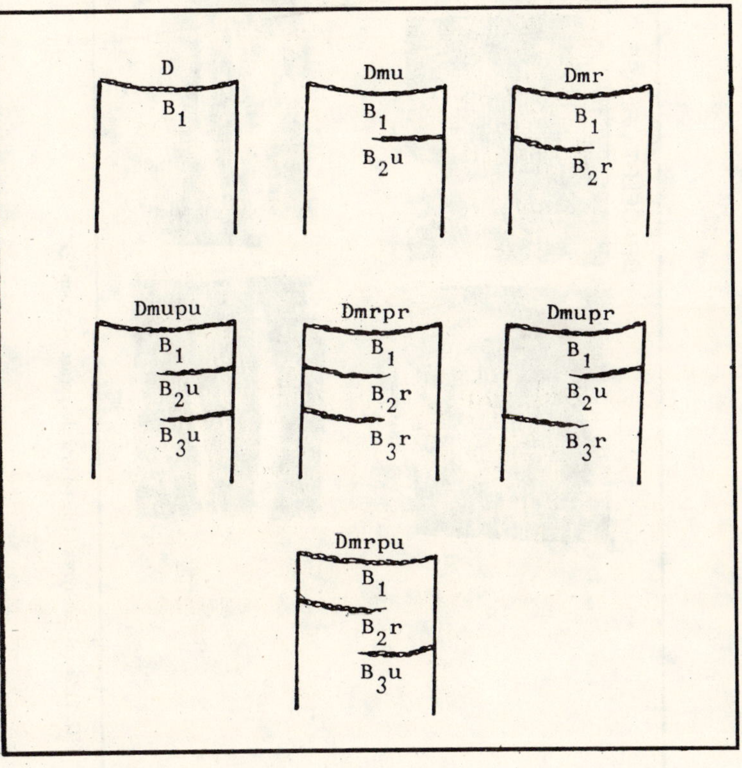

FIG. 11.2: Sub-types of "D" group

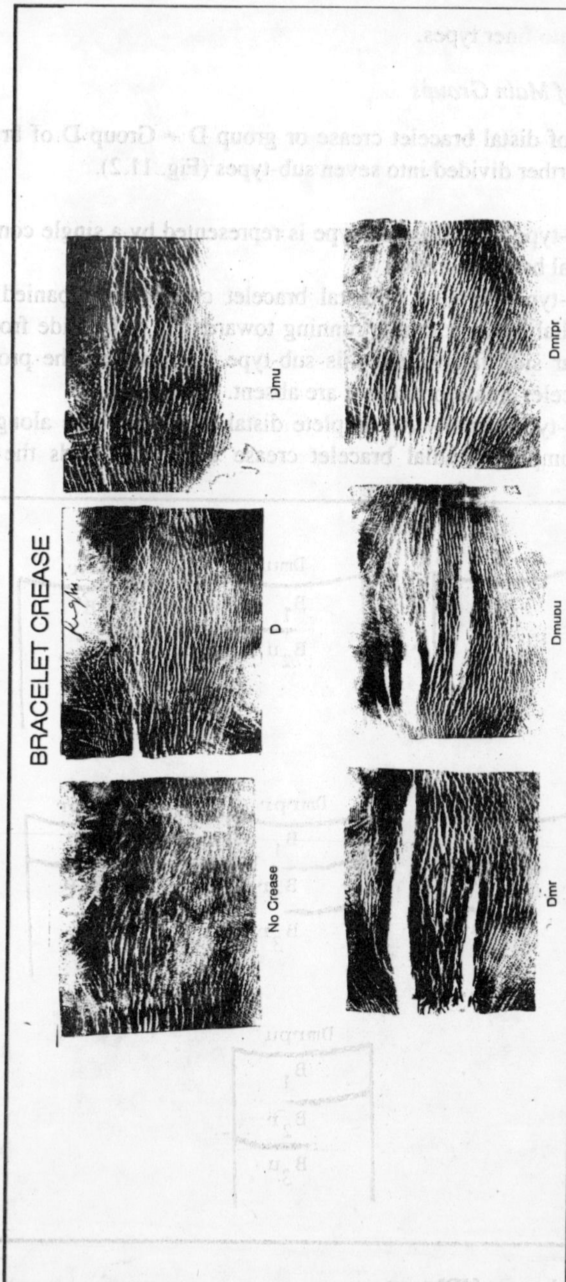

FIG. 11.2: (a) Sub-types of distal bracelet crease of group "D"

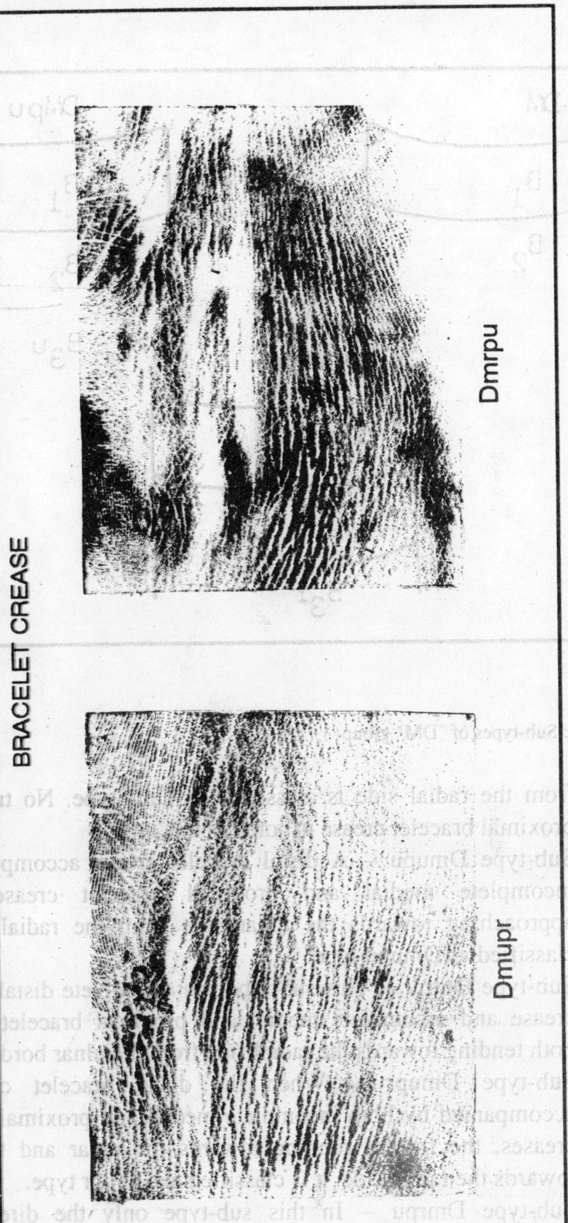

FIG. 11.2: (a) Sub-types of distal bracelet crease of group "D"

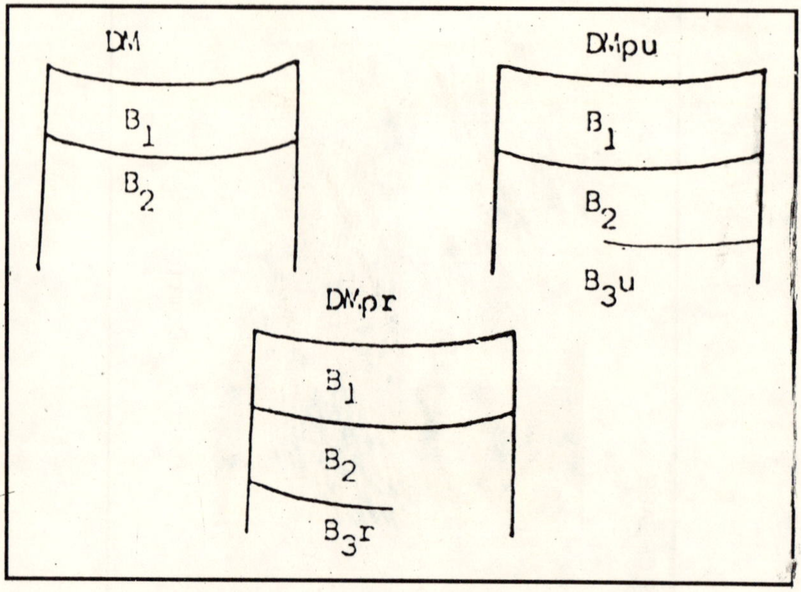

FIG. 11.3: Sub-types of "DM" group

from the radial side is classified as Dmr type. No trace of a proximal bracelet crease is noted in this type.

4. Sub-type Dmupu – A distal bracelet crease accompanied by incomplete medial and proximal bracelet creases, both approaching towards the ulnar side from the radial side, is classified as Dmupu type.
5. Sub-type Dmrpr – This sub-type has a complete distal bracelet crease and incomplete medial and proximal bracelet creases, both tending towards the radial side from the ulnar border.
6. Sub-type Dmupr – When the distal bracelet crease is accompanied by both incomplete medial and proximal bracelet creases, the former running towards the ulnar and the latter towards the radial side, it is classified as Dmupr type.
7. Sub-type Dmrpu – In this sub-type only the direction of incomplete creases, i.e., medial and proximal bracelet creases, is different from the type above.

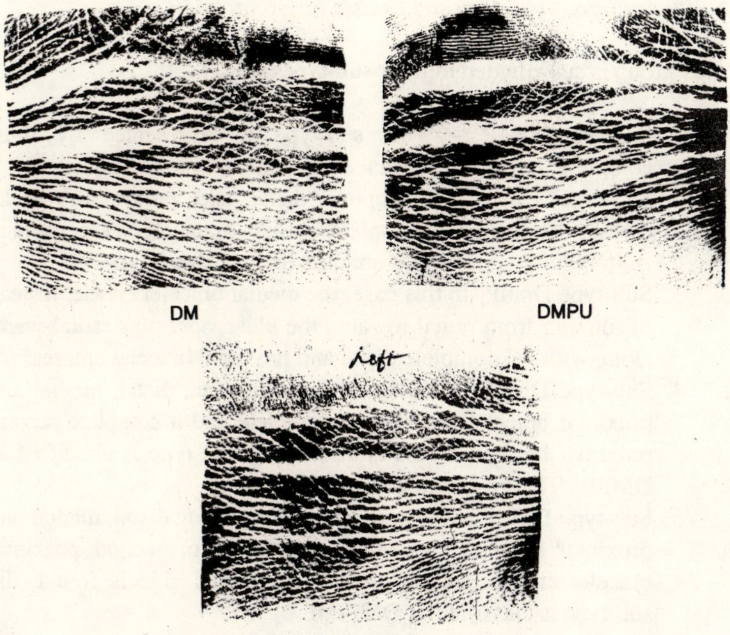

FIG. 11.3(a): Sub-types of medial bracelet crease or group 'DM'

Sub-type of Medial Bracelet Crease or Group DM

This group has been classified into three sub-types (Fig. 11.3).

1. Sub-type DM – This sub-type is represented by complete medial and distal bracelet creases only.
2. Sub-type DMpu – if both distal and medial bracelet creases are complete and are accompanied by an incomplete proximal bracelet crease tending towards the radial side from the ulnar border, they are classified as sub-type DMpu.
3. Sub-type DMpr – This sub-type differs from the above sub-type by an incomplete proximal bracelet crease tending ulnar-ward instead of radial-ward.

Sub-type of Proximal Bracelet Crease or Group DMP

This group is sub-divided into six sub-types (Fig. 11.4).

1. Sub-type DMP – This sub-type is represented by three complete, i.e., distal, medial and proximal bracelet creases.
2. Sub-type DmrP – Complete distal and proximal bracelet creases having an incomplete medial bracelet crease running from radial to ulnar-ward are classified as DmrP type.
3. Sub-type DmuP–In this case, the medial bracelet crease, instead of running from radial towards the ulnar side, runs radial-ward, along with the complete distal and proximal bracelet creases.
4. Sub-type $DMPP_1$ – When all the three, i.e., distal, medial and proximal bracelet creases are complete and a complete second proximal bracelet crease is also found, the type is classified as $DMPP_1$. This type is quite rare.
5. Sub-type $DMPP_1u$ – Along with the complete distal, medial and proximal bracelet creases, if the fourth or second proximal bracelet crease tending towards the radial side is found, the sub-type is classified as $DMPP_1u$.
6. Sub-type $DMPP_1r$ – This sub-type is similar to sub-type 5; the only difference is in the direction of the fourth crease or second proximal bracelet crease which is ulnar-ward.

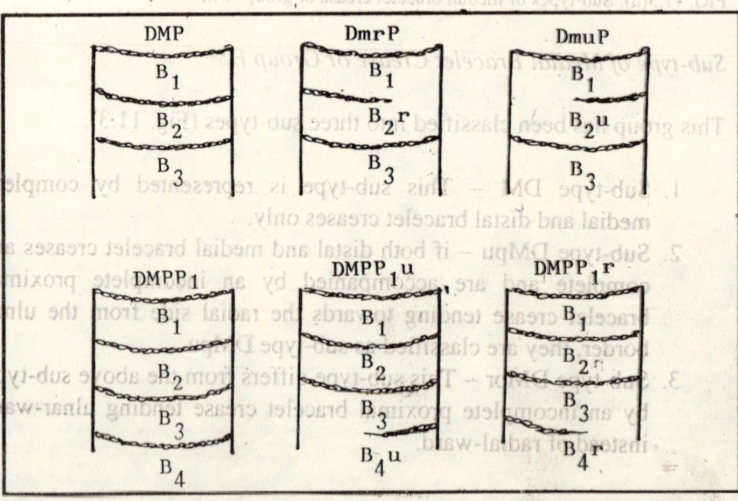

FIG. 11.4: Sub-types of "DMP" group

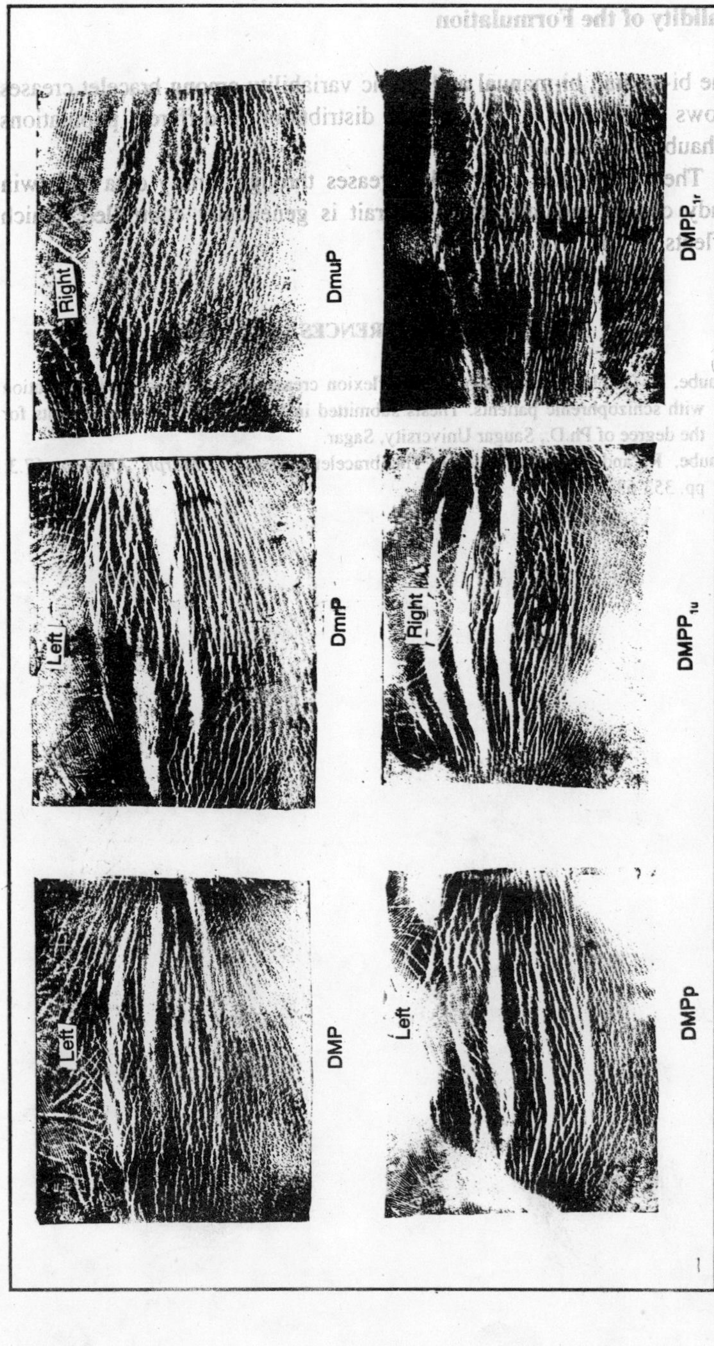

FIG. 11.4: (a) Sub-types of proximal bracelet crease or group "DMP"

Validity of the Formulation

The bi-sexual, bi-manual and ethnic variability among bracelet creases shows consistency of crease type distribution in different populations (Chaube and Bali, 1976).

The inheritance of bracelet creases through family data and twin study clearly indicates that the trait is genetically controlled, which reflects its utility in anthropology.

REFERENCES

Chaube, R. (1971): The study of palmar flexion creases — Inheritence and correlation with schizophrenic patients. Thesis submitted in fulfilment of the requirements for the degree of Ph.D., Saugar University, Sagar.

Chaube, R. and R.S. Bali (1976): The bracelet creases. Z. *Morph. Anthrop*. 67.3: pp. 353-63.

12

PHALANGEAL FLEXION CREASES

A GREAT number of researches on a very large material concerning dermatoglyphics of the distal phalanges (Finger ball) of human and non-human primates has been done. Their importance in Anthropology systematic, genetics and medicine has fully been realized.

But as regards basal and middle finger-section, our knowledge is scant. Ploetz-Radmann (1936), Basu (1968), Wasinski (1965) and a few others have shown their interest in this field of dermatoglyphics.

The genetic particularities of phalangeal traits, with special reference to dectylometry and phalangeal hair, find ample references.

The recent work of de Wilde (1980) on finger patterns and their total ridge system is somewhat provocative from future researchers in the field of phalangeal morphology.

The phalangeal creases on the individual phalanges find three flexion sites. The basal or metacarpo-phalangeal crease, the middle phalangeal crease and distal phalangeal crease occur at basal, middle and distal flexion of the phalangeal, respectively. The middle phalangeal crease is absent on thumb or may appear as a vestegial line and in certain cases it shows full form and size.

To define phalangeal crease Cummins and Midlo (1961) lay emphasis on localized ridge deficiencies which may have resulted into an ill-marked crease shape.

In the present context of crease definition the element of ridge interaction is of principal importance.

The phalangeal creases make their appearance amidst phalangeal dermatoglyphics and are devoid of dermal ridges and furrows. The phalangeal crease configuration shows pattern formation (Bali, 1980).

It may not be out of place to mention that a clear and complete phalangeal crease print is a pre-requisite for the analysis of crease patterns. It has, therefore, been felt necessary to explain the phalangeal crease technique once more.

Okajima (1966) gave a simple technique for procuring print cf metacarpo-phalangeal creases (Fig. 12.1). After smearing ink, fingers are made to revolve proximally along the bottle bearing printing paper.

Metacarpo-phalangeal crease. The accessory creases A on the forefinger from a configuration resembling a mane. RCIM is 75.2.

FIG. 12.1: Classification of interphalangeal flexion creases (Okajima, 1967)
A. accessory, B. boundary, R. ring creases

For our purpose, printing of radial and ulnar margin of individual phalanx is essential. To achieve this end each phalanx has to be revolved radial to ulnar margin or vice versa. Now, we have to couple the two techniques, i.e., Okajima's and Bali's (1980), the former for only basal crease and latter for middle and distal creases of individual phalanx. A separate print of each phalanx is then affixed just above, with gum, on a respective basal crease print of the individual finger (Figs. 2.3 & 2.4). The method provides a complete crease pattern without loosing the essential details of its margins.

Formulations of Phalangeal Flexion Creases

Cummins and Midlo (1943) made a casual reference of a phalanx showing absence of distal and middle phalangeal creases (Fig. 12.2).

Penrose (1931) was perhaps the first to arouse scientific interest in metacarpo-phalangeal creases.

Okajima's Formulation

The matacarpo-phalangeal creases tend to show characteristic patterns in each digit. The basal or metacarpo-phalangeal crease is situated close to the distal border of the palm and is usually composed of one main crease and some accessory small creases. The main crease was named as 'boundary crease' (Fig. 12.1). The boundary crease traverses at the base of the phalanx, while accessory creases are commonly located distally from the main crease and slant to the latter in a radial direction.

Two or more creases traversing the phalanx and separated from each other and usually observed on the middle finger were classified as 'boundary crease' and 'ring crease'. The boundary crease is situated at the base on the phalanx. Ring creases are located distally from the boundary crease (Fig. 12.1).

The above-quoted author calculated ring crease index for males and females. The index incorporates the distance between proximal boarders of boundary crease and middle phalanx crease and also ring crease distance from proximal border of middle phalangeal crease (Fig. 12.1).

Dejong and Platou (1967)

The extra crease concept among phalangeal distal creases was studied by these authors. They could define extra creases and also related them to sickle cell hemoglobinopathie.

Aue-Hauser's Formulation (1977)

This author gave a detailed account of the presence of extra-phalangeal crease. As reported by Cummins and Midlo (1943), Aue-Hauser also cited the total absence of phalangeal crease on one of the digits of hand. On the basis of above classification Lambson (1976) studied the extra crease displacement feature among phalangeal flexion creases (Fig. 12.3).

Rao (1980) studied metacarpo-phalangeal creases of Australian aborigines. His work was based on Okajima's classification of ring crease index on the middle finger.

Bali's Formulation (1980)

The author tackled this vexed problem of phalangeal flexion creases in two stages.

At stage one, instead of classifying crease the author resorted to classify the digits on the basis of phalangeal crease occurrence and non-occurrence at their respective sites, i.e., distal, middle and proximal of each digit of the hand.

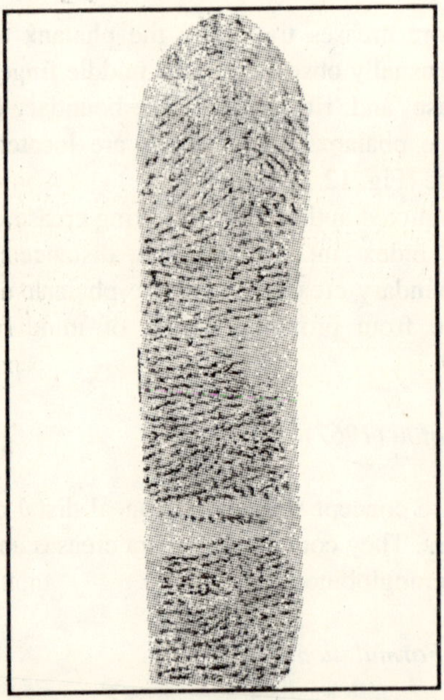

FIG. 12.2: Classification of phalangeal flexion creases (Cummins and Midlo, 1943)

Under the above-mentioned condition we are left with three probable chances of crease appearance on the individual phalanx. The crease may appear normally on distal, middle and proximal phalangeal crease sites. Or it may appear only at proximal and middle flexion sites or at proximal and distal flexion sites of the finger. The Third probability is of additional sites or extra crease sites.

On the basis of crease occurrence on the individual digit, the digit may be designated as 'Minus normal and extra' digit types.

In other words, a digit can be a 'minus' digit if it fails to carry phalangeal creases on normal three sites. The absence of the crease may be at one site or at two sites i.e., M(–) and M(=) conditions.

In normal conditions all flexion sites bear the creases at distal, middle and proximal flexion sites.

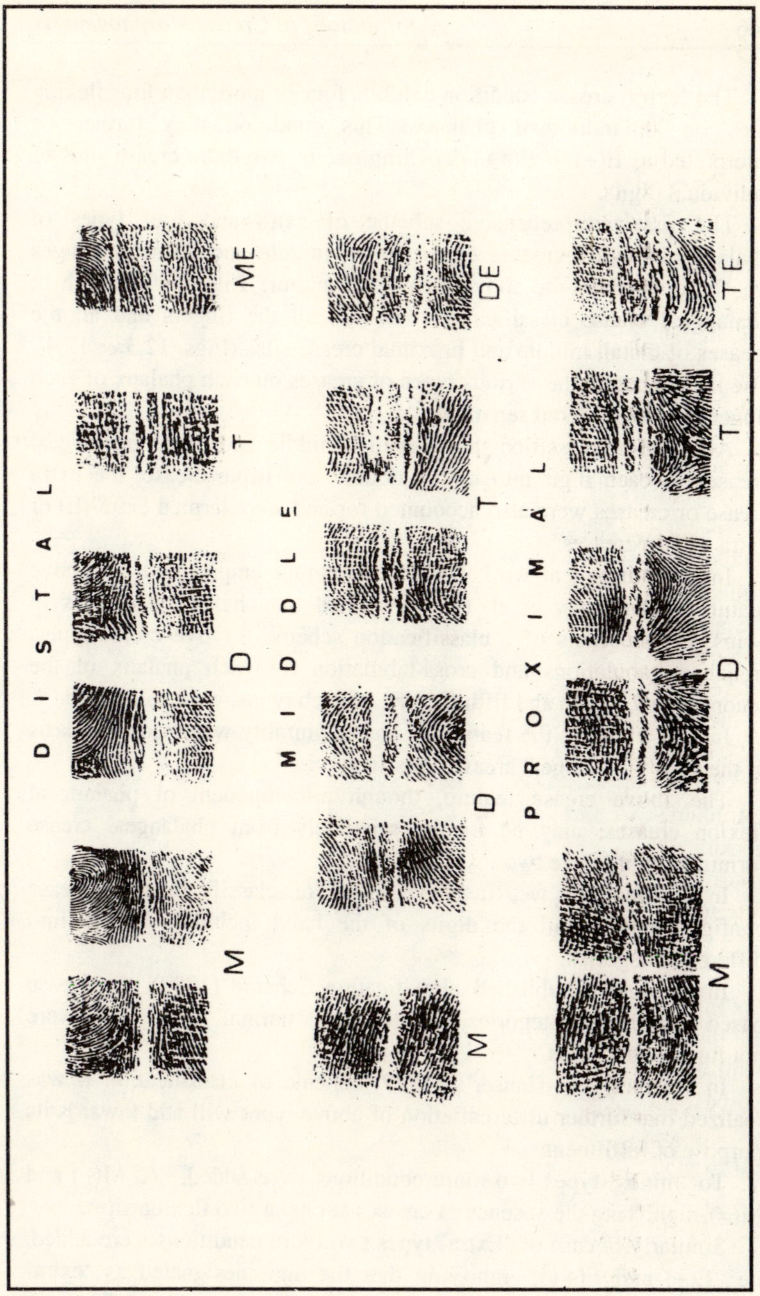

FIG. 12.3: Classification of interphalangeal flexion creases

The 'extra' crease condition exhibits four or more than four flexion sites on an individual phalanx. This condition may further be interpreted as E(+) or E(++) depicting one or two extra crease sites of individual digits.

The first comprehensive scheme of extra and four types of phalangeal flexion creases on proximal, middle and distal phalanges was introduced by the above-mentioned author. This breakthrough in phalangeal crease classification involved all the fingers and all the creases of distal, middle and proximal crease sites (Figs. 12.3 & 12.4). The incidences of the various types of creases on each phalanx of each finger were considered separately.

Aue-Hauser classified the proximal middle and distal phalangeal creases of each digit into mono, double and triple crease; the extra crease or creases were also accounted for and were termed extra (E) or extra + (E+) creases.

In her subsequent work (1980), the author emphasised the above feature. Aue-Hauser et al. (1978) studied the phalangeal creases in twins. On the basis of a classification scheme for five crease-types, frequency-tabulations and cross-tabulation for each phalanx of the second, third, fourth and fifth fingers, of each twins, were calculated.

Instead of form, the feature of crease plurality was made the basis of the above phalangeal crease classification.

The above crease feature, though a component of phalangeal flexion creases, may be treated separately from phalangeal crease formulation of 'stage two'.

In 'stage two' we, in fact, intend to classify various crease configurations of all the digits of the hand including thumb into different categories.

In previously published classification Scheme (1980), the crease based phalangeal categories, i.e., 'minus', 'normal' and 'extra' were not further sub-typed.

In view of Aue-Hauser's (1977) scheme of classification it was realized that further differentiation of above types will add towards its purpose of fulfilment.

To 'minus' types two more conditions were added, i.e., M(–) and M(=), signifying the absence of creases at one or two flexion sites.

Similarly in case of 'Extra' types two more conditions were added, i.e., E(+) and E(++), signifying that the digit designated as 'extra' crease type is also showing the number of these extra types. To avoid further complications their positional expression has deliberately been deleted.

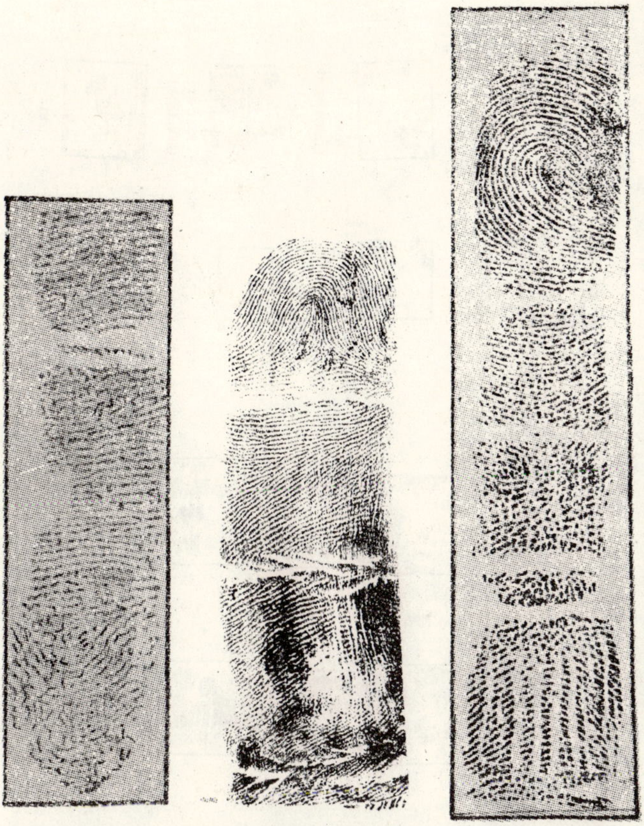

(a) Phalangeal flexion creases and digit types

FIG. 12.4: Formulation of phalangeal flexion creases base creases

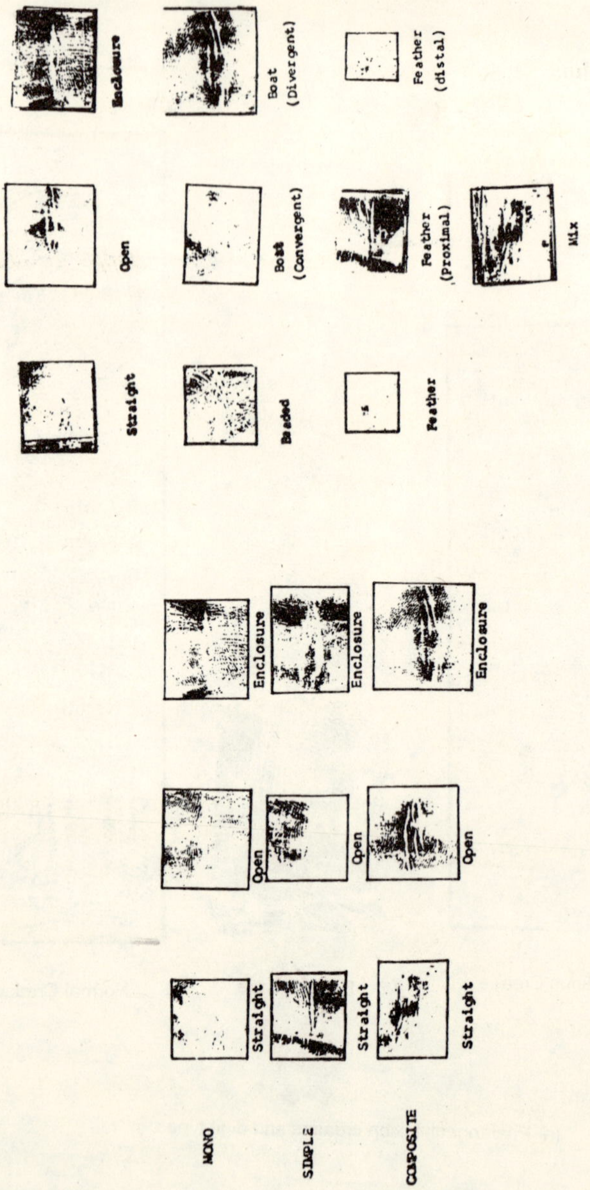

(b) Phalangeal flexion creases (Pattern types)

FIG. 12.4: Formulation of phalangeal flexion creases base creases (Bali 1980)

On the basis of crease number and the form of crease patterns, the phalangeal flexion creases are classified into three main types and seven sub-types.

According to the pattern, the phalangeal flexion creases can be divided into : straight type, beaded type, enclosure type, boat type, feather type, open type and mixed type (Figs. 12.4; 12.5 & 12.5a). The feather type can further be sub-divided into two sub-types, i.e., distal feather type and proximal feather type (Fig. 12.4). Similarly, the boat type of crease patterns may be divided into convergent boat types and divergent boat types (Fig. 12.4).

On the basis of the above crease types and their number on a particular phalangeal flexion site, the creases are classified into three main types :

1. Single phalangeal flexion crease (MPFC),
2. Simple phalangeal flexion crease (SPFC),
3. Composite phalangeal flexion crease (CPFC).

If a crease is represented by a single phalangeal pattern type the category is called Single Phalangeal Flexion Crease (Fig. 12.4).

When a phalangeal flexion crease site is represented by two or more than two of the same type of crease patterns the category is called Simple Phalangeal Flexion Crease (Fig. 12.4).

If the phalangeal flexion crease site is represented by two or more than two different crease types the category is called Composite Phalangeal Flexion Crease (Fig. 12.4).

For the purpose of classification, the composite crease take their nomenclature after basal or proximal crease type (Fig. 12.4). The composite creases take their classificatory nomenclature of the basal crease types, i.e., if beaded type of crease forms the base of the composite crease the category is called composite beaded phalangeal flexion crease.

Validity of the Formulation

Metacarpal phalangeal creases have been studied by Aue-Hauser and others. But the present classification is comprehensive and accommodates all digital creases including metatarsal phalangeal creases.

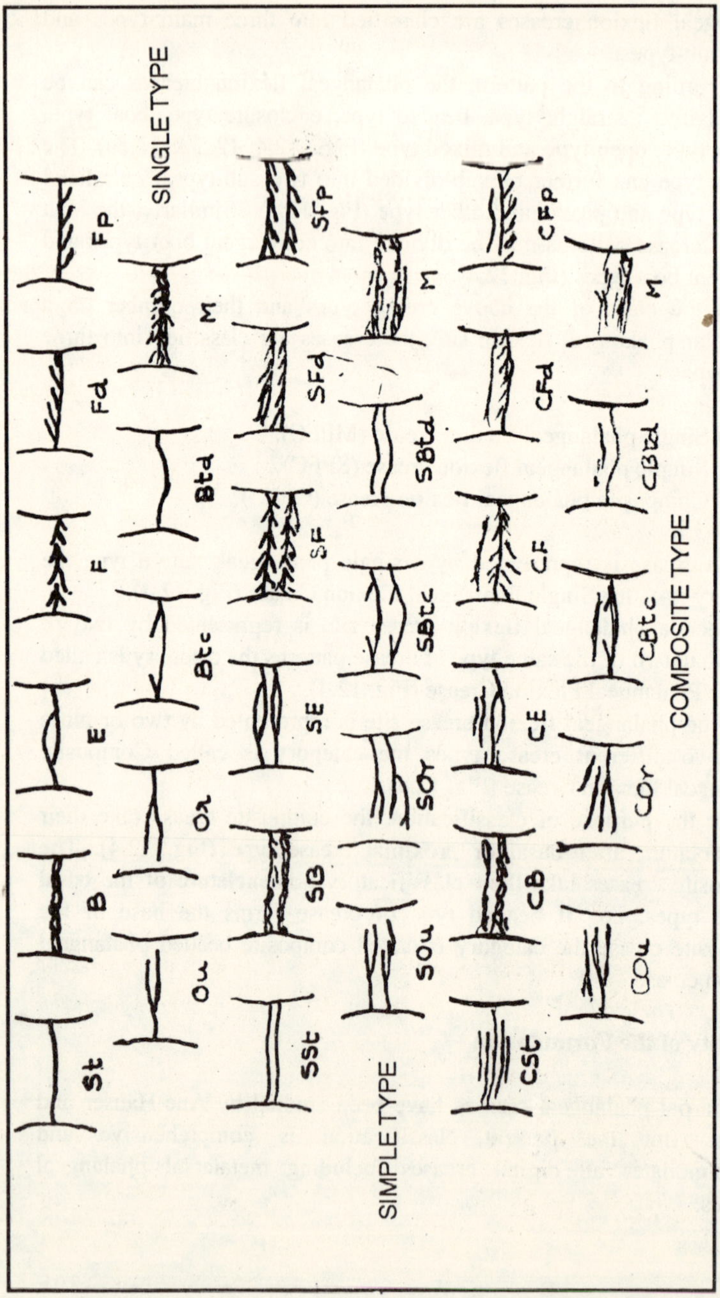

FIG. 12.5: Right hand: Phalangeal crease patterns
St-Straight, B-Beaded, E-Enclosure, F-Feather, Fd-Feather distal, Fp-Feather proximal, Ou-Open ulnar, Or-Open radial, Btc-Boat convergent, Btd-Boat divergent, M-Mixed

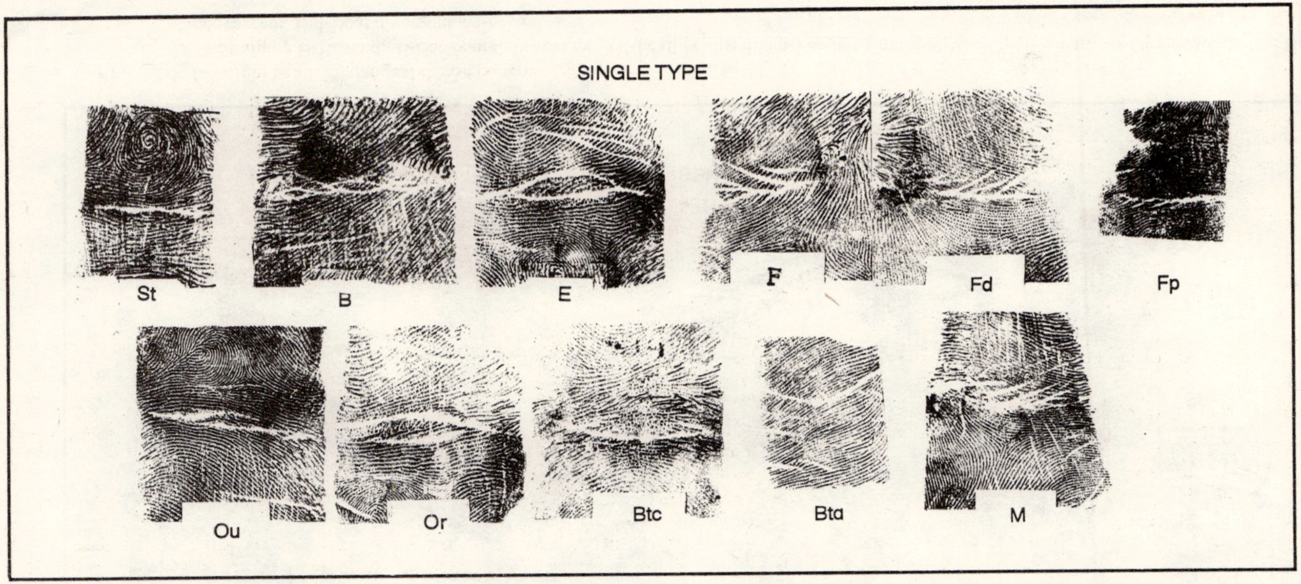

FIG. 12.5: (a) Right hand: Phalangeal crease patterns
St-Straight, B-Beaded, E-Enclosure, F-Feather, Fd-Feather distal, Fp-Feather proximal, Ou-Open ulnar, Or-Open radial, Btc-Boat convergent, Btd-Boat divergent, M-Mixed

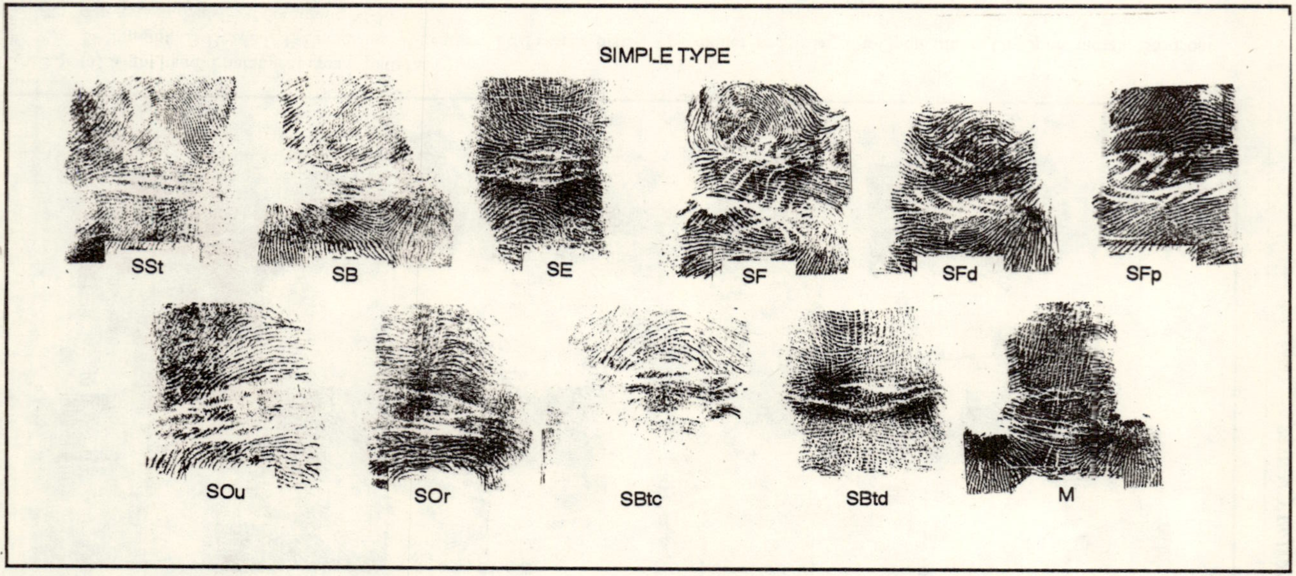

FIG. 12.5: (a) Right hand: Phalangeal crease patterns
St-Straight, B-Beaded, E-Enclosure, F-Feather, Fd-Feather distal, Fp-Feather proximal, Ou-Open ulnar, Or-Open radial, Btc-Boat convergent, Btd-Boat divergent, M-Mixed

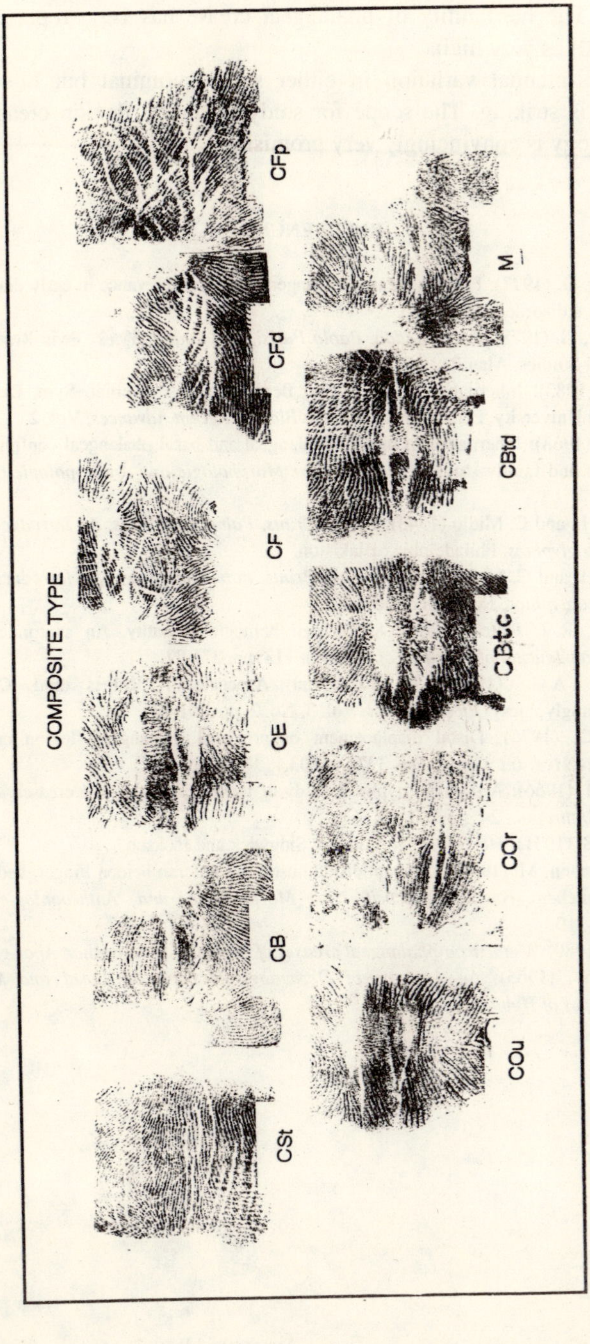

FIG. 12.5: (a) Right hand: Phalangeal crease patterns
St-Straight, B-Beaded, E-Enclosure, F-Feather, Fd-Feather distal, Fp-Feather proximal, Ou-Open ulnar, Or-Open radial, Btc-Boat convergent, Btd-Boat divergent, M-Mixed

The above formulation has been tried in populations, sexes and families. The heritability of phalangeal crease has been reported by Bali (1980) as very high.

The bi-manual variation in either sex is nominal but bi-sexual variation is striking. The scope for study of digital flexion creases in anthropology is convincingly very promising.

REFERENCES

Aue-Hauser, G. (1977): Flexion creases on fingers and their relevance in early diagnosis of mental disorders. (In press).

Aue-Hauser, G. (1978): *Luigi Gedda, Paolo Parisi, and Rudolf Wytek.* Twin Research : Clinical Studies. Alan R.

Bali, R.S. (1983): Inheritance of phalangeal flexion creases. Internat. Sym. Dermato. Punjabi University, Patiala, India. *Human Biology Recent Advances*, Vol. 2.

Basu, S.K. (1968): Inheritance of middle phalangeal and basal phalangeal configuration by twin and family studies. *Zeitscbrift fur Morphologie and Anthropologie* 60: pp. 85-99.

Cummins, H., and C. Midlo (1943): *Finger Prints, Palms, and Soles: An Introduction to Dermatoglyphics*, Philadelphia : Blakiston.

Cummins, H. and C. Midlo (1961): *Finger Prints, Palms and Soles: An Introduction to Dermatoglyphics*, New York: Dover.

Dejong, R., R.V. Platou (1967): Sickle cell hemoglobinopathy. An anatomic sign. *American Journal of Diseases of Children* 113: pp. 271-72.

de Wilde, A.G. (1980): Developmental Aspects of Ridges and Creases (Dermatoglyphics) *Oll. Anthropol.* Vol. 3, No. 2: pp. 201-10.

Lambson, G. (1976): Distal displacement of proximal phalangeal flexion creases. *Excerpta Med. Int. Congr. Ser.* 397 : p. 203.

Okajima, M. (1966): A dermatoglyphical study of metacarpophalangeal creases. *Am. J. Phys. Anthropol.*, 24: pp. 371-80.

Penrose, L.S. (1931): *Mental defect.* London: Sidgwick and Jackson.

Ploetz-Radmann, M. (1936): Die hautleistenmuster der unteren beiden Fingerglieder der menschilchen Hand. *Zeitscbrift fur Morphologie und Anthropologie*. 36: pp.281-310.

Rao, P.D. (1980): *Metacarpo-phalangeal creases of the palms of Australian Aborigines.*

Wasinski, W. (1965): *An Analysis of Dermatoglyphics on the Basal and Middle Phalanges of Human Fingers.*

13

TOE FLEXION CREASES

AMONG THE few reports on toe dermatoglyphics the work of Cummins and Midlo (1943), Takeya (1934), Newman (1936), Stiffen op. cit., Cummins and Midlo (1961), Hasebe (1918), Bhalla (1966), Bali (1963, 1967, 1973 and 1980) is worth mentioning.

The comparative study of finger and toe dermatoglyphics can reveal the genetic interdependence and the differential effect of their independent courses of evolutionary specialization (Bali, 1966, 1964).

There seems to be a general agreement that dermatoglyphic areas of foot and hand agree closely with the developmental sequences of foot and suggests that the factors that activate control and development of the terminal segments of the appendages are probably the same and both hand and foot grow together and increase with age.

The morphology of sole, according to Cummins & Midlo (1943), follows closely with that of palm and may be interpreted in the same way. It holds true for fingers and toes also. Newman (1936) has already given some dermatoglyphic correlation between the fingers and the toes of the same individuals.

It is widely known that correlations are highest between the characters effecting the same part, such as, pattern type, shape, direction and ridge count (Cummins, 1926, 1935). Correlation are lowest between non-corresponding parts of dermatoglyphic areas, i.e., toes and sole or palm and fingers, as compared to homologous parts, i.e., fingers and toes and palm and sole (MacArthur, 1938).

From the intra-individual relationship between the combined digits of hand and foot (Homolateral and heterolateral) it appears that there exists a positive correlation between the fingers and toe patterns in either sex. Thus, suggestive of the fact that both the dermatoglyphic regions may be controlled by a common set of factors, independent courses of specialization in evolution may have caused the differential trend of pattern reduction in toes and fingers. The delayed embryonic process in toes as compared with fingers could also be said to explain the re-capitulation of its phylogeny (Bali, 1968).

The objective of above discussion converges to a point that like dermal configurations, the toe crease patterns, too, conform topographically to the patterns of phalangeal flexion creases and are, thus, subject to identical methods of analysis.

As compared to other creases, the toe creases have been virtually neglected. As far as the review goes, there is hardly any reference of toe creases in the literature. The crease in general and toe creases in particular have failed to attract the attention of researchers.

In this volume attempt has been made to consolidate creases of all the areas and each area has been offered formulation technique and also the needed informations for initiating work in this field of anthropology.

It may be pointed out that digital creases of hands and feet show great departure from each other. Nevertheless, their typological conformity do not warrant a separate method of analysis.

Formulation of Toe Creases

It appears that the present formulation on toe creases is going to by a maiden attempt. The individual toe shows a marked departure of shape and size in comparison to its counterpart in finger.

The digital reduction in the size of toes has subsequently resulted into reduction of the flexion crease sites in each toe.

Greater toe or the first digit predominantly shows one flexion site that is proximal digital site. Occasionally the digit may show one or two straight creases or lines running across the middle of the digit are the sites for vestigeal and rudimentary types.

On the second and third digits, i.e., adjoining to the anatomical axis, the digital flexion crease sites are fully developed and crease configuration, to a greater extent, resembles with phalanges of the hand. But with regards to their number of flexion sites, they seldom agree with their counterpart in hands.

In toes the normal occurrence of crease site is of two, i.e., proximal and middle, crease flexion sites. The distal crease site is lost in process of reduction of digits of the foot. In certain digits we do find the rudimentary lines, perhaps representing vestigeal distal crease sites. Toes with two extra creases have also been cited.

On the basis of flexion crease site number, we can divide or classify digits into three types: 'minus', 'normal' and 'extra' digital

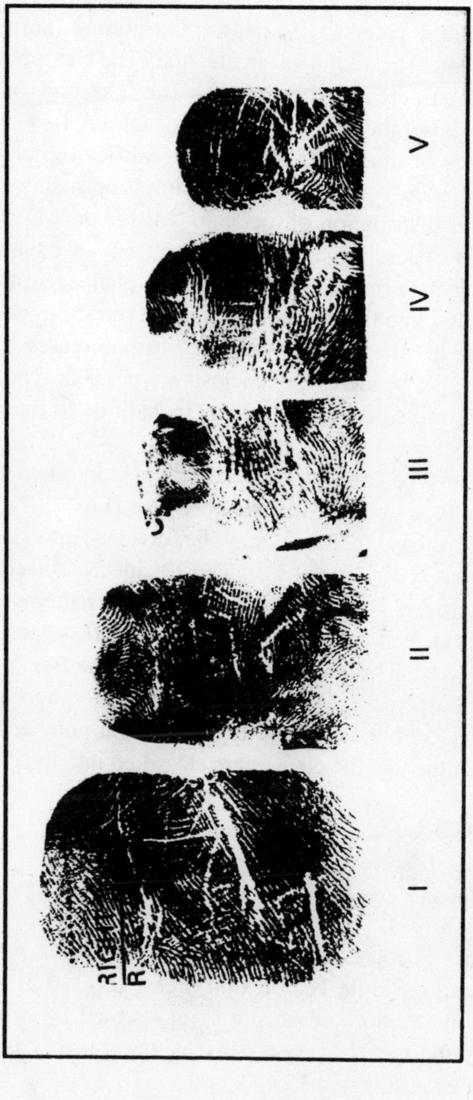

FIG. 13.1: Toe flexion creases

categories. The probability of occurrence of the third flexion site that is extra flexion crease of distal flexion crease site is much low in greater toe and small toe.

Under 'minus' category, i.e., lower to normal (normal for toes is two flexion sites) is found in greater toe. The rest of the toes show normal flexion crease sites (two). The second and third toes occasionally show the 'extra' crease or distal crease site (Figs. 13.1). The occurrence of three sites for phalangeal flexion crease is normal but in case of toes, occurrence of two sites is normal.

The further distribution of toes into 'M' (–) or 'M' (=) and 'E' (+) or 'E' (++) is of less application. On the basis of crease number and form of crease patterns, the toe creases like phalangeal flexion creases can be classified into three main types and seven sub-types.

According to the pattern, the toe flexion creases can be divided into straight type, beaded type, enclosure type, boat type, feather type, open type and mixed type (Fig. 13.2), in addition to flare type (only in toes).

The feather type can further be sub-divided into two sub-types i.e., distal feather type and proximal feather type (Fig. 13.2). Similarly the boat type of crease patterns may be divided into convergent and divergent boat types (Fig. 13.2). The incidence of convergent boat type of patterns is rare in toes. Sometimes, patterns in toes attain miniature form. Among toe crease patterns there appears an inflex of longitudinal lines. These lines flare out from the flexion site giving a star like shape to crease. This pattern is found only in toes (Flare type).

On the basis of above crease types and their number on a particular flexion site of the toe, the creases are classified into three main types:

1. Single Toe Flexion Crease
2. Simple Toe Flexion Crease
3. Composite Toe Flexion Crease

If a crease is represented by a single phalangeal pattern type, the category is called Single Toe Flexion Crease (Fig. 13.2).

When a toe flexion crease site is represented by two or more than two of the same type of crease patterns, the category is called Simple Toe Flexion Crease (Fig. 13.2).

If the toe flexion crease site is represented by two or more than two different crease types, the category is called Composite Toe Flexion Crease (Fig. 13.2).

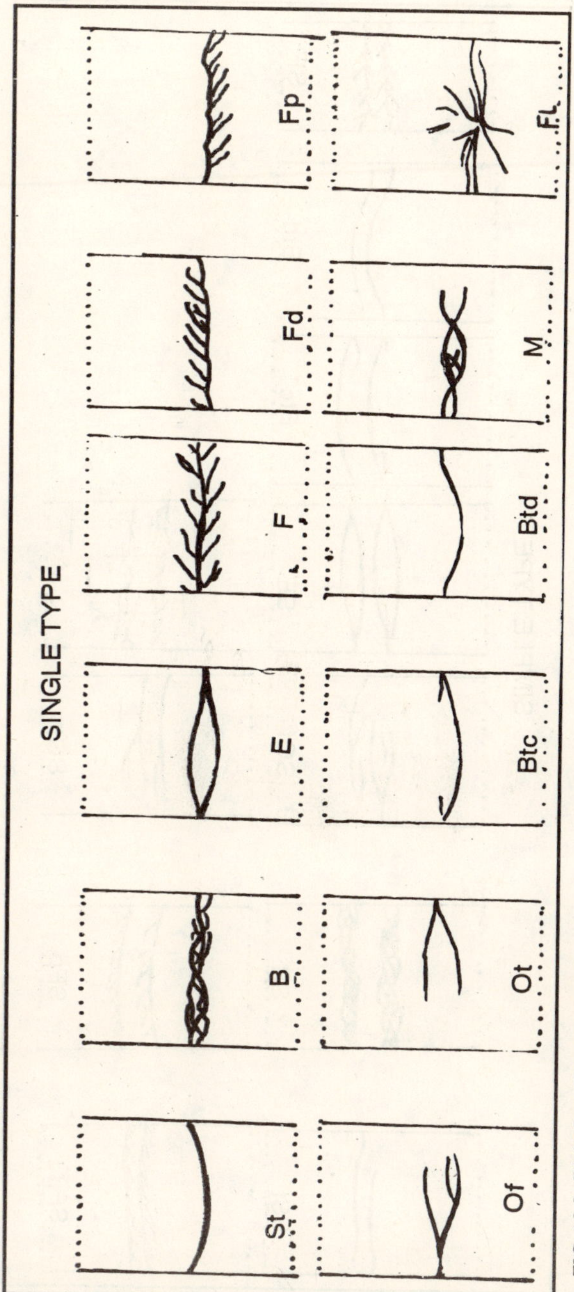

FIG. 13.2: Right foot: Toe crease patterns

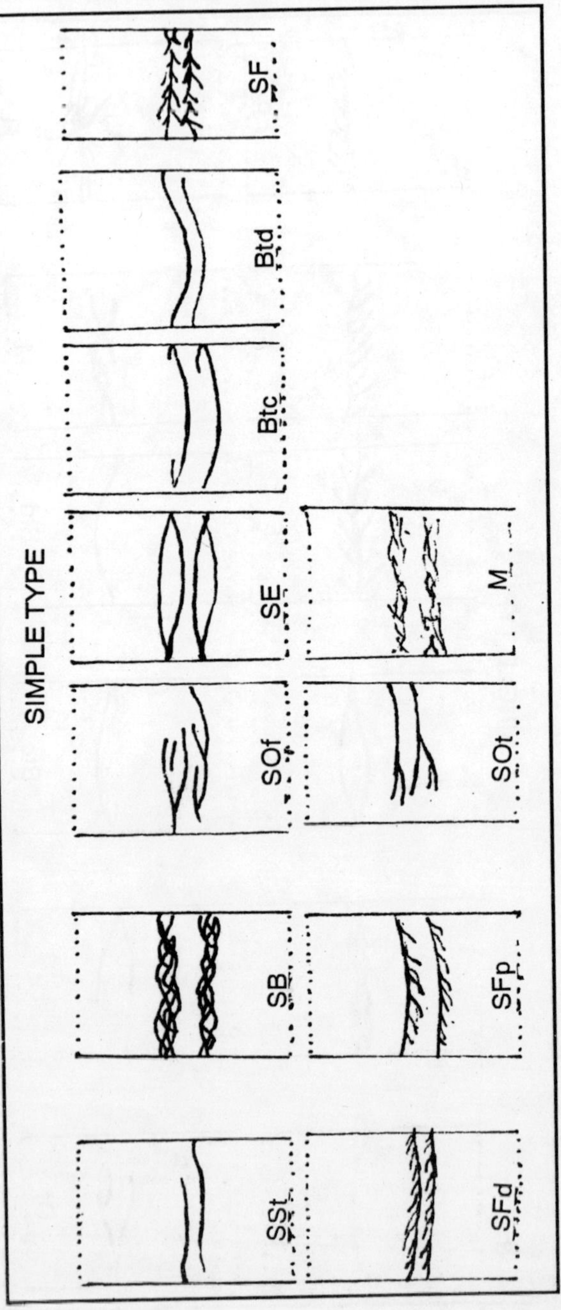

FIG. 13.2: Right foot: Toe crease patterns

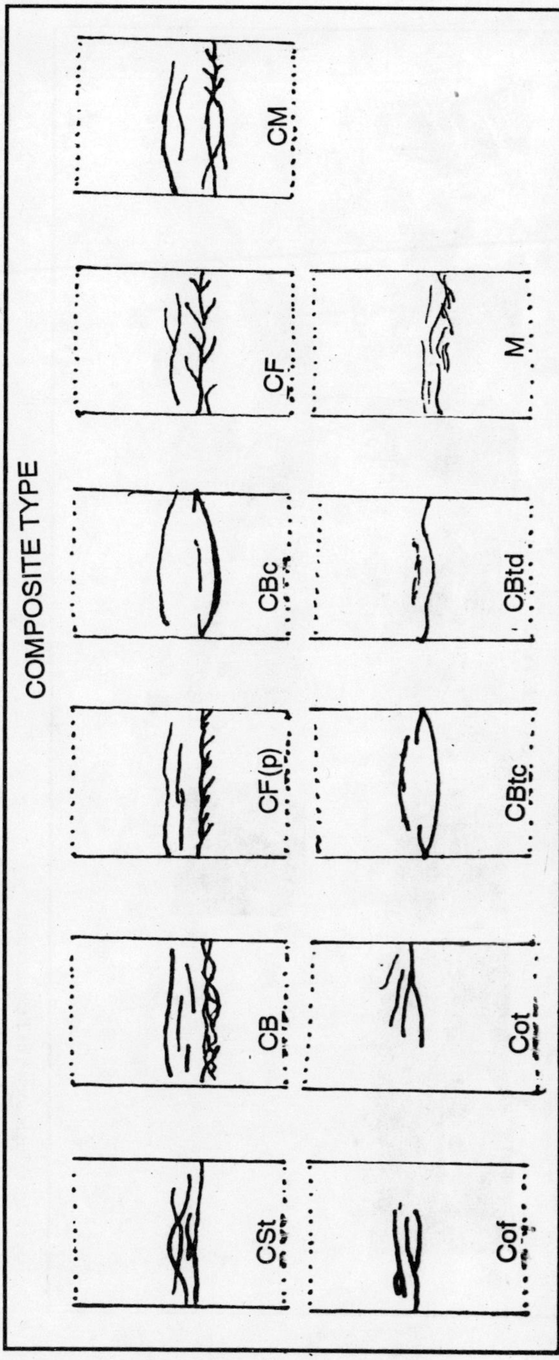

FIG. 13.2: Right foot: Toe crease patterns

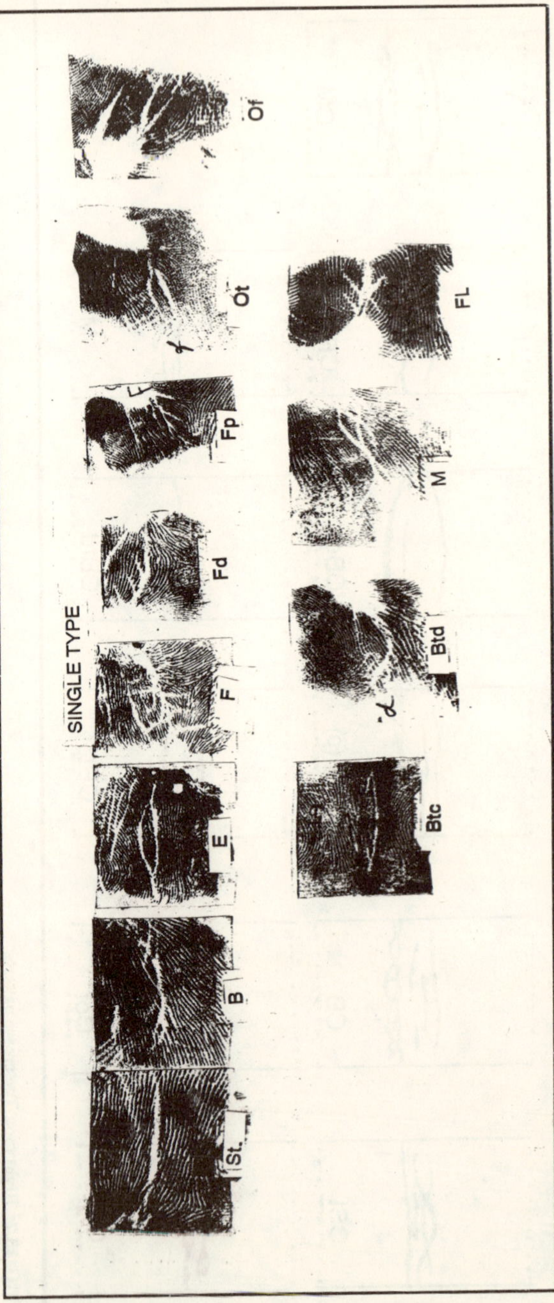

FIG. 13.2: (a) Right foot: Toe flexion crease
S-Straight, B-Beaded, E-Enclosure,, F-Feather, Fd-Feather distal, Fp-Feather proximal, Of-Open fibular, Ot-Open tibial, Btc-Boat convergent, Btd-Boat divergent, M-Mixed, Fl-Flare

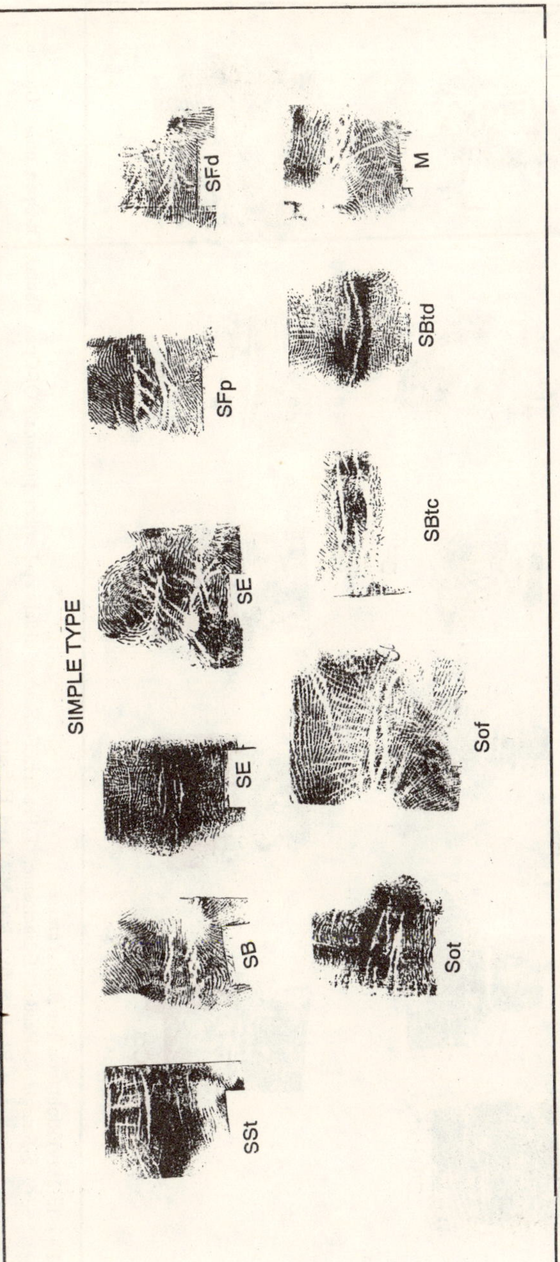

FIG. 13.2: (a) Right foot: Toe flexion crease
S-Straight, B-Beaded, E-Enclosure,, F-Feather, Fd-Feather distal, Fp-Feather proximal, Of-Open fibular, Ot-Open tibial, Btc-Boat convergent, Btd-Boat divergent, M-Mixed, Fl-Flare

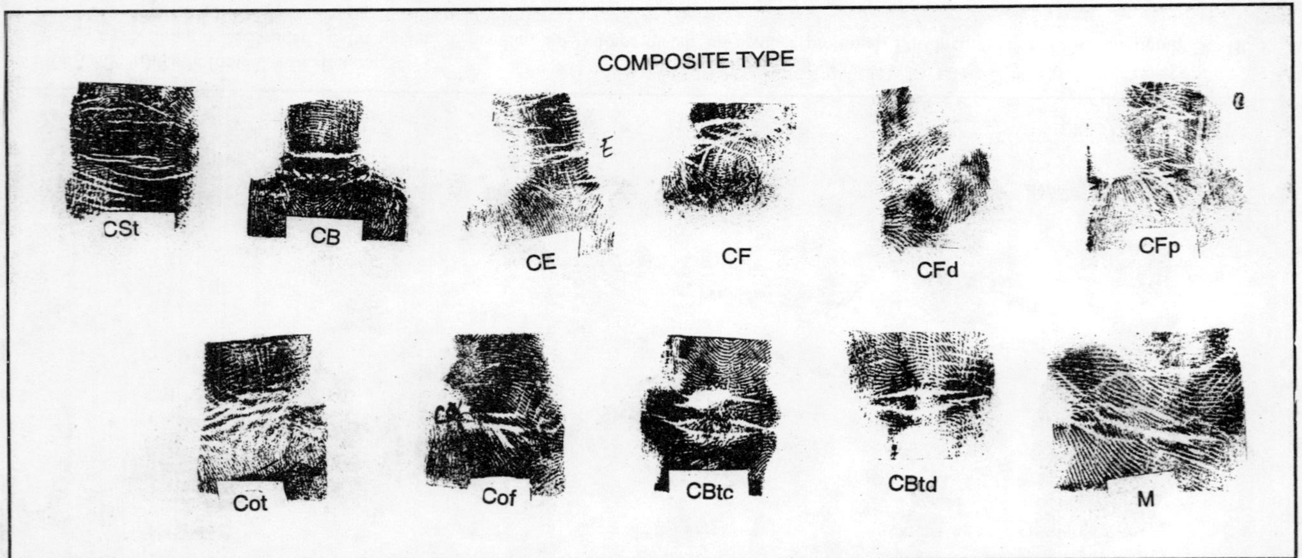

FIG. 13.2: (a) Right foot: Toe flexion crease
S-Straight, B-Beaded, E-Enclosure,, F-Feather, Fd-Feather distal, Fp-Feather proximal, Of-Open fibular, Ot-Open tibial, Btc-Boat convergent, Btd-Boat divergent, M-Mixed, Fl-Flare

For the purpose of further classification, the composite crease take their nomenclature after basal or proximal crease types (Fig. 13.2a).

Sub-types of Toe Flexion Crease

To accommodate all types of flexion creases occurring on different sites of the toes, the author proposed a binominal classificatory system of crease formulation on the same line as given under phalangeal crease classification (Figs. 13.2 & 13.2a).

As sated above the identical method of crease analysis is suitable for both, phalangeal flexion creases of the hands and flexion creases of the toes.

The above configurational types of crease patterns in case of toes show marked reduction, both in size and shape. In case of phalanges of the hand including the thumb the proximal crease site show higher frequency of composite types with enclosure, feather, boat and beaded types. In case of toes the composite patterns show much low frequency and, in shape, the most frequent form is straight, parallel, open or feather (proximal) types. The first toe exhibits beaded, enclosure or open types under a single category.

In case of toes, most of the boat and enclosure types have been transformed into open type of crease pattern.

The differential mode of occurrence of crease patterns shows agreement to a certain extent with the distribution of dermatoglyphic patterns. The frequency of whorls is much higher on II and III digits and that of arches on V digit. A similar is the case with crease patterns, the frequency of developed patterns, i.e., enclosure boat and feather type, is much higher on II and III toes as compared to the other toes.

In terms of three-fold expression of toe crease types, i.e., single, simple and composite, the formulation shows complete agreement with phalangeal creases. The incidence of simple and single creases is on higher side as compared to phalangeal creases.

REFERENCES

Bali, R.S. (1963): Symmetrical and asymmetrical occurrence of toe patterns of Kashmiri Muslims. *The Anthropologist* 10(1-2): pp. 49-54.

Bali, R.S. (1964): *Toe Dermatoglyphics-Inheritance & Comparison with the finger ball patterns*. Ph.D. Thesis, Delhi University, Delhi.

Bali, R.S. (1966): Some Genetic Observations on Dermatoglyphic Traits. *Internat. Symposium on Dermatoglyphics*, Delhi, India.

Bali, R.S. (1967): Heritable behaviour of dermal configurations of toes in relation to sex. *Acta Geneticae Medicae et Gemellologiae* 16: pp. 422-28.

Bali, R.S. (1968): Genetic inter-correlation between finger and toe patterns. *Zeitschrift fur Morphologie und Anthropologie* 59(3): pp. 244-72.

Bali, R.S. (1973): Correlation study between palmar creases, Schizophenia, Leprosy and Tuberculosis: IXth Internat. Congr. Anthrop. & Ethno. Sciences, Chicago, U.S.A.

Bali, R.S. (1983): Inheritance of phalangeal Flexion creases, *Human Biology Recent Advances*, Vol. 2, (Proc. Internat. Sym., Punjabi University).

Bhalla, V.C. (1966): Inheritance of loop patterns on Human Toes with a Short Note on a Comparative Study of Toe and Foot Prints. *Internat. Sym. on Dermato.*, Delhi, India.

Cummins, H. (1926): Epidermal-ridge configurations in developmental defects, with particular reference to the ontogenetic factors which condition ridge direction. *American Journal of Anatomy* 38(1): pp. 89-151.

Cummins, H. (1935): Morphology of the palmar hypothenar dermatoglyphics in man. *Human Biology* 7(1): pp. 1-23.

Cummins, H. (1935a): Dermatoglyphics in Eskimos from Point Barrow. *American Journal of Physical Anthropology* 20(1): pp. 13-17.

Cummins, H., C. Midlo (1943): *Finger Prints, Palms and Soles: An Introduction to Dermatoglyphics*. Philadelphia : Blakiston.

Cummins, H. and C. Midlo (1961): *Finger Prints, Palms and Soles: An Introduction to Dermatoglyphics*. New York, Dovar.

Hasebe, K. (1918): Uber das hautleistensystem der Vola und planta der Japaner und Aino. *Ark. Anat. Inst. Sendai* 1: pp. 13-88.

MacArthur, J.W. (1938): Reliability of dermatoglyphics in twin diagnosis. *Human Biology* 10(1): pp. 12-35.

Newman, M.T. (1936): A comparative study of finger prints and toe prints. *Human Biology* 8(4): pp. 531-52.

Takeya, S. (1934): Uber die Hautleistenfigur der Planta der Chinesen. *Journal of Oriental Medicine* 20: pp. 54-58 and pp. 495-523.

14

INHERITANCE OF PALMAR CREASES

THE IMPORTANCE of genetics in general among the biological and medical sciences is well-known, but the present interest and activity in human genetics has perhaps reached a peak never attained before. The study of genetics of dermatoglyphics and creases in particular stands a chance of being greatly enriched by researches on man.

It is true that the genetics of dermatoglyphics is hampered by the multi-factorial hereditary mechanism, thus causing variability within and among different patterns. In the present study, the observations converge upon the genetic particularities of crease traits as compared to the other morphological traits.

Like dermatoglyphics crease features are free from any paratypic influences and are not subject to age and sex influence (excepting the size and splits) as the differentiation of the features occurs during the first month of intra-uterine life and the certain characteristics of crease patterns remain constant throughout the life-span of an individual. Further, these features being free from assortative mating and not affected by genetic drift could be usefully employed for the study of population genetics.

If it is ever possible to know the genetic basis of all the human traits and in case we are able to grade them, it could be seen that the dermatoglyphic traits bridge the gap between the two schools of thought, that is the 'sero-monogenetic' and the 'phenotypic'.

While, advocating the merit of creases as partial polymorphic group of traits we mean that creases are sort of a genetic link between phenotypically stable and unstable human traits.

The study of inheritance of fluxion crease traits has greatly been enriched, but the obscurity in regard to their mode of transmission has not so far been removed. The inheritance of crease, like the inheritance of dermatoglyphic traits, is complicated by the multi-factorial hereditary mechanism, thus causing variability within and among the crease configurations.

On the formulation of palmar creases, Bali and Chaube (1971) investigated family and twin data to establish the heritability of palmar creases. They also investigated the inheritance of sub-type of creases. Chaube (1971) in his subsequent study confirmed the above results. Mishra (1980) also made observations on the study of palmar crease inheritance. The above study on palmar crease heritability embraces all the creases of the palm. As compared to single radial base crease the heritability of double and triple radial base crease is more convincingly established.

Familial Study of Crease Inheritance

The transmission of crease features through parents to their offspring is best known through familial data. Stiffen (1953) investigated 250 family members and inferred that the trait behaves as a Mendalian dominant. Portius (1937) advocated for the recessiveness of the trait. Becker (1952), Gruneberg (1928), Takanushi (1942) and Tillner (1956) studied simian crease inheritance through families and twins. Kimura and Hagiya (1958) investigated the inheritance of 'M figure' through family and twin data.

But for Kimura and above workers' main stress was on simian crease. The inheritance of sydney crease was carried out by Purvis-Smith and Menser (1968).

Advantages of Crease Features for the Study of Inheritance

Creases like dermatoglyphics are polygenic in nature. They show moderate to high heritability levels. With respect to age and sex, creases are less firm but some of their features remain constant through out the life span of an individual. Further, crease features are free from assortative mating and are not affected by genetic drift. Thus, indicating differential polymorphism among various morphological traits. In light of this fact we can provide group status to these morphogenic traits. By group status, the author means:

1. The group of traits with known mode of inheritance such as sero-genetic or sero-monogenetic traits.
2. Those traits which are polymorphic but phenotypically stable. In this group we can easily fit dermatoglyphic traits.
3. The third category is of those traits which are polymorphic but

phenotypically less stable, we can easily fit creases into this group.

4. Those traits which are polymorphic and phenotypically unstable can be accommodated in this group (other morphological variables).

To give an idea about the heritable behaviour of creases under fresh crease formulation of Bali and Chaube (1971) it is desirable to reproduce Tables as under.

The incidence of palmar flexion crease on the individual palm of the offspring born of respective parents show their heritable significance. The study is based on the family data (130 families, with two generations) derived from the homogenous population of Brahmins.

TABLE 14.1: Distribution of palmar flexion creases among father and offspring:

TABLE 14.1a: Father's right hand *vs* children's right hand

Children's right hand	Father's right hand			
	SRBC	DRBC	TRBC	Total
Present	20	294	21	335
Absent	25	61	13	99

$\chi^2 = 34.23$, C = 0.27, df = 2, P = ≤ .001

TABLE 14.1b: Father's right hand *vs* children's left hand

Children's left hand	Father's right hand			
	SRBC	DRBC	TRBC	Total
Present	15	283	13	311
Absent	30	72	21	123

$\chi^2 = 59.32$, C = 0.35, df = 2, P = ≤ .001

TABLE 14.1c: Father's left hand *vs* children's right hand

Children's right hand	Father's left hand			
	SRBC	DRBC	TRBC	Total
Present	16	285	18	319
Absent	35	69	11	115

$\chi^2 = 55.51$, C = 0.32, df = 2, P = ≤ .001

TABLE 14.1d: Father's left hand *vs* children's left hand

Children's left hand	Father's left hand			
	SRBC	DRBC	TRBC	Total
Present	16	287	14	317
Absent	35	67	15	117

$\chi^2 = 62.34$, C = 0.35, df = 2, P = ≤ .001

It could be seen from the Table 14.1a, b, c, d that offspring born of those fathers having single, double and triple radial base creases also exhibit the same types on their respective palms. The hetero-lateral mode of crease expression in parents and offspring have also been considered (Table 14.1a and 14.1b) the results are significant ($\chi^2 = 34.23$, C = 0.27, df = 2, P = ≤ .001, $\chi^2 = 59.32$, C = 0.35, df = 2, P = ≤ .001). Similar significant results are exhibited in Table 14.1c and 14.1d ($\chi^2 = 55.51$, C = 0.32, df = 2, P = ≤ .001, $\chi^2 = 62.34$, C = 0.35, df = 2, P = ≤ .001).

TABLE 14.2: Distribution of palmar flexion creases among mothers and offspring:

TABLE 14.2a: Mother's right hand *vs* children's right hand

Children's right hand	Mother's right hand			
	SRBC	DRBC	TRBC	Total
Present	32	235	31	298
Absent	66	37	33	136

$\chi^2 = 106.87$, C = 0.44, df = 2, P = ≤ .001

TABLE 14.2b: Mother's right hand *vs* children's left hand

Children's left hand	Mother's right hand			
	SRBC	DRBC	TRBC	Total
Present	31	234	28	293
Absent	67	38	36	141

$\chi^2 = 116.22$, C = 0.46, df = 2, P = ≤ .001

TABLE 14.2c: Mother's left hand *vs* children's right hand

Children's right hand	Mother's left hand			
	SRBC	DRBC	TRBC	Total
Present	28	232	27	287
Absent	72	42	33	147

$\chi^2 = 139.48$, C = 0.49, df = 2, P = ≤ .001

TABLE 14.2d: Mother's left hand *vs* children's left hand

Children's left hand	Mother's left hand			
	SRBC	DRBC	TRBC	Total
Present	36	243	26	305
Absent	64	31	34	129

$\chi^2 = 119.16$, C = 0.46, df = 2, P = ≤ .001

The transmission of these creases from mother to her offspring show significant result (Table 14.2a, b, $\chi^2 = 106.87$, C = 0.44, df = 2, P = ≤ .001, $\chi^2 = 116.22$, C = 0.46, df = 2, P = ≤ .001) Mother's left hand versus children's left and right hand (Table 14.2c and 14.2d $\chi^2 = 139.48$, C = 0.49, df = 2, P = ≤ .001, $\chi^2 = 119.16$, C = 0.46, df = 2, P = ≤ .001) exhibits significant resemblance.

The heritability of above crease traits, from Table 14.3, is further confirmed through the study of twins (15 MZ + 10 DZ).

The recent work of Khatoon (1986) on twins and reliability of creases in twin zygosity is an extension of the work carried out by the early workers. The author based her study on twin and family data. The crease classification was after Bali and Chaube (1971). Out of hundred pairs of twins, 19 were diagnosed as MZ, 62 DZ (like sex) and 19 as DZ (unlike sex).

TABLE 14.3: Concordance and discordance among MZ and DZ twins

(In percentage)

Twins	Concordance		Discordance		Right + Left	
	Right	Left	Right	Left	Concordance	Discordance
MZ	100	80	0	20	90	10
DZ	60	70	40	30	65	35

The concordance and discordance among MZ and DZ twins in respect to transverse palmar creases are 76.31 and 23.68 per cent, respectively. The like sex group of DZ twins show 62.09 per cent as concordance and in 37.90 per cent discordance. In case of unlike sex the concordance was 57.89 and discordance 42.10 per cent.

Inheritance of Longitudinal Creases

The classification of longitudinal creases of the palm are based on independent criteria. It is, therefore, natural to deal with their heritability under separate heading.

Through the system of parental combinations the affinity between parents and their offspring is investigated. The offspring form of different parental combinations show closer association with their parents.

Eswaraiah (1977) investigated longitudinal palmar creases from the standpoint of inheritance and found the trait as heritable.

Khatoon (1986) studied the inheritance of longitudinal creases on the basis of twin and family data.

The family data was treated on parental combination and offsprings born of these combinations were associated with their parents.

The concordance and discordance among MZ twins was 81.57 and 18.43 per cent, respectively.

The concordance and discordance among DZ twins (like sex) in respect to longitudinal palmar creases was 61.29 and 38.71 per cent, respectively. Among DZ, unlike twins, the concordance was 55.26 per cent and discordance 44.47 per cent.

The first study towards establishing heritability of longitudinal crease through twins was of Khatoon.

The inheritance of single carpal base crease and double carpal base crease shows convincing results but in case of triple carpal base creases the results are not much convincing. This may be because of the fact that frequency of the trait under discussion is very low.

In general the transmission of transverse and longitudinal creases from parents to their offspring show significant evidences of heritability. To conclude the above discussion it may be stated that palmar creases (transverse and longitudinal) are heritable traits, and can usefully be employed in complex population studies.

REFERENCES

Bali, R.S. and Ramesh Chaube (1971) : On the formulation of palmar creases. *Z. Morph. Anthrop.*, 63; p. 121.

Becker, E. (1952) : *Zur Verebung der Vierfingerfurche*. Homo, 3 : pp. 82-85.

Chaube, R. (1971) : *The Study of Palmar Flexion Creases — Inheritance and Correlation with schizophrenic patients*. Thesis submitted in fulfilment of the requirements for the degree of Ph.D., Saugar University, Sagar.

Eswaraiah, G. (1977) : *Palmar Creases and Diseases*. Thesis submitted in fulfilment of the requirement for the degree of Ph.D., Saugar University, Sagar.

Eswaraiah, G. (1977a) : *Palmar Flexion Creases of Muslims and their Symmetrical Occurrence* (R/L Combination), *Indian Anthropologist*.

Gruneberg, H. (1928) : Die verebung der menschlichen Tastfiguren. *Zeitschrift fur Induktiv Abstammungs und Vererbungslebre*. 46 : pp. 285-310.

Khatoon, S. (1986): Study of twins and Reliability of Creases in Twin Zygosity Diagnosis Ph.D. Thesis, Saugar University, Sagar.

Kimura, K. and Hagiya (1958) : A study of palmar creases in Ainus. *Jinruigaku Zassi*. 76 : pp. 60-74.

Mishra, R. (1980) : Inheritance of palmar creases. *Internat. Sym. Dermato.*, Punjabi University, Patiala, India.

Portius, W. (1937) : Beitrag zur Frage der Erblichkeit der vierfingerfurche. *Zeitschrift fur Morphologie und Anthropologie*. 36 : pp. 382-90.

Purvis-Smith, S.G. and M.A. Menser (1968) : Dermatoglyphics in adults with congenital rubella. *Lancet* 2 : pp. 141-43.

Stiffen, C. (1953) : *Zur Haufigkeit und verebung der vierfingerfurche*. Homo, 4, Band, 3 heft, pp. 126-39.

Takanushi, T. (1942): *Deux ou Trois observations sur lo genetique des dermatoglyphics digito-palmaires jinruigaku Zassbi* 52(7): pp. 303-20.

Tillner, I. (1956) : Die vierfingerfurche in Beziehung zum verlaug der handleisten. *Anthrop. Anzeiger*. 22 : pp. 260-76.

15

INHERITANCE OF PLANTAR CREASES

THE FRICTION ridges have played a vital part in Primate evolution in as far as their functional usage is considered. It is more so in view of the fact that the anatomical part of the body bearing the dermatoglyphic characters (viz., the hands and feet) have undergone a significant change in their mode of operation in the course of evolution in man. The relative complexity of patterns in different regions, as such, be counted as a reflection of the extent of evolutionary modification undergone in different regions. Subsequently in the total crease analysis of various regions of the human body as a whole the problem of evolution *vis-a-vis* pattern complexity provides the actual field for an understanding of the genetic significance of creases as a morphological variable in man.

As compared to palmar creases the work on plantar creases is in paucity. But for the work of Patten (1953), Nokiela (1972), Schenk and Patzer (1959) and Schauman and Alter (1976) we are left with very few references in this field for citation. Penrose (op. cit. Alter, 1976) studied the inheritance of sandal crease in sole. The author also reported the clinical significance of sandal crease.

It is a known fact that proper crease formulation has a vital role to play for making the basis of all future studies. In view of this, Bali and Mishra (1978) introduced a three-fold classification of plantar creases. These authors have tried to show the element of genetic unity among the various types. While establishing the validity of above given formulation, the work on families and twins was undertaken by these workers to show the trend of plantar crease inheritance.

Mishra (1979) independently investigated plantar creases from the standpoint of inheritance. On the basis of three-fold plantar crease classification, he arrived at the conclusion that plantar creases like palmar creases are heritable traits. The inheritance of plantar crease traits was studied with the help of twins and familial data (130 families with two generations).

TABLE 15.1: Distribution of plantar creases among the child's right foot born of parental combination having isopedal feet

Sl. No.	Parental combination P×M	No. of families		Male Children			Female Children			Total			Grand Total
				SMBC	DMBC	TMBC	SMBC	DMBC	TMBC	SMBC	DMBC	TMBC	
1.	SMBC × SMBC	20	Ab.	14	12	0	13	13	0	27	25	0	52
			Pc.	51.85	48.00	0.00	48.14	52.00	0.00	51.92	48.07	0	99.99
2.	DMBC × DMBC	18	Ab.	12	13	0	13	12	1	25	25	1	51
			Pc.	48.00	52.00	0.00	52.00	48.00	100.00	49.01	49.01	1.96	99.98
3.	TMBC × TMBC	0	Ab.	—	—	—	—	—	—	—	—	—	—
			Pc.	—	—	—	—	—	—	—	—	—	—

TABLE 15.2: Distribution of plantar creases among the child's left foot born of parental combination having Isopedal feet

Sl. No.	Parental combination F×M	No. of families		Male Children			Female Children			Total			Grand Total
				SMBC	DMBC	TMBC	SMBC	DMBC	TMBC	SMBC	DMBC	TMBC	
1.	SMBC × SMBC	20	Ab.	12	15	0	13	12	0	25	27	0	52
			Pc.	48.00	55	0	52.00	44.44	0	48.07	51.92	0	99.99
2.	DMBC × DMBC	18	Ab.	13	13	1	12	13	0	25	26	1	52
			Pc.	52.00	50.00	100.00	48.00	50.00		48.07	50.00	1.92	99.99
3.	TMBC × TMBC	0	Ab.	—	—	—	—	—	—	—	—	—	—
			Pc.	—	—	—	—	—	—	—	—	—	—

The children born of parents having similar trait on all four feet where referred as having isopedal feet. Offspring with isopedal feet showed greater affinity with their parents. On the basis of similarity the three similar feet or two similar feet of parents were compared with their offspring having similar condition on their feet. The relationship showed closer association between parents and their offspring (Tables 15.1 & 15.2).

Valotzkoy (1936) expresses pleotropy of like pattern on both hands as genetically governed trait. The isopedal relationship between parents and offspring is a useful index of plantar crease inheritance. The frequency of a single medial and double medial base creases shows heritable transmission while, triple medial base crease do not indicate such a trend.

On the basis of various parental combinations and offspring born of these combinations, it could be concluded that plantar crease traits are polygenic in nature and their inheritance is free of sex influence.

The homolateral and heterolateral affinities between parents and offspring appear to be real.

Mishra (1979) studied plantar crease inheritance through several possible parental combinations. The homolateral and heterolateral consideration between parents and offspring was to find out the bilateral heritable trend of pattern expression.

The study of MZ and DZ twins conclusively establishes that plantar creases are heritable traits but obscurity regarding their mode of transmission remains as such (Table 15.3).

TABLE 15.3: Heritability estimate among MZ and DZ twins

Trait	Twins	Prec. Conc.		Herita.	Estimate	Total for both feet
		Right	Left	Right	Left	
Plantar	MZ	80.00	80.00	0.400	0.400	0.800
Creases	DZ	66.66	66.66			

Heritable estimate, i.e., percentage of variations within population, was considered by the above-quoted author through Rife's formula (1959)

$$H = \frac{(CI - CF)}{(100 - CF)},$$

where it stands for the heritability of a trait, *CI* for concordance in identical twins and *CF* for concordance in fraternal twins.

A similar attempt of Khatoon (1986), with a larger data on twins (100 pairs), confirmed the early results. Concordance and discordance in plantar creases among MZ and DZ twins revealed that main type of plantar creases show 78.94 per cent concordance and 21.06 per cent discordance in MZ twins, numbering 19 pairs. The DZ like sex twins (62) show concordance and discordance as 66.93 per cent and 33.07 per cent, respectively. In DZ (unlike sex) twins it is 50 per cent. Apart from the study of twins, the above work on plantar crease inheritance was also supported by familial data. The result again showed higher similarity between parents and offspring. Singh (1980) investigated plantar creases as ethnic variable among Rajput and compared this population with other populations and showed the variation for comparing the ethnic inheritance limiting the trend of variability of unlike frequencies within the respective population.

The available work on three populations is not sufficient to arrive at any conclusive prediction with regards to plantar creases as ethnic variable.

Table 15.3 reveals high estimate value of plantar crease heritability.

REFERENCES

Alter, M. (1967): *Medicine* (Baltimore) 46(1): pp. 35-57.

Bali, R.S. and R. Mishra (1978): The plantar creases and their formulation, Xth Internat. Congr. Anthrop. & Ethno. Sciences, New Delhi, India.

Khatoon, S. (1986): *Study of Twins and Reliability of Creases in Twin Zygosity Diagnosis*. Ph.D. Thesis, Saugar University, Sagar.

Mishra, R. (1979): *Inheritance and Methodological Study of Plantar Creases*. Thesis submitted in part fulfilment for the requirements of the degree of Ph.D., Saugar, University Sagar.

Nokiela, J. (1972): Flexion furrows of the feet in Poles. *Folia. Morphol.* (Warsz), 31: p. 301.

Patten, B.M. (1953): *Human Embryology*, Blakistan, New York, 19.

Schaumann, B., M. Alter (1976): Dermatoglyphics in cerebral gigantism, in Dermatoglyphics: An International perspective. Edited by J. Mavalwala, *World Anthropology*. The Hague : Mouton.

Schenk, H. and H. Patzer (1959): Das fussfurchenbild des Neugeborenen. *Kinderarztliche Praxis* 27(4) : pp. 169-73.

Singh, N.R. (1980): *A Study of Plantar Creases Among Rajputs*, M.Sc. Thesis, Saugar University, Sagar.

Valotzkoy, M.V. (1936): On the genetics of fingerprints. *Proceedings of the Maxim Gorky Medico-Genetical Research Institute* 4: pp. 404-39.

16

INHERITANCE OF PHALANGEAL AND TOE CREASES

THE GENETIC particularities of phalangeal traits with special reference to dectylometry, phalangeal dermatoglyphics and mid-phalangeal hair find abundant evidence.

Among the few reports on phalangeal creases as cited in Chapter 11, there are only two studies on phalangeal crease inheritance that is of Okajima (1967) and Aue-Hauser (1977).

The above-cited work of Okajima is essentially a study of the metacarpo-phalangeal area of the middle fingers.

Okajima (1966) on the study of metacarpo-phalangeal creases stated the need for investigation of inheritance through twins and family studies.

The author in his subsequent effort reported his work on twins for investigation of metacarpo-phalangeal crease inheritance. His work was restricted to the metacarpo-phalangeal area of four fingers. He could not consider the thumb for certain reasons. Nevertheless, his pioneer contribution towards the study of phalangeal creases is noteworthy.

Aue-Hauser's work on phalangeal creases is comprehensive and sound. Aue-Hauser (1977) gave a scheme of the four types of digital flexion creases on proximal, middle and distal phalanges (see Chapter 11).

The subsequent work of the above-mentioned authors on digital flexion creases in twins (Aue-Hauser et al., 1978) provides sufficient details regarding the classification as well as on the study of inheritance of digital flexion creases.

The study was based on bilateral ink prints of 62 pairs of monozygotic and 112 pairs of dizygotic twins of both sexes.

The authors studied twins with respect to hereditary dependence between digital flexion creases of five-crease type scheme of classification. In spite of convincing result of concordance in monozygotic twins the authors desired further studies in this direction.

Khatoon (1986) repeated the work of Aue-Hauser et al. by employing the technique of classification prescribed by Aue-Hauser (1977).

Bali (1983) studied inheritance of phalangeal creases on the basis of his own formulation (see Chapter 11).

The familial data on phalangeal creases of both the hands was procured from 50 families (Brahmins).

The method of printing has already been described in early chapters.

The formulation of phalangeal flexion creases of all the digits and of all flexion sites of the hand has already been discussed. The binomial system of crease classification of Bali (1983) has been adopted to accommodate all types of phalangeal creases of all the phalangeal sites. The relationship between the main three types and the seven sub-types of phalangeal flexion creases forms the basis of the present classification.

The phalangeal crease may be a straight type, beaded type, enclosure type, boat type, feather type, open type and mixed type (Figs. 12.5 and 12.5a).

If a crease is represented by any of the above patterns occurring singly on the site the crease will be designated as single type of phalangeal crease. Similarly double pattern combination of same type is called simple crease while combination of one or more pattern types is called composite type of phalangeal crease. The composite type of phalangeal crease takes its classificatory nomenclature after basal crease types. If beaded type crease forms the base of the composite crease the category is called beaded composite type of phalangeal crease.

Apart from studying the three main types of phalangeal creases, the study of digit type is also important. To avoid the number of tables, the result regarding the heritability of normal, extra and minus types of digits have been deleted, more ever, they do not show convincing results of heritability. The reason being simple, the size of sample is inadequate and the extra type crease bearing individuals were very few in number and minus crease type individuals are absent in our data.

The classification of sub-types of phalangeal creases though essential could not be undertaken because of data size.

To trace the heritability of phalangeal flexion creases the data appropriated was on 50 families and 20 pairs of twins. The probe for the study of phalangeal creases was made for single, simple and composite patterns.

TABLE 16.1a: Distribution of basal phalangeal creases (Right+Left) hands of father and offspring

Offspring	Father (Basal)			Total
	S	SP	Com	
Present	670	—	350	1,020
Absent	175	35	225	435
Total	845	35	575	1,455

[χ^2 = 114.970 (Significant)]

TABLE 16.1b: Distribution of basal phalangeal creases (Right+Left) hands of mother and offspring

Offspring	Father (Basal)			Total
	S	SP	Com	
Present	630	5	440	1,075
Absent	130	30	260	420
Total	760	35	700	1,495

[χ^2 = 131.328 (Significant)]

TABLE 16.2a: Distribution of middle phalangeal creases (Right+Left) hands of father and offspring

Offspring	Father (Middle)			Total
	S	SP	Com	
Present	190	10	520	720
Absent	115	65	140	320
Total	305	75	660	1,040

[χ^2 = 145.20 (Significant)]

TABLE 16.2b: Distribution of middle phalangeal creases (Right+Left) hands of mother and offspring

Offspring	Mother (Middle)			Total
	S	SP	Com	
Present	145	10	485	640
Absent	75	155	170	400
Total	220	165	655	1,040

[$\chi^2 = 259.60$ (Significant)]

TABLE 16.3a: Distribution of distal phalangeal creases (Right+Left) hand of father and offspring

Offspring	Father (Distal)			Total
	S	SP	Com	
Present	990	—	25	1,015
Absent	240	100	145	485
Total	1,230	100	170	1,500

[$\chi^2 = 452.01$ (Significant)

TABLE 16.3b: Distribution of distal phalangeal creases (Right+Left) hands of mother and offspring

Offspring	Mother (Distal)			Total
	S	SP	Com	
Present	1,020	10	15	1,045
Absent	245	105	105	455
Total	1,265	115	120	1,500

[$\chi^2 = 459.85$ (Significant)]

The phalangeal crease inheritance is treated separately for basal, middle and distal phalangeal creases in Tables 16.1a,b, 16.2a,b and 16.3a,b. All the basal phalangeal creases of five phalanges of both hands are appropriated and their relationship with parents and offspring is traced through the presence or absence of the trait. The relationship is further interpreted in term of chi-square value.

Considering the heritability of single phalangeal basal flexion crease, it could be seen from the above Tables that the incidence of crease transmission is quite high. A similar trend is exhibited by simple and composite types of phalangeal flexion creases. Chi-square value shows significant results.

The closer affinity of basal creases between fathers and their offspring shows that the trait is heritable in nature. A similar trend is exhibited by mothers and their offspring.

The presence and absence of single, simple or composite type of middle phalangeal flexion creases on the hands of fathers and their offspring show greater affinity of the trait between parents and their children. It could be seen from Table 16.2 a,b that the trait exhibits a clear cut heritable behaviour. This is further supported by the chi-square values.

The significant chi-square value of resemblance between mothers and their offspring show a close association between children and their male parents (Tables 16.1a, 16.2b, 16.3b).

Considering the transmission of distal phalangeal flexion creases from fathers to their offspring, it could be seen from Table 16.3a,b that the trait shows heritable behaviour.

The incidence of distal single, simple and composite phalangeal creases on the hands of fathers and their offspring show greater affinity (Table 16.3a,b).

The chi-square results are significant, thus, suggestive of the fact that the traits are transmissible.

A similar trend of pattern transmission is exhibited by mothers to their offspring. The significant chi-square value shows that trait is heritable.

It is safe to conclude that phalangeal flexion creases are heritable traits and the proposed formulation is valid for any subsequent morphometric investigation in Man.

Inheritance of Toe Flexion Creases

In the absence of data on the heritability of toe flexion creases the study on inheritance could not be carried out. The only toe flexion prints of two pairs of MZ twins, diagnosed for some other purpose, were observed. On the basis of our observation of the prints it was realised that the inheritance of toe flexion creases warrants a fresh probe for validating the proposed formulation of toe flexion creases.

REFERENCES

Aue-Hauser, G. (1977): *Flexion creases on fingers and their relevance in early diagnosis of mental disorders.*

Aue-Hauser, G., Luigi Gedda, Paolo Parisi and Rudolf Wytek, (1978): *Twin Research: Clinical Studies.* Alan R.

Bali, R.S. (1983): Inheritance of phalangeal flexion creases. *Internat. Sym. Dermato,* Punjabi University, Patiala, India.

Bali, R.S. (1983): *Human Biology, Recent Advances,* Vol. 2, Dermatoglyphics.

Khatoon, S. (1986): Study of Twins and reliability of Creases in Twin Zygosty diagnosis, Ph.D. Thesis, Saugar University, Sagar.

Okajima, M. (1966): A dermatoglyphical study of metacarpo-phalangeal creases. *Am. J. Phys. Anthropol.*, 24 : pp. 371-80.

Okajima, M. (1967): Metacarpo-phalangeal and ring crease in twins. *Am. J. Phys. Anthropol.*, 26 : pp. 349-55.

17

INHERITANCE OF BRACELET CREASES

THE PUBLICATION of Chaube and Bali (1976) first time revealed the scientific informations on bracelet creases, a least studied field among creases.

In the strict sense of the definition, bracelet creases do not qualify as creases. Bracelet creases are more closer to the skin folds. The closer approximation of distal bracelet crease makes it appear like other creases of the palm or phalanges. A crease must occur in dermal ridged surface. This condition is absent in bracelet creases. However, certain essential crease features are shared by bracelet creases, which qualify them to be treated under creases.

The bracelet area, a junction of proximal and distal ends of palm and forearm, falls beyond the area of palmar dermatoglyphics and distinctly differs from other skinfolds of the forearm.

Bracelet creases extend quite prominently towards the pronation of palm from the stylion to the radial points. Of all the bracelet creases, the distal crease is the most prominent and shows beaded appearance of classical nature. Out of several types and sub-types the reliable types fall closer to the proximal margin of the palm. The other types are not phenotypically stable. In old age they get merged in skinfolds.

For the purpose of inheritance, only the main groups of bracelet creases are considered, i.e., distal bracelet crease (D), medial bracelet crease (DM) and proximal bracelet crease (DMP).

The study of inheritance in bracelet creases is based on familial and twin data. Chaube (1971) investigated bracelet creases from the standpoint of heritability. The work was based on family and twin data. The author showed high to moderate heritability of bracelet creases. Out of three main types the distal bracelet crease exhibited high heritability and moderate to low heritability was exhibited by medial and proximal bracelet creases, respectively.

It has already been emphasised that those bracelet creases which fall beyond the dermatoglyphics of the palm are mere skinfolds and are liable for change both under age and nutritional stress. The testing of heritability will allow us to restructure our classification. The author leaves this area for future evidences.

Chaube and Bali (1976) initiated the study of bracelet crease heritability. The study of inheritance of bracelet creases was also made by Khatoon (1986). The work of Chaube and Bali (1976) was based on familial data of 130 families with two generations and properly diagnosed five pairs of MZ and ten pairs of DZ twins. The twin diagnosis of 'similarity method' was after Siemens (1927) and Verschuer (1939); however, help was also taken from Rife (1933), Berry et al. (1955) and Lund (1933). The work is being cited as under (Table 17.1).

TABLE 17.1: Bi-manual distribution of bracelet creases among two sexes

Sex	Groups	Right hand		Left hand		Right+Left hand	
		Absolute number	Percentage	Absolute number	Percentage	Absolute number	Percentage
Male	D	6	4.61	7	5.38	13	4.99
	DM	66	50.77	66	50.77	132	50.77
	DMP	58	44.61	57	43.84	115	44.22
	Total	130	99.99	130	99.99	260	99.98
Female	D	13	10.00	4	3.07	17	6.53
	DM	71	54.61	67	51.54	138	53.07
	DMP	46	35.38	59	45.38	105	40.38
	Total	130	99.99	130	99.99	260	99.98

The incidence of bracelet creases of the offspring born of respective parents show their heritable significance.

It could be seen from the Tables 17.2a,b,c and 17.2d that the offspring born of fathers, having any of the above-mentioned type of bracelet creases, exhibit greater affinities with each other on their respective side. Distribution of bracelet creases among the father's right hand and the children's right hand shows an obvious inheritance ($\chi^2 = 26.59$, C = 0.24, df = 2, $P \leq 0.001$). A similar trend could also be noticed in father's left hand and the children's left hand. Table 17.2d, the χ^2 value shows closer relationship as indicated by right hand ($\chi^2 = 20.95$, C = 0.22, df = 2, $P \leq 0.001$).

TABLE 17.2a: **Distribution of bracelet creases among father and offspring: Father's right hand *vs* children's right hand**

Children's right hand		Father's right hand			
		D	DM	DMP	Total
Present	Ab.	12	156	97	265
	Pc.	33.33	71.88	53.59	61.06
Absent	Ab.	24	61	84	169
	Pc.	66.67	28.12	46.41	38.94
Total	Ab.	36	217	181	434
	Pc.	100	100	100	100

$\chi^2 = 26.59$, $C = 0.24$, $df = 2$, $P \leq 0.001$

TABLE 17.2b: Father's right hand *vs* Children's left hand

Children's left hand		Father's right hand			
		D	DM	DMP	Total
Present	Ab.	9	148	106	263
	Pc.	25.00	68.20	58.55	60.59
Absent	Ab.	27	69	75	171
	Pc.	75.00.	31.80	4.45	39.41
Total	Ab.	36	217	181	434
	Pc.	100	100	100	100

$\chi^2 = 20.29$, $C = 0.21$, $df = 2$, $P \leq 0.001$

The opposite hand relationship of fathers and their offspring shows a lesser degree of affinity (Tables 17.2b and 17.2c) ($\chi^2 = 20.29$, $C = 0.21$, $df = 2$, $P \leq 0.001$; $\chi^2 = 15.68$, $C = 0.18$, $df = 2$, $P \leq 0.01$).

A similar distribution of various types of bracelet crease among the mother's right hand and the children's right hand presents a closer relationship.

It is apparent from Tables 17.3a, b, c and d that in the transmission of bracelet creases from mothers to their offspring reflects heritability of the trait (Tables 17.3a and 17.3b) ($\chi^2 = 21.38$, $C = 0.22$, $df = 2$, $P \leq 0.001$; $\chi^2 = 21.33$, $C = 0.22$, $df = 2$, $P \leq 0.001$).

TABLE 17.2c: Father's left hand *vs* Children's right hand

Children's right hand		Father's left hand			
		D	DM	DMP	Total
Present	Ab.	11	136	95	242
	Pc.	31.43	60.46	51.63	55.76
Absent	Ab.	24	79	89	192
	Pc.	68.57	39.54	48.37	44.24
Total	Ab.	35	215	184	434
	Pc.	100	100	100	100

$\chi^2 = 15.68$, $C = 0.18$, $df = 2$, $P \leq 0.01$

TABLE 17.2d: Father's left hand *vs* Children's left hand

Children's left hand		Father's left hand			
		D	DM	DMP	Total
Present	Ab.	10	147	114	259
	Pc.	28.57	68.37	61.95	62.44
Absent	Ab.	25	68	70	175
	Pc.	71.43	31.63	38.05	37.56
Total	Ab.	35	215	184	437
	Pc.	100	100	100	100

$\chi^2 = 20.95$, $C = 0.22$, $df = 2$, $P \leq 0.001$

Mother's left hand versus children's left and right hand (Tables 17.3c and d; $\chi^2 = 24.46$, $C = 0.23$, $df = 2$, $P \leq 0.001$; $\chi^2 = 17.15$, $C = 0.19$, $df = 2$, $P \leq 0.01$) exhibits significant resemblance.

The concordance and discordance between MZ and DZ twins both for the right and the left hand exhibit a striking resemblance showing heritability of trait (Table 17.4).

Table 17.4 exhibits the concordance among MZ twins (Rt-100, LT-80 per cent) and 0 per cent discordance in their right and 20 per cent in their left hand. In DZ twins the concordance in the right and left hand is 60 per cent and 50 per cent, respectively, and discordance is 40 per cent and 50 per cent for right and left hand, respectively.

TABLE 17.3a: Distribution of bracelet creases among mother and offspring

Mother's right hand *vs* children's right hand

Children's right hand		Mother's right hand			
		D	DM	DMP	Total
Present	Ab.	15	169	107	291
	Pc.	35.71	72.53	67.29	67.05
Absent	Ab.	27	64	52	143
	Pc.	64.29	27.47	32.71	32.95
Total	Ab.	42	233	159	434
	Pc.	100	100	100	100

$\chi^2 = 21.38$, C = 0.22, df = 2, $P \leq 0.001$

TABLE 17.3b: Mother's right hand *vs* Children's left hand

Children's left hand		Mother's right hand			
		D	DM	DMP	Total
Present	Ab.	9	133	96	238
	Pc.	21.43	57.08	60.38	54.84
Absent	Ab.	33	100	63	196
	Pc.	78.57	42.92	39.62	45.16
Total	Ab.	42	233	159	434
	Pc.	100	100	100	100

$\chi^2 = 21.33$, C = 0.22, df = 2, $P \leq 0.001$

TABLE 17.3c: Mother's left hand *vs* Children's right hand

Children's right hand		Mother's left hand			
		D	DM	DMP	Total
Present	Ab.	8	155	100	263
	Pc.	28.57	70.45	53.76	60.59
Absent	Ab.	20	75	86	181
	Pc.	71.43	29.55	46.24	39.41
Total	Ab.	28	230	186	434
	Pc.	100	100	100	100

$\chi^2 = 24.46$, C = 0.23, df = 2, $P \leq 0.001$

TABLE 17.3d: Mother's left hand *vs* Children's left hand

Children's left hand		Mother's left hand			
		D	DM	DMP	Total
Present	Ab.	9	159	118	286
	Pc.	32.14	72.27	63.44	65.89
Absent	Ab.	19	61	68	148
	Pc.	67.86	27.73	36.56	34.11
Total	Ab.	28	220	186	434
	Pc.	100	100	100	100

$\chi^2 = 17.15$, $C = 0.19$, $df = 2$, $P \leq 0.01$

TABLE 17.4: Concordance and discordance among MZ and DZ twins.

(*In percentage*)

Twins	Concordance		Discordance		Right + Left	
	Right	Left	Right	Left	Concor.	Discor.
MZ	100	80	0	20	20	10
DZ	60	50	40	50	55	45

The inheritance of bracelet creases through family data and twin study clearly indicates that the trait is genetically controlled and supports the proposed method of bracelet creases formulation.

The ethnic variation in the distribution of bracelet creases show scant material. It is, therefore, not possible to investigate ethnic inheritance on the basis of population studies. So far, only one ethnically homogeneous population of Brahmins (males and females) has been investigated by the above-cited author.

The concluding remarks about bracelet crease heretability converges to a single point that the work available in this field is much less and it is too early to ask for the claims.

Khatoon (1986) made an attempt to investigate reliability of bracelet creases in twins. The author based her work on 100 pairs of twins, of which 19 were diagnosed as MZ and rest as DZ types. The concordance and discordance in the bracelet creases among MZ and DZ twins was 60.52, 39.48 per cent and 35.48, 64.52 per cent, respectively. The above author made her observation on family data and found that bracelet crease is a heritable phenotypic variable.

REFERENCES

Chaube, R. (1971): *The Study of Palmar Flexion Crease — Inheritance and Correlation with Schizophrenic patients.* Thesis submitted in fulfilment of the requirements for the degree of Ph.D., Saugar University, Sagar.

Chaube, R. and R.S. Bali (1976): The bracelet creases. *Z. Morph. Anthrop.* 67.3 : pp. 353-63.

Khatoon, S. (1986): *Study of Twins and Reliability of Creases in Twin Zygosity Diagnosis.* Ph.D. Thesis, Saugar University, Sagar (M.P.).

Lund, S.E.T. (1933): A psycho-biological study of a set of identical girl triplets. *Human Biology* 5 : pp. 1-34.

Parisi, P., M. di Bacco (1967): Finger prints in twins. A quali-quantitative analysis. (Methodological note). *Acta Geneticae Medicae et Gemellologie* 16(1) : pp. 71-100.

Rife, D.C. (1933): Genetic studies of monozygotic twins. I.A. diagnostic formula. *Journal of Heredity* 24: pp. 339-45.

Rife, D.C. (1933a): Genetic studies of monozygotic twins. II. Finger-patterns and eye-colour as criteria of monozygosity. *Journal of Heredity* 24 : pp. 406-14.

Siemens, H.W. (1927): The diagnosis of identity in twins. *Journal of Heredity* 18 : pp. 201-9.

Verschuer, O.Von (1939): Twin research from the time of Francis Galton to the present day. *Proceedings of the Royal Society* (London) 128 : pp. 62-81.

18

INHERITANCE OF MORPHOGENIC ATTRIBUTES OF PALMAR CREASE

THE STUDY of inheritance in crease morphogenesis is as important as the study of palmar and plantar creases. In our early discussion on crease morphology and crease morphometry we have dealt, in details with the importance of individual primary crease of the palm.

It is, therefore, desirable to discuss the inheritance of morphogenic attributes of palmar creases.

Besides others, Bali and Rawat (1980) made an extensive study in this direction.

The bilateral inked prints of 400 individuals belonging to the 100 Jain families with two generations have been appropriated for the above study. The data is drawn exclusively from the Sagar district.

The study of inheritance of phenotopic traits in man has remained an obscure field of study and the knowledge concerning their mode of inheritance is fragmentary. Certain important evidences have begun to explain the inheritance of some morphological traits.

The crease morphogenesis, in fact, is the study of crease morphology in term of its length, length formula, breadth, depth, surface area, crease transversality and positioning of its radial base point between digits first and second.

The present study is an attempt to investigate the heritability of crease transversality and positioning of radial base point between digits first and second.

The crease transversality is the angle contained by *a* - *d* line and *a* line joining the base and terminal end of crease. Their angle can be measured separately for each crease (Fig. 18.1).

The crease transversality and positioning of radial base point is of embryonal nature and their inheritance appears to be of much value. The heritability of above crease traits has been investigated through the study of family data.

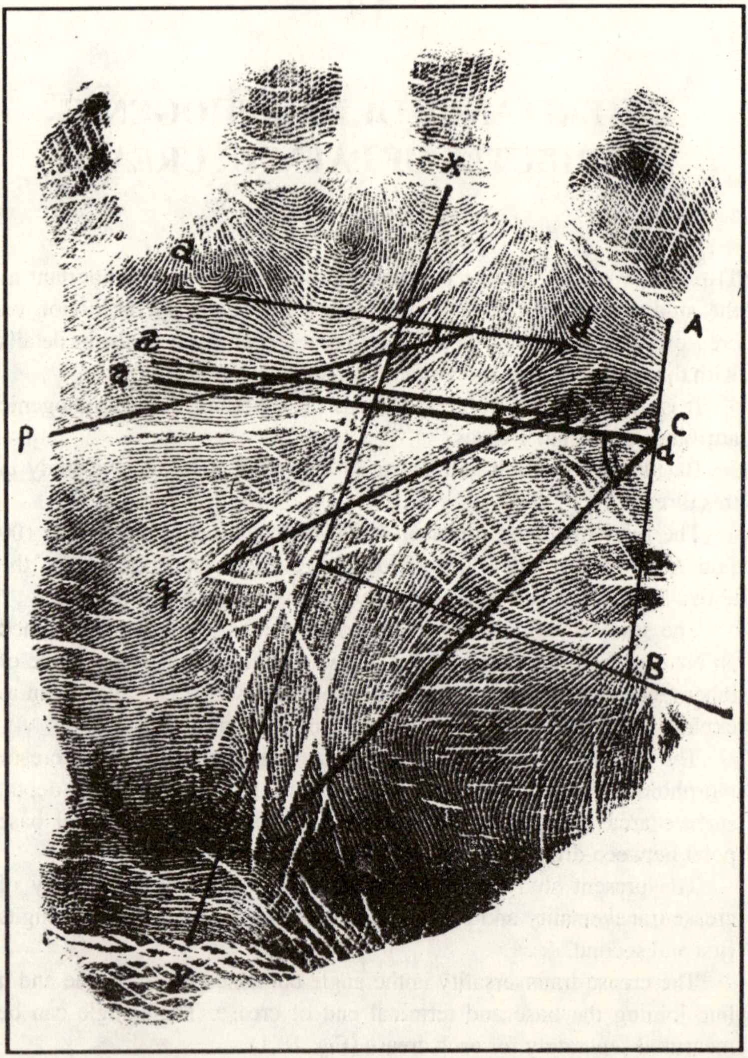

FIG. 18.1: Crease transversality angles and positioning of radial base point

Methodology for Measuring Crease Transversality

The crease transversality is never same for the two individuals, even the identical twins show variability in crease transversality. The bending of crease with respect to *a - d* line and the line joining the base and terminal point of the crease provide the required angle.

The transversality angle for distal transverse crease, proximal transverse crease and radial longitudinal crease is *a d' p, a d' q, and a d' r,* respectively. The line joining the base and terminal point is in fact the transversality indicating axis of the crease, while line joining *a - d* tri-radius provides the reference line for calculating the angles of creases transversality.

Methodology for Measuring the Relative Length of Base Points

The radial margin has been found of much value for formulating palmar crease (Bali and Chaube, 1971). It has also been noticed that the positioning of radial base point shows fairly consistent results. To assess the positioning of base point with special reference to point A, which is marked on the medial and proximal margin of the inter-phalangeal basal crease of digit two is not difficult. The second reference point is *B* which divides the anatomical axis into two equal halves. This point falls between the basal crease of third digit and distal margin of distal bracelet crease.

The positioning of point *C,* which is a basal point of radial longitudinal crease provides three relative length for calculating the positioning of radial base point. These lengths are *AB, AC* and *BC.*

Considering the positioning of radial base point, it is imperative to deal *AB, AC* and *BC* lines separately.

Results and Discussion

Parental Combination on Crease Transversality

The nine parental combinations are between normal, medium and high ranges. The angles show a general trend of crease affinity between parent and offspring (Table 18.1).

Inheritance of Radial Longitudinal Crease

The crease transversality of crease angle refers to a angle which is formed by *a d'* and *r d'* lines (Fig. 18.1). The radial longitudinal crease is a primary crease and its orientation on the palm remains almost constant. The heritability of this trait is assessed by comparing transversality of radial base crease in parents and their offspring.

TABLE 18.1: Offspring born of parental combinations (Radial longitudinal crease angle)

Parental combination	No. of family			Offspring N Ab	N Pc	M Ab	M Pc	H Ab	H Pc	Total
N×N	Rt	12	M	6	(21.43)	19	(67.86)	3	(10.71)	28
			F	6	(30.00)	13	(65.00)	1	(15.00)	20
	Lt	16	M	13	(43.34)	15	(50.00)	2	(6.33)	30
			F	13	(38.24)	19	(55.88)	2	(5.88)	34
N×M	Rt	20	M	16	(32.00)	34	(68.00)	—		50
			F	13	(38.24)	17	(56.66)	—		30
	Lt	17	M	12	(31.58)	26	(68.42)	—		38
			F	12	(40.00)	17	(56.67)	1	(3.33)	30
N×H	—		M	—		—		—		—
			F	—		—		—		—
	—		M	—		—		—		—
			F	—		—		—		—
M×N	Rt	24	M	24	(38.71)	37	(59.68)	1	(1.61)	62
			F	9	(26.47)	22	(64.70)	3	(8.82)	34
	Lt	25	M	22	(32.35)	45	(66.18)	1	(1.47)	68
			F	12	(37.50)	17	(53.13)	3	(9.37)	32
M×M	Rt	40	M	20	(22.73)	65	(73.86)	3	(3.41)	88
			F	23	(31.94)	44	(61.11)	5	(6.95)	72
	Lt	35	M	19	(23.17)	61	(74.39)	2	(2.44)	82
			F	19	(32.76)	36	(62.07)	3	(5.17)	58
M×H	Rt	2	M	—		2	(50.00)	2	(50.00)	4
			F	4	(100.00)	—		—		4
	Lt	1	M	1	(50.00)	—		1	(50.00)	2
			F	—		2	(100.00)	—		2
H×N	Rt	1	M	—		—		—		—
			F	2	(50.00)	2	(50.00)	—		4
	Lt	1	M	—		3	(75.00)	1	(25.00)	4
			F	—		—		—		—
H×M	Rt	1	M	—		—		—		—
			F	1	(25.00)	3	(75.00)	—		4
	Lt	5	M	2	(16.67)	10	(83.33)	—		12
			F	2	(25.00)	6	(75.00)	—		8
H×H	—	—	M	—		—		—		—
			F	—		—		—		—
	—		M	—		—		—		—
			F	—		—		—		—

Range: N: Normal = 35 — 50; M: Medium = 51 — 65; H: High = 66 — 80.

Considering the high range of variability, of the crease angle, the angles have been grouped into three different ranges; i.e., normal (30-50), medium (51-65) and high (66-80).

Considering parental combination (N × N) between right hands, it is seen that the combination shows closer association between parents and offspring.

The combination N × M and N × H is not represented by the adequate number of children and their results are not convincing.

The combination between M × N and M × M shows that offspring follow their parents and the frequency of their alikeness indicate that the trait is heritable in nature (Table 18.1).

The other combinations are meagrely represented and their results are of less importance.

Inheritance of Proximal Transverse Creases

The transversality angle of proximal transverse crease and its inheritance show that the trait follows the parental line.

The parental combinations between normal (1-15), medium (16-30) and high (31-45) ranges show that the combination (N × N) and (N × M) is not represented by majority of the families. Nevertheless, both male and female offspring exhibit closer association with their parents. This relationship is best marked by N × N, combination in right hand, while left and right hand combination of N × M parents show 67.86 per cent and 60.71 per cent offspring having normal counts of transversality angle.

The most prominent expression of transversality angle's inheritance is represented by M × N, M × M and M × H parental combinations. It could be seen from Table 18.2, that offspring born of above parental combinations show closer association with the parents who bear M and N ranges of the angles. The expressivity of inheritance is best indicated by the male and female children of M × M combination.

Inheritance of Distal Transverse Crease

The inheritance of transversality angle of distal transverse crease (ranges – Normal 1-10, Medium 11-20 and High 21-30) shows high variability range. The parental combinations N × N, N × M, M × N and M × M are represented by (Rt 18; Lt 16), (Rt 21; Lt 13) and (Rt 10; Lt 19), respectively. But for the last the other combinations follow their parental line (Table 18.3).

TABLE 18.2: Offspring born of parental combinations (proximal transverse crease)

Parental combination	No. of family			Offspring						Total
				N		M		H		
				Ab	Pc	Ab	Pc	Ab	Pc	
N×N	Rt	11	M	17	(70.83)	7	(29.17)	—		24
			F	8	(40.00)	11	(55.00)	1	(5.00)	20
	Lt	11	M	12	(46.15)	10	(38.47)	4	(15.38)	26
			F	11	(61.11)	6	(33.33)	1	(5.56)	18
N×M	Rt	7	M	3	(21.43)	11	(78.57)	—		14
			F	3	(21.43)	9	(64.28)	2	(14.29)	14
	Lt	14	M	17	(60.71)	11	(39.29)	—		28
			F	19	(67.86)	9	(32.14)	—		28
	—		M	—		—		—		—
			F	—		—		—		—
N×H	—		M	—		—		—		—
			F	—		—		—		—
M×N	Rt	29	M	27	(37.50)	45	(62.50)	—		72
			F	16	(36.36)	27	(61.36)	1	(2.27)	44
	Lt	25	M	31	(43.05)	39	(54.17)	2	(2.78)	72
			F	12	(42.86)	16	(57.14)	—		28
M×M	Rt	46	M	33	(31.73)	67	(64.42)	4	(3.85)	104
			F	27	(33.75)	51	(63.75)	2	(2.50)	80
	Lt	46	M	31	(30.39)	68	(66.67)	3	(2.94)	102
			F	30	(36.58)	52	(63.41)	—		82
M×H	Rt	3	M	2	(33.34)	4	(66.66)	—		6
			F	1	(16.67)	4	(66.66)	1	(16.67)	6
	Lt	2	M	—		2	(100.00)	—		2
			F	2	(33.33)	3	(50.00)	1	(16.67)	6
H×N	Rt	1	M	—		3	(75.00)	1	(25.00)	4
			F	—		—		—		—
	Lt	1	M	1	(50.00)	1	(50.00)	—		2
			F	—		2	(100.00)	—		2
H×M	Rt	1	M	2	(50.00)	2	(50.00)	—		4
			F	—		—	(100.00)	—		—
	Lt	1	M	1	(50.00)	1	(50.00)	—		2
			F	—		1	(50.00)	1	(50.00)	2
H×H	Rt	2	M	—		5	(83.33)	1	(16.67)	6
			F	1	(50.00)	1	(50.00)	—		2
	—		M	—		—		—		—
			F	—		—		—		—

Range: N: Normal = 1 — 15; M: Medium = 16 - 30; H: High = 31 — 45.

TABLE 18.3: Offspring born of parental combinations (Distal transverse creases)

Parental combination	No. of family		Offspring						
			N		M		H		Total
			Ab	Pc	Ab	Pc	Ab	Pc	
	Rt 18	M	30	(53.57)	20	(35.71)	6	(10.72)	56
		F	10	(62.50)	5	(31.25)	1	(6.25)	16
N×N	Lt 16	M	16	(47.06)	13	(38.25)	1	(14.70)	34
		F	11	(36.67)	10	(33.33)	9	(30.00)	30
	Rt 21	M	19	(45.24)	16	(38.10)	7	(16.66)	42
		F	19	(45.24)	14	(33.33)	9	(21.43)	42
N×M	Lt 13	M	12	(42.86)	9	(32.14)	7	(25.00)	28
		F	14	(58.33)	7	(29.17)	3	(12.50)	24
	Rt 4	M	2	(16.67)	4	(33.33)	6	(58.00)	12
		F	—		1	(25.00)	3	(75.00)	4
N×H	Lt 8	M	5	(31.25)	8	(50.00)	3	(18.75)	16
		F	5	(31.25)	10	(62.50)	1	(6.25)	16
	Rt 22	M	15	(31.25)	25	(52.08)	8	(16.67)	48
		F	10	(25.00)	21	(52.50)	9	(22.50)	40
M×N	Lt 20	M	20	(40.00)	25	(50.00)	5	(10.00)	50
		F	7	(23.33)	16	(53.24)	7	(23.33)	30
	Rt 10	M	9	(34.61)	10	(38.46)	72	(28.26)	26
		F	5	(35.72)	7	(50.00)	2	(16.67)	14
M×M	Lt 19	M	13	(28.26)	20	(43.48)	13	(28.26)	46
		F	10	(33.33)	15	(50.00)	5	(16.67)	30
	Rt 8	M	6	(60.00)	3	(30.00)	1	(10.00)	10
		F	8	(36.36)	8	(36.36)	6	(27.28)	22
M×H	Lt 4	M	2	(25.00)	4	(50.00)	2	(25.00)	8
		F	5	(62.50)	3	(37.50)	—		8
	Rt 10	M	3	(11.54)	16	(61.54)	7	(26.92)	26
		F	4	(28.57)	8	(57.14)	2	(14.29)	14
H×N	Lt 10	M	7	(26.92)	10	(38.46)	9	(34.62)	26
		F	1	(7.14)	10	(71.43)	3	(21.43)	14
	Rt 4	M	2	(25.00)	2	(25.00)	4	(50.00)	8
		F	—		5	(62.50)	3	(37.50)	8
H×M	Lt 6	M	1	(6.25)	10	(62.50)	5	(31.25)	16
		F	—		2	(25.00)	6	(75.00)	8
	Rt 3	M	—		6	(100.00)	—		6
		F	1	(16.67)	1	(16.67)	4	(66.66)	6
M×H	Lt	M	4	(40.00)	6	(60.00)	4		10
		F	2	(33.34)	—		4	(66.66)	6

Range: N: Normal = 1 — 10; M: Medium = 11 — 20; H: High = 21 — 30

H × N and H × M parental combinations do not represent heritable expression. It may be stressed that crease transversality is a heritable trait and show constant resemblance between parents and their offspring.

Inheritance of Radial Base Point

Considering the heritable nature of radial base point, it is essential to evaluate this point in relation to line *AB, BC* and *AC*. This relative distance is compared by forming separate ranges among parents and offspring. The *AB* line is the most human feature of the palm and its importance in crease formulation has already been realised.

The inheritance of line *AB* is based on parental combinations and their relation with the offspring born of the combinations shows that the trait is heritable.

The combinations N × N and M × N are more predominant. It could be seen from Table 18.1 that offspring born of N × N and M × N combinations follow their parental lines. The combination N × M Also shows the same trend.

The parental combinations N × M, M × N and H × N, although are not represented by adequate number of families but closer association between parents and their offspring shows that the trait is heritable in nature.

The inheritance of *AC* line like *AB* line shows that trait follows the familiar lines. The parental combinations, *N* × N, N × M, M × N and M × M, show greater affinities between parents and their offspring. (Table 18.1).

The combinations, M × H, N × H and H × H are not represented by any family. The other combinations, too, are meagrely represented and fail to throw any light on heritability of *AC* line.

The *BC* line is very important as far as the location of radial base point is concerned. This distance is somewhat stable and its reference points are *B* and *C*.

Out of nine probable parental combinations, our data is represented by all the combinations. The majority of the families are accommodated under N × N, M × N and N × M parental combinations.

It could be seen from Table 18.1, that parental combination M × N and M × N are represented by majority of the families.

The offspring born of the above parental combinations show convincing results of parental and offspring association. The majority of the offspring follow their parental line and the deviation is not much.

It appears from the above results that the line *BC* is heritable and gives position to a point which is taken as most stable and highly evolved.

This point is, in fact, a manifestation of evolutionary stresses which human hand has undergone in the past.

The distance lines between point *AC, AB* and *BC* show their relative position and their subsequent role in hand appositely and as a crease stable trait.

REFERENCES

Bali, R.S. and Ramesh Chaube (1971): On the formulation of palmar creases. *Z. Morph. Anthrop.*, 63: p. 121.

Bali, R.S. and S.K. Rawat (1980): Inheritance of morphogenic attributes of palmar creases. *National Symposium* on child with handicap and VII Annual Conference of I.S.H.G., Ranchi University, Ranchi, India.

PART III

CREASES IN HUMAN BIOLOGY, ETHNIC VARIATION AND MEDICINE

19

RELIABILITY OF CREASES IN TWIN DIAGNOSIS

Palmar Creases in Twins

THE IDENTICAL (monozygotic) twins, arising from one fertilized egg, share identical genotypes while non-identical twins share identical pre-natal environment. The environmental differences between MZ and DZ twins are comparable, and the difference is generally lower than for the normal sibs because they share pre-natal as well as post-natal conditions.

Scientists like Siemmen (1932), Stocks (1930), Newman (1931a, b), Cummins (1930, 1936), Von Verschuer (1932), MacArthur (1936), Whichmann (1953), Smith and Penrose (1955), Suttan et al. (1962) and Shields et al. (1969) have tried to establish reasonably dependable ways of diagnosing twins. Most systems for distinguishing 'identical' from fraternal twins are based on the study of serology, total finger ridge counts, PTC, somatometric measurements, somatoscopic observations and a variety of other traits.

'The advantages of emphasizing dermatoglyphic features in diagnosis are that they comprise a large group of diverse characters requiring in common somewhat similar, though special, methods of study, that they are so easily, accurately recorded; and that their formulated characters, like sex, blood groups, are fixed early and remain constant in all environmental conditions throughout life, and are thus always directly comparable in subjects of any race and of either sex at any age' (MacArthur, 1938).

Like dermatoglyphics, the reliability of palmar, plantar, bracelet and phalangeal creases has fully been realised. In this context the author has made a detailed study on twin pairs (Bali, 1971, 1976, 1978). Chaube (1971) and Mishra (1979) studied palmar, bracelet and plantar creases in twins.

Apart from the formulation of crease types and sub-types, the creases of palm, sole, bracelet and phalangeal areas have been compared among the twins from the standpoint of crease morphogenesis. The data on crease features, such as crease core, crease borders, crease split and crease length formula along with the morphometric (quantitative) details of crease length, crease breadth (maximum), crease depth, crease surface area, crease transversality and positioning of 'base points', have been appropriated as diagnostic tools in the study of twins.

The homolateral and heterolateral differences between hands, feet and phalanges among twins agree with genetic expectations. The homolateral difference is less in identical twins but among fraternal twins it is more.

The comparisons made on the basis of morphometric traits appear to offer an additional means of distinguishing identical pairs from the non-identical ones. Moreover, material for the study of creases and dermatoglyphics is the same and does not involve additional labour. The crease features like dermatoglyphics are universally comparable regardless of race, sex, or surroundings; and their reliability in twin diagnosis appears to be quite high.

Transverse Crease

Twins are the best known tool for knowing the role of heredity in the transmission of palmar crease traits. The work on simian, sydney and other known types of creases have extensively been studied in twins. It is desirable to restrict our discussion only to those crease types, whose significance is of primary importance for the present work.

Monozygotic twins are known to have more similar genetic composition than the dizygotic twins. On the basis of relative genetic distance the hereditary transmission of transverse crease shows a genetic unity of various crease types.

The study of transverse creases in twins have been studied by Bali and Chaube (1971), Chaube (1971) and Khatoon (1986).

The tabulated expression of Bali and Chaube's work has already been referred under inheritance of transverse creases (Chapter 14). Chaube (1971) independently arrived at the similar results which were reported earlier by Bali and Chaube. The earlier study was restricted to main types of transverse creases but the work on sub-types in twins was undertaken by the later author.

In the recent years, Khatoon (1986) made extensive studies on creases of twins and their reliability for zygosity diagnosis. The work is based on 100 pairs of twins of which 19 are MZ, 62 DZ (like sex) and 19 DZ (unlike sex).

The concordance and discordance among MZ and DZ twins with respect to the main types of transverse palmar creases show 76.31, 62.09 and 57.89 per cent concordance for the above twins, respectively.

The element of discordance among the above said twin groups showed 23.68, 37.90 and 42.10 per cent variation for each group.

The consistency of results in the case of twins in various studies show the validity of transverse crease types for the study of diseases and complex population problems.

Longitudinal Creases

The basis of formulations of transverse and longitudinal creases are on two independent criteria. It is, therefore, desired to treat longitudinal creases under a separate group.

In the light of the above fact the study of twins with respect to longitudinal creases has been dealt under the separate heading.

The study of longitudinal creases in twins has been investigated only by Khatoon (1986). On the basis of 100 twin pairs, it was found that longitudinal creases like transverse creases show closer approximity towards the transmission of its heredity. The study of longitudinal palmar creases in twins has been considered by the above-quoted author on main as well as on its sub-types. For our present discussion we will restrict to main types only.

The three main types of longitudinal creases are: single carpal base crease, double carpal base crease and triple carpal base crease. Out of above three main types, the incidence of triple radial base crease is very low. The other two types show higher incidence of heredity transmission.

The concordance among MZ twins is 81.57 per cent, while in DZ twins it is 61.29 per cent. This concordance in relation to unlike DZ twins is more. In DZ twins, with unlike sex, the incidence of concordance is 55.26 per cent.

It could thus be said that heredity transmission of longitudinal creases is real, but mode of its transmission is still unknown. Rife (1933) is pessimistic for finding any answer in this complex problem.

Bracelet Creases in Twins

Bracelet creases have false borders and cores but still from their appearance and closer association with dermatoglyphic area make them qualify into the family of creases. Bracelet creases or crease extend from stylion towards the radial point on supination position of the hand.

Only main types of bracelet creases, i.e., distal, medial and proximal, have been appropriated in the study of twins.

The bracelet crease study in twins finds three references: Chaube and Bali (1976), Chaube (1971) and Khatoon (1986).

The work conducted by Chaube and Bali is predominantly formulation oriented. The author's stress is to probe the validity of bracelet crease classification. The study in twins further added evidences of validity for bracelet crease classification.

Chaube (1971) independently investigated the role of twins in bracelet creases. On the basis of 30 pairs of twins he also established that bracelet crease traits are of heritable nature.

Khatoon (1986) subjected bracelet creases in twin study on the basis of 100 pairs of twins. Out of these 100 pairs, 19 were MZ, 62 DZ (like sex) and 19 DZ (unlike sex). The bracelet creases among MZ and DZ twins show that main type of bracelet creases in twins show concordance 60.52 and discordance 39.48 per cent. While concordance in DZ (like sex) twins is 35.48 per cent, discordance is 64.52 per cent. The concordance and discordance in DZ twins (unlike sex) show 52.64 per cent and 47.36 per cent, respectively.

Although bracelet creases are not creases in the true sense of the definition but their heritability is a valid reality.

Plantar Creases in Twins

Like transverse and longitudinal creases of the palm the plantar creases, too, have been formulated on the basis of their terminations and origins. In case of plantar creases instead of origin we find union at a terminal point or points. The main plantar creases, i.e., medial longitudinal crease, tibial distal transverse crease and fibular distal transverse crease generally approximate towards the distal thenar region of the anatomical axis, and tend to meet at a point or points which is named as 'Distal Medial Base Point'.

On the basis of terminal meeting of the above creases at distal medial base point we can divide creases into three main types:

Single Medial Base Crease
Double Medial Base Crease
Triple Medial Base Crease

The study of above main types of plantar creases in twin has been carried out by Bali and Mishra (1978), Mishra (1979) and Khatoon (1986).

The sub-types of plantar creases have not been incorporated in the present text. We have considered only the above main types in the present study of twins. The available material on twin study with respect to present formulation is restricted to three reports. Bali and Mishra (1978) studied twins from the standpoint of plantar crease formulation and its validity. But in the context of present discussion we will like to consider the work of Mishra (1979) and Khatoon (1986).

The Mishra's work was based on 20 pairs of twins out of which five pairs were diagnosed as MZ and rest as DZ twins. The incidence of concordance and discordance of main type of plantar creases in MZ and DZ pairs of twins show that the traits under investigation are heritable.

The MZ twins show concordance in both hands as 80 per cent and discordance about 20 per cent.

On the basis of heritability estimate among MZ and DZ twins the author speaks about high estimate value of heritability of main type of plantar creases.

Based on the above given formulation of plantar creases, Khatoon studied the heritability estimate of plantar creases with the help of 100 pairs of twins. The crease application in population study has been possible only after the trait was tested in twins.

Both main types and sub-types were considered for the estimation of heritability through the study of twins. In the diagnosis made into MZ, DZ (like sex) and DZ (unlike sex), twins showed that plantar crease traits are of heritable nature.

Concordance and discordance in plantar creases among MZ twins is 78.94 per cent and 21.06 per cent respectively. The concordance and discordance among DZ (unlike sex) twins is 50 per cent and 50 per cent, respectively.

From the above percentages it could be concluded that plantar creases (main types) show high probability value of heritability. From the above discussion it appears that plantar creases as morphological variables stand a chance for their application in complex population problems.

Phalangeal Creases in Twins

Twin studies in phalangeal flexion creases show paucity of reference, nevertheless, work of Au-Hauser et al. (1978) provides comprehensive details.

In the context of phalangeal crease formulation given by Bali (1980), the work does not find relevance. Study of phalangeal flexion creases with reference to the present classification has three main types and seven sub-types, besides, the type of digit, carrying minus, normal or extra creases, is also considered.

We have restricted the study of phalangeal flexion crease to its main types only.

The concordance and discordance among MZ and DZ twins with respect to phalangeal creases, i.e., single, simple and composite types, show that crease formulations are dependable morphological variable for conducting any sort of anthropological studies.

Out of 25 pairs of twins, 18 were diagnosed as DZ and seven as MZ twins.

The concordance and discordance among DZ twins in respect to phalangeal flexion creases are 61.30 per cent and 38.70 per cent of combined hands.

The concordance and discordance among MZ twins in respect to phalangeal creases show 63.16 per cent and 36.84 per cent respectively.

It may be conceded that any phenotypic variable of polymorphic nature takes its own time to attain precision of technique and treatment of data and then it can be tested in the field.

A single unit action in this direction falls short of its goal. It is felt that only future researches can make creases as a viable morphological variable for undertaking complex population problems both in human and non-human primates.

REFERENCES

Aue-Hauser, G., Luigi Gedda, Paolo Parisi, and Rudolf Wytek (1978): *Twin Research: Clinical Studies*. Alan R.

Bali, R.S. (1971a): Palmar creases and Schizophrenia, *Internat. Sym. Hum. Genet.*, Andhra University, Waltair, India.

Bali, R.S. (1971b): *Palmar Creases and Diseases*. S.C. Roy Centenary Celebration held in Ranchi, Bihar, India.

Bali, R.S. (1980): Inheritance of phalangeal flexion creases. *Internat. Sym. Dermato.*, Punjabi University, Patiala, India.

Bali, R.S. and R. Mishra (1978): The plantar creases and their formulation, Xth Internat. Cong. of Anthrop. and Ethno. Sci., New Delhi.

Bali, R.S. and R. Mishra (1978): The study of morphological change in hand, palm and palmar flexion creases of one to eleven years old boys and girls. Xth Internat. Congr. Anthrop. & Ethno. Sciences, New Delhi, India.

Bali, R.S. and Ramesh Chaube (1971): On the formulation of palmar creases. *Z. Morph. Anthrop.*, 63(121).

Chaube, R. (1971): *The Study of Palmar Flexion Creases: Inheritance and Correlation with Schizophrenic Patients.* Thesis submitted in fulfilment of the requirement of the degree of Ph.D., Saugar University, Sagar.

Chaube, R. and R.S. Bali (1970): The bracelet creases. *Z. Morph. Anthrop.* 67.3: pp. 353-63.

Cummins, H. (1930): Dermatoglyphics in twins of known chronic history, with reference to diagnosis of the twin varieties. *Anatomical Record.* 46: pp. 179-98.

Cummins, H. (1936): Finger prints in 'Siamese' twins. *Eugenical News* 21: pp. 89-95.

Khatoon, S. (1986): *Study of Twins and Reliability of Creases in Twin Zygosity Diagnosis*, Ph.D. Thesis. Saugar University, Sagar.

Komai, T. (1928): Criteria for distinguishing identical and fraternal twins. *Quart. Rev. Biol.*, 3: pp. 408-18.

MacArthur, J.W. (1936): A measure of similarity in finger and palm prints aiding diagnosis of identical and fraternal twins, Royal Soc. of Canada, Abstracts, pp. 52.

MacArthur, J.W. (1938): Reliability of dermatoglyphics in twin diagnosis. *Human Biology* 10(1): pp. 12-35.

Mishra, R. (1979): *Inheritance and Methodological Study of Plantar Creases.* Thesis submitted in part fulfilment for the requirements of the degree of Ph.D., Saugar University, Sagar.

Newman, H.H. (1931): Palm print patterns in twins. *Journal of Heredity* 22: pp. 41-9.

Newman, H.H. (1931a): Differences between conjoined twins. *Journal of Heredity* 22: pp. 201-05.

Rife, D.C. (1933): Genetic studies of monozygotic twins. I. A diagnostic formula. *Journal of Heredity* 24: pp. 339-45.

Rife, D.C. (1933a): Genetic studies of monozygotic twins. II. Finger patterns and eye-colour as criteria of monozygosity. *Journal of Heredity* 24: pp. 406-14.

Shields, J., E. Slater and P. Slater (1969): A quadratic discriminant of Zygosity from finger prints. *J. Med. Genet.* 1: p. 142.

Siemmen, H.W. (1932): Die allgemeinen der menschlichen Mehrlings forschung. *Zeits. f. ind. Abst. und Verebungsl.*, 61: pp. 208-22.

Smith, S.M. and L.S. Penrose (1955): Monozygotic and dizygotic twin diagnosis. *Annals of Eugenics.* 19: pp. 273-90.

Stocks, P. (1930): A biometric investigation of twins and their brothers and sisters. *Annals of Eugenics.* 4: pp. 49-108.

Suttan, H.E., S.G. Vandenberg and P.J. Clark (1962): The heriditary abilities studies. Selection of twins, diagnosis of zygosity and programme of measurements. *Amer. J. Hum. Genet.* 14: pp. 152.

Verschuer, O.V. (1932): Die biologischen Grundlagen der menschlichen Mehrlingsforschung. *Zeits. f. ind. Abst. und Vererbungsl.* 61: pp. 147-205.

Whichmann, D. (1953): Zur, Genetik Hautleist ensystems des Fuss-sohle. 2. Morph. Anthrop. 47: 331-81.

20

PHENOTYPIC VARIATION IN CREASES

THE STUDY of human variation ultimately aims at knowing the inter and intra-group variations in human race. Besides culture, language or geographic distribution, the founding element of various phenotypic traits are not only valid but most tried and trusted tools in ethnographic research.

Among physical characters, instead of finding a resolved we get conflicting results, it is more so when the mass of data is increased.

Dermatoglyphic traits to a certain extent have steered out of this conflict by displaying variations which in general are in accord with the classification based upon other traits of human variation. Only simian, sydney or 'M Figure' crease types have found some ground in the study of normal or abnormal complex population problems. Their accord with dermatoglyphic traits is of convincing nature.

The ethnic status of creases is yet at infancy stage, nevertheless it promises a good deal of hope. The number of simian crease traits so far used in the study of human variation is very small. We will discuss about the available work of simian creases on various population in a separate chapter. Here we will like to plead for a firm and stable place of creases in anthropological investigation on the following grounds:

The creases as an objective criteria can help to classify individuals, but in the absence of a uniform scheme of classification the work remains as individual and not a collective force to make crease acceptable for the study of human biology and anthropology.

In the light of the present work, creases appear to have released a score of new phenotypic traits not yet known to the workers. After the long wait of more than a century this morphological variable has reluctantly been accepted. By adding new tools into the ethnographic kit it is hoped that in future work will find a ground to answer some of the problems of human variation and adaptability. The less extensive environmental modifications increase, their obscurity of genetic mechanism are necessary handicaps but, as compared to other phenotypic traits, crease as criteria for ethnic comparisons stands a chance for its application in population studies. Because method and handling of material is simple. The already accumulated material on dermatoglyphic can also be utilized for the study of creases.

The Variability Trends in Creases

Edward's (1978) remark:

> "Three factors–polygenic inheritance moderate to high heritability, inter-population and intra-population variabilities have made dermatoglyphic analysis a useful tool for population biology and physical anthropology" regarding dermatoglyphic trait suits equally well for creases.

In the light of above statement we will discuss few modalities of crease behaviour and its application in population studies.

Bilateral Distribution in Transverse Creases

Palmar creases as morphological variable have been tried by several workers. Creases like other phenotypic traits show bi-sexual and bilateral variations. The consistency in bilateral variation is indicative of crease being a biological human trait which can usefully be employed in population study.

Palmar crease formulations of two groups, i.e., transverse palmar creases and longitudinal palmar creases, are dealt under separate headings.

The three main types of transverse creases are: Single Radial Base Crease (SRBC), Double Radial Base Crease (DRBC) and Triple Radial Base Crease (TRBC). The sex-wise bilateral distribution of each type is considered separately as under:

Males: Rt. Hand: 13.30; 15.00, 14.00, 10.00, 14.67 = 13.50
(SRBC) Lt. Hand: 16.70, 12.50, 14.00, 12.30, 18.67 = 14.85

The distribution of single radial base creases in right and left hand of males among five different populations show less deviational trend both in right hand and left hand frequencies. The bilateral distribution of SRBC shows sinistral dominance which is highest in the last population (Rt: 13.50, Lt: 18.67).

Males: Rt. Hand: 78.00, 75.00, 76.30, 82.30, 77.30 = 77.98
(DRBC) Lt. Hand: 76.70, 80.00, 82.30, 80.77, 77.33 = 81.42

Frequency distribution of double radial base creases among five representative samples, in their right hand as well as left hand, shows consistency of trend by showing nominal variation in frequency distribution. The bi-manual distribution of double radial base crease types in left hand shows dominance over right hand.

Males: Rt. Hands: 8.70, 10.0, 9.70, 7.70, 8.00 = 8.82
(TRBC) Lt. Hands: 6.70, 7.50, 3.80, 6.92, 4.00 = 5.78

The right hand frequencies of five male populations show dextral dominance. It could be seen from the above figures that right hand frequency of TRBC, in all the populations, is strikingly more.

Female: Rt. Hand: 22.30, 17.33, 19.30, 15.70, 19.80 = 18.88
(SRBC) Lt. Hand: 23.84, 16.00, 16.70, 17.40, 15.80 = 17.94

The bi-manual distribution of SRBC in five different female populations do not show much variation of SRBC in left and right hands. The total frequency is little more in right hands as compared to the left hands of the females.

Female: Rt. Hand: 64.62, 72.00, 74.00, 72.00, 71.60 = 68.84
(DRBC) Lt. Hand: 63.08, 72.00, 79.30, 75.40, 80.60 = 74.08

The incidence of DRBC in left hand of female populations is more, as compared to SRBC and DRBC type of creases show inverse relationship with SRBC. It could be seen from the above figures that the distribution trend among five populations exhibits consistency and the variation do not show much deviation.

Female: Rt. Hand: 13.08, 10.67, 16.70, 14.30, 18.60 = 14.68
(TRBC) Lt. Hand: 13.08, 12.00, 14.00, 15.10, 13.60 = 13.56

Considering the bilateral distribution of TRBC, among five different populations it could be seen that the trait under discussion does not show wide range of inter-population difference with respect to bilateralism.

Longitudinal Creases

It has already been pointed out that longitudinal group of palmar creases is different from the transverse types. Only three representative populations represent these creases.

Males: Rt. Hand: 43.30, 42.50, 23.60 = 36.46
(SCBC) Lt. Hand: 49.30, 38.00, 37.60 = 41.97

It could be seen from the above frequencies of longitudinal crease type (SCBC) that for the exception of one male population all other show higher incidence of the trait in their left hands. The bi-manual difference is repeating the trend as indicated by single radial base crease among the male populations.

Male: Rt. Hand: 50.00, 55.00, 72.60 = 59.20
(DCBC) Lt. Hand: 41.30, 58.00, 59.70 = 53.00

The frequency distribution of double carpal base crease in three male populations shows dextral dominance. In the case of longitudinal creases the relative incidence of single radial base crease is much higher as compared to transverse crease type of single base category.

Male: Rt. Hand: 6.70, 2.50, 3.80 = 4.33
(TCBC) Lt. Hand: 9.30, 4.00, 2.70 = 5.33

The incidence of triple carpal base crease in above given male populations show bi-manual difference. The distributional trend of the trait shows a regular feature.

Female: Rt. Hand: 24.00, 28.60, 18.80 = 23.80
(SCBC) Lt. Hand: 26.70, 30.90, 25.70 = 27.76

Considering the female populations with respect to the distribution of single carpal base crease, it could be noticed that females like males, show higher incidence of the crease in left hand. The trait maintains the consistency in all the populations.

Female: Rt. Hand: 62.70, 64.60, 72.30 = 66.53
(DCBC) Lt. Hand: 61.30, 60.60, 67.30 = 63.66

The bilateral incidence of double carpal base creases in females show dextral dominance. The sexual dimorphism in longitudinal creases as compared to transverse creases is well marked.

The right and left hand variations among transverse and longitudinal crease types show consistency of trend as exhibited by other biological traits. The bilateral difference is a biological attribute.

Bi-sexual Distribution of Crease Types

(SRBC): Male: Rt. Hand: 13.30, 15.00, 14.00 10.00, 14.67 = 13.50
Female: Rt. Hand: 22.30, 17.33, 19.30, 15.70, 19.80 = 18.88

The bi-sexual variation of any phenotypic trait has to be tested against sexes. The sexual variation of human morphological variable shows that the trait is a biological attribute.

The distribution of SRBC in the above five male populations shows lesser frequencies as compared to the females. This trend of bi-sexual variation of SRBC is shown by all the populations.

(SRBC): Male: Lt. Hand: 16.70, 12.50, 14.00, 12.30, 18.67 = 14.85
Female: Lt. Hand: 12.84, 16.00, 16.70, 17.40, 15.80 = 17.94

Considering the left hand frequencies of SRBC in males and females the sexual dimorphism of the left hand is more striking than the right hand.

(DRBC): Male: Rt. Hand: 78.00, 75.00, 76.30, 82.30, 77.30 = 77.98
Female: Rt. Hand: 64.62, 72.00, 74.00, 72.00, 71.60 = 68.84

The bi-sexual dimorphism with respect to DRBC shows male dominance. All the five populations of males exhibit higher incidence of DRBC as compared to SRBC and DRBC types. The sexes show inverse relationship.

(DRBC): Male: Lt. Hand: 76.70, 80.00, 82.30, 80.77, 77.33 = 81.42
Female: Lt. Hand: 63.08, 72.00, 79.30, 75.40, 80.60 = 74.08

The left hand frequency of males and females show the same trend of sexual dimorphism as exhibited by the right hand. Bi-sexual variation in both types of creases is well marked.

(TRBC): Male: Rt. Hand: 8.70, 10.00, 9.70, 7.70, 8.00 = 8.82
Female: Rt. Hand: 13.08, 10.67, 16.70, 14.30, 18.60 = 14.68

The sex-wise distribution of TRBC type of crease in right hands of females show strikingly higher incidence of the trait as compared to males. All the five female populations show higher frequency of TRBC.

(TRBC): Male: Lt. Hand: 6.70, 7.50, 3.80, 6.92, 4.00 = 5.78
Female: Lt. Hand: 13.08, 12.00, 14.00, 15.10, 13.60 = 13.56

A similar trend is exhibited by left hand of the above

populations. It could be seen from the above figures that TRBC shows bi-sexual variation as a biological attribute. On the basis of bi-sexual and bilateral distribution of transverse creases it appears that these crease types are genetically inter-dependent on each other.

Female: Rt. Hand: 13.30, 6.80, 8.90 = 9.33
(TCBC) Lt. Hand: 12.00, 8.60, 6.90 = 9.11

All the three types of longitudinal creases show clear sexual difference. The difference is more striking in the case of triple carpal base creases. The trait does not show clear cut bilateral difference.

On the basis of above observation, it is amply clear that longitudinal creases like transverse palmar creases qualify as a tool for the study of ethnic or other anthropological studies.

Isolateral and Non-isolateral Hands

Those hands which possess a same crease type are designated as isolateral hands. When this feature is absent the hands are called non-isolateral. This situation can be known both for sexes and populations.

The palmar creases are represented by two sets of creases and symmetry between the sets can be seen on the same palm. The hands bearing similar crease types (transverse and longitudinal) are called isolateral hands.

Plantar Creases

There are a few reports available in the study of plantar creases. The present work is on the basis of the formulation given by Bali and Mishra (1978). It is desirable to investigate the bi-sexual and bi-pedal trend of the traits as under:

Male: Rt. Foot: 57.69, 70.64 = 64.15
(SMBC) Lt. Foot: 65.11, 65.13 = 65.12

From the above two male populations it could be observed that the incidence of single medial base crease show nominal bi-pedal difference. The distributional trend shows consistency in either sides.

The incidence of single medial base crease in female populations reflects a striking bilateral difference. The incidence of crease under discussion exhibits higher frequencies in males as compared to females.

Male: Rt. Foot: 42.30, 25.68 = 33.99
(DMBC) Lt. Foot: 33.33, 31.19 = 32.26

A similar bi-pedal trend is exhibited by double medial base crease as shown by SMBC types. The bilateral difference is more in first population and least in the second.

Male: Rt. Foot: 0, 3.66 = 1.83
(TMBC) Lt. Foot: 1.55, 3.66 = 2.60

The triple medial pase crease shows rare incidence both in left and right hands of above populations.

Female: Rt. Foot: 41.53, 59.25 = 50.39
(SMBC) Lt. Foot: 44.61, 68.51 = 56.56

Out of three different female populations, the frequency of SMBC is more in the second population. The bilateral difference is more in the second population. Sexual dimorphism is not well marked.

Female: Rt. Foot: 56.16, 31.48 = 43.82
(DMBC) Lt. Foot: 53.84, 24.07 = 38.95

In the case of the double medial base crease the second female population shows more bi-manual difference. The female populations exhibit higher frequencies as compared to the males. From bi-sexual and bi-pedal difference of the trait it could be seen that creases of the plantar surface stand a chance for their application in ethnic study.

Female: Rt. Foot: 2.30, 9.25 = 5.77
(TMBC) Lt. Foot: 1.54, 7.40 = 4.47

Triple medial base crease in relation to other creases shows low incidence, a condition also true for sexes.

Isopedal and Non-Isopedal Feet

As we have designated hands in isolateral and non-isolateral types, a similar type of expression is devised for plantar creases. Isopedal feet signify the occurrence of the same type of creases on both the feet.

REFERENCES

Bali, R.S. and R. Mishra, (1978): The plantar creases formulation, X Internat. Congr. Anthrop, and Ethnic Science, New Delhi, India.

Edwards, C.R. (1978): A comparison of Dermatoglyphic and Genetic similarity Indices in Rhesus Monkeys. *Dermatoglyphics: An International Perspective*, Mouton Publishers.

21

ETHNIC VARIABILITY IN CREASES

ONE OF the main objectives of anthropologists is to study the variations in different population groups in relation to ethnic and geographic distribution. At present, there is little data on crease trait distribution. The reports on simian crease have been studied very sporadically from different countries of the world.

Crease traits like dermatoglyphic traits are controlled by polygenic factors and stand a chance to be used in the study of ethnic and geographic distribution. With the accumulation of records for many ethnic series, it is now assured that racial differences in creases are real. As a result of intense recent interest in creases, several descriptive methods are being rapidly put in currency, thus creating the need for standardizing of a method, so that consistency in data interpretation is properly maintained.

In case of phalangeal, bracelet and sole creases, the material on crease prints is rather meagre and the question of their ethnic utility does not arise. But palmar creases, especially simian creases, stand a chance for re-interpretation on the basis of the present superseded methodology.

The status of ethnic variation in palmar creases may be better appreciated in the light of current schemes of palmar, plantar, bracelet and phalangeal crease formulations.

The existing material on different population, formulated under different schemes of crease classification, has been accommodated under the current palmar crease classification. Thanks to the work on transverse crease in Europe by Lestrange (1969) that we are able to interpret at least one crease (transverse crease) for evaluating its ethnic importance. The reported work on transverse crease in Europe was of varied nature and purpose and against heavy odds the above-mentioned author could consolidate the work of several researchers in Europe. Taking into consideration the total number of creases (palm, sole, phalanges, toe and bracelet) we just could relate only one crease of the palm for its ethnic purpose, this shows the amount of progress made in this direction.

To gather the work of all sorts on creases a brief review is desired. To avoid repetition those authors who have been referred in the proceeding table are not included here.

Crease Appraisal

Ito et al., (1956) studied transverse crease among Japanese. Chakravartti and Basu (1960) made their observation on simian crease of Tripura Indians, Büchi (1965) investigated the frequency of simian crease in Tabitians and on Indian population (1965). Naffah (1974) studied simain crease of Lebanese, while Marshal and Jephcott (1969) and Tunakan (1954) studied the prevalence of simian creases in Turkish population. Chamla and Sahley (1973) investigated transverse crease in Tunisians. Obata's work (1956) on longitudinal flexion crease of Kyushi islanders is a solitary reference on longitudinal crease.

Apart from specific ethnic work several reports are available on simian crease or transverse line with respect to its phenotypic behaviour. Kutsuna (1929), Lasinski and Urbanowicz (1960) and Gomila et al. (1967) studied simian creases with purpose other than ethnic variation. Wiel (1953) and Wendt (1959) studied simian creases. Wiel's work was on transverse line.

Purvis-Smith (1972) related sydney line with Down's syndrome and reported significant results. Davies and Smallpiece (1963) investigated transverse crease among infants. Debrunner (1957) studied transverse crease in children. Nassau and Kallner (1958) made observation of flexion creases on diseased children while Erne (1953) studied simian crease in relation to mangolism. Eriksson (1958) studied simian crease in relation to Swedish population.

The work on simian and transverse creases in relation to certain abnormalities, diseases and syndrome of special importance was conducted by Erne (1953), Goodman et al. (1972), Hirsch (1977) and Sottner et al. (1968). Hook et al., (1974) studied the effect of maternal smoking during gestation period on infant morphology in relation to transverse line.

The frequency of transverse palmar crease among European populations has been studied by Lestrange (1969). The author's Table (21.1) with essential details is given as under:

TABLE 21.1: Frequency of transverse creases among various unselected groups

S.No.	Country of origin	Percentage of bearers of at least one T.C.		Authors
		Men	Women	
(1)	(2)	(3)	(4)	(5)
1.	Germany	188/4639=4.05		Portius and Schiller in Walter 1952
2.	England	14/811=1.73		Davies and Smallpiece, 1963
3.	England	232/6299=3.68		Davies, 1966
4.	Finland	51/983=5.19		Kervinen, 1954
5.	Finland	242/4742=5.10		Kervinen, 1954
6.	Turkey	38/323=11.176		Tunakan, 1954
7.	U.S.A. (New York)	11/500=2.20		Achs, Harper and Harrick, 1966
8.	Germany	11/100=11.00	6/100=6.00	Bettmann, 1932 in Rittmeister, 1936
9.	Germany	25/325=7.69	6/264=2.27	Becker, 1952
10.	Germany	13/400=3.25	—	Geipel, 1961
11.	Germany	15/302=4.97	—	Schroeder in Van der Wiel, 1953
12.	Austria (Principally Vienna)	39/986=3.96	25/862=2.90	Weninger and Navratil, 1957
13.	Austria (Principally Vienna)	45/1122=4.01	18/815=2.21	Weninger and Navratil, 1957
14.	Belgium	18/663=2.71	14/545=2.57	Vrydagh-Lasureux, 1967
15.	Denmark	7/150=4.67	5/150=3.33	Bjork in Walter, 1957
16.	Spain	15/390=3.85	2/105=1.50	Jordan and Pons in Walter, 1957
17.	Finland (Helsinki)	12/348=3.45	5/375=1.33	Brander in Van der Wiel, 1953 and Kervinen, 1954
18.	France	7/100=7.00	—	C.Fere in Rittmeister, 1936
19.	France (Paris)	8/388=2.06	5/279=1.79	Kherumian, 1957
20.	Holland (West)	7/826=0.85	—	Rittmeister, 1936
21.	Hungary (Debrecan & neighbourhood)	20/480=4.17	13/568=2.99	M.Papp, 1964
22.	Ireland	1/91=1.10	2/130=1.54	Rashad, Morten & Scally, 1964

(Contd.)

TABLE 21.1 (*Contd.*)

(1)	(2)	(3)	(4)	(5)
23.	Italy	1/97=1.03	—	Gobesso & Piazzi, 1962
24.	Italy	10/62=6.17	—	Carrara, 1893
25.	Poland	20/580=3.45	—	Lasinsky in Walter, 1957
26.	Portugal	19/541=3.51	13/415=3.13	Almeida Santos, 1960
27.	Romania (Banat)	28/521=5.37	15/557=2.69	Weninger, 1953
28.	Romania (Hunedoara & Olthenie)	91/2,535=3.59	53/2,659=1.99	Dumitrescu-ciovirnache
29.	Sweden	20/346=5.80	8/319=2.51	Eriksson and Norinder, 1958
30.	Sweden	1/95=1.05	3/97=3.09	Beckman *et al.* 1962
31.	Switzerland (Zurich)	3/230=1.30	—	Rittmeister, 1936
32.	Turkey	5/120=4.17	4/140=2.86	Tunakan, 1954
33.	India (Saugar District)	21/630=3.33	31/630=4.92	Ramesh Chaube, 1971

The distribution of transverse crease in 40 European populations were first tabulated by Lestrange (1969). On the basis of sample size and other scrutinies the author selected only representative populations. In spite of much care still the result do not agree with accepted classification of anthropologists and author desires a genetically based creases classification.

Simian crease frequency among various unselected groups, as listed in Fischer's table (1949), shows varied and unsuggestive distribution of simian crease (Table 21.2).

A similar attempt on Hungarian population (four groups) was made by Gyula (1974).

Ethnic Variability Among Creases

Palmar flexion creases are not the sole representative of crease science. Creases in fact, are the components of entire dermatoglyphic regions and should not be treated as indiscrete units of non-biological aspects. Instead, a uniform approach is recommended.

The present work is an attempt towards this direction. The creases of palm, sole phalanges and bracelet areas are treated for their ethnic variability under separate headings.

Transverse Palmar Creases

Transverse Palmar creases are the separate group of palmar creases which are classified on independent criteria i.e., base point.

TABLE 21.2: Simian crease frequency among various unselected groups

Group	Number	Sex	Simian Crease		Author
			Complete	Transition	
Germans	3,646	M	1.5	—	Steffens, 1953
	3,508	F	0.2	—	
Germans	1,030	M	1.65	5.15	Portius, 1937
Germans	1,502	M	3.20	—	Schiller, 1942
		F	2.35	—	
Germans	325	M	7.8	—	Becker, 1952
	264	F	2.2	—	
Jews	108	M	4.6	—	Schiller*
	92	F	0.0	—	
Arabs & Kabyls	530	M	7.9	—	Nanhart, 1936
Amerinds	41	M+F	7.1	16.7	Mayntzhusen-Fischer*
Eskimos	74	M+F	1.35	5.41	Peters-Abel*
Chinese	100	M	13.00	2.00	Kings*
Basua	191	M rt.	17.8	—	Abel, 1940
		M lt.	16.2	—	
	104	F rt.	18.2	—	
		F lt.	17.2	—	
Indians*	630	M	0.95	10.16	Ramesh Chaube, 1971 (Present Study)
	630	F	1.43	15.55	

* Cited after Fischer (1949).

TABLE 21.3: Ethnic variability in transverse palmar creases

S.No.	Authors	Sample	Place of origin	No.	Male			No.	Female		
					SRBC	DRBC	TRBC		SRBC	DRBC	TRBC
1.	Bali & Chaube (1971)	Punjabi Brahmins	Punjab	95	6.80	85.80	7.40	95	5.30	64.20	30.50
2.	Bali & Chaube (1971)	Bhangi	Sagar (M.P.)	75	16.70	77.30	6.00	75	16.70	72.00	11.30
3.	Chaube (1977)	Brahmins	Sagar (M.P.)	260	11.16	80.53	7.31	260	23.07	66.85	10.08
4.	Eswaraiah (1977)	Sale	Karnataka	150	15.00	77.30	7.70	150	8.00	76.70	15.30
5.	Eswaraiah (1977)	Devanga	Karnataka	200	13.80	77.50	8.70	175	6.60	77.50	15.90
6.	Eswaraiah (1977)	Thogata	Karnataka	186	14.00	79.30	6.70	101	7.80	76.10	16.10
7.	Eswaraiah (1978)	Muslim	Karnataka	213	11.50	83.50	5.00	—	—	—	—
8.	Eswaraiah (1978)	Reddi	Karnataka	146	13.00	83.20	3.80	—	—	—	—
9.	Eswaraiah (1978)	Balija	Karnataka	118	8.10	84.30	7.60	—	—	—	—
10.	Jain (1978)	Brahmins	Sagar (M.P.)	346	9.39	80.21	10.40	311	3.54	68.65	27.81
11.	Patel (1981)	Jain	Sagar (M.P.)	200	26.00	71.50	2.50	200	26.00	69.50	4.50
12.	Safiya (1986)	Mixed Population	Sagar (M.P.)	182	19.78	70.22	9.90	180	20.00	65.84	14.16
13.	Mondal (1987)	Gonds	Sagar (M.P.)	299	11.90	75.52	12.58	119	13.44	73.12	13.44

The frequencies listed in the Table (21.3) are of transverse palmar crease after the formulation given by Bali and Chaube (1971). It could be seen from this table that bi-manual and bi-sexual trend is fairly similar for all population.

The higher incidence of SRBC shows inverse relationship with TRBC. A situation common for all the populations.

It could be concluded that above three main types of transverse creases are indicative of common genetic interaction.

Longitudinal Palmar Creases

Longitudinal group of palmar creases is independent of transverse creases. Although, radial longitudinal crease is the common factor but its distal end which forms the carpal base point is distinctly different from radial base point.

The ethnic variability among the population studied is less known because only few populations have been studied from ethnic point of view. It could be seen from the Table (21.4) that longitudinal palmar creases are indicative of the fact that these creases could usefully be employed for ethnic investigation. But for one mixed population, rest three populations are mendalian in nature.

Plantar Creases

Ethnic distribution of plantar creases is based on three separate groups (Table 21.5). Brahmins and Rajputs are endogamous groups and are nearer to the mendalian population categories. The mixed group is not suitable example for ethnic study.

The three main crease types have only been considered. From the frequency of single, double and triple medial base crease it appears that there exists a mutual trend of frequency distribution which shows genetic interdependence among above main three types of plantar creases.

Phalangeal creases occur on three flexion sites. Each site is independent ethnic trait. The incidence of crease types on distal, middle and proximal sites show variation. The ethnic variability has not been studied so far, only one population is represented by phalangeal crease types. The bi-manual and bi-sexual variations indicate that phalangeal crease is an effective ethnic tool. Toe creases are represented by a single population, i.e., Bangali Brahmins, an endogamous caste group.

TABLE 21.4: Ethnic variability in longitudinal palmar creases

S.No.	Authors	Sample	Place of origin	No.	Male			No.	Female		
					SCBC	DCBC	TCBC		SCBC	DCBC	TCBC
1.	Eswaraiah (1977)	Sale	Karnataka	150	46.40	45.60	8.00	150	25.30	62.00	12.70
2.	Eswaraiah (1977)	Devanga	Karnataka	200	40.20	56.50	3.30	175	29.70	62.60	7.70
3.	Eswaraiah (1977)	Thogata	Karnataka	186	30.60	66.10	3.30	101	22.30	69.80	7.90
4.	Safiya (1986)	Mixed population	Sagar (M.P.)	182	58.79	41.21	0.00	180	51.66	48.34	0.00

TABLE 21.5: Ethnic variability in plantar creases

S.No.	Authors	Sample	Place of origin	No.	Male			No.	Female		
					SMBC	DMBC	TMBC		SMBC	DMBC	TMBC
1.	Mishra (1979)	Brahmins	Rewa (M.P.)	130	61.39	37.83	0.78	130	43.08	55.00	1.92
2.	Singh (1983)	Rajputs	Sagar (M.P.)	218	67.88	28.44	3.68	108	63.80	27.87	8.33
3.	Safiya (1986)	Mixed population	Sagar (M.).)	182	61.82	32.14	6.04	180	36.12	42.22	21.66

The ethnic validity of creases is an emerging field of anthropology. Each crease is a trait and its several biological attributes are discreet units of genetic expression, which also have collective phenotypic behaviour thus making creases an effective ethnic tool. A serious and extensive investigation only can establish creases in anthropology. It is too early to think of crease anthropology as a viable branch of human science.

REFERENCES

Bali, R.S. and Ramesh Chaube (1971): On the formulation of palmar creases, *Z. Morph. Anthrop.*, 63 : p. 121.

Büchi, E.C. (1954): The Simian crease in India. *Bulletin of the Indian Department of Anthropology*, 3(1): pp. 39-49.

Büchi, E.C. (1965): Anthropologie des Tibetains. Paris: Ecole Francaise d' Extreme-Orient, Maisonneuve.

Chakravartti, M.R. and S.K. Basu (1960): A note on the simian crease of the Riangs of Tripura, *Science and Culture* 26: 41-45.

Chamla, M.C. and A. Sahley (1973): Le pli palmaire transverse chez (les tunisiens). *L' Anthropologie* (Paris) 77(1-2) : pp. 107-18.

Davies, P.A. and V. Smallpiece (1963): The single transverse palmar crease in infants and children. *Developmental Medicine and Child Neurology*, 5(5) : pp. 491-96.

Debrunner, I.M. (1957): Zur Morphologie der Transversalfurche (Vierfingerfurche). *Deutsches Gesellschaft fur Anthropologie*, 5 : pp. 52-56

Ernè, H. (1953): *Uber das pappillarleistensystem und die palmafurchen in Familien mit einem order mehreren Fallen von Mòngolismus und ein Beitrag zum problem der Vierfingerfurche.* Thesis, Zurich.

Eriksson, S.A. (1958): Systematik der Fingerspitzenmuster. *Nordic Criminology Magazine*, 27 : pp. 275-87 (in Swedish).

Eswaraiah, G. (1977): *Palmar creases and diseases.* Thesis submitted in fulfilment of the requirement for the degree of Ph.D., Saugar University, Sagar.

Eswaraiah, G. (1978): Palmar creases - Criteria for ethnic variation. *Indian Journal of Physical Anthropology and Human Genetics.* IV. 7.

Gomila, J., L. Per-Laborde, M. Lestrange (1967): Dermatoglyphics digitopalmaires et plis de flexion dans 1' isolat Bedik, S'enegal (oriental). *Akten des antropologischen Kongresses* (Brno) 19 : pp. 103-18.

Goodman, R.M., M. Batmiriam Katzrelson, M. Frydman (1972): Evolution of palmar skin creases in the Ehlers - Danlos Syndrome. *Clinical Genetics* (K benhavn) 3(1) : pp. 67-72.

Goodman, R.M., M. Batmiriam Katznelson, E. Manor (1972): Camptodactyly: occurrence in two new genetic syndromes and its relationship to other syndromes. *Journal of Medical Genetics*, 9(2) : pp. 203-12.

Gyula, G. (1974): A Négyujjasredö és a Sidney-redö gyakorisága néhány magyarországi populációban. *Anthróp közl.* 18: pp.69-77.

Hirsch, W., (1977): Dermatoglyphics and creases in their relationship to clinical syndromes. A diagnostic criterio, in Dermatoglyphics : an international perspective, Edited by J. Mavalwala. *World Anthropology*. The Hague: Mouton.

Hook, E.B., S. Selvin, J. Garfinkel, M. Greenberg (1974): "Maternal smoking during gestation and infant morphologic variation : Preliminary report concerning birth, weight and incidence of transverse palmar creases", in *Congenital Defects : New Directions in Research.* Edited by D.T. Janerich, R.G. Skalko and I.H. Porter, London: Academic Press, pp. 171-84.

Ito, K., T. Kogata, M. Murai, H. Osugi (1956): The transverse crease among the Japanese. Classification of *Affenfurche* among the Japanese. *Transactions of Tottori University* (Department of Anatomy), 4.

Jain, D.K. (1978): *Age change - Morphology of hand and palmar flexion creases among Brahmin Girls.* Thesis submitted in part fulfilment for the requirement of the degree of M.Sc., Saugar University, Sagar.

Khatoon, S. (1986): *Study of Twins and Reliability of Creases in Twin Zygosity Diagnosis.* Ph.D. Thesis, Saugar University, Sagar.

Kutsuna, S. (1929): On "Bewegungslinie" of the human hand. *Jinruigaku Zasshi,* 44(504): pp. 471-89.

Lasinski, W., M. Urbanowicz (1960): The system of skin furrows on the human palm. *Folia Morphologica,* 11 : pp. 115-24 (in Polish).

Lestrange, M. de (1969): The transverse crease in Europe - index and comparative study of different samples cited in the literature. *American Journal of Physical Anthropology,* 30 : pp.173-82.

Marshall, I.B., J. Jephcott (1969): The prevalence of simian lines in a sample of the Turkish population. *Turkish Journal of Pediatrics,* 11(3) : pp. 91-97.

Mishra, R. (1979): *Inheritance and Methodological Study of Plantar Creases.* Thesis submitted in part fulfilment for the requirements of the degree of Ph.D., Saugar University, Sagar.

Mondal, R.C. (1987): *Palmar Creases in Gonds of Sagar.* Thesis submitted in part fulfilment for the requirement of the degree of M.Sc., Saugar University, Sagar.

Naffah, J. (1974): Dermatoglyphics and flexion creases in the Lebanese population. *American Journal of Physical Anthropology,* 41(3) : pp. 391-409.

Nassau, E., A. Kallner (1958): Observations on the deep furrows of the palm of the hand and the sole of the foot in diseased children. *Annales de Pe'diatrie* (Basel), 191: pp. 295-307.

Obata, Y. (1956): Studies on the longitudinal flexion crease. 1. The South Kyushu Islanders. *Medical Journal of Kagoshima University,* 7(5).

Patel, A.B. (1981): *The Study of Inheritance of Palmar Creases and their Base Point Positioning.* M.Sc. dissertation, Saugar University, Sagar.

Purvis-Smith, S.G. (1972): The Downs syndrome dermatogram - a clinical evaluation. *Australian Journal of Mental Retardation,* 2 : pp. 51-53.

Purvis-Smith, S.G. (1972a): The Sydney line : a significant sign in Down's syndrome. *Australian Paediatric* Journal, 8 : pp. 198-200.

Singh, N.R. (1983): *A Study of Plantar Creases among Rajputs.* M.Sc. dissertation, Saugar University, Sagar.

Sottner, L., J. Pospisil, A. Syrovatka (1968): Observation of karyotype changes in person with simian line. *Ceskoslovenska Pediatrie,* 23(12) : pp. 1096-1100.

Tunakan, S. (1954): A study on the simian creases in Turkish people and convicts. *Turk Tarib Kurumu Basimevi* (Ankara) 12 (1-2): 117-26.

Wendt, G.G. (1959): Untersuchunger an den Handfurchen des Menschen. *Homo* 10 : pp. 276-83.

Wiel, H.J. Van der (1953): On the fourfinger line. *Verhanddelingen (Koninklijke). Nederlandse Akademie van Wetenschappen.* 56(5) : pp. 666-72.

22

SIMIAN CREASE RELATION TO CLINICAL SYNDROMES

THE MAXIMUM work on simian or sydney crease finds citation under the heading 'dermatoglyphics' because of its close topographical association, which is carried to the level of prints, is of conjugal nature.

In the light of above facts a short review on 'dermatoglyphic in medicine' will provide to the reader the magnitude of the work carried out in the field.

The work on chromosomal anomalies and dermatoglyphics is plenty. After Lejeune, Turpin and Gautier (1959), the contributors are Geipel (1961), Penrose (1963), Uchida and Soltan (1963). Kumbnani and Pfeiffer (1969), Holt (1964, 1965), Uchida (1966) and several others have added greatly towards the knowledge of dermatoglyphic of patients with trisomy 21.

A rapidly growing body of data is now becoming available to provide information regarding relationship between dermatoglyphics, chromosomal aberration disorders and clinical syndromes.

The contributions of Geipel and Hirsch (1960), Weninger et al. (1965), Weninger et al. (1966), Brehme and Schroler (1967), Rott (1971), Bartsocas et al. (1970), Fauchier et al. (1971), Kumbnani (1971) and Schaumann and Pantke (1978) are noteworthy.

The clinical importance of dermatoglyphic traits is an established fact and the above cited work is a further lead for future work.

The present work is essentially on creases and the literature available on diseases and congenital disorders is mostly available with reference to simian crease. It is, therefore, desirable to make a review of the existing work with reference to simian crease or sydney line. The author is aware that the reader is being loaded with a number of citations giving minimum information on their individual contributions. A full detail of the work is beyond the scope of this Chapter. Nonetheless in the next Chapter we will deal with diseases under the formulations which include almost all creases of palm. Hanhart (1936) and Tunakan (1954) studied abnormal human traits with simian crease. Davies and Smallpiece (1963) showed more simian creases among the newborn children of prematurity, neo-natal death, still birth and cases of congenital abnormalities.

Nassau and Kallner (1958) made observations on the simian line of the hand and foot in diseased children. Hook et al. (1974) studied in detail the effect of smoking during gestation on infants and incidence of transverse palmar creases in congenital defects. The clinical significance of simian crease was also worked out by Johnson (1971).

Purvis-Smith (1972) made observation on Down's syndrome in relation to sydney crease and showed higher frequency of the crease in affected persons. The relationship of simian line with psoriasis was studied by Verbov (1967).

Sottner, Pospisil and Syrovatka (1968) made observation of karyotype changes in persons with simian line.

Mehas (1972) indicated higher frequency of simian lines in subject with some inborn errors of metabolism and congenital disorders.

Biswas and Bardhan (1966) studied simian crease in relation to schizophrenia.

Simian Creases in Medicine

Langdon-Down (1866) described certain typical features in mentally retarded children which are indistinguishable morphologically from those of Mongols. This syndrome is also known as Down's syndrome. The person afflicted by the syndrome show certain outstanding features on his/her fingers, palm and sole.

Langdon-Down (1909) was first to stir up interest among scientists in the study of simian crease. He found higher incidence of the single transverse crease among mongoloid idiots. Rittmeister (1936) found higher frequency of the simian crease among mongoloid idiots. Kervinen (1954) studied the simian crease among feeble minded children of Finland.

Hale et al. (1961) observed more simian lines and sydney lines in congenital heart disease. Erne (1953) observed mongoloid relation of simian crease. Forbes (1964) studied flexion crease relation with gonadal dysgenesis, and pseudo-hypoparathyroidism and Klinefelter's syndrome. Geipel (1961) also studied simian line in relation with abnormal human traits.

REFERENCES

Bartsocas, C.S., A.L. Weber, J.D. Crawford (1970): Acrocephalosyndactyly type III: Chotzen's syndrome. *Journal of Pediatrics* 77: pp. 267-72.

Biswas, P.C. and A. Bardhan (1966): Palm prints and Schizophrenia. *The Anthropologist* pp.13(1-12).

Brehme, H, R. Schroler (1967): Dermatoglyphics of 15 patients with Russell-Silver syndrome. *Humangenetik* 5: pp. 28-35 (in German).

Davies, P.A. and V. Smallpiece (1963): The single transverse palmar crease in infants and children. *Developmental Medicine and Child Neurology* 5(5).

Erne, H. (1953): *Uber das Papillarleistensystem und die Palmar-furchen in Familien mit einem oder mehreren Fallen won Mongolismus und ein Beitrag zum Problem der Vierfingerfurche*. Thesis, Zurich.

Fauchier, C., J.M. Regy, J.P. Lamagnere, P. Combe (1970): Gigantisme cerebral., *Annales de pediatrie* (Paris) 17: pp. 870-75.

Forbes, A.P. (1964): Fingerprints and palm prints (dermatoglyphics) and palmar flexion creases in gonadal dysgenesis, pseudo-hypoparathyroidism, and Klinefelter's syndrome. *New England Journal of Medicine* 270(24): pp. 1268-77.

Geipel, G. (1961): Ein Beitrag zur Verteilung der Winkel and auf der inneren Handflache. *Zeitschrift fur Morphologie und Anthropologie* 51(3): pp. 333-38.

Hale, A.R., J.H. Phillips, G.E. Burch (1961): Features of palmar dermatoglyphics in congenital heart disease: report on variants frequently associated with congenital lesions of heart. *Journal of the American Medical Association* 176: p. 41.

Hanhart, E. (1936): Uber die Bedeutung der Vierfingerfurche (sogen. Affenfurche) also Merkmal konstitutionellr nervoser Minderwertigkeit und ihr vorkommen in mitteleuropaischen und nordafrikanischen Ressen gemischen. *Verbandlungen der Schweizischen Naturfors chung Gesellschaft* 117: pp. 365-66.

Hirsch, W. and G. Geipel (1960): Das Papillarieistensystem der Hand und seine Beziehung ze cerebralen Storungen. *Acta Genetica et Statistica Medica* 10(1-3): pp. 103-82.

Holt, S.B. (1964): The role of dermatoglyphics in medical Biology. *Medical World* (London) 101: pp. 112-25.

Holt, S.B. (1965): Dermatoglyphics of congenital Malformations. *Developmental Medicine and Child Neurology* 7: pp. 568-69.

Hook, E.B., S. Selvin, J. Garfinkel, M. Greenberg (1974): 'Maternal smoking during gestation and infant morphologic variation: preliminary report concerning birth, weight and incidence of transverse palmar creases,' in *Congenital Defects: New Directions in Research*. Edited by D.T. Janerich, R.G. Skalko, and I.H. Porter, 171-84. London: Academic Press.

Johnson, C.F., E. Opit (1971): The single palmar crease and its clinical significance in a child development clinic. *Clinical Pediatrics* (Philadelphia) 10: pp. 392-404.

Kervinen, V. (1954): The incidence of the four-finger groove in Finland. *Annales Academiae Scientiarum Fennicae* (Helsinki) 40: pp. 1-12.

Kumbnani, H.K. (1971): Main-line index and transversality in a German population afflicted with Down's Syndrome. *International Symposium on Human Genetics* Waltair, India.

Kumbnani, H.K., R.A. Pfeiffer (1969): Partial trisomy in a child with features suggesting mongolism. *Journal of Medical Genetics* 6: pp. 201-05.

Lejeune, J.R., Turpin, M. Gautier (1959): Le mongolisme premier example d'aberration autosomique humaine. *Annales de Genetique* 1: p. 241.

Langdon-Down, R.L. (1909): Mongolian Imbecility, *Brit. Med. J.*, 12: p. 665.

Mehas, K. (1972): Simian Crease, *Acta Pediatra. Acad. Sci. Hung.* 13, 4: p. 335.

Nassau, E., A Kallner (1958): Observation on the deep furrows of the palm of the hand and the sole of the foot in diseased children. *Annales de pediatrie* (Basel) 191: pp. 295-307.

Penrose, L.S. (1963): Fingerprints, palms, and chromosomes. *Nature* 197(4871): pp. 933-38.

Purvis-Smith, S.G. (1972): The Down's syndrome dermatogram — clinical evaluation. *Australian Journal of Mental Retardation* 2: pp. 51-53.

Rittmeister, J.F. (1936): Uber die Affenfurche (Vierfingerfurche) mit besonderer Beruchsichtigung der Mikrodegeneration en und des Problems des Mongolismus. *Zeitschrift fur Anatomie und Entwicklungsgeschichte* 106(2): pp. 276-314.

Rott., H.D. (1971): Hautleistenstorungen bei verschiedenen Krankheiten. *Hautleisten und Krankbeiten* 2: pp. 247-54.

Schaumann, B., O.A. Pantke (1978): 'Dermatoglyphics in dyscephaly Saethre-Chotzen (Acrocephalosyndactyly type III, Chotzen syndrome),' in *Dermatoglyphics: An International Perspective.* Edited by J. Mavalwala. World Anthropology. The Hague: Mouton.

Sottner, L., J. Pospisil, A. Syrovatka (1968): Observation of Karyotype changes in persons with simian line. *Ceskoslovenska Pediatrie* 23(12): pp. 1096-1100.

Tunakan, S. (1954): A study on the simian crease in Turkish people and convicts. *Turk kurumu Basimevi* (Ankara) 12(1-2): pp. 117-26.

Uchida, I.A. (1966): Dermatoglyphics and chromosomes. *Alabama Journal of Medical Science* 3(4): pp. 432-34.

Uchida, L.A., H.C. Soltan (1963): Evaluation of dermatoglyphics in medical genetics, *Pediatric Clinics of North America* 10(2): pp. 409-22.

Verbov, J.L. (1967): Simian line and psoraisis. *Lancet* 2: p. 779.

Weninger, M., F. Kaindl, G. Rothenbuchner, B. Schober (1966): Skin ridge studies in congenital defects of the heart and the large vessels. *Wiener Klinische Wocbenschrift* 798(51): pp. 905-06.

Weninger, M., G. Rothenbuchner, B. Schober (1965): Dermatoglyphics finding in thyroiditis lymphomatose Hashimoto. *Humangenetik* 1(7): pp. 676-80.

23

PALMAR CREASES IN MEDICINE

THERE IS ample evidence now available to show that certain diseases bear relationship with palmar creases. There exists a well documented association between several diseases, congenital malformations and palmar crease variations.

The work cited in the previous Chapter is restricted only to simian crease relationship and the role of other creases of the palm has not been fully realized, for the obvious reason that all the available palmar crease formulations do not embrace all the creases of the palm.

In the light of the above limitation, a fresh approach towards this problem is recommended. The principal element of the change in the approach is the use of crease formation suggested by the author.

In this Chapter, only those reports are being considered which deal crease relationship with diseases, on the basis of transverse and longitudinal crease classification. These classifications embrace all the creases of the palm irrespective of their being simian or non-simian types.

Both transverse and longitudinal palmar crease classifications find their independent status and are dealt on a separate basis in their applications. The central theme of our discussion will be based on crease variation among the patients and the control (normal population).

Here we have included only those reports which are based on a uniform formulation system for better clarity and also for involving all creases of the palm for their relationship with diseases.

Palmar Radial Creases and Schizophrenia

Bali (1971) first applied radial crease or transverse crease classification on schizophrenic patients of Delhi mental hospital. The bilateral ink prints of 90 male schizophrenic patients were compared with a control of 150 individuals. The author interpreted his result only on the basis of three-fold classification of transverse crease types, i.e., single radial base crease, double radial base crease and triple radial base crease.

Highly significant relationship of single radial base crease was discovered by comparing patients with the normal control.

Chaube (1971), independently, arrived at above result in his study of schizophrenic patients. The above-quoted author interpreted his data in terms of sub-types and found significant result for the sub-type which is akin to the simian crease. Later, employing the same classification Eswaraiah (1977) made comprehensive study of diagnosed schizophrenic patients. Palmar prints of 127 patients and 536 normal individuals were derived from the same ethnic region. Out of three main transverse crease types, SRBC type of palmar creases indicated significant association. The least association was exhibited by TRBC type of crease. The DRBC creases type did not show much deviation from the control population. Only male patients were tested. The chi-sequare value was indicated as $\chi^2 = 15.98$, df 2, $P < 0.001$, C = 0109 oE.

Bali (1983) tested his early finding by using fresh control and arrived at the similar results.

On the basis of statistical association between creases and schizophrenic patients, it can be deduced that some underlying biological mechanism may be operative for this associational behaviour, otherwise the possibility of arriving at a similar result through three different studies is least probable, because the data were procured from three populations living under different circumstances.

Palmar Radial Creases and Congenital Deafness

Congenital deafness is due to various intra-utrine factors. Its rubella relation has long been indicated. The material appropriated for this study comprises 86 males and 38 females showing congenital deafness. The control population was of 536 males and 426 females. Out of three main types, only DRBC shows positive association at significant level. This condition is also maintained by female patients; showing chi-square value as $\chi^2 = 8.48$, df 2, $P > 0.01$ C = 0.095 S and male the value is $\chi^2 = 4.24$, df 2, $P > 0.10$ N.S. For male patients the value is significant and for female patients insignificant.

The size of data being small, the sub-type results are less reliable.

Palmar Radial Creases and Congenital Blindness

There are several clinical causes of congenital blindness. Only 45 male cases could be studied against a fixed control of 536 normal individuals. The sample size being small, the reliability of the result remains questionable. The significant value is indicated as, $\chi^2 = 6.11$ df 2, $P > 0.02$, $C = 0.07$. The above work of Eswaraiah (1977) has not been confirmed by any other worker.

Palmar Radial Creases and Leprosy

Bali (1973) investigated 70 leper patients alongwith the normal control and found suggestive statistical association between disease and creases.

Gupta (1985) studied 800 lepers from the standpoint of palmar creases and dermatoglyphics and showed statistical association of creases with leprosy.

Eswaraiah (1977) utilized 115 palmar print of male lepers and prints of 536 normal individuals to work out association value between the two populations.

The palmar prints of female lepers, numbering 48, were also observed and compared with the control. The author showed significant value of association between main types of radial creases and the disease.

Male $\chi^2 = 29.5$, df 2, $P < 0.001$ $C = 0.148$ S.
Female $\chi^2 = 15.23$, df 2, $P < 0.001$ $C = 0.1264$ S.

From the above investigation it is concluded that in spite of showing higher statistical values, the results do not show consistency to the level from which we can predict crease relation with leprosy. The only trait, i.e., SRBC, shows some convincing results.

Palmar Radial Creases and Cancer

Eswaraiah's work on cancer patients has a pitfall. We combined all type of cancer patients into a single group of 127 males and 124 females.

The higher incidence of SRBC crease type among patients and lower of DRBC indicate associational trend between creases and the disease:

Male: $\chi^2 = 49.8$, df 2, $P < 0.001$, $C = 0.1900$ S.
Female: $\chi^2 = 57.63$, df 2, $P < 0.001$, $C = 0.2229$ S.

Based on radial base crease formulation, there is no second work through which the above result could be confirmed.

Palmar Radial Creases and Diabetes Mellitus

This disease of impairment has often been associated with several phenotypic traits. Palmar crease prints of 108 males and 65 females were appropriated for this purpose (Eswaraiah and Bali, 1976).

The association of SRBC shows higher incidence in males as well as in females.

Male: $\chi^2 = 51.42$, df 2, $P < 0.001$, $C = 0.1962$ S.
Female: $\chi^2 = 55.23$, df 2, $P < 0.001$, $C = 2306$ S.

Eswaraiah (1977) independently arrived at the similar conclusion and confirmed the above results.

Palmar Radial Creases and Pulmonary Tuberculosis

Pulmonary tuberculosis is the most clinically extensive known disease.

Bali (1973) found significant association of palmar creases (SRBC) with tuberculosis. But Eswaraiah and Bali (1976) failed to arrive at the similar result as earlier indicated by Bali.

Eswaraiah (1977) again investigated the associational link between palmar creases and the diseases and found his result different from the early findings. The result among male patients showed χ^2 value as,

$\chi^2 = 5.8$, df 2, $P > 0.05$, N.S.

From the above discussion we can conclude that palmar transverse creases or radial creases, when compared with other attributes like diseases, etc. show consistency of trend. This was judged by comparing the work of different workers. But for few anomalies, the result, by and large, showed the validity of the crease formulation system in its application for the study of diseases.

Palmar Longitudinal Creases and Diseases

The palmar longitudinal creases (Carpal creases) consist of radial longitudinal crease, sagittal crease and ulnar crease. These creases emerge from a base at the proximal region of the palm, called carpal base point.

When these three creases show union at carpal base point the crease is called single base carpal crease (SCBC), when they emerge from two separate points, the crease is designated as Double Carpal Base Crease (DCBC) and when they emerge from three separate bases the crease is called Triple Carpal Base Crease (TCBC).

The relationship study of palmar carpal base creases and diseases is an exclusive work of Eswaraiah (1977). All those diseases which we have discussed in previous Chapter, are being discussed again in the present Chapter.

It has already been made clear that both systems of palmar crease classification, i.e., radial base system and carpal base system, are governed by independent criteria of classification. It is, therefore, essential to deal with them separately for their application in anthropology or medicine.

Palmar Longitudinal Creases and Congenital Deafness

The strength of congenital deaf patients and of control of either sex has already been indicated in our previous discussion.

The incidence of SCBC in congenital deafs, both males and females, show nominal deviation from control population. A slight bilateral difference of no significance has been noticed. The chi-square values are given as under:

Male: $\chi^2 = 0.17$, df 2, $P > 0.90$ NS.
Female: $\chi^2 = 3.64$, df 2, $P > 0.10$ NS.

Longitudinal Creases and Congenital Blindness

The detail about the material is already given under the transverse creases and congenital blindness.

The present discussion on longitudinal creases and congenital blinds shows higher incidence of SCBC in blinds and low of TCBC in normal control. The incidence of DCBC in more in blind and less in control population.

Male: $\chi^2 = 8.2$, df 2, $P > 0.01$, $C = 0.08$ S.

Longitudinal Creases and Schizophrenia

The strength of the data remains the same as given earlier. All the three types of longitudinal creases do not show any associational indication. The chi-square value is also not significant.

In the case of transverse creases the associational value between creases and schizophrenia showed significant association. But the condition is reverse in the case of longitudinal carpal crease. We can form better opinion by tallying the result of both transverse as well as longitudinal creases.

Palmar Longitudinal Creases and Diabetes Mellitus

The disease is caused by the impairment of the secretion of insulin by Langerhans islands present in the pancreas.

Among the male patients both SCBC and TCBC show difference of frequencies. The trend is maintained by females in SCBC. The chi-square value shows no significant results.

Palmar Longitudinal Creases and Cancer

The strength of the material being the same, we can compare the results indicated by two groups of crease formulations. In the majority of cases it has been noticed that when transverse creases fail to indicate or show feeble relationship with the control the same is better indicated by longitudinal creases. There exists a sort of inverse relationship between the creases of longitudinal types and transverse types when we relate them to various types of diseases.

In the case of cancer patients the associational values of SCBC and DCBC is strikingly high in males. A similar trend is maintained by female patients. The chi-square value in both the creases is significant.

Palmar Longitudinal Creases and Leprosy

The leprosy patients, when compared with the longitudinal creases, showed significant result. A similar condition was observed also in radial creases.

In the case of leprosy, longitudinal as well as transverse creases of the palms have indicated similar level of association between creases and leprosy. The condition is true for both the sexes.

Male: $\chi^2 = 35.26$, df 2, $P < 0.001$, $C = 0.1627$ S.
Female: $\chi^2 = 16.6$, df 2, $P < 0.001$, $C = 0.1315$ S.

Palmar Longitudinal Creases and Tuberculosis

Pulmonary tuberculosis is due to tubercle bacteria which infects lungs and produces tubercles. It is an extensively investigated disease.

The relationship between creases and patients, in the case of transverse crease, was of insignificant nature. But in case of longitudinal crease, it is quite prominent and indicates significant results.

Male: $\chi^2 = 8.3$, df 2, $P > 0.01$, $C = 0.08$ S.

While concluding this Chapter we had two points in mind. The first to evolve relationship between creases and diseases and the second to find out the differential mode of behaviour of longitudinal and transverse creases towards each disease.

'The polygenic heredity, multifactorial genesis of the illness, in which the series of genes have combined with environmental factor and experience' (Hirsch, 1978).

The above statement sums up the magnitude of our problems, handicaps and outcome of our efforts towards a goal which is distant but inspiring for the future researchers.

REFERENCES

Bali, R.S. (1971a): Palmar Creases and Schizophrenia. *Internat. Sym. Hum. Genet.* Andhra University, Waltair, India.

Bali, R.S. (1971b): *Palmar Creases and Diseases*. S.C. Roy Centenary Celebration held in Ranchi, Bihar, India.

Bali, R.S. (1973): Correlation study between palmar creases, Schizophrenia, Leprosy and Tuberculosis. IXth Internat. Cong. Anthrop. & Ethno. Sciences, Chicago, U.S.A.

Chaube, R. (1971): *The Study of Palmar Flexion Creases: Inheritance and Correlation with Schizophrenic Patients*. Thesis submitted in fulfilment of the requirements for the degree of Ph.D. Saugar University, Sagar.

Eswaraiah, G. (1977): *Palmar Creases and Diseases.* Thesis submitted in fulfilment of the requirement for the degree of Ph.D., Saugar University, Sagar.

Eswaraiah, G. and R.S. Bali (1976): Palmar Dermatoglyphics among congenital deaf people, *Madhya Bharati*, Saugar University Journal.

Hirsch, W. (1978): Dermatoglyphics and creases in their relationship to clinical syndromes. A diagnostic criterion, in *Dermatoglyphics: An International Perspective*, Edited by J. Mavalwala. World Anthropology. The Hague: Mouton.

Gupta, D.K. (1985): *Dermatoglyphics, Palmar Creases and other Genetic Markers in Leprosy*. Ph.D. Thesis, Rani D.V.V., Jabalpur (M.P.).

PART-IV

APPLICATIONAL ASPECTS OF THE CREASES

24

FORENSIC AND CRIMINOLOGICAL ASPECTS OF CREASES

THE COMPUTABLE quantitative expressions such as ridge count relation to the crease borders provide a new set of infallible tools for their application in criminology and forensic science. The creases of the phalangeal metacarpal area show a greater potentiality. The vernier matching of adjacent ridges on crease borders provides a highly sensitive tools for personal identification. The ridge relation to the creases shows a greater precision and the system can be perfected to the limit of its requirement.

Creases occur on the palmar, plantar and phalangeal surfaces with distinct features of their own. Creases are devoid of dermal configuration, thus giving true and pseudo forms to the crease. A true type of crease core is not intercepted by dermal ridges, while pseudo type shows dermal interception.

On the basis of crease origin and crease form the creases are classified into primary, secondary and tertiary. The primary creases are embryonic in nature and have pre-ordained shape with a distinct base and terminal end. The core is surrounded by crease borders formed of ridges or ridge endings. The core of a crease determines its prominance and traceability into primary, secondary and tertiary crease. The secondary creases are secondary manifestation of crease configurations while tertiary creases are of non-specific shape and size.

A systematic analysis of an individual crease in relation to adjacent dermal ridges can provide practical and infallible means of personal identification. The dermal ridge ending on crease borders may show or may not show alignment of ridges on the adjacent crease borders. Another feature of relating ridge number to creases is an important tool for identification.

Based on the above feature of ridge relation with creases it has been observed that ridge angle with crease borders is immutable and persists throughout the life span of an individual.

On micro-examination the feature of ridge relation with crease provides a number of fresh criteria for forensic and criminological investigations. The dermal configurational and crease bearing areas of hands and feet are the most potent ones for forensic and criminological investigation. Among these areas the most important is the phalangeal surfaces.

The manual involvement of phalanges is relatively more as compared with the rest of the hand. The imprints of phalangeal creases under varied muscle pressures and directions are bound to vary which in turn can help to speculate on the mode and nature of a particular act for tracing the offender. The work on forensic importance of creases was first taken up by Bali and Sharma (1980) and Bali (1983).

The forensic interpretation of phalangeal, palmar and plantar creases is based on independent norms which are considered separately.

It is desired to give the details pertaining to the phalangeal crease classification and other marks of identification. It may be stated that each crease pattern in itself is a mark of identification. It is, therefore, importive to discuss the types of phalangeal flexion creases.

The phalangeal flexion creases are classified into three main and seven sub-types (Bali, 1980). The earlier attempts of classification by Penrose (1931), Cummins and Midlo (1943), Zizmor (1973), Okajima (1966-67), Lambson (1976) and Aue-Hauser (1977) do not find relevance to the author's classification because the above-cited formulations are based on crease plurality, rather than on its form, according to the occurrence of metacarpal phalangeal creases, the digit may be designated as zero crease, minus crease, normal crease or extra crease digit.

The phalangeal flexion creases can be divided into straight type, enclosure type, boat type, feather type, open and mixed type (Fig. 13.2). The feather and boat categories have further two sub-types, i.e., distal feather, proximal feather, convergent boat and divergent boat types, respectively.

On the basis of above crease types along with their number on a particular phalangeal site, the creases are classified into three main types. Thus the existing phalangeal crease formulation is based on a bi-nomial system of crease classification, i.e., the type as well as their number of occurrence on a particular site (Fig. 13.1).

Forensic Interpretation of Phalangeal Creases

Based on the aligned and non-aligned ridge characters of two adjacent crease borders, the creases for identification purpose may be divided into non-aligned and aligned forms. The former is further divided into 'border ridge type' and 'ridge angle type', while the latter shows ridge angle and straight angle type of alignment. The ridge types show ulnar and radial ridges (Fig. 24.1).

The border ridge type creases show ridge or ridges creeping along the crease borders. For finer accuracy the counting of ridges on the adjacent crease borders is recommended. This quantitative expression of ridge alignment between the two adjacent crease borders serves as a vernier for further accuracy.

Forensic Interpretation of Palmar Creases

The counts of dermal ridge in relation to primary creases is an embryonic feature and the ridge counts from crease borders to the reference lines is immutable in nature and persists throughout the life time of an individual (Fig. 24.1).

With reference to 'a' 'd' line the distal transverse crease shows maximum and minimum counts of the ridges. Similar ridge counts between the 'a' 't' line and border of longitudinal crease may be counted. The reference line for the sagittal crease is 'd' 't' (Fig. 24.2). The maximum and minimum ridge counts are between reference line formed by joining the 'a', 't', 'd' tri-radii of the palm. A ridge relation to the specific crease provides a dependable human mark for personal identification.

Thus palmar creases in forensic science and criminology can provide us the maximum and minimum ridge count index. But each primary palmar crease has to own a reference line, i.e., lines formed by joining 'a', 't', 'd' tri-radii.

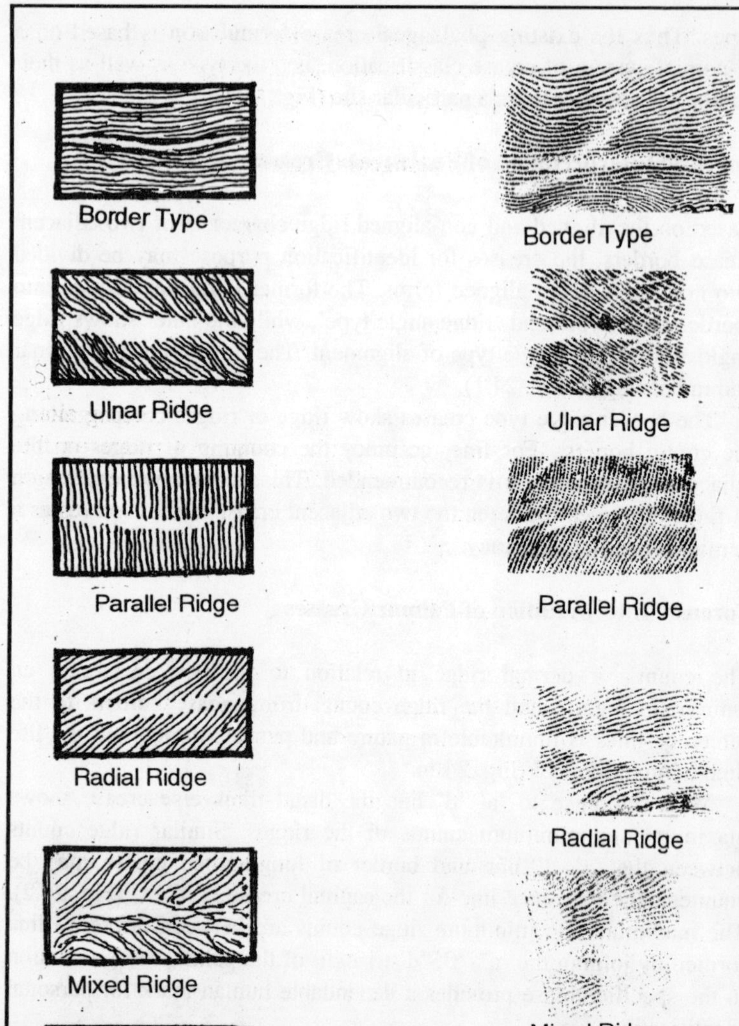

FIG. 24.1: Phalangeal creases in identification – Crease border and ridge relation

Forensic Interpretation of Plantar Creases

The marks of foot prints, like finger prints, could usefully be employed for personal identification. The ridge relation to the borders of the individual plantar crease serves as an important identification tool.

The medialward distal portion of the plantar surface accommodates all the three primary creases and is the area of greater functional use, thus leaving its imprints on the surface of its contact. The imprints to toes are least probable and are difficult comparables. On the other hand, the halucal area, Th/I, is more probable area of touch and is easy to print.

However, the major three primary creases of the sole, i.e., medial, tibial and febular creases, make their configuration in the same region of the foot.

FIG. 24.2: Palmar creases in identification — Crease border and ridge relation

To count the ridges from the respective crease border to its reference line which is formed by joining two tri-radii provides us the minimum and maximum ridge counts (Fig. 24.3).

In case of plantar creases the procedure of counting ridges is the same as described in palmar creases.

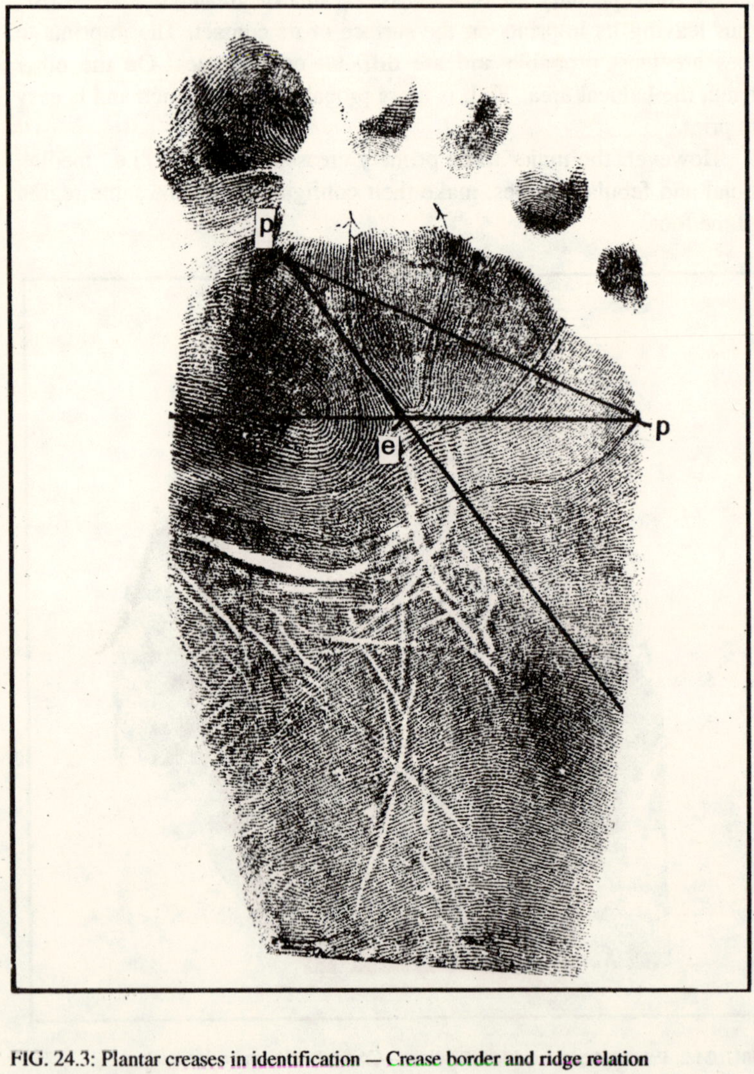

FIG. 24.3: Plantar creases in identification — Crease border and ridge relation

REFERENCES

Aue-Hauser, G. (1977): Flexion creases on fingers and their relevance in early diagnosis of mental disorders.

Bali, R.S. and A.N. Sharma (1980): Creases as a diagnostic tool for personal identification. National Symposium of I.S.H.G., Ranchi University, Ranchi.

Bali, R.S. (1980): Inheritance of phalangeal flexion crease, International Sym. Dermato., Punjabi University, Patiala.

Bali, R.S. (1983): *Creases in Forensic and Criminological Investigations. Anthropology in Indian Context,* Today and Tomorrow's Publishers, pp. 187-94.

Cummins and Midlo (1943): *Finger Prints, Palms and Soles: An Introduction to Dermatoglyphics*. Dover Publications, New York.

Lambson, G. (1976): Distal displacement of proximal phalangeal flexion creases. *Excerpts Med. Int. Congress Seminar* 397: p. 203.

Okajima, M. (1966): A dermatoglyphical study of metacarpophalangeal creases. *American Journal of Physical Anthropology* 24(3): 371-80.

Okajima, M. (1967): Metacarpophalangeal and ring creases in twins, *American Journal of Physical Anthropology* 26: 349-55.

Penrose, L.S. and M.D. Camb. (1931): The creases on the minimal digit in mongolism. *Lancet* 2: 585-86.

Zizmor, J. (1973): The extra transverse digital crease, a skin sign found in sickle cell disease. *Cutis* (New York) 11: pp. 447-49.

25

BEHAVIOURAL ATTRIBUTES OF CREASES

THE EVOLUTIONARY interpretation of human behaviour is currently attracting a great deal of attention from psychologists, ethnologists, socio-biologists and anthropologists. The recent renaissance in understanding human behaviour came via ethology, a study of behaviour from the zoological viewpoint. They seek to establish that social behaviour, human as well as animal, has a biological basis and is evolved from the animal past. The nature of human aggressiveness has deeper implication in modern society, and the contribution made by Frisch (1950), Timbergen (1964), Lorenz (1966), Ardrey (1967) and Storr (1968) in the above field has raised innumerable academic eye-brows.

Socio-biologist's hyper-kinetic syndrome and development of anti-social behaviour in childhood, adolescence and adulthood received attention of Wilson (1975).

The chromosomal interpretation of crime was investigated by Bartlett et al. (1968), Benezect et al. (1973), Harvey et al. (1970) and Niclson and Fischer (1965) who specified their work on criminals to extra 'X' chromosome and extra 'Y' chromosome.

The deviant behaviour exhibited by criminals and juvenile delinquents may find its biological base but reflexion of their social consequences and their interaction with that particular social group appears to be a pertinent factor.

Biological Studies of Criminals

Crime is as old as human society. The old expression on crime, from Baccaria's (1764) doctrine of pleasure and pain genesis to Lombroso's (1896) biological interpretation of crime, was latin for criminology into scientific courts. Sheldon et al. (1949) studied body types in delinquents. The mesomorphic body from link of crime was studied by Sheldon (1956). Cartes and Gatti (1972) also made a similar observations. Longe (1930) studied behaviour traits through twins while Christiansen (1968) made comprehensive studies on twins and their environmental history.

The physical basis of criminality was emphasised by Lombroso (1911), Sheldon (1949) and Glueck and Glueck (1956). Several physical features showing genetical pre-disposition have been related to abnormal human behaviour and disordered personality. For understanding the cause of deviant behaviour, out of several physical traits, the dermatoglyphic traits find greater recognition in the modern scientific literature. The work of Portius (1937), Schiller (1942), Biswas (1945), Tillnar (1958) and Mahapatra (1960, 1966) is worthy of mention.

Dermatoglyphic studies on criminals show varied results. Ascarelli (1906) studied finger prints of prostitutes. Abel (1936) observed defect of ridge formation in criminals. Usha Deka (1966) carried out study on dermatoglyphics on German criminals. Welch et al. (1979) and Alicia (1979), on the bases of whorls and loops, associated criminal tendencies to dermatoglyphics.

The study of simian crease relation with criminality, delinquency and mental disorders has been carried out by several workers. The contributions of Kervinen (1954), Tunakan (1954), Rittmeister (1936, b), Crookshank (1924), Langdon-Down (1909) and Penrose (1949) are noteworthy.

It is the Simian crease, and not creases in general, which often represents the science of creases. Palmar and plantar creases have very recently been found significant for the study of various normal and abnormal human traits.

On the basis of the above methodology, Rawat (1980) studied palmar creases among murderers. Chaube (1980) studied palmar creases in criminals. Bali and Sharma (1980) studied plantar crease features in juvenile delinquents. The same authors have made observations on palmar creases of mentally retarded children (1980).

A comprehensive study of palmar creases among criminals and juvenile delinquents/mentally retarded children is being conducted by Rawat.

Sharma and Bali (1980) in their subsequent work compared palmar creases with mental retardedness. Bali and Rawat (1980) studied in detail the attributes of crease morphogenesis among criminals on the basis of crease surface area, crease transversality, crease length, crease breadth and positioning of base point.

Rawat (1983) studied palmar dermatoglyphics and palmar creases among murderers. The three main transverse crease types, i.e., single radial base crease, double radial base crease and triple radial base crease of the murderers of various jails were compared with the normal control. The frequency distribution is given in the Table (25.1). In spite of significant n^2 result the size of the sample does not show confidence and desires a future probe.

TABLE 25.1: Frequency distribution of palmar flexion creases among murderers and the control

Crease Formula		Right Hand		Left Hand	
		Murderers	Control	Murderers	Control
SRBC	Ab	69	13	41	9
	Pc	34.5	8.66	20.5	6
DRBC	Ab	115	122	144	130
	Pc	57.5	81.33	72	86.66
TRBC	Ab	16	15	15	11
	Pc	8	10	7.5	7.33

$\chi^2 = 31.990$ (*Result*: Significant) $\chi^2 = 14.970$ (*Result*: Significant)

Rawat and Bali (1980) tried to investigate the morphogenesis of primary creases of the palm among murderers (60) and compared their result with the normal control (150) individuals.

The crease morphogenesis is a study of individual crease with respect to its absolute and projectile lengths. The study of crease length formula, crease breadth, crease depth, crease surface area, crease transversality and positioning of crease 'base points' is called crease morphogenesis.

The three main primary creases of the palm, i.e., radial longitudinal crease, distal transverse crease and proximal transverse crease, have been considered for the present study. The crease morphogenesis involves a quantitative description of primary creases with reference to crease length, crease length formula, crease breadth, crease depth, crease surface area, crease transversality and positioning of crease 'base point' on inter-digital area between 1st and 2nd digits.

The above crease features have been utilized to investigate the variations among palmar creases of murderers in relation to the creases of normal individuals.

Crease Length

The length of primary palmar creases, such as, distal transverse, proximal transverse and radial longitudinal creases could be expressed in term of absolute crease length and projectile crease length. The absolute crease length is the absolute distance of a crease between base and terminal ends. The distance is measured by planimeter, measurer or steel wire.

TABLE 25.2: Distribution of absolute crease length among murderers and the control

Crease Type	Right Hand						Left Hand					
	Murderer			Control			Murderer			Control		
	Mean	S.D.	S.E.	Mean	S.D.	S.E.	Mean	S.D.	S.E.	Mean	S.D.	S.E.
D.T.C.	6.44	0.87	±0.11	7.17	0.65	±0.04	6.54	0.79	±0.10	6.92	0.87	±0.05
P.T.C.	5.64	1.04	±0.13	7.25	1.10	±0.06	6.58	0.93	±0.12	7.13	1.12	±0.05
R.L.C.	8.64	0.94	±0.12	8.66	1.02	±0.06	8.64	1.00	±0.12	8.90	1.01	±0.05

It could be seen from Table 25.2 that length of distal transverse crease is less among murderer both in right and left hand, as compared to the control.

The absolute length of proximal transverse crease shows higher incident in control as compared to the murderers. A similar trend is indicated by radial longitudinal crease on either palm of murderers and control group.

The projectile length is given in Table 25.3. The Table 25.3 exhibits creases with longer projectile length in normal individuals as compared to the murderers.

If radial longitudinal crease is longer than the distal transverse crease and the latter is longer than the proximal transverse crease, the formula is stated as L>D>P. In our data the formula L>D>P is more frequent in murderers as compared to the control.

The formula L>D>P shows equal incidence both in control and the murderers.

TABLE 25.3: Distribution of projectile length among murderers and the control

Crease Type	Right Hand						Left Hand					
	Murderer			Control			Murderer			Control		
	Mean	S.D.	S.E.	Mean	S.D.	S.E.	Mean	S.D.	S.E.	Mean	S.D.	S.E.
D.T.C.	6.24	0.79	±0.10	7.05	0.61	±0.03	6.31	0.71	±0.09	6.82	0.85	±0.04
P.T.C.	5.48	1.01	±0.13	7.05	1.04	±0.06	6.33	0.93	±0.12	6.97	1.06	±0.06
R.L.C.	7.78	0.76	±0.09	8.01	0.84	±0.07	7.77	0.91	±0.11	8.19	0.83	±0.07

Crease Breadth

The maximum breadth of creases is given in Table 25.4. It could be seen from the Table 25.4 that distal transverse crease shows higher value as compared to proximal transverse and radial longitudinal creases in right and left hands of murderers and the control.

TABLE 25.4: Distribution of crease breadth among murderers and the control

Crease Type	Right Hand						Left Hand					
	Murderer			Control			Murderer			Control		
	Mean	S.D.	S.E.	Mean	S.D.	S.E.	Mean	S.D.	S.E.	Mean	S.D.	S.E.
D.T.C.	0.18	0.04	±0.005	0.19	0.04	±0.06	0.15	2.00	±0.00	0.16	0.03	±0.00
P.T.C.	0.15	0.01	±0.001	0.14	0.02	±0.00	0.12	0.02	±0.00	0.13	0.01	±0.00
R.L.C.	0.14	0.00	±0.00	0.14	0.02	±0.00	0.15	0.02	±0.00	0.15	0.01	±0.00

TABLE 25.5: Distribution of crease depth among murderers and the control

Crease Type	Right hand				Left hand			
	Murderer		Control		Murderer		Control	
	Mean	S.D.	Mean	S.D.	Mean	S.D.	Mean	S.D.
D.T.C.	0.09	0.00	0.09	0.00	0.07	0.00	0.08	0.00
P.T.C.	0.07	0.00	0.07	0.00	0.06	0.00	0.06	0.00
R.L.C.	0.07	0.00	0.07	0.01	0.07	0.00	0.07	0.00

Crease Depth

The Table 25.5 exhibits crease depth. The greater crease depth is exhibited by distal transverse crease both among murderers and control.

Surface Area

The crease surface area is an area occupied by crease core between base point and the terminal point of the crease and the crease margin. This crease feature is expressed in term of square centimetre as well as per unit ridge counts area of the crease. The crease surface area in term a cm is given in Table 25.6.

TABLE 25.6: Distribution of crease surface area among murderers and the control

Crease Type	Right Hand						Left Hand					
	Murderer			Control			Murderer			Control		
	Mean	S.D.	S.E.	Mean	S.D.	S.E.	Mean	S.D.	S.E.	Mean	S.D.	S.E.
D.T.C.	0.91	0.25	±0.03	1.06	0.38	±0.02	0.81	0.20	±0.02	0.88	0.23	±0.01
P.T.C.	0.69	0.16	±0.02	0.82	0.32	±0.02	0.73	0.18	±0.02	0.69	0.25	±0.01
R.L.C.	1.16	0.23	±0.03	1.12	0.29	±0.02	1.20	0.29	±0.03	1.01	0.32	±0.01

Comparing crease surface area among radial longitudinal crease in both hands of murderers and the control it could be seen that the frequencies are more among murderer as compared to the control.

Considering the surface area of proximal transverse crease it is noticed that control shows higher incidence in right hands and murderers show higher incidence in left hands.

The surface area of distal transverse crease of both, right and left, hands shows higher frequencies of control group as compared to murderers.

Ridge Counts

The crease surface area in term of ridge counts expresses the age stable relationship of the crease core. This morphometric expression is given in Table 25.7.

TABLE 25.7: Distribution of ridge count among murderers and the control

Crease Type	Right Hand						Left Hand					
	Murderer			Control			Murderer			Control		
	Mean	S.D.	S.E.	Mean	S.D.	S.E.	Mean	S.D.	S.E.	Mean	S.D.	S.E.
D.T.C.	17.67	1.80	±0.23	17.40	0.79	±0.04	15.67	1.59	±0.20	17.52	0.86	±0.04
P.T.C.	17.72	1.79	±0.23	16.90	0.81	±0.04	16.72	1.84	±0.24	16.70	1.05	±0.06
R.L.C.	17.77	2.05	±0.26	19.78	1.46	±0.08	16.85	1.70	±0.21	19.77	1.34	±0.07

It could be noticed from this Table that radial longitudinal creases show higher value as compared to the transverse creases among the murderers. The similar trend is exhibited by the control.

Crease Transversality

The morphogenesis of crease finds best interpretation in term of crease transversality. The crease transversality shows (Table 25.8) that the distal transverse crease in both right and left hands of murderers shows higher values.

TABLE 25.8: Distribution of crease transversality among murderers and the control

Crease Type	Right Hand						Left Hand					
	Murderer			Control			Murderer			Control		
	Mean	S.D.	S.E.	Mean	S.D.	S.E.	Mean	S.D.	S.E.	Mean	S.D.	S.E.
D.T.C.	15.17	7.02	±0.90	12.60	5.67	±0.32	15.52	6.52	±0.84	12.87	5.85	±0.33
P.T.C.	21.05	6.05	±0.78	19.35	6.69	±0.38	18.68	7.14	±0.92	19.12	6.15	±0.35
R.L.C.	54.48	6.31	±0.81	52.35	6.17	±0.35	52.88	6.70	±0.86	53.03	6.66	±0.38

TABLE 28.9: Distribution of radial base area among murderers and the control

Crease Type	Right Hand						Left Hand					
	Murderer			Control			Murderer			Control		
	Mean	S.D.	S.E.	Mean	S.D.	S.E.	Mean	S.D.	S.E.	Mean	S.D.	S.E.
AB	4.94	0.35	±0.04	5.29	0.49	±0.02	5.05	0.37	±0.04	5.19	0.55	±0.03
AC	1.67	0.24	±0.03	1.80	0.27	±0.01	1.67	0.22	±0.02	1.80	0.28	±0.01
BC	3.27	0.36	±0.04	3.49	0.44	±0.02	3.37	0.39	±0.05	3.39	0.48	±0.02

The value of proximal transverse and radial longitudinal creases are higher in right hands of murderers and left hand of control.

Radial Base Area

The relative distance of base point shows the position of radial base point in relation to the proximal and distal lengths.

The Table 25.9 shows that AB, AC and BC distances are less among murderers as compared to control in both right and left hands.

REFERENCES

Abel, W. (1936): Uber storungen der Papillarmuster. I. Gestorte Papillarmuster in Verbindung mit einigen korperlichen und geistigen anomalien. *Zeitschrift fur Morphologie und Anthropologie* 36: pp. 1-37.

Ardrey, R. (1967): *The Territorial Imperative*. London: Collins.

Ascarelli, A. (1906): Le impronte digitali nelle prostitute, *Arch. di. Psichiat*, vól. 27, pp. 812-21.

Baccaria, L. (1764): *Crime and Punishment*.

Bali, R.S. and A.N. Sharma (1980): On the formulation of calcar plantar creases. National Symposium on child with handicap and VII Annual Conference of I.S.H.G., Ranchi University, Ranchi, India.

Bali, R.S. and A.N. Sharma (1980): Creases as a diagnostic tool for personal identification. National Symposium of I.S.H.G., Ranchi University, Ranchi, India.

Bali, R.S. and S.K. Rawat (1980): Inheritance of morphogenic attributes of palmar creases. National Symposium on child with handicap and VII Annual Conference of I.S.H.G., Ranchi University, Ranchi, India.

Bartlett, D.J., W.P. Hurley, C.R. Brand, et al. (1968): Chromosomes of male patients in a security prison. *Nature* 219: pp. 351-54.

Benezect, M., G. Robert, B. Noel and R. Zintilini (1973): Aggressive delinquence psychopathique d longer chromosome aberrations in a child psychiatric hospital. *Clin. Genet.* 5: pp. 205-10.

Biswas, P.C. (1945): Finger and palm prints of the Indian juvenile criminals. *Science and Culture* 9.

Chaube, R. (1980): *Palmar Creases and Criminality* (In press).

Cortes, J.B. and F.M. Gatti (1972): Delinquency and Crime. *British Medi. J.* 30: pp. 1752-53.

Crookshank (1924): *The Mongol in our Midst, a Study of Man and his Three Faces*, Duffon & Co., New York.

Frisch, K. von (1950): *Bees, their Vision, Chemical Senses and Language*. Ithaca, N.Y.

Glueck, S. and E. Glueck (1956): *Physique and Delinquency*. New York, Hory Holt.

Harvey, P.W., S. Muldal and O. Wauchob (1970): *Anti. Social Behaviour and Larger Y Chromosome Lancet* 1: p. 887.

Kervinen, V. (1954): The incidence of the four-finger groove in Finland. *Annales Academiae Scientiarum Fennicae* (Helsinki). 40: pp. 1-2.

Langdon-Down, R.L. (1909): Mongolian Imbecility, *Brit. Med. J.*, 12: p. 665.

Lombroso, C. (1896): *Crime, Its Causes and Remedies*, translated by H.P. Horton, Boston Little Brown (1911).

Lombroso, C. (1911): *Crime: Its Causes and Remedies*, translated by H.P. Horton, Boston: Little Brown.

Lorenz, K. (1966): *On aggression*. Methues, London.

Mahapatra, U.D. (1960): *Studies an Handabdruecken von verbrechen und Deutschland*. Thesis for f. Dr. rer. nat. in Kiel.

Mahapatra, U.D. (1966): Palmar Dermatoglyphics of the German criminals in *Proceedings* volume of International Sym. on Dermato. Edited by P.C. Biswas and A. Sharma, New Delhi, India.

Penrose, L.S. (1949): *Mental Defect*. London: Sidgwick and Jackson.

Portius, W. (1937): Beitrag zur Frage der Erblichkeit der vier fingerfurche. *Zeiotschrift fur morphologie und Anthropologie*. 36: pp. 382-90.

Quintana, A. (1979): *Dermatoglyphic study in a Spanish Penal Population in Dermatoglyphics* - fifty-year later edited by Wladmir Wertelecki and Chris C. Plato. New York: Alan R. Liss.

Rawat, S.K. (1980): The study of palmar creases and palmar dermatoglyphics of murderers. Internat. Sym. Dermato., Punjabi University, Patiala, India.

Rittmeister, J.F. (1936): Uber die Affenfurche (Vierfingerfurche) mit besonderr Beruchsichtigung der mikrodegenerationen und des Problems des Mongolismus. *Zs. Anat. u. Entwicklungsgesch.* Bd. 106, H. 2: pp. 276-314.

Schiller, M. (1942): Realitaet und Problematic der menschlichen Handfuerchen, insbesondere der Affenfuerche. *Z. Morph. Anthrop.* 25.

Sharma, A.N. and R.S. Bali (1980): The study of creases and crease morphogenesis among mentally retarded children. National Sym. on child with handicap and VII, Annual Conference of I.S.H.G., Ranchi University, Ranchi, India.

Sheldon, W.H. (1949): *Varieties of Delinquent Youth*. New York, Harper and Brothers.

Storr, A. (1968): *Human Aggression*. London: Atheneum.

Tillner, I. (1958): Die Vierfingerfurche in Beziechung zum Verlauf der Handleisten. *Anthropologischer Anzeiger* 22(3-4): pp. 260-76.

Timbergen, N. (1964): The evolution of signalling devices. In Etkin, W. (ed.) *Social Behaviour and Organization among Vertebrates*. Chicago: University of Chicago Press.

Tunakan, S. (1954): Turklerde ve Turk Suclularinda et ayas indaki dort parmack Cizgisi (Maymun Cizgisi) Uzerinde arastirma. Ankara Universitiesi Dil ve Tarih-Coqratya Fakultesi Dergisi XII - Cilt, 1-2 *Sayilardan Ayribasim*, Mart Haziran: pp. 117-226.

Wilson, W.A. and S. Zieler (1976): Some tests of intermodality transfer of intensity in squirrel monkeys. *Neuropsychologia* 14: pp. 237-41.

26

CREASES – THEIR SCOPE AND GOALS

A POTENTIAL area of specific research on the genetic particularities of crease warrants a probe for determining the genetic interdependence between two different homologous crease areas.

There seems to be a general agreement that dermal area of foot and hand agree closely with the developmental sequences of the embryo. Davenport (1933) has ably discussed the growth of human foot and suggests that the factors, that activate control on the development of the terminal segments of the appendages, are probably the same and both hand and foot grow together and increase with age.

The morphology of sole, according to Cummins and Midlo (1961), follows closely with that of palm and may be interpreted in the same way. It holds true for fingers and toes also. The distal plantar and palmar morphology reflects parallel features. Creases unlike dermatoglyphics show age change. Crease morphology follows the rhythm of growth of palm and hand but still has its fixed features. This characteristic feature of creases makes them a more effective biological variable.

It is widely known that correlations are lowest between the non-corresponding part, i.e., toes and sole or palm and fingers, as compared to the homologous parts, i.e., fingers and toes and palm and sole. It is true both for dermatoglyphic and crease features (MacArthur, 1938).

The correlation of crease morphology between homologous parts both in human and non-human primates can reveal the cause and effect of deviation under the functional stresses during the course of evolution. Morphology of creases in monkeys and other primates reveal the existence of major similarities between the living primates, including man.

The comparative study of finger and toe or palm and sole, when considered from a genetic point of view, leads to the conclusion that the several crease features are controlled by polygenic factors and are partially independent of each other. A systematic study of crease can lead us for better understanding of primate relation as well as genetic interrelationship between human and non-human primates.

The morphogenesis of individual crease configuration on different crease areas, if studied from an evolutionary point of view, could evolve better classification norms which will reveal to us the various stages in crease pattern modification due to the independent course of specialization in evolution.

Towards the study of ethnic relation of creases, the account for localization of particular crease configuration or its relative complexity in different regions as such may be treated as a reflection of the evolutionary modification which acts as a selective measure. Little is known of the inheritance mechanisms accounting for crease morphometry or crease type differentiation. The relative high correlations between various crease features found in twins and siblings suggest the action of genetic expression which may have modified by intra-utrine environmental effects. Little is known of the inheritance of crease types in man.

The variability and loose genetic make-up of crease characteristics do not qualify creases as effective ethnic tool but as compared to other phenotypic traits creases have a role in ethnic study. The number of crease feature is quite large (palmar creases, plantar creases, phalangeal creases and toe flexion creases) and morphology and morphometry of individual crease can also be ethnic criteria of some value. Only future investigations can lead creases in the field of ethnic study.

The mode of crease inheritance is still obscure and it is likely to intrigue researchers for quite some time. Crease, like dermatoglyphic features are free from any paratypic influences and are not subject to age and sex influence as the differentiation occurs during early intra-utrine life and the characteristic of primary crease origin remains fairly stable. Further, these features being free from assortative mating and not affected by genetic, drift could be usefully employed for the study of population genetics.

Among the traits with known genetic mode of inheritance and those phenotypic traits which are least stable to paratypic influences, after dermatoglyphics, creases fall second to none and their application in the study of population and disease association can be of use in anthropology.

Edwards (1978), while comparing dermatoglyphics and genetically known traits, reveals valuable clues and informations towards understanding of phenotypically defined population and role of certain traits like dermatoglyphic or creases as a reliable phenotypic markers to a roughly known limit.

A statistically based crease relation with diseases is of genetic origin and is a valuable tool in understanding certain clinical syndromes. Comparing creases with structural, physiological and psychological traits, the role of environment is worth considering. This includes the intrinsic environment which operates within the body from inception onwards. Different traits vary in susceptibility to environmental influences. Human creases stabilize during the early embryonal months and from a firm base for scaling the traits which are prone to higher rate of variability.

Pronouncements on the association of creases with character and temperament are bound to remain questionable. But future researches on crease features, such as crease surface area, crease splits, crease length, and crease borders, may perhaps throw some light on the relationship. The crease surface area, in term of centimetre counts, cell counts and ridge counts, makes a sufficiently sensitive scale for marking change under differential, physiological, psychological or social stresses. This interesting area of investigation remains to be explored by future researchers.

Dermatoglyphics and creases are inseparable, instead creases are manifestation of ridge action and share a same pre and post-natal environment.

As compared to creases, dermatoglyphics have great value as a screening device for diagnosis of congenital and other anomalies. The investigations are simple and more economical as compared to examining of chromosomes.

The growth of this field has been very rapid and the bulk of the material on dermatoglyphics is much large. The data on dermatoglyphics can be re-used for crease investigation. The collection and preservation or recording is simple both in case of dermatoglyphic and crease prints.

But for simian crease the work on crease is less extensive. In spite of the fact that work on crease has been appearing in the world literature for over a century, but international concensus on crease methodology is still being sought. Once such a consensus is achieved the anthropological and medical importance of creases can find their due place in anthropology because all those elements of crease science potential are present. The crease phenotype is very complex and its inheritance is yet to be fully explained.

REFERENCES

Cummins, H. and C. Midlo (1961): *Finger Prints, Palms and Soles. An Introduction to Dermatoglyphics.* New York: Dover.

Davenport, C.B. (1933): The Growth of Human Foot. *Am. J. Phys. Anthrop.* 17: p. 167.

Edwards, C.R. (1978): "A comparison of dermatoglyphic and genetic similarity indices in rhesus monkeys (Macaca mulatta)", in *Dermatoglyphics: An International Perspective.* Edited by J. Mavalwala. *World Anthropology.* The Hague: Mouton.

MacArthur, J.W. (1938): Reliability of Dermatoglyphics in twin diagnosis. *Hum. Biol.* 10: pp. 12-35.

BIBLIOGRAPHY

Abel, W. (1936): Uber storungen der Papillarmuster. I. Gestorte Papillarmuster in Verbindung mit einigen korperlichen und geistigen anomalien. *Zeitschrift fur Morphologie und Anthropologie* 36: pp. 1-37.

Alter, M. (1967): *Medicine* (Baltimore) 46(1): pp. 35-51.

Ardrey, R. (1967): *The Territorial Imperative*. London: Collins.

Ascarelli, A. (1906): *Le impronte digitali nelle prostitute*, Arch. di. Psichiat, vol. 27, pp. 812-21.

Aue-Hauser, G. (1977): *Flexion creases on fingers and their relevance in early diagnosis of mental disorders.*

Aue-Hauser, G. (1978): *Luigi Gedda, Paolo Parisi, and Rudolf Wytek. Twin Research : Clinical Studies.* Alan R.

Aue-Hauser, G. (1979): Magna Brush Technique in Dermatoglyphic Research. *American Journal of Physical Anthropology*. 5 : I.

Baccaria, L. (1764): *Crime and Punishment.*

Bali, R.S. and Ramesh Chaube (1971) : On the formulation of palmar crease. *Z. Morph. Anthrop.*, 63 : p. 121.

Bali, R.S. and S.K. Rawat (1980): Inheritance of morphogenic attributes of palmar creases. *National Symposium* of child with handicaps and VII Annual conference of I.S.H.G. Ranchi University, Ranchi, India.

Bali, R.S. (1963): Symmetrical and asymmetrical occurrence of toe patterns of Kashmiri Muslims. *The Anthropologist* 10(1-2): pp. 49-54.

Bali, R.S. (1964): *Toe Dermatoglyphics-Inheritance and Comparison with the finger ball patterns*. Ph.D. Thesis, Delhi University, Delhi.

Bali, R.S. (1965): Finger Dermatoglyphic Study of Kashmiri Muslims. *Madhya Bharati*, 14-16, pp. 104-10.

Bali, R.S. (1966): Some Genetic Observations on Dermatoglyphic Traits. *Internat. Symposium on Dermatoglyphics*, Delhi, India.

Bali, R.S. (1967): Heritable behaviour of dermal configurations of toes in relation to sex. *Acta Geneticae Medicae et Gemellologiae* 16: pp. 422-28.

Bali, R.S. (1968): Genetic inter-correlation between finger and toe patterns. *Zeitschrift fur Morphologie and Anthropologie* 59(3): pp. 244-72.

Bali, R.S. (1971a): Palmar creases and Schizophrenia. *Internat. sym. Hum. Genet*. Andhra University, Waltair, India.

Bali, R.S. (1971b) *Palmar Creases and Diseases*, S.C. Roy Centenary Celebration held in Ranchi, Bihar, India.

Bali, R.S. (1973): Correlation study between palmar creases, Schizophrenia, Leprosy and Tuberculosis. IXth Internat. Congr. Anthrop. & Ethno. Sciences, Chicago, U.S.A.

Bali, R.S. (1980): Inheritance of phalangeal flexion creases. *Internat. Sym. Dermato*. Punjabi University, Patiala, India.

Bali, R.S. (1983) : *Inheritance of phalangeal flexion creases* (Human Biology Recent Advances Vol. 2) (Proc. Internat. Sym. Punjabi University, Patiala.

Bali, R.S. (1983): *Creases in Forensic and Criminological Investigations: Anthropology in Indian Context,* Today and Tomorrow's Publishers, pp. 187-94.

Bali, R.S. (1983): *Human Biology, Recent Advances* Vol. 2, Dermatoglyphics.

Bali, R.S. and A.N. Sharma (1980): Creases as a diagnostic tool for personal identification. National Symposium of I.S.H.G. Ranchi University, Ranchi, India.

Bali, R.S. and A.N. Sharma (1980): On the formulation of calcar plantar creases. National Symposium on child with handicap and VII Annual Conference of I.S.H.G., Ranchi University, Ranchi, India.

Bali, R.S. and D.K. Jain (1983): The study of pre-natal and postal Development of creases in Man. *Human Biology Recent Advances*, 2 (Proc. Intermat. Sym. Punjabi University).

Bali, R.S. and R. Mishra (1980) : Age change and crease morphogenesis. *Internat. Sym. Dermat*. Punjabi University, Patiala, (India).

Bali, R.S. and R. Mishra (1978) : The study of morphological change in hand, palm and palmar flexion creases on one to eleven year old boys and girls. *Xth Internat. Congr. Anthrop. & Ethno, Sciences*, New Delhi, India.

Bali, R.S. and R. Mishra (1980): Age change and crease morphogenesis. *Internat. Sym. Dermat,* Punjabi University, Patiala, India.

Bali, R.S. and R. Mishra (1978): The plantar creases and their formulation, *Xth Internat. Congr. Anthrop. & Ethno. Sciences,* New Delhi, India.

Bali, R.S. and Ramesh Chaube (1971): On the formulation of palmar creases. *Z. Morph. Anthrop.*, 63: p. 121.

Bali, R.S. *et al.* (1980): On the formulation of calcar plantar creases. National Symposium on child with handicap and VII Annual Conference of I.S.H.G., Ranchi University, Ranchi, India.

Bali, R.S. *et al.* (1983): Intra-Individual relationship between palmar creases and plantar creases. Human Biology Recent Advances, (*Proc. Internat. sym.* Punjabi University).

Bali, R.S., S. Koley, K. Bannerjee and S. Bannerjee (1989): The study of Syndactyly and Polydactyly in Relation to phalangeal creases. *Internat. Conf. on Progress and Trends in Dermatoglyphic Research.* Calcutta.

Bali, R.S., S. Koley, K. Bannerjee and S. Bannerjee (1989): Transverse and longitudinal creases in Relation to syndactyly and polydactyly. *Internat. Conf. on Progress and Trends in Dermatoglyphic Research.* Calcutta.

Bali, R.S.; A.N. Sharma and R. Chaube (1983) : The Intra-Individual Relationship between Palmar and Plantar creases (Human Biology Recent Advances, Vol. 2) *Proc. Internat Sym.* Punjabi Univerty.

Bartlett, D.J., W.P. Hurley, C.R. Brand, *et al.* (1968): Chromosomes of Male Patients in a Security Prison. *Nature* 219: pp. 351-54.

Bartsocas, C.S., A.L. Weber and J.D. Crawford (1970): Acrocephalosyndactyly type III: Chotzen's syndrome. *Journal of Pediatrics* 77: pp. 267-72.

Basu, S.K. (1968): Inheritance of middle phalangeal and basal phalangeal configuration by twin and family studies. *Zeitscbrift fur Morphologie and Anthropologie* 60: pp. 85-99.

Becker, E. (1952) : *Zur Verebung der Vierfingerfurche.* Homo, 3 : pp. 82-85.

Benezect, M., G. Robert, B. Noel and R. Zintilini (1973): Aggressive Delinquence Psychopathique d Longer Chromosome Aberrations in a Child Psychiatric Hospital. *Clin. Genet* - 5, pp. 205-10.

Bettman, S. (1932) : *Zs Anat.* U. Entwicklungsch.

Bhalla, V.C. (1966): Inheritance of Loop Patterns on Human Toes with a Short Note on a Comparative Study of Toe and Foot Prints. *Internat. Sym. on Dermato.*, Delhi, India.

Bhanu, V.V. (1973): Simian Creases in Man: Some Methodological Considerations. *Journal of Human Evolution*, 2: pp. 153-60.

Biegert, J. (1961): *Volarhaut der Hande und Fusse. primatologia* 1 (suppl. 2) pp. 4-326.

Biswas, P.C. (1945): Finger and Palm Prints of the Indian Juvenile Criminals. *Science and Culture* 9.

Biswas, P.C. and A. Bardhan (1966) : Palm Prints and Schiozophrenia. *The Anthropologist* 13(1-2) : pp. 1-12.

Blümel, P. (1911) : *Papillarmuster and psychische Eigenschaften*, Vol. 9. pp. 180-92.

Blümel, P. and H. Poll (1922): *Gingerliniemuster und Geistige Norm Medizinische Klinik*, 24 pp. 1428-30.

Böök, J.A. (1948) : Finger-print Method for Genitical Studies. *Hereditas* 34 : 368 - 39.

Bonnevie, K. (1927): Die ersten Entwick Lungsstadicn der Papillarmuster der Menschlichen Finger ballen. *Nyt Mag f. Nuturv*, 65. pp. 10-56.

Brehme, H. and R. Schroler (1967): Dermatoglyphics of 15 Patients with Russell-Silver Syndrome. *Humangenetik* 5: pp. 28-35 (in German).

Broca, P. (1877) : *Le pli transversal du Singe dans la main de l'homme, Bull. soc. Anthr.* Paris, Ze Serie, t. XII, pp. 431-32.

Büchi, E.C. (1954) : The Simian Crease in India. *Bulletin of the Indian Department of Anthropology*, 3(1) : pp. 39-49.

Büchi, E.C. (1965): *Anthropologie des Tibetains. Paris.* Ecole Francaise d' Extreme-Orient, Maisonneuve.

Carrara, (1893) : *Anomali dei Sochi Palmari hei normali e nei Criminale* (Roma.).

Chakravartti, M.R. and S.K. Basu (1960): A note on the simian crease of the Riangs of Tripura, *Science and Culture* 26: 41-45.

Chamla, M.C. and A. Sahley (1973): Le pli palmaire transverse chez (les tunisiens). *L' Anthropologie* 77(1-2) (Paris) : pp. 107-18.

Chanderia, A.K. (1981): *The Study of Inheritance of Palmar Creases and Crease Transversality*. M.Sc Thesis. Saugar University, Sagar.

Chaube, R. (1971) : *The Study of palmar flexion creases – Inheritance and Correlation with schizophrenic patients*. Thesis submitted in fulfilment of the requirements for the degree of Ph.D., Saugar University, Sagar.

Chaube, R. (1980): *Palmar Creases and Criminality* (In press).

Cheiros (1966) : *Language of Hand*, Taraporewala, Bombay.

Cortes, J.B. and F.M. Gatti (1972): Delinquency and Crime. *British Medi. J.*, 30: pp. 1752-53.

Cotterman, C.W. (1951): A Scotch-tape India Ink Method for Recording Dermatoglyphics. *American Journal of Human Genetics* 3(4). pp. 376-79.

Crookshank (1924) : *The Mongol in our Midst, a study of man and his three faces*. Duffon & Co., New York.

Cummins and Midlo (1943): *Finger Prints, palms and soles: An Introduction to Dermatoglyphics*. Dover Publications, New York.

Cummins, H. (1926): Epidermal-ridge configurations in developmental defects, with particular reference to the ontogenetic factors which condition ridge direction. *American Journal of Anatomy* 38(1): pp. 89-151.

Cummins, H. (1930): Dermatoglyphics in twins of known chronic history, with reference to diagnosis of the twin varieties. *Anatomical Record*. 46: pp. 179-98.

Cummins, H. (1935): Morphology of the palmar hypothenar dermatoglyphic in man. *Human Biology* 7(1): pp. 1-23.

Cummins, H. (1935a): Dermatoglyphics in Eskimos from Point Barrow. *American Journal of Physical Anthropology* 20(1): pp. 13-17.

Cummins, H. (1936): Finger prints in 'Siamese' twins. *Eugenical News* 21: pp. 89-95.

Cummins, H. and C. Midlo (1927): Dermatoglyphics in Jews. *American Journal of Physical Anthropology*, 10: pp. 91-113.

Dar, H., R. Schmidt and H.M. Nitowsky (1977): Palmar crease variants and their clinical significance: A study of new borns at risk. *Pediat. Res.* 11: pp. 103-08.

Datta, P.K. (1964): The symmetry of the plantar main-life formula in an Indian population. *Acta Geneticae Medicae et Gemellologiae*, 13(3): pp. 305-12.

Davenport, C.B. (1933): The growth of Human foot. *Am. J. Phys. Anthrop.*, 17: pp. 167ff.

Davies, P.A. and V. Smallpiece (1963): The single transverse palmar crease in infants and children. *Developmental Medicine and Child Neurology*, 5(5) : pp. 491-96.

de Wilde, A.G. (1979) : *Developmental Aspects of Ridges and Creases (Dermatoglyphics) Coll. Anthrop*. 3, 2: pp. 201-10.

Debrunner, I.M. (1957): Zur Morphologie der Transversalfurche (Vierfingerfurche). *Deutsches Gesellschaft fur Anthropologie*, 5 : pp. 52-56

Dejong, R. and R.V. Platou (1967): Sickle cell hemoglobinopathy. An anatomic sign. *American Journal of Diseases of Children* 113: pp. 271-72.

Dubey, N.M. (1981): The study of inheritance of crease and crease surface area — Morphogenesis and their Attributes. M.Sc. Thesis Saugar University, Sagar.

Duckworth, W.L.H. (1915) : *Morphology and Anthropology*, Cambridge.

Duel, Sloan and Pearce (1900) : *The Laws of Scientific Hand Reading*. New York.

Edwards, C.R. (1978) : A Chalk and Tape method for lifting the palm prints of Non-human Primates. *Dermatoglyphics. An Introductional Perspective*. Moutan Publishers, Paris.

Edwards, C.R. (1978): "A Comparison of Dermatoglyphic and Genetic Similarity Indices in Rhesus Monkeys (Macaca mulatta)", in *Dermatoglyphics: and international perspective.* Edited by J. Mavalwala. *World Anthropology.* The Hague: Mouton.

Eriksson, S.A. (1957): *Systematik der Fingerspitzenmuster. Nordic Criminology Magazine*, 27 : pp. 275-87 (in Swedish).

Eriksson, S.A., and A. Norinder (1958) : *En frekvensundersokning ar handflatans papillari injemonster i thenar-och hypothenarzonerna samt av den s.k. fyrfingerfaran. Nordic Criminology Magazine*. 28: pp. 257-70.

Erne, H. (1953): *Uber das pappillarleistensystem und die palmafurchen in Familien mit einem order mehreren Fallen von Mongolismus und ein Beitrag zum problem der Vierfingerfurche.* Thesis, Zurich.

Eswaraiah, G. (1977) : *Palmar creases and diseases*. Thesis submitted in fulfilment of the requirement for the degree of Ph.D., Saugar University, Sagar.

Eswaraiah, G. (1978): Palmar prints and schizophrenia. *Indian J. Psychiat. 20*: pp. 347-53.

Eswaraiah, G. (1978): Palmar creases - Criteria for ethnic variation. *Indian Journal of Physical Anthropology and Human Genetics.* IV. 7.

Eswaraiah, G. and R.S. Bali (1976): Palmar Dermatoglyphics among congenital deaf people, *Madhya Bharati*, Saugar University Journal.

Fauchier, C., J.M. Regy, J.P. Lamagnere and P. Combe (1970): Gigantisme cerebral. *Annales de pediatrie* (Paris) 17: pp. 870-75.

Fērē, C. (1900a): *Les lines papillaires de la plante du pied. Journal de l' Anatomic et de la physiologie* 36: pp. 602-18.

Fērē, C. (1900) : *Notes sur les plis de flexion de la paume de la main. C.R. et Mem. Soc. Biol.* Paris, T., 52 : pp. 309-11.

Fischer, E. (1949) : *Bemerkung uber die vierfingrfurche. Zeitschrift fur Morphologie and Anthropologie*. 41 : pp. 268-74.

Forbes, A.P. (1964): Fingerprints and palm prints (dermatoglyphics) and palmar flexion creases in gonadal dysgenesis, pseudo-hypoparathyroidism, and Klinefelter's syndrome. *New England Journal of Medicine* 270(24): pp. 1268-77.

Frisch, K. von (1950): *Bees, their vision, chemical senses and language*. Ithaca, N.Y.

Geipel, G. (1961): Ein Beitrag zur Verteilung der Winkel and auf der inneren Handflache. *Zeitschrift fur Morphologie und Anthropologie* 51(3): pp. 333-38.

Glueck, S. and E. Glueck (1956): *Physique and Delinquency*. New York, Hory Holt.

Goafar (1964) : *Ilm-ul-Kaff*.

Gomila, J., L. Per-Laborde and M. Lestrange (1967): *Dermatoglyphics digitopalmaires et plis de flexion dans 1' isolat Bedik, S'enegal (oriental). Akten des antropologischen Kongresses* (Brno) 19 : pp. 103-18.

Goodman, R.M., M. Batmiriam Katzrelson and M. Frydman (1972): Evolution of palmar skin creases in the Ehlers - Danlos Syndrome. *Clinical Genetics* (K benhavn) 3(1) : pp. 67-72.

Goodman, R.M., M. Batmiriam Katznelson, E. Manor (1972): Camptodactyly: occurrence in two new genetic syndromes and its relationship to other syndromes. *Journal of Medical Genetics*, 9(2) : pp. 203-12.

Grunberg, H. (1928) : *Die vererbung der menschlichen Tastfiguren. Zeitschrift fur Induktive Abstammungs and Vererbungslebre*. 46 : pp. 285-310.

Gupta, D.K. (1985): *Dermatoglyphics, Palmar Creases and other Genetic Markers in Leprosy*. Ph.D. Thesis, Rani D.V.V., Jabalpur (M.P.).

Gyenis, G. (1975): Dermatoglyphics of three Hungarian populations. *American Journal of Physical Anthropology* 45(2): pp. 229-32.

Gyenis, G. and G. Hera (1971): Investigation of the hand creases in the random sample of subjects in Baranya Province of South Hungary. *Anthropologiai Kozlemenyek* (Budapest) 15(1): pp. 29-47.

Gyula, G. (1974): A Négyujjasredö és a Sidney-redö gyakorisága néhány magyarországi populációban. Anthróp közl. 18: pp.69-77.

Hale, A.R., J.H. Phillips and G.E. Burch (1961) : Features of palmar dermatoglyphics in congenital heart disease: report on variants frequently associated with congenital lesions of heart. *Journal of the American Medical Association*. 176 : p. 41.

Hanhart, E. (1936): Uber die Bedeutung der Vierfingerfutche (sogen. Affenfurche) also Merkmal konstitutionellr nervoser Minderwertigkeit und ihr vorkommen in mitteleuropaischen und nordafrikanischen Ressen gemischen. *Verbandlungen der Schweizischen Naturfors chung Gesellschaft* 117: pp. 365-66.

Harvey, P.W., S. Muldal and O. Wauchob (1970): *Anti. Social Behaviour and Larger Y chromosome Lancet* 1, p. 887.

Hasebe, K. (1918): Uber das hautleistensystem der Vola und planta der Japaner und Aino. *Ark. Anat. Inst. Sendai* 1: pp. 13-88.

Henckel, K.O. (1938): *Contribuciones al estudio de la antropologie Chilena. III. La disposicion de las crestas papilares de las falangitas en los indigenas de la provincia de Cautin. Boletin de la sociedad de Biologia de Concepcion* (Chile) 7: pp. 35-60.

Hepburn, D. (1895): The papillary ridges on the hands and feet of monkeys and men. *Scientific Transactions of the Royal Society of Dublin*, 5: pp. 525-38.

Hirsch, W. (1978): Dermatoglyphics and creases in their relationship to clinical syndromes. A diagnostic criterion, in *Dermatoglyphics: An International Perspective*, Edited by J. Mavalwala. World Anthropology. The Hague: Mouton.

Hirsch, W. and G. Geipel (1960): Das Papillarieistensystem der Hand und seine Beziehung ze cerebralen Storungen. *Acta Genetica et Statistica Medica* 10(1-3): pp. 103-82.

Holt, S.B. (1964): The role of dermatoglyphics in medical Biology. *Medical World* (London) 101: pp. 112-25.

Holt, S.B. (1965): Dermatoglyphics of congenital Malformations. *Developmental Medicine and Child Neurology* 7: pp. 568-69.

Hook, E.B., S. Selvin, J. Garfinkel and M. Greenberg (1974): "Maternal smoking during gestation and infant morphologic variation : Preliminary report concerning birth, weight and incidence of transverse palmar creases", in *Congenital Defects : New Directions in Research.* Edited by D.T. Janerich, R.G. Skalko and I.H. Porter, London: Academic Press.

Iagolnitzer, E.R. and J. Iagolnitzer (1983): Pseudo Symmetry in the Palmar Flexion Crease System. Human Biology Recent Advances, 2 (*Proc. Int. Sym.* Punjabi University).

Ito, K., T. Kogata, M. Murai and H. Osugi (1956): The transverse crease among the Japanese. Classification of "*Affenfurche*" among the Japanese. *Transactions of Tottori University* (Department of Anatomy), 4.

Jain, D.K. (1978): *Age change – Morphology of hand and palmar flexion creases among Brahman girls.* Thesis submitted in part fulfilment for the requirement of the degree of M.Sc., Saugar University, Sagar.

Johnson, C.F. and E. Opit (1971): The single palmar crease and its clinical significance in a child development clinic. *Clinical Pediatrics* (Philadelphia) 10: pp. 392-404.

Kervinen, V. (1954) : The incidence of the four-finger groove in Finland. *Annales Academiae Scientiarum Fennicae* (Helsinki). 40 : pp. 1-2.

Khatoon, S. (1978): Study of twins and Reliability of Creases in Twin Zygosity Diagnosis Ph.D. Thesis. Saugar University, Sagar.

Kimura, K. (1957) : A study of palmar dermatoglyphics in inhabitants of Sado island *Anthropological Reports* (Niigata) 18 : pp. 51-66 (in Japanese).

Kimura, K. (1968) : A study of palmar creases in Ainus. *Jinruigaku Zassi*. 76 : pp. 60-74.

Kimura, K. and S. Hagiya (1958) : *A Study on the handlines of twins. Jinruigaku Zasshi*. 66 (718) : pp. 209-15.

Kirchmair, M. (1935): *Der Fingerabdruck im Dienste der Rassen und Konstitutionsforschung Munchener Medizinische Wochenschrift* 82(1): pp. 529-31.

Kollmann, A. (1883): *Der Tastapparat der Hand der menscblichen Rassen und der Affen*. Hamburg: Leopold Voss.

Komai, T. (1928): Criteria for distinguishing identical and fraternal twins, *Quart. Rev. Biol.*, 3: pp. 408-18.

Kumbnani and H.K. (1971): Main-line index and transversality in a German population afflicted with Down's Syndrome. *International Symposium on Human Genetics* Waltair, India.

Kumbnani, H.K., R.A. Pfeiffer (1969): Partial trisomy in a child with features suggesting mongolism. *Journal of Medical Genetics* 6: pp. 201-05.

Kutsuna, S. (1929): On "Bewegungslinie" of the human hand. Jinruigaku Zasshi, 44(504): pp. 471-89.

Lambson, G. (1976) : Distal displacement of proximal phalangeal flexion creases. *Excerpta Med. Int. Congr. Ser.* 397. p. 203.

Langdon-Down, R.L. (1909): Mongolian Imbecility. *Brit. Med. J.,* pp. 12-65.

Lasinski, W. and M. Urbanowicz (1960): The system of skin furrows on the human palm. *Folia Morphologica* 11: pp. 115-24 (in Polish).

Leiber, B. (1960) : *Zur systematic und klinischen Bedentung des menschlichen Handfurch-enbildes. Z. menschi. vererb. u. Konstitution slehre.* 35, pp. 205-32.

Lejeune, J.R., Turpin and M. Gautier (1959): Le mongolisme premier example d'aberration autosomique humaine. Annales de Genetique 1: p. 241.

Lestrange, M. de (1969) : A propos des plis de flexion de la paume : Classification et rapports entre les differents types decrits. *Bulletin et memoires de la Sociele d Anthropologie de Paris.*

Lestrange, M. de: (1969a) : The transverse creases in Europe-index and comparative study of different sample cited in the Literature. *Amarical Journal of Physical Anthropology*, 30-173-182.

Lestrange, M. de. (1969b): *A propos des plis de flexion de la paume: classification et rapports entre 'l'es different types decrits. Bulletin et memoires de la societe d' Anthropologie de Paris* 5(12): pp. 251-67.

Loeffler, L. (1969): *Papillarleistren und Hautfurchensystem in Human genetik Enkurzes Handbuch in funt Banden* Edited by P.E. Becker, 1-2: pp. 205-408.

Loeffler, L. (1969): *Spezielle Morphologie und Indizwert der Befunde bei personnenmit chromosomalen Aberrationen. Haut leisten und Krankbeiten*, p. 105.

Lombroso, C. (1896): *Crime, Its causes and Remedies*, translated by H.P. Horton, Boston Little Brown (1911).

Lorenz, K. (1966): *On aggression*. Methues, London.

Lund, S.E.T. (1933): A psycho-biological study of a set of identical girl triplets. *Human Biology* 5 : pp. 1-34.

Lynn, R. and J. Murray (1978) : *An inkless method of recording dermal ridges: An introductional perspective.* Moutan Publishers, Paris.

MacArthur, J.W. (1936): A measure of similarity in finger and palm prints aiding diagnosis of identical and fraternal twins, Royal Soc. of Canada, Abstracts, pp. 52.

MacArthur, J.W. (1938): Reliability of dermatoglyphics in twin diagnosis. *Human Biology* 10(1): pp. 12-35.

Mahapatra, U.D. (1960): *Studies an Handabdruecken von verbrechen und Deutschland.* Thesis for f. Dr. rer. nat. in Kiel.

Mahapatra, U.D. (1966): Palmar Dermatoglyphics of the German criminals in *Proceedings* volume of International Sym. on Dermato. edi. by P.C. Biswas and A. Sharma, New Delhi, India.

Marshall, I.B., J. Jephcott (1969): The prevalence of simian lines in a sample of the Turkish population. *Turkish Journal of Pediatrics,* 11(3) : pp. 91-97.

Mavalwala, J. (1971): *The heredity of dermatoglyphic traits in non-human primates and man; in comparative genetics in monkeys, apes, and man* ed. by B. Charelli, 43-63. London: Academic Press.

Mavalwala, J. (1978) : *Methodology for dermatoglyphics: Finger and Palms. An introductional perspective.* Moutan Publishers, Paris.

Mehas, K. (1972) : Simian Crease, Acta Pediatra. *Acad. Sci. Hung.* 13, 4 : p. 335.

Menser, M.A. and S.G. Purvis-Smith (1969) : Dermatoglyphic defects in children with Leukaemia, *Lancet* 1(7605) : pp. 1076-78.

Methews, H.H. (1928) : Vide Montgomery, R.B. (1925) : Sole Prints of newborn babies; *Am. Jour. Med. Sci.*; clxix.

Meyer-Heydenhagen, G. (1934): *Zur Erbbiologie der Papillarleisten der Handflache. (Zeitschrift fur Induktive Abstammungs und Vererbungslebre)* 67: pp. 302-05.

Midlo, C. and H. Cummins (1942): Palmar and plantar dermatoglyphics in primates. *American Anatomical Memoirs* 20 : pp. 1-98.

Mishra, R. (1979): *Inheritance and Methodological Study of Plantar Creases.* Thesis submitted in part fulfilment for the requirements of the degree of Ph.D., University of Saugar, Sagar.

Mishra, R. (1980): Inheritance of palmar creases. *Internat. Sym. Dermato.* Punjabi University, Patiala, India.

Mondal, R.C. (1987): *Palmar creases in Gonds of Sagar.* Thesis submitted in part fulfilment for the requirement of the degree of M.Sc., Saugar University, Sagar.

Naffah, J. (1974): Dermatoglyphics and flexion creases in the Lebanese population. *American Journal of Physical Anthropology,* 41(3) : pp. 391-409.

Nakiela, J. (1972) : Flexion furrows of the feet in poles. *Folia Morphol.* (Warsz.), 31 : p. 301.

Nassau, E. and A Kallner (1958): Observation on the deep furrows of the palm of the hand and the sole of the foot in diseased children. *Annales de pediatrie* (Basel) 191: pp. 295-307.

Newman, H.H. (1931): Palm print patterns in twins. *Journal of Heredity* 22: pp. 41-9.

Newman, H.H. (1931a): Differences between conjoined twins. *Journal of Heredity* 22: pp. 201-05.

Newman, M.T. (1936): A comparative study of finger prints and toe prints, *Human Biology*, 8(4): pp. 531-52.

Obata, Y. (1956): Studies on the longitudinal flexion crease. 1. The South Kyushu Islanders. *Medical Journal of Kagoshima University,* 7(5).

Okajima, M. (1966) : A dermatoglyphical study of metacarpophalangeal creases. *Am. J. Phys. Anthropol.*, 24 : pp. 371-80.

Okajima, M. (1967) : Metacarpo-phalangeal and ring crease in twins. *Am. J. Phys. Anthropol.*, 26 : pp. 349-55.

Okajima, M. (1976) : *A new technique for examining Primate dermatoglyphics*. Dermatoglyphics an introductional perspective; Moulton Publishers, Paris.

Parisi, P. and M. di Bacco (1967): Fingerprints in twins. A qualiquantitative analysis. (Methodological note). *Acta Geneticae Medicae et Gemellologie* 16(1) : pp. 71-100.

Patel, A.B. (1981): *The study of inheritance of palmar creases and their base point positioning.* M.Sc. dissertation, Saugar University, Sagar.

Patten, B.M. (1953): *Human embryology*, Blakistan, New York, p. 19.

Penrose, L.S. (1931) : The creases on the minimal digit in Mongolism. *Lancet* ii : p. 583.

Penrose, L.S. (1933): *Mental defect.* London: Sidgwick and Jackson.

Penrose, L.S. (1963): Finger-prints, palms, and chromosomes. *Nature,* 197(4871): pp. 933-38.

Penrose, L.S. (1967) : *A suggested use of dermatoglyphic analysis in mongolism in mongolism.* Boston: Little, Brown.

Penrose, L.S. (1973): Finger Prints and Palmistry. *Lancet* 1(7814) pp. 1239-42.

Penrose, L.S. and M.D. Camb. (1931): The creases on the minimal digit in mongolism. *Lancet* 2: 585-86.

Plato, C.C. (1970): Dermatoglyphics and flexion crease of the Cypriots. *American Journal of Physical Anthropology*, 33(3): pp. 421-27.

Plato, C.C. (1970): Polymorphism of the c. line of palmar dermatoglyphics with a new classification of the c. line terminations, *American Journal of Physical Anthropology*, 33(3): pp. 413-19.

Ploetz-Radmann, M. (1937): Die hautleistenmuster der unteren beiden Fingerglieder der menschilchen Hand. *Zeitscbrift fur Morphologie und Anthropologie*. 36: pp.281-310.

Pöch, H. (1925): *Uber Handlinien. Mitteilungen der Anthropologischen gesellschaft in Wien* 55; pp. 133-59.

Portius, W. (1937) : Beitrag zur Frage der Erblichkeit . der vierfingerfurche. *Zeitschrift fur Morphologie und Anthropologie*. 36 : pp. 382-90.

Purvis-Smith, S.G. (1972) : The Sydney Lines: a significant sign in Down's syndrome. *Australian Paediatric Journal 8* : pp. 190-200.

Purvis-Smith, S.G. (1972): The Downs Syndrome dermatogram - a clinical evaluation. *Australian Journal of Mental Retardation,* 2 : pp. 51-53.

Purvis-Smith, S.G. and M.A. Menser (1968) : Dermatoglyphics in adults with congenital rubella. *Lancet* 2 : pp. 141-43.

Quintana, A. (1979): *Dermatoglyphic study in a Spanish Penal Population in Dermatoglyphics* - fifty-year later edited by Wladmir Wertelecki and Chris C. Plato. New York: Alan R. Liss.

Rai, A.K. (1980): Intra-individual relationship between palmar creases — Dermatoglyphics of newborn. M.Sc. Thesis, Saugar University, Sagar.

Rai, A.K. and D.K. Jain (1980): *Age change and crease morphology*, Madhya Pradesh Vigyan Academy, Jabalapur (M.P.).

Rao, P.D. (1980): *Metacarpo-phalangeal creases of the palms of Australian Aborigines*.

Rawat, A. (1983): Study of attributes of palmar creases and phalangeal flexion crease. M.Sc. Thesis, Saugar University, Sagar.

Rawat, S.K. (1980): The study of palmar creases and palmar dermatoglyphics of murderers. *Internat. sym. Dermato*. Punjabi University, Patiala, India.

Rawat, S.K. and R.S. Bali (1980): Morphogenesis of crease among murderers. *National Sym. on Child with Handicap and VII Annual Conference of I.S.H.G.*, Ranchi University, Ranchi, India.

Renes, R.C. (1946): Symmetrical and asymmetrical occurrence of papillary patterns. *American Journal of Physical Anthropology*, 4(2): pp. 169-91.

Rife, D.C. (1933): Genetic studies of monozygotic twins. I.A. diagnostic formula. *Journal of Heredity* 24: pp. 339-45.

Rittmeister, J.F. (1936): Uber die Affenfurche (Vierfingerfurche) mit besonderer Beruchsichtigung der Mikrodegeneration en und des Problems des Mongolismus. *Zeitschrift fur Anatomie und Entwicklungsgeschichte* 106(2): pp. 276-314.

Rott, H.D. (1971): Hautleistenstorungen bei verschiedenen Krankheiten. *Hautleisten und Krankbeiten* 2: pp. 247-54.

Ruth Achs, Rita and Happer (1966) : Unusual dermatoglyphics associated with Rubella embryopathy, *New England Journal of Medicine*, 274, 3 : p. 148.

Safia (1987): Study of twins and Reliability of creases in twin zygosity diagnosis. Ph.D. Thesis, Saugar University, Sagar.

Saha and Dermat (1983): *Population Genetics.*

Sarkar, S.S. (1961) : The Simian crease. *Zeitschrift fur Morphologie und Anthropologie*. 51(2) : pp. 212-19.

Schaeuble, J. (1933): Die Entstehung der palmaren digitalen Triradien. Ein Beitrag Zur Entwicklung der Hautleistenzuge der distalen palma. *Zeitschrift fur Morphologie and Anthropologie*. 31(3) pp. 403-38.

Schaumann, B. and M. Alter (1976) : *Dermatoglyphics in Medical Disorders*. Springer-Verlag, New York. pp. 118-22.

Schaumann, B. and M. Alter (1977): Dermatoglyphics in cerebral gigantism, in Dermatoglyphics: An International perspective. Edited by J. Mavalwala, *World Anthropology*. The Hague : Mouton.

Schaumann, B. and O.A. Pantke (1977): 'Dermatoglyphics in dyscephaly Saethre-Chotzen (Acrocephalosyndactyly type III, Chotzen syndrome),' in *Dermatoglyphics: an international Perspective*. Edited by J. Mavalwala. World Anthropology. The Hague: Mouton.

Schawman, B. and M. Alter (1976): *Dermatoglyphics in medical disorders*. Springer-Verlag, New York, pp. 118-22.

Scheimann, E. (1972) : *A doctors' guide To Better Health Through Palmistry*. Vikas Publishing House.

Schenk, H. and H. Patzer (1959): Das fussfurchenbild des Neugeborenen. *Kinderarztliche Praxis* 27(4) : pp. 169-73.

Schiller, M. (1942): Realitaet und Problematic der menschlichen Handfuerchen, insbesondere der Affenfuerche. *Z. Morph. Anthrop.* 25.

Schultz, A.H. (1937): Foetal growth and development of the rhesus monkey. *Contributions to Embryology* (Carnegie Institute) 26: pp. 71-97.

Sen, S.K. (1969) : *Hast Samudrika Shastra, Indian Science of Hand Reading*, Taraporewala, Bombay.

Sharma, A. (1960): Symmetry of four palmax main lines collectively and of modal types in the Burmn Series. *The Anthropologist,* 7(1-2): 21-31.

Sharma, A.N. and R.S. Bali (1980): The Occurrence of Symmetrical and Asymmetrical Palmar Creases: Human Biology Recent Advances 2 (*Proc Int. Sym.*) Punjabi University, Patiala.

Sharma, A.N. and R.S. Bali (1980): The study of creases and crease morphogenesis among mentally retarded children. *National Sym.* on child with handicap and VII, Annual Conference of I.S.H.G., Ranchi University, Ranchi, India.

Sheldon, W.H. (1949): *Varieties of Delinquent Youth.* New York, Harper and Brothers.

Shields, J., E. Slater and P. Slater (1969): A quadratic discriminant of Zygosity from finger prints. *J. Med. Genet.* 1: p. 142.

Shuttle Worth, G.E. (1909): Mongolian Imbecility. *Brit. Med. J.,* 12 : p. 665.

Siemmen, H.W. (1927): The diagnosis of identity in twins. *Journal of Heredity* 18 : pp. 201-9.

Siemmen, H.W. (1932): *Die allgemeinen der menschlichen Mehrlings forschung. Zeits. f. ind. Abst. und verebungsl.*, 61: pp. 208-22.

Singh, N.R. (1983): *A study of plantar Creases Among Rajputs*, M.Sc. Thesis, Saugar University, Sagar.

Smith, S.M. and L.S. Penrose (1955): Monozygotic and dizygotic twin diagnosis. *Annals of Eugenics* 19: pp. 273-90.

Sonntag, C.F. (1924): *The morphology and evolution of the Apes and man*, London.

Sottner, L., J. Pospisil and A. Syrovatka (1968): Observation of karyotype changes in person with simian line. *Ceskoslovenska Pediatrie*, 23(12) : pp. 1096-1100.

Stiffen, C. (1953) : *Zur Haufigkeit und verebung der vierfingerfurche.* Homo, 4, Band, 3 heft, pp. 126-39.

Stocks, P. (1930): A biometric investigation of twins and their brothers and sisters. *Annals of Eugenics*. 4: pp. 49-108.

Storr, A. (1968): *Human Aggression*. London: Atheneum.

Suttan, H.E., S.G. Vandenberg and P.J. Clark (1962): The heriditary abilities studies. Selection of twins, diagnosis of zygosity and programme of measurements. *Amer. J. Hum. Genet.* 14: pp. 152.

Takanushi, T. (1942): *Deux ou Trois observations sur lo genetique des dermatoglyphics digito-palmaires jinruigaku Zassbi* 52(7): pp. 303-20.

Takeya, S. (1934): Uber die Hautleistenfigur der Planta der Chinesen. *Journal of Oriental medicine* 20: pp. 54-58 and pp. 495-523.

Tillner, I. (1953) : *Zur Entstehung dev vierfingerfurche. Zeitschrift fur Menscheliche verebungs und Konstitutionslehre* 32 : pp. 56-7.

Tillner, I. (1956) : Die vierfingerfurche in Beziehung zum verlaug der handleisten. *Anthrop. Anzeiger*. 22 : pp. 260-76.

Timbergen, N. (1964): The evolution of signalling devices. In Etkin, W. (ed.) *Social Behaviour and Organization among Vertebrates*. Chicago: University of Chicago Press.

Tunakan, S. (1948) : *Etude anthropologique des empreintes digitales et palmaires chez les Tures*. Publication de l' universite d' Ankara 15.

Tunakan, S. (1954): A study on the simian crease in Turkish people and convicts. *Turk kurumu Basimevi* (Ankara) 12(1-2): pp. 117-26.

Tunakan, S. (1954): Turklerde ve Turk Suclularinda et ayas indaki dort parmack Cizgisi (Maymun Cizgisi) Uzerinde arastirma. Ankara Universitiesi Dil ve Tarih-Coqratya Fakultesi Dergisi XII - Cilt, 1-2 *Sayilardan ayribasim,* Mart Haziran, pp. 117-226.

Uchida, I.A. (1966): Dermatoglyphics and chromosomes. *Alabama Journal of Medical Science* 3(4): pp. 432-34.

Uchida, L.A. and H.C. Soltan (1963): Evaluation of dermatoglyphics in medical genetics, *Pediatric Clinics of North America* 10(2): pp. 409-22.

Usher, R., F. McLean and K.E. Scott (1966) : Judgement of fetal age. II. Clinical significance of gestational age and an objective method for its assessment. *Pediatr. Clin. North Am.*, 13 : 835.

Valotskoy, M.V. (1936): On the genetics of fingerprints. *Proceedings* of the Maxim Gorky Medico-Genetical Research Institute 4: pp. 404-39.

Verbov, J.L. (1967): Simian line and psoraisis. *Lancet* 2: p. 779.

Verschuer, O. Von (1932): Die biologischen Grundlagen der menschlichen Mehrlingsforschung. *Zeits. f. ind. Abst. und Vererbungsl.* pp. 147-205.

Verschuer, O.Von (1940): Twin research from the time of Francis Galton to the present day. *Proceedings* of the Royal Society (London) 128 : pp. 62-81.

Volotzkoy, M.V. (1936): On the genetics of finger prints. *Proceedings* of the Maxim Gorky Medico-Genetical Research Institute.

Volotzkoy, M.V. (1936a): Dactyloscopic graphs and formulae. *Anthropologicbeskii Zburnal (Moskva)* 4: pp. 428-37.

Walker, N.S. (1957) : Inkless methods of finger, palm and sole printing. *Journal of Pediatrics* 50 : pp. 27-9.

Walter, H. (1952) : *Betrachtungen, uber die verteilung der vierfingerfurche. Zs. f.* Morphol. u. Anthrop, Bd. XLIV. heft 3-s. pp. 362-68.

Wasinski, W. (1965): *An Analysis of Dermatoglyphics on the Basal and Middle Phalanges of Human Fingers.*

Weinand, H. (1937): *Familienuntersuchungen uber der Hautleistenverlauf der Hand-flache. Zeitschrift fur Morphologie und Anthropologie* 36: pp. 418-42.

Wendt, G.G. (1959): *Untersuchunger an den Handfurchen des Menschen. Homo* 10 : pp. 276-83.

Weninger, M. and L. Navratil (1957) : *Die Vierfingerfurche in atiologischer Betrachtung. Anthrop. Gesellsch.* in Wien. Bd., LXXVII : pp. 1-21.

Weninger, M., F. Kaindl, G. Rothenbuchner and B. Schober (1966): Skin ridge studies in congenital defects of the heart and the large vessels. *Wiener Klinische Wocbenschrift* 798(51): pp. 905-06.

Weninger, M., G. Rothenbuchner and B. Schober (1965): Dermatoglyphics finding in thyroiditis lymphomatose Hashimoto. *Humangenetik* 1(7): pp. 676-80.

Whichmann, D. (1956): Zur, Genetik Hautleist ensystems des Fuss-sohle. 2. *Morph. Anthrop.* 47: 331-81.

Whipple, I. (1904): *The ventral surface of the mammalian chiridium, with special morphologie und Anthropologie* 7: pp. 261-368.

Wiel, H.J. Van der (1953): On the fourfinger line. *Verhanddelingen (Koninklijke). Nederlandse Akademie van Wetenschappen.* 56(5) : pp. 666-72.

Wilson, W.A. and S. Zieler (1976): Some tests of intermodality transfer of intensity in squirrel monkeys. *Neuropsychologia*, 14: pp. 237-41.

Wood-Jones, F. (1929) : *Man's place among the mammals*, London.

Wurth, A. (1937): Die Entstehung der Beugefurchen der menschlichen Hohlhand. 2. *Morph. Anthrop.*, 36 : pp. 187-214.

Zizmor, J. (1937) : The extra transverse digital crease asking sign found in Sickle cell disease. Cutis (New York) 11 : pp. 447-49.

INDEX